Duquesne Studies
LANGUAGE AND LITERATURE SERIES

[VOLUME THIRTEEN]

GENERAL EDITOR:

Albert C. Labriola, *Department of English, Duquesne University*

ADVISORY EDITOR:

Foster Provost, *Department of English, Duquesne University*

EDITORIAL BOARD:

Judith H. Anderson
Donald Cheney
Patrick Cullen
French R. Fogle
A.C. Hamilton
S.K. Heninger, Jr.
A. Kent Hieatt
Robert B. Hinman
William B. Hunter
Michael Lieb
Waldo F. McNeir
Thomas P. Roche, Jr.
John T. Shawcross
James D. Simmonds
John M. Steadman
Humphrey Tonkin
Robert F. Whitman

John Milton's Writings
in the Anglo–Dutch Negotiations

John Milton's Writings in the Anglo-Dutch Negotiations, 1651-1654

by
Leo Miller

DUQUESNE UNIVERSITY PRESS
Pittsburgh, Pennsylvania

Copyright © by Duquesne University Press
All Rights Reserved.

No part of this book may be used or reproduced,
in any manner whatsoever, without written permission,
except in the case of short quotations
for use in critical reviews and articles.

Published in the United States of America.

by
DUQUESNE UNIVERSITY PRESS
600 Forbes Avenue
Pittsburgh, Pennsylvania 15282-0101

Library of Congress Cataloging-in-Publication Data

Miller, Leo. 1915-1990.
   John Milton's writings in the Anglo-Dutch negotiations, 1651-1654.
/ by Leo Miller.
   p. cm. -- (Duquesne studies. Language and literature series :
vol. 13)
   Includes Milton's translations into classical Latin of diplomatic
correspondence to European rulers from the revolutionary government of
England.
   Includes bibliographical references and index.
   ISBN 0-8207-0232-3.
   1. Milton, John, 1608-1674--Political and social views.
2. Milton, John, 1608-1674--Knowledge--Language and languages.
3. English language--Translating into Latin--History--17th century.
4. Diplomatics--Great Britain--Translations into Latin. 5. Great
Britain--Foreign relations--Netherlands. 6. Netherlands--Foreign
relations--Great Britain. 7. Great Britain--Foreign
relations--1649-1660. 8. Netherlands--Foreign
relations--1648-1714. 9. Anglo-Dutch War, 1652-1654--Sources.
Selections. 1992. II. Title. III. Series.
PR3592.P64M48   1992
821'.4--dc20
                                                      92-33554
                                                         CIP

Dedicated
to
THEO THOMASSEN
of the
Algemeen Rijksarchief, The Hague,
Scholar-Archivist,
for generous and unfailing cooperation
in these labors
above and beyond the call of duty.

> So easy seem'd
> Once found, which yet unfound most would have
> thought Impossible
>
> (*Paradise Lost*, 6.499–501)

Contents

Foreword	xv
A Note on Textual Readings	xvii
A Brief Guide to the Manuscript Sources	xviii
An Abstract in Place of a Preface	xxi

PART ONE
Milton in the Anglo-Dutch Negotiations, 1651–1654

1. Milton as Secretary for Foreign Correspondence	3
The Real Picture	3
The Anglo-Dutch Competition: Milton's Workaday World	8
The Negotiations Begin and Milton is Involved	10
2. Authenticating Miltonic Texts and Those of his Colleagues	14
Milton's Creative Classical Neo-Latin	14
The *Paper of Demands* and Milton's Colleague, Lewis Rosin	21
The Thirty-six Counter-articles; Milton Revises the Latin of the Dutch	30
A New Letter by Milton and Two by Weckherlin	35

3. May & June 1652: More Negotiations
   and the Onset of War   41
      Milton's Time of Trouble   41
      The *"Answer"* and the *"Narrative"*   46
      The Mission of Adrian Pauw   49

4. Milton at Work: Identifying More
   Milton Compositions   56
      The *Declaration/Scriptum*: How Milton
         and His Colleagues Did Their Work   56
      Two More Milton Letters: To the
         Danish Envoys on the Dutch War   67
      Peace Negotiations in 1653–1654:
         More Milton Letters Found   70

   A Postscript: Judging or Understanding   77

   Appendix A: The Treatment of Names in
      Milton's Latin Texts   79

   Appendix B: Milton's *Thesaurus Linguae
      Latinae*   82

   Appendix C: A Caveat   86

PART TWO

*The New Published Writings of Milton
and Related Documents*

Van Vliet's *Cum Nihil Prius*   94
*Concilium Status Parlamenti Republicae
   Angliae*   98
Scriptum ab Excellentijs Vestris   103
The *Paper of Demands*   112
   The Covering Letter   114
   The *Summarium Damnorum*, Milton's
      Earlier Text   121
   The *Summarium Damnorum*, The Final
      Text, B1 and B2   125

The Fifteen Articles, B3	133
The Catalogue, B4	142
The Thirty–six Counter-articles	154
The Letter of 16/26 April 1652	180
The Letter of 27 April/7 May 1652	185
The Letter of 28 April/8 May 1652	194
The *Declaration* of July 1652	196
The *Scriptum* of July 1652	232
The Letter of 8 July 1652	270
The Letter of 19 October 1652	273
The Letter of 13 July 1653	278
The Letter of 1 August 1653	289
Notes	294
Index	336

Foreword

This book, unfortunately, is a posthumous publication, its author having died in April 1990. My poignant regret is that Leo Miller did not live to see his dream realized, a dream that included the publication of materials that add significantly to the Milton canon. Many of the documents published in this book have not been known heretofore and thus did not exist in print in any form; some documents, though known, were not available in print; still others have been available but in printed texts sometimes abbreviated or erroneous. Therefore, the texts in this book replace or supplement what appear in the following works: *The Works of John Milton*, gen. ed. Frank Allen Patterson (New York: Columbia University Press); *Complete Prose Works of John Milton*, gen. ed. Don M. Wolfe (New Haven: Yale University Press); and *The Life Records of John Milton*, ed. J. Milton French (New Brunswick: Rutgers University Press).

Most of the research for this book was conducted in European archives, cited in the author's "A Brief Guide to the Manuscript Sources," p. xvi. Because of Mr. Miller's untimely death, which occurred even before his manuscript was copyedited, we were disadvantaged in our quest for total accuracy, notably in the transcriptions of documents in European archives. After Mr. Miller died, Mrs. Diana Miller, his widow, donated his books and journals on Milton, as well as his original research files, including microfilm and copy-flo reproduction of documents and books, to the Department of Special Collections, the University of Colorado at Boulder. These materials, now known as the Leo Miller John Milton Collection, are invaluable to the research of scholars in seventeenth century studies.

Through the splendid cooperation of Mrs. Diana Miller and Mr. James F. Williams, II, Dean of Libraries at the University of Colorado at Boulder, we have had access to numerous documents in the Leo Miller John Milton Collection, enabling us to check the accuracy of Mr. Miller's typescript against his handwritten transcriptions or photocopies. Our regret, however, is that all of the materials used in compiling this book were not yet available, since the process of reading, sorting, and cataloguing Mr. Miller's lifetime collection on Milton will continue indefinitely.

In view of the circumstances outlined above, we have been as diligent as possible to insure the highest degree of accuracy in the documents transcribed in this book. Indeed, the accuracy to which I refer reflects Ms. Susan Wadsworth-Booth's extraordinary service. An editor at Duquesne University Press, she personally has spent many of her days in the past two years on this book. Dr. John W. Smeltz, associate professor of English at Duquesne, has also been involved in checking the original documents, especially those written in Latin. If some errors remain, they were impossible to detect. All abbreviations and notations have been fashioned to approximate the appearance of the original documents, according to Mr. Miller's preferences. All things considered, I am confident that this book reflects Leo Miller's finest professional standards and, by doing so, becomes a tribute to his lifelong commitment to scholarship of the highest order.

Albert C. Labriola, General Editor
Language & Literature Series

A Note on Textual Readings

This work is based on firsthand study of original seventeenth century manuscript sources, in the handwriting of many different persons. Utmost care has been expended to reproduce the original texts accurately, even though anomalies result. Even within one document by one scribe, spellings, diacritical marks and accidentals may be inconsistent, and there is no consistency from one document to another. Idiosyncrasies among amanuenses are chronic, and it has not been possible to reproduce every idiosyncrasy. Where essential, preference has been given to clarity. Serious difficulties in textual readings and outright errors are indicated by annotations.

Where clarity may require supplying one or more letters omitted in a word by a scribe, these are supplied in italics. Italics are used to designate the seventeenth century squiggle for terminal *-que* and *-us*, but ū and ā for -um and -am are retained. Initial F is sometimes written ff. The œ ligature in *Fœdus, Fœderatus* (not used or used inconsistently by some) has been regularized throughout.

In 1652 the English still used the Old Style Julian calendar (designated O.S.), while the Dutch used the New Style Gregorian calendar (designated N.S.). Therefore dates are often given double, as in 6/16 April. In England the official New Year began on 25 March, so that dates between 1 January and 24 March are designated 1651/52.

A Brief Guide to the Manuscript Sources

The primary achievement of this study is the recovery from the original manuscripts, largely untapped in archival oblivion, of John Milton's *literary* contributions to the official documents of the English government in its diplomatic relations with the Dutch between 1651 and 1654.

To the best of my knowledge, there is no complete or well-organized set of these documents in England. The papers that are available are fragmentary and scattered. The Public Record Office, London, retains the manuscript Order Books of the Council of State, and transcripts of some diplomatic papers, catalogued in its SP series. Related data is located through the *Calendar of State Papers, Venetian*, and the *Calendar of State Papers, Colonial, East Indies*, etc. Many original manuscripts removed from government files during the seventeenth century have found their way into the Bodleian Library, Oxford: the Nalson Papers (used here by permission of Lady Anne Bentinck) and the Tanner Papers. A third collection there, a huge mass of state documents taken and concealed by John Thurloe at the Restoration, the Rawlinson MSS, has been extensively though imperfectly edited by Thomas Birch, *A Collection of the State Papers of John Thurloe*, 1742 (not including Rawl. C 129, the 1651 mission journal of Strickland and St. John).

Documents at one time held by Philip I. Hardwicke were transferred to the British Museum (now British Library) by Thomas Birch and are now in its Add. MSS. collection; the Library also has extensive nineteenth century transcriptions from Dutch sources. At Westminster, the House of Lords Record Office preserves the original manuscript Journals of both the House of Lords and the House of Commons; both have been committed to print by eighteenth century standards.

The holdings of the Algemeen Rijksarchief at the Hague are much more complete, in originals received from the British and in transcripts of documents transmitted by the Dutch. The Dutch envoys sent reports not only to the States General, but voluminous duplicates to provincial States and to individual public figures, adding up to thousands of pages. The *Verbael vande Ambassade naer Engelant*, 1652, the report of Ambassadors Cats, Schaep and Van de Perre for 15 December 1651 to 10 July 1652, NS, supplies most of the pertinent papers for that period in MS. S.G. 8460, about 550 pages; the rest are largely in MS. Aitzema 86, which partly duplicates that *Verbael*, and includes materials from the Strickland-St. John 1651 mission, and transcripts of essential papers for 1653, deriving from originals in MS. S.G. 8483 and 8484, which supply the final report of the 1653–1654 peace negotiations. MS. S.G. 8461 duplicates much of S.G. 8460, including the Latin Letters dictated by Milton. MS. S.G. 8462 is another duplicate but breaks off in the middle of Article 21 of the Thirty-six Counter-articles, so it has Milton texts only before that point. MS. Arch. St. v Holl. Inv. Nr. 2813.1 includes 1652 duplicates sent to Johan de Witt.

Detailed citations and more precise descriptions are given in the text and notes, together with citations to other manuscript collections in the Rijksarchief; in the Amsterdam Gemeentearchief; the Rigsarkivet, Copenhagen (notably T.K.U.A, A. II. 16); the manuscript diary of Lodweijck Huygens; and the diary and papers of Hermann Mylius in the Niedersächsisches Staatsarchiv, Oldenburg.

Some of the documents from 1651–1654 were printed in Latin by Leo ab Aitzema, *Historia Pacis*, 1654, incompletely, and edited into third person discourse. His vast *Saken van Staet en Oorlogh* has some Dutch translations. The 1653–1654 treaty papers were printed extensively by H. Scheurleer, *Verbael* (1725). In none of these sources, however, were Milton's contributions ever identified by his name.

An Abstract in Place of a Preface

For 11 long years, the great poet John Milton devoted his literary talents to translating into classical Latin prose the diplomatic correspondence addressed to European rulers by the revolutionary government of England. Milton lives today in his great poems, and even scholarly specialists hardly ever look into his state papers. Yet in his own century, these Latin letters were published at least three times as truly *belles-letters*, and were read with appreciation for their stylistic merits. It is time to end our neglect of these years in Milton's life and his achievement in that era when the English people struggled to create and maintain a republic. Milton was a passionate participant in those historical events, and that participation was central to his life and work during those 11 years.

Until now, Milton's labors as secretary for foreign correspondence have been known only fragmentarily, and published accounts are marred by serious errors and omissions. Valuable sources such as the Dutch archives have been ignored. I have been engaged in extensive endeavor exploring this public phase of Milton's career. My book *John Milton and the Oldenburg Safeguard*, by making available for the first time all of the Mylius papers and their correct interpretation, made it possible to precisely define Milton's status and activity in office, and to form a clear picture of his practice in composing his translations of official state letters. This study eliminated many previous misconceptions and exaggerations.

The present monograph continues this exploration. Part One is a narrative reconstruction of the day-by-day diplomatic fencing between England and the Netherlands leading up to their naval war of 1652–1654 and a recreation of the day-by-day functioning by Milton in that agitated milieu. Part 2 reproduces in full the official English-language originals of his state papers, the texts of Milton's Latin versions, and certain related documents. Many of these are either being published now for the first time or, in some instances, for the first time correctly.

Beginning with a precise definition of Milton's role as revealed by the Mylius papers, and with a review of the conflicts leading to the negotiations of 1651–1652, we turn to Milton's first assignment, his translation of the Netherlander's letter *Cum nihil prius*, and then examine his Latin translation of two British state papers dated 29 January 1651/52. In this examination, I do not rely only on the circumstantial evidence in coincidental Council of State minutes, as Milton's editors have previously; instead, the internal evidence is tested to authenticate and confirm Milton's authorship, and to establish the methodology needed to do so. Immediately the methodology reveals the presence of a collaborating hand: an aide, Lewis Rosin, entirely overlooked until now, who shares with Milton the written work of these proceedings.

Next, the British *Paper of Demands* is elucidated. I have recovered the full four-part document and its covering letter, in English and Latin texts, investigating Milton's share and Rosin's. This clarifies the significance of the *Summarium Damnorum*: although that bill of claims was printed in 1676 as Milton's work, it has been wholly misunderstood in the past.

It was Milton's toiling on this complex *Paper of Demands* and the burgeoning of foreign affairs, and not just his blindness, which led to his need for a colleague with status to help, and therefore to the appointment of Georg

Rudolph Weckherlin as Milton's secretary-assistant.

The proposals for a treaty follow: the Dutch draft *Thirty-six Articles*, the British draft *Thirty-six Counter-articles*. Here, as elsewhere in his state papers, Milton is seen in character, reacting to unclassical terminology with a lexicographer's sensitivities. The *Oldenburg Safeguard* study demonstrated how Milton struggled to maintain a standard of pristine classical Latin, in sharp distinction from the neo-Latin foisted on his drafts by his colleagues. From his preferences, vividly demonstrated throughout these negotiations, we can now infer the nature of the lost Latin dictionary on which he labored for many years: most likely, a thesaurus not aiming to be all-inclusive, but restricted to authors most authentically classical and preferably native to ancient Rome. Milton's peculiar usages also serve as a method for recognizing, identifying and recovering works hitherto not known as Milton's, which can now be attributed to him with considerable assurance. Identifying other habitual usages that Milton avoids now enables us to distinguish papers done by his colleagues.

Continuing, this study demonstrates that *Ut tandem*, a document erroneously printed in the Columbia edition as Milton's work, was in fact a paper submitted by the Dutch envoys. The British state paper of 16/26 April 1652, assigned by the Council of State to Milton for translation, is now recovered and considered for inclusion in the Milton canon. Two other Council documents from that April are shown by style and by handwriting to be by Weckherlin, whose state papers have never been identified before.

Here, Milton's time of trouble intervenes—the death of his young wife and, soon after, of his year-old son. These events coincide with the first clashes at sea between the English and the Dutch navies. Milton's letter to the Athenian Philaras, which has been treated by biographers *in vacuo*, is here read in the context of the impending war. The mission of Willem Nieupoort to England is also brought to light and connected to the garbled recollections in Edward Phillip's 1694 *Life of Milton*.

The supplementary mission of Adrian Pauw, the final ambassador sent by the Netherlands, is analyzed paper by paper. Milton's peculiar remark about Pauw's messages to him is noted as an instance of Milton's foible, his occasional tendency to dramatize facts about himself, to satisfy his hunger for the recognition he knew he deserved but rarely received in his lifetime.

Finally at the end of June, the politicians called off their redundant mummery, and both sides unleashed their sea dogs in war. The British launched a major public relations effort in a *Declaration of Parliament* (published along with statements issued by both sides during May and June), issued in four languages in July. Some Milton scholars, with no evidence, have attributed to Milton the bulk of that publication in the English and Latin booklets, each about 70 pages long. Other Milton scholars, also with no evidence, have flatly denied any participation by Milton. In this study, these papers are examined for internal evidence, establishing that Milton did not compose the primary English documents, and that Rosin was responsible for editing the French booklet. It is suggested that Theodore Haak translated the only part that was published in Dutch. An analysis of the Latinity leads to identifying Milton's share in the *Scriptum* booklet; and an extraordinarily peculiar change in style in mid-booklet is noted, which allows us to reconstruct the operating procedures in which Milton was involved. Further, the manuscript diary of Leo ab Aitzema, previously overlooked, gives us confirming testimony for crediting the Latin of the Parliament's *Declaration* to Milton, and the French version to Rosin.

The same Latinity tests also now serve to identify and recover two hitherto unknown letters about the Anglo-Dutch war translated by Milton for the Anglo-Dutch negotiations, in July and October 1652.

Proceeding, I give attention to the mid-war negotiations in 1653. Three British letters to the Dutch, dated

1 April and 6 May 1653, are examined; evidence for the author of their Latin versions is inconclusive. A series of eight documents submitted by the British in July and August 1653 is recovered from manuscript obscurity; applying our tests, it is now possible to attribute six of these eight Latin papers to Milton's colleague Philip Meadowes, while two can be assigned to Milton himself. The draft treaty of 18 November 1653, and the final peace treaty of 5 April 1654, are studied in parallel, and in them I tabulate the persistence of phraseology carried over from Milton's Latin *Thirty-six Counter-articles* of 1652—but these treaties are stripped of his admonitions against current unclassical usages.

My study concludes with a review of Milton's public statements at various times, showing his ambivalence and feelings of conflict as an official in the government of England. Milton was not in favor of war against the Dutch, but he "went along," and was most happy when it came to an end.

To convey my findings in brief and easily digestible form, I have separated the story line into a Part One, and placed the newly recovered Milton works and other essential documents into Part Two, where they may be scrutinized at leisure. In the notes section, as well as in the appendices, the careful reader will find a great deal of other new and significant data derived from these researches.

A Personal Note on My Work and Previous Studies by Others

In my *John Milton and the Oldenburg Safeguard* (1985) I intentionally refrained from calling attention to the failings of previous studies by others, which would have required multitudinous notes identifying their errors, many arising from their neglect of the original sources, to which I was able to gain access. Reviewers generally commented on my restraint with approval, but some missed my prefaced explanation and then drew erroneous conclusions. Others, while friendly, wished to be alerted wherever previously published accounts required revisions. In this current book, I again present much new material from archival sources that have not been previously explored, thereby superseding past published accounts, and here I have tried to strike a balance between courtesy and calling attention to corrections.

Since as yet there is no concordance to Milton's Latin prose, I have had to rely on memory for locating parallel usages in his various works. The development of a proper and all-inclusive concordance will, I trust, confirm and expand the findings here presented.

Leo Miller
1990

PART ONE

*Milton in the Anglo-Dutch Negotiations,
1651–1654*

1

Milton as Secretary for Foreign Correspondence

❧ The Real Picture

At once a passionate lover and a dauntless fighter for freedom, John Milton composed the most poignant lyrics ever murmured between man and woman, and equally brilliantly he moves readers from idyllic garden scenes in Eden to blazing celestial battlefields, and back again to the Earthly Paradise. For the liberation of the human individual in matters of faith and of intellect and as a citizen in a free commonwealth, he wielded a dynamic pen in English and Latin prose during the turbulent decades of the English Revolution. He set standards for versifying in epic, tragedy and sonnet, unequalled since. And he was also, for 11 long years, a most extraordinary *literary* secretary for foreign languages in the diplomatic service of the English Commonwealth and Protectorate, 1649–1660.

In the corridors and chambers of Whitehall, where army generals and parliamentary statesmen of a regicide republic managed the business affairs of a burgeoning England, they were intermittently aware of the former schoolmaster and eloquent pamphleteer whom they employed to present their best face to the powers of continental Europe. For them, his Latin versions of their *pronunciamentos* were important momentarily in the pursuit of their state policies; but the cultured reading public of that age recognized in those same papers the qualities of true literature. Milton's Latin state letters were admired and published at least three times in his century for their literary qualities as Latin prose, and twice published in English translation. In the splendor of Milton's poetic achievement, his great English-language prose is overshadowed and neglected, and so it comes as a surprise even to scholarly specialists that these historical documents have intrinsic artistic merit. In addition, these documents also yield rich biographical data and new insights into Milton's mind and creativity.

Milton's career in public office is well documented, and yet has so many tantalizing gaps and indefinite aspects as to leave us with a less than satisfactory account. We have no knowledge of anyone who kept a daily log or regular record of Interregnum activities in international relations. Milton himself left no journal. For our knowledge of his role, we have had to depend mainly on two sources. In the handwritten Order Books of the Council of State, the official mandates for Milton to translate specified state papers are preserved, but these minutes are far from complete, and extend only from March 1649 to April 1652. These fragmentary notes also show Milton called upon for sundry ephemeral tasks, often in intelligence and counterintelligence functions.[1] The other source has been the state papers themselves, collected by contemporaries, incompletely: in two manuscript compilations, circa 1659 and 1674, and in two printed versions, the *Literæ Pseudo-Senatûs Anglicani*, 1676. These offer very uneven texts, some derived from Milton's rough drafts, some from interim drafts in varying stages of revision, some from near-final drafts. None of his original papers survive.[2]

In recent years, research into other sources has yielded a large amount of additional documents and data. In particular, my monograph *John Milton and the Oldenburg Safeguard* (1985), by recovering the manuscripts of Hermann Mylius, has made it possible to correctly and clearly define Milton's role as secretary.[3]

Until recently, Milton's status in office has been described in distorted terms. While his secretaryship was central to his own life for those 11 years, it is now quite clear that he did not function at the top level where policy was made and decided. Did he ever participate in a session of the Commonwealth Council of State when it was deliberating or debating any issue of foreign policy, or was he ever called into a meeting of the Council to be consulted? For 1649–1651 there is recorded testimony for only *one* such occasion, the day when the Council discussed Claudius Salmasius's *Defensio Regia* and decided to let Milton attempt a rebuttal to its heavy blast of royalist propaganda. From early 1651 onward, there are strong indications that he was *not* present at Council policy sessions. On 19 February 1650/51, the Council ordered "That after ye Councell is set noe Minister of the Councell shall be present at any debates but onely the Secretary and his Assistant without speciall order of the Councell."[4] Those two were, at that time, Gualter Frost, senior, and Gualter Frost, junior. There is no record of such a special order for Milton.

The Council, during Commonwealth days, 1649–1653, had a committee on foreign affairs, chosen from among its members, and, as necessary, the Council appointed as hoc committees to handle specific matters or to meet with envoys. On 10 February 1650/51, a Council order directed "That Mr. Milton the Secr for forreigne languages be appointed to attend this com̄ittee at their meetings."[5] Otherwise it appears that Milton was expected to be available on call, in some office chamber at the Council premises or at his home, to receive orders through the principal secretary, first Gualter Frost (to March 1652) and John Thurloe thereafter.

Such an order might be to meet with a Continental envoy to work out details, as Milton does with Hermann Mylius of Oldenburg in 1652 (although that specific order is not recorded). More often it was a direction to turn into Latin a paper more or less already drafted in English. From the Oldenburg negotiations, it has become evident that Milton sought to dictate his versions in what he considered purist classical Latin, or in the original neoclassical neo-Latin he created to meet the new needs of the seventeenth century. In this effort he constantly had to contend with his colleagues who did not hesitate to revise his texts, substituting their current neo-Latin terminologies in the final officially signed and sealed texts.

From the Mylius papers, we have learned that Milton could try to exercise a personal influence with top level men—in a private meeting with Council President John Bradshaw, or by making a suggestion in a letter to Bulstrode Whitelocke, Keeper of the Great Seal. Yet with regard to the most decisive final arbiter of policy, Oliver Cromwell, we cannot cite any *recorded* occasion when Milton and Cromwell came close enough to exchange a greeting of simple courtesy, let alone join in a policy discussion, even though many such occasions should have been possible.

Hermann Mylius describes for us, how, at his official reception by a committee of commissioners designated from the Council membership, on 20 October 1651, Milton was present, serving as interpreter, standing at one side, while Oliver Fleming, Master of the Ceremonies (chief of protocol), stood at the other. The councillors and Mylius were seated.[6]

This is the only reception of this kind for which there appears to be a surviving record. In contrast is the account by Leo ab Aitzema, envoy from the Hanse cities, of his welcome on 27 February/8 March 1651/52. Spelling the names of the commissioners phonetically as he heard them, Aitzema mentions *Lile, Traver, Pembrooke, Morley,*

Raleigh, Ingelsby, Ipsly, Strickland, Nevile, Chaloner as being seated at one side of a table. As at Mylius's audience, one seat on the opposite side was reserved for Aitzema. Aitzema recounts that Fleming (who had escorted him from his lodgings to Whitehall) three time made reverence (a sweeping bow?). Aitzema took off his glove and, speaking in Latin, handed his letter of credentials to Fleming. Aitzema put his glove back on; his head having been uncovered, he put his hat back on, the others put their hats on, and he proceeded to deliver his message in Latin. Lisle responded in English, of which Aitzema had a good grasp. Again there were three bows, and Aitzema withdrew. In all this detailed account, there is no mention of Milton's being present, or of any oral translation from the Latin.[7]

At other embassy receptions that are on record as being conducted with particular formality—Portuguese, Dutch, Danish, Swedish, Genoese—there is no indication of Milton's presence. Yet we would infer that Milton may have participated in several such ambassadorial audiences with Council committees in 1649–1651, before his total blindness, and perhaps after. That follows from his apologetic disclaimer when he had been a full year sightless, in his letter to John Bradshaw, "I find noe encumberances of that wch belongs to me, except it be in point of attendance at Conferences w.th Ambassadors, wch I must confess, in my Condition I am not fit for."[8]

It is time to discard the distortions that have been fostered by a misguided desire to magnify Milton's status in the Commonwealth administration, and to concentrate on an intensive study of that work he actually did perform. That focus will be found to yield much information—new, valid, and most significant—on the day-to-day events of Milton's life, on his scholarly and literary activity, and on texts of his hitherto unknown writings.

❧The Anglo-Dutch Competition: Milton's Workaday World

Milton's nomination as Council secretary was proposed on 13 March 1648/49, accepted 15 March, and in full force by 22 March. For the next two years, many records preserved his work on diplomatic papers addressed to Spain, Hamburg, Portugal, Danzig, Tuscany and the Spanish (Belgian) Netherlands, but *none* addressed to the Dutch Netherlands. Yet all indications are that during those two years there was a considerable volume of British diplomatic correspondence with the Dutch provinces. Someone prepared a letter of credence for Issac Dorislaus, who went as envoy to the Netherlands on 30 April 1649, and when Dorislaus was assassinated there, exchanges ensued with Dutch representative Albert Joachimi and continued to September 1650. From March 1650 into mid-1651, Gerard Scheap was in London on behalf of the Dutch provinces of Holland and West Friesland, addressing Parliament, submitting documents and receiving replies. In February 1651, credentials and other papers were needed for the major mission headed by Oliver St. John and Walter Strickland. In connection with that embassy, on 28 March 1651, Sir Henry Vane was directed to supply the Latin text of the 1495 *Intercursus Magnus* treaty for Milton to translate. Several transcripts must have been made of his English version, which was needed well into 1652, yet none are known to be extant now.[9]

By far the most crucial English diplomatic negotiations for that era were the talks held at Westminster between the Council's committees and the extraordinary Dutch embassy headed by three ambassadors—Jacob Cats, Gerard Schaep and Paulus van de Perre—from December 1651 to June 1652. These talks were supplemented in May by talks with Willem Nieupoort and in June with Adrian Pauw. For both countries, these parleys were political maneuvers, preliminary to transferring their commercial competition to trial naval warfare.

In this era, it had become less profitable to snatch wealth by barefaced piracy and more profitable to engage in the regular accumulation of wealth by transporting and trading goods across the seas. To the enterprising merchants in Amsterdam and in London, there was no doubt that it was fitting and proper to use their influence on their respective governments to promote their own prosperity and to damage competitors. In place of lawless piracy, legally authorized letters of marque and reprisal and legally functioning Admiralty Courts permitted preying on the shipping and commerce of "foreign" competition. Diplomatic missions spoke pious platitudes as they fenced with rival chancelleries while seeking to wangle the most advantage with the least cost and risk.

The newly established English Commonwealth, aiming to assert its power, moved first with the negotiation gambit. The Strickland-St. John embassy was sent to the Netherlands with an offer of close union, and there they were stalled for the three months. The momentary advantage was then with the Dutch. In the early months of 1651, it seemed shrewd policy in Amsterdam to wait for the outcome of Charles II's Scottish ploy. If he secured his throne in London as he seemed to have secured his crown in Scotland, he might reverse English policy, or at least he might again convulse the English in civil war. These calculations crumpled, however, when Cromwell crushed Charles and his forces at Worcester on 3 September 1651.

The London speculators then saw that it was their turn. Quickly they threw down their challenge. In October 1651, Parliament passed the Navigation Act, barring the ships of any country from carrying into British realms any goods not originating in that country, and restricting aliens from British fisheries. It was obvious to all that the Navigation Act was primarily aimed at the Dutch. The Dutch then took their turn at diplomacy. Petty internal politics and local scandals slowed their choice of ambassadors, but finally on 15 December the triple-headed embassy came sailing up the Thames, with a retinue of 90 dignitaries and servitors.¹⁰

The full story of this mission would take many pages, and has its own intrinsic interest. Here we shall be concerned with trying to determine Milton's day-to-day role, but that will still require telling a good deal of the surrounding story.

❧The Negotiations Begin and Milton Is Involved

In various recorded sources we see that the Dutch flotilla casts anchor at Gravesend, 16 December 1651; the principals are welcomed in state at Tower Hill by the Earl of Pembroke, Lord Lisle, Sir Peter Wentworth, on 17 December; and their chief secretary Jan van Vliet (Janus Vlitius) is dispatched on 18 December to make the formal request for their audience.¹¹

Milton is not mentioned. We do know that he is not well. He is suffering from the harsh and hopeless surgical treatments mistakenly prescribed in futile efforts to save his failing sight. Because of petty politics in Parliament, he is under distressing pressure to vacate his Whitehall apartments; on 17 December he is moving his household to other lodgings in the street called Petty France, for the comfort of his pregnant wife and their three little children.¹² He is continuing old business, the slow-moving *Safeguard* for the Count of Oldenburg, and long overdue responses owed by the Council to the Doge of Tuscany. And, because of his worsening eyesight, until the end of the month he is not even sure that he will be reappointed to his post.

On 19/29 December the three Dutch ambassadors are formally received by Parliament. Jacob Cats makes a supreme effort at conciliatory oratory. In his own country he was regarded as a great poet. Even today his Latin oration for this occasion may be regarded as a model of baroque eloquence, but from the manipulators of policy in Westminster the word went out to the purveyors of public opinion to sneer at his artistry as academic, pedantic high-sounding nonsense.¹³

It was now the turn of the English to be dilatory. Not until 1/11 January are the ambassadors received by the Council of State (Christmas and New Year's Day were no holidays for the Puritans). On 6/16 January at Parliament,

> The Lord Com*missioner* Whitelock reports, from the Counsell of State the Proceedings of the Lords Ambassadors Extraordinary from the States Generall of the United Provinces, upon their addresse to the Counsell of State, contayned in severall Papers, whereof the first was, The copie of the Com*mission* to the Lords Ambassadors from the High and Mighty Lords, the States Generall of the United Provinces, both in French and English; wh<u>i</u>ch were read, The Second being a Paper delivered into the Counsell by the Lords Ambassadors, in Latine; w<u>i</u>th a Translation thereof in English whi<u>c</u>h were read.¹⁴

Since the Dutch envoys supplied English versions of their speeches and papers, Milton's service as translator was not needed. No Wednesday, 7/17 January, the House of Commons—perhaps some 50 members—officially recognized those papers and authorized the Council to proceed further.

At that Council session of 1/11 January, the Dutch ambassadors suggested that discussions resume at the point where they had been interrupted the previous spring in Holland. In a somewhat propitiatory manner, they presented their three key demands: suspension of the Navigation Act; suspension of letters of marque and reprisal; and restitution of captured Dutch ships, with compensation.¹⁵

Of these three demands, the most urgent was the status of captive Dutch ships in danger of being sold, and the condition of their skippers and crews in detention. More Dutch ships were liable to be seized under cover of letters of marque and reprisal issued "to the administrator of

Anna Paulet" back in 1635 during the reign of Charles I, long in abeyance but recently renewed. On 12/22 January, 18 of the captive Dutch skippers, acting on their own initiative, submitted a petition to the Council asking for action: either their cases should be adjudicated, if there were legal grounds, or else they should be set free with their goods restored. This petition was read that day in Council, who forwarded it to the Court of Admiralty to decide.

Meanwhile, these same issues were taken separately to the Admiralty Court on behalf of the ambassadors by their secretary Van Vliet and a junior member of their staff, Lodewijck Huygens. Obtaining no resolution from the Court, on 16/26 January the ambassadors filed a written protest at the Council, *Exposuerunt nuper*.* In response, the Council voted that day to suspend the *Paulet* letters of marque and reprisal, and directed the judges of Admiralty to publish the suspension. As of 20/30 January the Court had not acted, so Huygens was sent there to seek an explanation. Although, after a bit of haggling, he was given some assurances, further discussions were needed on 21/31 January between Gualter Frost and Bulstrode Whitelocke on the one side, Van Vliet and Huygens on the other, with more memoranda written from the Dutch to the Council of State.[16]

It is quite likely that Milton was already involved in the proceedings at this point. We can infer this from the note in Hermann Mylius's diary that on 20/30 January he saw a Dutch visitor arriving at Milton's home; but Milton is not yet named in any records of the negotiations. On 22 January, in response to a Latin note signed by Vlitius on 11/21 January, the Council's reply was written in English over the signature of Gualter Frost, and so delivered, apparently not yet turned into Latin.[17]

In effect, the Council retorted that the Admiralty judges

---

* These diplomatic documents are identified by their opening words.

were conducting their court proceedings precisely because of the petition submitted by the captured skippers. Vexed, the Dutch ambassadors sent Vlitius and Huygens bearing a strongly worded expostulation, in Latin (23 January/2 February). They found Oliver Fleming with four or five others smoking their pipes in a small room near the Council chamber, delivered their document, waited nearly an hour and a half, only to be then told that the Council would consider their presentation and respond in its own time.[18]

What went on behind the closed doors of the Council, we can only guess. There were some members present who could read Latin well enough to understand the urgent Dutch message. Nonetheless, the Council's Order Book for that 23 January/3 February enters as its decision:

> That Mr. Milton doe make a translate of the paper this day sent in to the Councell from the Lords Ambassadrs from the High and mighty Lords the States generall of the united Provinces, which the Comitte for foreigne affaires are to take into consideracon and prepare an answere thereto to be reported to the Councell.[19]

The ambassadors' paper, *Cum nihil prius*, signed by Janus Vlitius, is not known to be extant, but transcripts do survive. It is especially regrettable that no copy of Milton's English version is known to survive. In Part Two, I reproduce Vlitius's Latin letter, and supply my own version in English, in the hope that this might lead someone to recognize Milton's text in some neglected pile of old papers.[20]

2

Authenticating Miltonic Texts and Those of his Colleagues

❧ *Milton's Creative Classical Neo-Latin*

The captured Dutch ships were specific and concrete problems within the whole conflict between English and Dutch merchants and shipowners. The ships represented only one of the three points at issue, as submitted by the Dutch on 1/11 January. To pick up the other threads, we must step back to 19/29 January. On that Monday, the three ambassadors met with six commissioners from the Council of State and reiterated their three prime points in writing, in a paper beginning *Quæ tam a Parlamento*.[21] On 20 January, the Council asked its committee on foreign affairs to prepare answers to all three items. This reply was drawn up by Monday, 26 January/5 February, when the Council directed "That Mr. Milton doe translate into Latin the Answere of the Councell to the first paper of the Lord Ambassadrs of the united Provinces conteyning three Articles."²²

The official text of this letter, in its original English, dated 29 January 1651, in British style, is written in elegant script by a Council amanuensis and signed by Council President Arthur Hesilrige, who was elected 26 January for the ensuing month. It is preserved in the Algemeen Rijksarchief at The Hague in MS. S.G. 8460 under no. 16. With it, also under number 16, is preserved the authorized Latin translation done by Milton, beginning *Concilium Status Parlamenti Reipub: Angliæ*, in the hand of the same amanuensis, but unsigned.²³ Both texts, new to Milton studies, are now reproduced in Part Two.

This reply to the Dutch paper of 19/29 January politely agrees to consider any proposals based on the *Intercursus Magnus* or otherwise, but brushes aside any connection with the aborted 1651 talks in the Netherlands. With a brevity that is almost curt, it flatly rejects any repeal or suspension of the Navigation Act. In contrast, the reply goes to great length as it implies that blame for any need for letters of marque and reprisal rests with the other side, cites their own recent suspension of the *Paulet* letters, and justifies the referral of pending cases to the Admiralty Court as proper legal procedure.

The Latin text of this reply has been known since 1938 from photostats supplied to Professors Mabbott and French by The Hague archives.²⁴ Although it is not found among any of the seventeenth century compilations, they accepted it as Milton's version because its contents fit the Council of State's order of 26 January. That is strong circumstantial evidence, but that attribution can now be confirmed by considering certain stylistic features.

Our most critical evidence is Milton's purist adherence to the standard of Latin that he considered authentically native to ancient Rome in its heyday. In that spirit, he had roundly belabored the eminent Salmasius for having used *persona* in its seventeenth century vernacular sense of "person," instead of its classical sense of "actor's mask";

and when Hermann Mylius used the neo-Latinism *projecta* for "drafts," Milton wrote back *"projecta illa, quæ vocas,"* "those drafts, as *you* call them." Milton adhered to a purist standard of "correct" Latin, while his colleagues on the Council staff preferred current unclassical neo-Latin terminology. These differences, now recognized, make it possible to distinguish Milton's Latin from that of his colleagues and thereby to identify state papers done by Milton.[25]

Four times in the 1651 letter, the English text refers to "letters of marque and reprisal." Three times in the concurrent Latin, certain interpolated cautionary phrases appear, which are not included in the English: *literas quas vocant Merc et Represales* "letter *which are called* of marque and reprisal"; *literæ, quas vocant* and *literas Merc et Represales vulgò dictas*, "letters *commonly called* of marque and reprisal."

Over a span of decades up to his last days, Milton compiled materials intended for a Latin dictionary; for the Mylius papers we have learned to recognize these phrases as his sensitive lexicographer's protest against terms not known in ancient Rome and not used in classical Latin.

The English text of this letter also refers to the "Admiralty Court." At that time there was in customary use a law-Latin unclassical term, *curia admiralitatis*, but the Latin text of the Council's reply offers instead a different expression, minted from classical vocabulary: *curia maritimarum causarum*, "court of maritime cases."

In yet another example of this, we see that the English text uses "navigation" and "shipping" rather as synonyms. Adam Littleton's 1684 *Linguæ Latinæ Liber Dictionarius Quadripartitus* accepted *navigatio* in its English-Latin pages for "navigation," but only with a restrictive asterisk. But in ancient Rome a *navigatio* was a particular voyage, not an abstract generality, and so the Latin text here uses *as navigandi studium* for "navigation," and *res navalis* for its synonym "shipping."

That these choices of locution are the critical confirmation that this Latin letter was indeed the work of Milton will be reconfirmed many times over by the recurrence of similar choices among his state papers.[26]

These phrasings, which at times displeased Milton's business-oriented colleagues who were concerned with the task of the moment, remind us that the learned reading public in Europe read these state papers as a work of artistry in the great tradition of epistolary stylists from Cicero to Petrarch to Erasmus. In his preface to the 1690 edition, J.G. Pritius marveled at their elegance, their polished felicity: "I must honestly confess," he writes, "that when I first came across them, they took me so greatly that I could not lay them down until I had read them all through." We must remember that Milton had here a quite limited field for creativity. He was bound to texts composed by a regime of lawyers, merchants and shipowners; but what he could do, and did do, was to supply the most appropriate level of literary phrasing, conforming to the best classical models. Unfortunately, in our century, many who most highly value Milton's literary genius have been insensitive to the scope of his achievement here.

Turning its attention again to Vlitius's *Cum nihil prius* and Milton's English translation, on 28 January/7 February the Council directed:

> That the paper now read in answer to the paper from the Dutch Ambassad.[rs] sent by them to the Councell on the 23th instant be passed & approved off. And M.[r] Milton is to translate it into latine in order to be signed by the Lord President of the Councell.[27]

This letter, in its final official form in English, dated 29 January British style, is written in elegant script by a Council amanuensis and signed by Arthur Hesilrige. It is preserved in the Hague Rijksarchief in MS. S.G. 8460 under no. 17. With it likewise is preserved Milton's authorized Latin translation, *Scriptum ab Excellentijs*

Vestris, unsigned, but in the hand of the same amanuensis. Both texts, previously unrecorded in Milton studies, are now printed in Part Two.[28]

This reply voices pained innocence of the allegations made in the Netherlanders' note of 23 January/2 February; it further reproduces in full the petition of the Dutch skippers, the Council's decree thereon 12/22 January, the Council order of 16/26 January suspending the *Paulet* letters of marque, and their further response of 22 January (including and expanding the paragraph signed by Gualter Frost on 22 January) to expedite Admiralty Court decisions on other pending cases of captured ships.

Like the preceding letter, this Latin text *Scriptum ab Excellentijs Vestris* has been known since the 1930s from a photostat of the 1652 text, and it was attributed to Milton by Mabbott and French because it matches orders in the Council's minutes. Once again that attribution can now be confirmed by the master touches of Milton's Latin prose style.

Four times this English letter refers to the "Court of Admiralty," but Milton dictated his *curia maritima* four times, and once *judices maritimarum causarum,* in appropriate grammatical declensions. Four times the English text refers to the current (present) month as "instant." Milton's contemporaries among composers of state papers commonly used the word *currentis,* a locution not used in the days of Augustus Caesar. Milton does differently: he uses *hujus* (mensis).

In the Dutch skippers' petition, submitted in English, there were five names of ships and five names of ship masters. In the Latin text, two of the ship names are put into Latin, one remains in English, two show *of* rendered as *de;* and three of these names are introduced by the formula *cui nomen,* while two are not, remaining in simple apposition. First names of the five captains are made Latin, family names are not. (In the companion letter of the same date, the ship's name is in Latin, with *cui nomen;* the captain's given name is Latin, not his family name). These patterns, and their inconsistencies, are characteristic of the *Literæ* text of Milton's state papers.[29]

Summarizing the Dutch complaint, Milton borrows some Latin phrases from Vlitius's *Cum nihil prius*. Perhaps the English equivalents in the Council's English reply came from Milton's translation.[30]

While Milton was primarily a translator, and not the formulator, of the state papers, he did have some leeway in phraseology, and on this occasion he seems to have taken advantage of this liberty. The Council's English text bluntly asserts that the paper submitted by Vlitius "is grounded upon great mistakes." In Milton's Latin, this is softened to read, "relies on certain inaccurate preceptions, as if they were true." We know that Vlitius had eagerly arranged in advance for personal introductions to meet Milton. Had Vlitius, by this time, already come to pay his respects?

One other peculiarity in the Latin of this letter is especially notable. The United (Dutch) Provinces had a joint governing body, the States General. In Dutch it was called *Staten Generael* and in their own Latin usage, *Ordines Generales*. They also used *Ordines* to designate each province's governing "States." In the same way, in the preface to his *Pro Populo Anglicano Defensio*, printed early in 1651, Milton used *Ordines* both for the joint States General and for the provincial States of Holland, *Illustrissimi Fœderatorum Ordines*, and *Hollandiæ Ordines*. However, in this letter *Scriptum ab Excellentijs Vestris* in January 1652, the joint body is designated, in the ablative case, as *Statibus Generalibus*. This is a quite out of the ordinary form, which will appear again in two or more of these Anglo-Dutch documents and will be seen *nowhere else*. In sharp contrast, later, in the July 1652 *Scriptum* text, the expression that appears to be Milton's preference is something else again: *Potestates Generales*, used some 21 times, and the same term *Potestates Generales* reappears eight times in two presumably Miltonic letters of 1653.

His later preference for *Potestates* can be understood: it has strong classical justification. Milton was strong-willed and obstinate enough to ignore the practice of the Dutch even when addressing a letter *to* the Dutch. But neither *Status* nor *Statibus Generalibus* was classical in this sense, and so can hardly be construed as Milton's preference. Rather, this usage suggests the participation of a different mind, a mind given to literal substitutions in translating one language to another, the mind of a particular person who had previously completed official translations for the English government, and who, in a few days, would be officially appointed as a colleague to Milton: Lewis Rosin.

We have no way of knowing; we can only try to visualize the scene. Milton, almost totally blind, sits listening to a clerk read the English language draft, and dictates his characteristic classical Latin. One or more others are present; Rosin, under consideration for appointment, is one. Milton halts at *States General*. In 1651 he had not given it a second thought, but lately he has been sparring with his colleagues over just such word choices. Now he is dissatisfied with *Ordines*; the Dutch themselves may use it, but that word reminds him of the three ranks in Cicero's Rome, *senator, equester, plebeius*, and in his mind this does not fit the Dutch federal assembly. He hesitates. Rosin speaks up: Dutch diplomats commonly render *States General* in their French correspondence as *Estats Generaux*, and surely the closest to both in Latin would be *Statibus Generalibus*. Milton is not really at all satisfied, but he lets it pass and makes a mental note to have someone re-read to him some appropriate passages from Suetonius and Cicero for their use of *potestates*.

It would be better, certainly, if we had written testimony for that January day, but something of this kind is clearly implied by the records we do have. When *Statibus Generalibus* recurs, twice, it is in contexts attributable to Rosin; while by the second week in March, when Milton is translating Article 7 in the Thirty-six

Counter-Articles, he notices that the Netherlanders' draft uses *Status* for [nation-] "states," but he rejects this and dictates *potestatibus* instead.³¹

On Thursday, 29 January, the Council directed that these two papers be ready for examination between seven and eight the next morning, and accordingly both were transmitted by the commissioners to the ambassadors at their meeting on 30 January/9 February.³²

❧*The Paper of Demands and Milton's Colleague, Lewis Rosin*

In the course of preparing these two replies to the Dutch, the Council decided to draw up a *paper of demands*, a bill of claims for damages suffered by English business interests, to offset the claims being pressed by the Netherlands, and perhaps to serve as an effective barrier against reaching an agreement. The Council's first thought was to submit this set of accounts together with those other two documents, but on 28 January the Council decided to separate it, and ordered instead:

> 6. That the paper now read to be of Demands to the Dutch Ambasdrs be referred to the Comittee for fforeigne affaires to consider of the damages done to the people of this Nation, and the tymes, and to report it to the Councell to morrow in the afternoone.
>
> 7. That the paper prepared to be a paper of Demands to be given to the Dutch Ambassadrs shall not be presented to them with the two other papers which the Councell hath passed to be given unto them in answere to two papers of theirs.
>
> 8. That it be referred to the Comittee for forreigne affaires to peruse the last clause of the last paper of the Councell which makes mention of a paper of Demands to be given to the Dutch Ambassadrs, and to amend it soe as it may not relate to the present sending of a paper of Demands, the Councell haveing ordered the not goeing of it at present.

On Thursday, 29 January, the Council specified:

> 3. That the paper of Demands be referred to the consideraĉon of the Comittee for fforeigne affaires who are to perfect the same and to bring in any other particulars of the like nature, and they are to report it to the Councell on Monday next in the afternoone.
> 4. That the Comittee for fforeigne affaires doe meet on Saturday morning in reference to the business of the paper of Demands.[33]

On Thursday, 12 February, the Council set Wednesday, 18 February, for the committee on foreign affairs to report, and on 20 February (SP 25/66, p. 369) ordered "That the paper now read to bee sent to the Dutch Ambass^{rs} bee approved off, translated into Latine and sent to the said Ambassado^{rs} the English paper to bee signed and the latine to go as a Copie." This last paper, otherwise not there specified, seems to refer to the cover letter for the *Paper of Demands*.

These fragmentary Order Book entries often prematurely imply that a document has reached its final form. Ordained the Council, 25 February/6 March,

> That the paper now read of demands to be made to the Dutch Ambass^{rs} be translated.
> That the English copie of the said Demands be signed by the lord President.[34]

Milton is *not* named, here or in the 20 February order, although he has been and is the Council's expert for that function of translation into Latin.

However, the Council was not quite finished. The next day, it voted again, "That the Paper now read conteyning a Sixth Article of Demand be approved of and translated," when someone remembered that there was still another old bill of claims outstanding, although he could not remember its exact date. This old account was therefore added, "That soe much of the Particulars demanded by Parlam.^{t} in the yeare—, be alsoe translated and sent with the other paper" (26 February, PRO, SP 25/66, pp. 381-82). This old account is not further described, but we can identify it as a catalog of claims by individuals, drafted in English by Thomas Eden, doctor of laws and burgess for Cambridge in the Long Parliament. This was compiled pursuant to an order of the House of Commons, 21 January 1644/45, during negotiations with the earlier Dutch embassy of Willem Boreel and Johan van Reede van Renswoude: "That Doctor Eden do prepare a Brief of the Complaints of the English, and their desire of Redress from the States General, for Damages done unto them from Subjects of the States General."[35]

These composite sets of claims were finished on 11/21 March, and so the Council ordered them to be delivered on Monday, 15/25 March (together with another long document translated by Milton, which will be discussed shortly): "That the papers of demands agreed on at the Councell together wth the answere to the 36 Articles be delivered to the Ambassd^{rs} from the United Provinces on Monday morning by the Com^{rs} of the Councell" (PRO, SP 25/66, p. 440).

Until now this *Paper of Demands* has been overlooked by Miltonists, although an earlier version of one part, the *Summarium Damnorum*, was printed in the 1676 *Literæ Pseudo-Senatûs Anglicani* as a paper done by Milton. From the originals in the Dutch archives, we can now reconstruct the entire document. In its bare form, it reads like the kind of invoice that might be submitted by a people whom Napoleon is said later to have called a *nation* of *shopkeepers*. It is also a classic document of nascent nationalism, in which private and public economic interests are blended with jingoistic distortion and pride. In its final form, as delivered to the ambassadors, it had four main parts: a cover letter, two sets of claims in the *Summarium Damnorum*, another table of claims in 15 articles, and the 1645 catalogue of complaints.

The cover letter, written in English, signed by Philip [Sidney, Lord] Lisle, together with its translation in four pages of Latin manuscript, tabulated six numbered articles and a string of further unnumbered claims:

1. Reparations to the Muscovy Company for wrongs suffered at Greenland in 1618, £22,000.
2. Punishment of any perpetrators of the "Amboyna massacre" of 1622/23 who might still be living. [That was an affair which the Dutch described as a trial and executions pursuant to law.]
3. Reparation to the East India Company, as itemized in the *Summarium Damnorum* and in the table of 15 articles.
4. Restoration to English control of the East Indies island of Poolaroon, and the port of Pooloway, with a quantity of spices derived thence.
5. Reparations for depredations on merchant ships since 1648, in particular for the case of the *Mary and John*, Francis Hardedge, master.
6. Reparations for the claims in the 1645 catalog.

The cover letter also reiterated complaints made to Boreel and Renswoude in 1645, protested mistreatment suffered by English envoys Strickland and St. John in 1651, and denounced the murder of Dorislaus. With the letter went four enclosures marked B1, B2, B3 and B4.

In B1 and B2 are two tables, one of six articles and one of four. These are itemized claims *revised* from a previous draft (preserved in the Miltonic text printed as the *Summarium Damnorum* in the 1676 *Literæ*), together with a translation of four pages in Latin manuscript, spelling out on detailed figures the financial losses suffered by English interests in the East Indies and Persia, plus a claim for 32,899 pounds of pepper worth £6,000 sterling taken from the ship *Endimion* in 1649.

B3 is a table of 15 articles, reduced from a previous 16, of claims dating from 1621–1627 in the East Indies, totaling £48,900 15s. This fills two pages in the Latin translation, covering claims for money and property seized by Dutch nationals, for bad debts, and for the cash value of about 150 *slaves*. The keepers of the liberty of England saw no inconsistency in buying and selling men and women of alien races as chattel, or in English sailors hijacking cargos of such slave property as "lawful prizes," but they objected strenuously to the Dutch hijacking of British slave cargos.[36]

B4 is the 1645 English-language catalog of complaints, 13 articles in minute detail, with six pages of Latin translation.[37]

In all, the *Paper of Demands* encompassed 16 pages of Latin text, with many names of individual persons, places and ships, and many figures in English currency and continental currency, several times revised and refigured. It makes dreary labor to trace out and to transcribe all of this dismal matter now and to reproduce it in Part Two, but we must do so to put ourselves into Milton's presence in March 1651/52, and to understand with what dreary labor he was sometimes expected to cope.

What becomes clearer, in this context, is that it was not only the closing in of Milton's total blindness, but the sudden increase in the demand for his services and the necessity of precise attention to detail, which must have impelled him to ask for help. These Anglo-Dutch exchanges were a full-time activity. The Oldenburg *Safeguard*, just concluded, had been a daily drain. A major Danish mission had also arrived in London, beginning a six-month process of negotiation. Leo ab Aitzema had come to normalize relations on behalf of the Hanse cities. In between everything else, Milton had translated a letter to the Senate of Hamburg (by 5 March) and to Queen Christina of Sweden (by 10 March). So Georg Rudolph Weckherlin, Milton's predecessor in office, was recalled, nominated on 9 March to be Milton's *secretary-assistant*, and appointed 11 March.[38]

As we have seen, Milton had already been given another aide to relieve him of one phase of his burdens, a close colleague who deserves much notice. A Council order of 2 February 1651/52 proposed

That Monsieur Rosin bee made use of for the translating of such papers out of the ffrench tongue into English as the Comittee for fforeigne affaires shall have occasion to make use of or direct to bee translated.

Lewis Rosin had served with the Strickland-St. John mission in the Netherlands in 1651, and some of its papers written in French are signed by his name.[39]

The appointment of Weckherlin was official on 11 March, and the *Papers of Demands* (*papers* plural in the Council order of that date) were all ready on that date. Therefore the cover letter was not translated by Weckherlin. And it was not done by Milton: it shows no specific Miltonisms, and there are too many occurrences of non-Miltonic vocabulary in it. However, the translator would seem to have known of Milton's blast against Salmasius's use of *persona*, because the words *in person* in the letter's English text do not appear in the Latin version. (One peculiarity must be noticed. The Latin letter uses *uti* rather than *ut*, seven times, and *ut* only once as *utque*.) Rosin is most likely the translator of this letter.[40]

Included in the 1676 *Literæ*, the *Summarium Damnorum* (parts B1 and B2) may be with assurance attributed in that Latin to Milton. It may have been drafted early in 1651 for the Strickland-St. John mission; it has a reference to 1650 which, by the British calendar, would run through 25 March 1651. When used in 1652, this document was somewhat revised, either by Milton or Rosin, or both.[41]

The English text of the 15 articles in part B3 is essentially copied word for word from the original 16-article table of claims as it was prepared about 1627. The Latin text in the 1652 *Paper of Demands* uses a Miltonic vocabulary, with a number of typical Miltonisms: *cui nomen* inserted before the unfamiliar name *Nelacca*; *vulgo dictis* appended to *octonis*, used for "pieces of eight"; "sterling" is *nostræ montæ*, as in the *Summarium Damnorum*. Some technical terms are necessarily unclassical:

"gunpowder" required the addition of *nitrati* before *pulveris*; for "spices," *species* [sc. *aromaticae*, as in Littleton's dictionary]; *fiscalis* for the functionary "fiscal"; *caryophyllum* for the spice "clove"; and Far Eastern place names unknown to the ancients in Rome. The fourth article makes a distinction between the English people and "his majesties Subjects at Polloroone" (not English), reflecting the 1622 status of this group; this is carried over into the Latin without modification. The earlier draft of the *Summarium* Damnorum, completed before 25 March 1651, refers to this table in its previous 16-article format as *pridem exhibita*, "formerly delivered," which could mean 1627, but could also suggest that at this time, the table was completed first. The weight of the evidence favors the inference that the Latin of this 15-article document was composed or revised by Milton.

The catalog of individual complaints in enclosure B4 was given in 1645 to the Dutch envoys in English and in French, and survives in those original manuscripts. The English text also appeared in print in *A Second Declaration* of the Lords and Commons dated 18 September 1645. No version in Latin from 1645 is known, neither in English nor in Dutch archives. Only from 1652 are translated Latin copies extant.

The 1652 Latin version of B4 is an exceedingly complex problem. It does repeatedly manifest indications of Milton's own practice. Ship names are six times turned into Latin equivalents, each with *cui nomen*. One that remains in English, the *Cygnet*, is labeled *vulgo dictam*, "commonly called." The latter formula is seen in place names: The *Flye vulgo dictum* twice, although "commonly called" is not in the English, and "within the Boyes" [buoys] becomes *intra indices quos Boyos vocant*. "Court of Admiralty" is rendered as *curia maritima*. These usages are all characteristic of Milton and not characteristic of his colleagues.

"Your Lordship" appears here translated as *Dominationes Vestræ*. One month earlier, Milton had had a problem with that title. In translating "Your Lordship" for the *Recreditif*, which commended envoy Hermann Mylius as he returned to his ruler the Count of Oldenburg, Milton used *Amplitudo Vestra* (literally, "Your Grandeur"), most likely because *dominatio* rang in his ear with the connotations of tyranny and despotism it had conveyed in republican Rome. His colleagues, chief secretary Gualter Frost and chief of protocol Oliver Fleming, saw to it that the final text was changed to *Dominatio Vestra*. Milton had been "edited" similarly on other occasions. Whether Milton first dictated *Amplitudo* here again, or chose not to repeat a dispute, we cannot know, but it is certain that *Dominationes Vestrae* was not his choice, but the preference of his colleagues.

Since the characteristics that we regard as tests of authenticity are examples of classical purism, it is essential to consider the presence of other usages in B4. *Mercator Adventurarius*, "Merchant Adventurer," is matched in Milton's writings once by *Societas Adventuraria* in the 2 April 1649 state paper to Hamburg, but it was common in diplomatic correspondence at that time. In those years, new terms of a technical character sometimes could be rendered by late Latin words that had been adapted (as *solidus*, once a coin in the later Roman Empire, for "shilling"). Such adaptations in the B4 catalog are *sclopus*, for "musket"; and with a classical adjective, *sclopus minusculus*, for "pistol"; *bombarbas*, for "pieces of ordnance." Official titles of specific functionaries necessarily required their *neo*-Latin form, *balivus* for "bailiff" of the Prince of Orange, and *advocatus fiscalis*. Such terms permitted little or no choice, whereas "ammunition" could still be treated by a Ciceronian circumlocution as *armis et instrumento bellico*.

Naval titles were another challenge. In B4, "admiral" is once rendered by the classical *præfectus*, but when a particular commander is named, the title is the nonclassical *Admirallus*. Milton's personal preference for the supreme naval commander was *præfectus*, seen in his letter of 27 April 1650 to Portugal (where he avoids "captain" by *dux*), in the letter of same date to Spain, and again in his letter of 11 November 1652 to Spain. For "captain," he used either *præfectus* or *navarchus* (11 November 1652 letter to Spain, 14 December 1652 letter to Tuscany). At that time, two other words were in use for "admiral," variant borrowings from the Greek. Mylius used *archithalassus*, which Milton had to accept, just as he had to swallow Mylius's half-Gothic *Salvaguardia*. Dutch envoy Pauw used *thalassiarcha*, but Milton regarded such adoptions from Greek as a corruption of Latinity.[42] Therefore the conspicuous appearance in this B4 catalog of the word *telonium* for "custom house"—an outright borrowing from the Greek, and a word shunned by Milton in other state documents—points to collaboration by another hand.

The States General of the Netherlands is here, once, in that unusual form as *Statibus Generalibus* (as in the cover letter) and several times as *Ordines*. The Dutch themselves always used *Ordines*, as did Milton's colleagues (and did Milton also after 1654). Here those two forms again point to a collaborating hand.

Most troubling is the emphatically literal sound and style of *Domus Dominorum and Domus Communium* for "House of Lords" and "House of Commons," used in B4 several times. That is sharply different from Milton's usage in his *Pro Populo Anglicano Defensio* (composed 1650, revised 1658), where he regularly used *ordo plebeius* for "House of Commons," and *ordines* for "Houses" of Parliament.[43]

From these particulars it would seem that B4 was translated into Latin by a colleague who read his draft to Milton, with Milton tolerating what had to be tolerated. But Milton must have required *cui nomen* and *curia maritima*, and may have insistently interjected *vulgo dictum* and *quos vocant* for those words that were not in any way Latin.

Further, in B4 *ut* is used seven times and *uti* three times, a disproportion that recalls the cover letter attributed to Rosin. And in introducing each claim, the Latin version uses the word *queritur* or *queruntur*: "complains." That word is not seen in the English text of 1654, but it is used throughout the derivative French version of 1645. It seems that the primary translator of B4 found the latter helpful, hence someone whose first language was French: Rosin.

In this composite *Paper of Demands* (a piece of bureaucratic hackwork if there ever was one) we see Milton at work side by side with the obscure Lewis Rosin. Milton is responsible, but Rosin carries the papers through to the finish. In Milton's personal file, there remained only his original *Summarium Damnorum*, which was later picked up and incorporated incongruously among the state letters of the *Literæ* edition.

The Thirty-six Counter-articles: Milton Revises the Latin of the Dutch

We return to the Anglo-Dutch negotiating teams. In playing their diplomacy games, both sides liked to present their respective positions in the guise of updating the Thirty-six Articles of the "Burgundian" treaty, the famous *Intercursus Magnus* of 24 February 1495 O.S., between the Low Countries and England. Under other circumstances, this pose might have contributed to a new agreement. In his first pamphlet, *Of Reformation*, Milton had written: "Hence it is that the prosperous, and prudent states of the united Provinces, whom we ought to love ... whom the similitude of manners and language, the commodity of traffick, which founded the old Burgundian League betwixt us, but chiefly Religion should bind us immortally...."[44] The reasons Milton asserted in 1641 for Anglo-Dutch friendship were essentially the same as those voiced by Jacob Cats in his opening address in December 1651.

On 11/21 February, at a meeting they requested, the Dutch ambassadors formally handed over *their* draft of the Thirty-six Articles to the English commissioners; this draft was substantially the same as the one they had submitted to Strickland and St. John in June 1651. An English version had been prepared, perhaps partly by John Thurloe and partly by Lewis Rosin, and so was ready to hand.[45]

The Council of State was occupied for several weeks with examining each of these Thirty-six Articles point by point. On Monday, 8/18 March, having rewritten many of these articles to suit themselves, the Council ordered

> That the remainder of the Articles to bee offered to the Dutch Ambassrs: wch were not taken up this day be taken up to morrow in the afternoone the first businesse.
>
> That soe many of the Articles as are already passed bee sent to Mr Milton to be translated into Latine.

The next day, Tuesday, 9/19 March, the Council further directed

> That the Articles now read in answere to the thirty six Articles offered to the Councell by the Dutch Ambassrs: bee translated into Latine by Thursday next in the afternoone.[46]

Milton's work was done by that Thursday. On 11 March, the Council directed that their own Thirty-six Counter-Articles, in English signed by Philip Lisle, along with (Milton's) Latin translation, should be given to the Dutch on Monday, 15/25 March, together with the complete *Paper of Demands*.[47]

That official English text, written in elegant script by a Council amanuensis, is preserved and is available in the Hague Rijksarchief, MS. S.G. 8460, no. 21; and the officially authorized Latin version is in MS. Aitzema 86, no. 21. Both have been unrecorded in Milton studies. Both manuscripts have suffered damage at the margins, with some loss of text, but another transcript (of the Latin only) is preserved in MS. S.G. 12589.62. Both the Council's

English and Milton's Latin texts are reproduced in Part Two.[48]

In their reply, the English accepted some of the Dutch proposals, partially modified some, drastically changed some and rejected some. They skirted rather than confronted the real issues. Like the Dutch, they spoke of friendship and alliance, but they still refused to void the Navigation Act; declined to give access to their colonial "plantations" located between Virginia and Newfoundland, barely conceding that there might be a few Dutch settlers along the Hudson Rives; refused to join in combined naval action against pirates; were equivocal or unhelpful with regard to the fisheries on which many Netherlanders depended, and so also with reference to Portugal, whose Brazilian colonies were then still partly and shakily in Dutch hands. Some points were accepted, but were hedged with technical and legalistic reservations. The Dutch had proposed mutual rights for their respective nationals to enter and reside in each other's countries; the English, knowing that the Dutch were then the most tolerant nation in matters of religion, proposed to restrict that privilege to Protestants only. This may have been motivated primarily by anti-Catholic sentiment, but this provision effectively continued the official exclusion of Jews from England for the time being.

The Dutch Thirty-six Articles follow the pattern of the 1495 *Intercursus Magnus*, and some articles relate to similar subject matter, but as a whole they constitute an entirely different document. The British counterproposals follow the same pattern, but even where there was some agreement with Dutch offers, the answers are couched in different terms.

In its deliberations the Council presumably worked from Milton's English version of the *Intercursus Magnus* and from (Thurloe/Rosin's?) English version of the Netherlanders' Latin text, drawing up their answer in English for Milton to put into Latin. In the process, a few words and phrases were carried over from the ambassadors' Latin draft, but clearly Milton preferred his own vocabulary and construction, adhering far more strictly to his classical models.

The Dutch draft, for instance, spoke of cities "walled or unwalled" as *vallata vel non vallata;* Milton substituted *sive muro cincti sive sine mœibus* (Article 3). In his own dictionary, he very likely restricted *vallo* and *vallum* to palisades or earthen ramparts, as in Caesar's time. The Dutch spoke of "contraband" as *mercibus illegitimis,* but *illegitimus* was not spoken in ancient Rome, so Milton (Articles 5 & 6) uses the circumlocution *merces ullæ publicæ prohibitæ.* (Adam Littleton felt the same way, offering *bona edicto publico prohibita* in his 1684 dictionary). As previously, Milton said *res navalis* where the Dutch wrote *navigatio* (Article 2). Referring to shoreline safety, the English draft used the word *beakon,* while the Dutch used *Phari.* Milton apparently restricted *Pharus* to the ancient lighthouse near Alexandria and the island on which it stood, and so dictated *speculatorios ignes* (Article 15), which was also the equivalent given for *beacon* by Littleton.

Further, the Dutch used *telonia* for "customs duties." This was the word used for "customs duties" in the 1495 *Intercursus Magnus* and for "river tolls" in the 1648 Treaty of Westphalia. The word *telonium* came from church Latin, having entered through the Vulgate from the Greek text of Luke 5.27, Matthew 9.9 and Mark 2.14, where Joseph and Mary go to pay their taxes. Milton may have had to tolerate *telonium* for customs house on B4 of the *Paper of Demands,* but here for "customs duties" he insists on the classical *portorii, censûs and vectigalium* (Article 15).[49]

Where the Dutch spoke of arms *ad defendendum quam offendendum apta,* Milton went along with *defendenda causa* but balked at *offendere* in that sense (Article 16), offering instead *aut se protegere aut vim propulsare.* Here again, whenever Milton is required to employ a word that he regards as grossly unclassical, he signals his deprecation. On the payment of salvage money, he dictates *salvagium vulgò dictum* (Article 33); for letters of marque and reprisal (Article 35), *literæ repræsales, vulgo dictæ mercæ*. No phrase is so qualified by the Dutch ambassadors in their draft.[50]

We may wonder whether Jacob Cats or Janus Vlitius, in their concern with the serious objectives of their mission, were ever sensitive to these nuances in the texts given them. Milton, whose classical Latinity was at times overridden by his colleagues, could hardly effect a revolution in Continental diplomatic discourse, but his stubborn adherence to these principles remains on record. In his later advocacy of blank verse as an alternative to couplet rhyme, his example will ultimately be more influential.

While Latinity in the Thirty-six Counter-articles *is* Miltonic, Milton was now blind. Someone else therefore had to prepare the fair copy, and traces of this hand may perhaps remain in the final text. Several times we have noticed, in Rosin texts, the frequency of the Latin doublet *uti*. *Ut* and *uti* have the same meaning and may be used interchangeably, independent of context. Milton's usage, in his longer Latin works, is sufficiently habitual that it can be defined statistically (although not with absolute precision, because quotations interface, and because Milton revised his first *Defensio* twice). In the 1651 *Pro Populo Anglicano Defensio*, *ut* appears 13 to 14 times as often as *uti*. In *Defensio Secunda* (1654) and in *Pro Se Defensio* (1655), the ration is about 20 times for *ut* for each use of *uti*. In the Thirty-six Counter-articles, the ration is only 2 to 1 for *ut* over *uti*. Thus, we must weigh the possibility that Rosin may have been responsible for preparing the fair copy after Milton finished dictating his translation, and that his more habitual *uti* unconsciously replaced Milton's more habitual *ut*.

⊱A New Letter by Milton and Two by Weckherlin

On 15/25 March, the Dutch ambassadors received several documents from the Council commissioners: the English counter to the Thirty-six Articles; the composite *Papers of Demands;* and one additional item, a "preliminary article," specifying that any one or another article that might be agreed upon would not take effect unless the entire treaty were concluded and brought into effect. This single sentence in English and in Latin was substantially the same as previously formulated in the Strickland-St. John negotiations, 25 March 4 April 1651. Ultimately, it was the only point on which agreement was reached.[51]

While commissioners and ambassadors were playing out their roles at the conference table, decisions of a more concrete nature were being brought into effect in other quarters. On 24 January at the House of Commons, the Navy Committee had reported on plans for expanding the fleet. Over in the Netherlands, similar planning was underway. Lodewijck Huygens wrote in his diary for 5/15 March that he "translated something into English which Mr. Van Vliet and I were to bring to Sir Oliver Fleming in Whitehall towards midday, to be delivered to the Council of State. We did not find him at home, however, and left it there in a sealed envelope."[52]

This message, carefully if not perfectly put into English by Huygens, was an announcement, already public in the Netherlands, that the States General had decided to outfit an additional 150 ships for their navy. Thoughtfully they added assurances that this armada need give the English no concern. On 10/20 March, Vlitius and Huygens repeated this solemn affirmation in its official Latin addressed to Parliament. Needless to say, the tacticians in Westminster could do their own naval arithmetic. On that same 10/20 March, speaker Lenthall had this message read in the Commons in Latin and in English, and thereupon it was "Ordered, that it be referred to the Council of State, to increase the Number of Ships for this Summer's Guard; if they shall think fit."⁵³

Weeks elapse. The Dutch ambassadors have sent the British responses home, and await instructions. On 20/30 March, Huygens learns that Gualter Frost is ill. A few days later, Frost dies, and in his place John Thurloe is appointed, on 29 March/8 April. On that same Monday, 29 March, in the same month when Milton became completely blind, a long total eclipse of the sun, the second solar eclipse during Milton's lifetime, took place. It was so dark that it was named Black Monday or Mirk Monday, with preachers that day preaching and people praying, and John Milton thinking that for those others around him the dark would pass, but for him there would be

> O dark, dark, dark, amid the blaze of noon,
> Irrecoverably dark, total eclipse
> Without all hope of day!
>
> (*Samson Agonistes*, 80–82)

Word comes from the States General. On 2/12 April, the Council sets Monday, 5/15 April, to hear their replies. The ambassadors hand them over in a brief writing, *Ut tandem*: they accept the proposed Preliminary Article; they do not respond to the demands for compensation; and they request an explanation of the final paragraph following British Counter-article 36, which seems to hint at other questions to be resolved. The ambassadors ask for a negotiating session to work on the points of disagreement. This Dutch ambassadors' document was printed in the Columbia edition of Milton's *Works* vol. 18, pages 124–26, erroneously, as Milton's State Paper 167F, but obviously it was not Milton's at all.⁵⁴

That afternoon of 5/15 April, the Council heard the Dutch reply reported on by the commissioners, deliberated, and set down no fewer than four orders (PRO 25/66, p. 541):

That a Conference bee had wth the Dutch Ambass^rs upon

the answer given to the thirty-six Articles.

That a Conference bee had wth the Dutch Ambass.^rs upon the paper of Demands given to them from the Councell.

That in this Conference wth the Dutch Ambass.^rs upon the paper of Demands, It is ordered that it be insisted upon that an Answer bee given by the said Ambassad^rs to the paper of Demands.

That it bee referred to the Comittee for fforegine affairs to prepare a paper to bee given in to the Dutch Ambassad.^rs at the Conference now resolved on wherein it is to bee signified unto them that the Councell doe insist upon an answer to be given by them to the paper of Demands given in to them from the Councell.

This conference was set for Friday, 9/19 April, and that Committee paper was prepared. But for reasons not recorded, the commissioners did not deliver it, and so reported back to the Council, which approved. Perhaps they felt it had been worded too brusquely.[55]

On 12/22 April, the ambassadors jointly sign a note: they have been instructed to obtain an absolutely clear interpretation of what possible pending issues might be implied in that British Counter-article 36. Responding the same day, the Council calls on the committee for foreign affairs to prepare a reply to the last two Dutch papers; on 14/24 April it directs that this draft be reviewed at its session of 15/25 April, and 15/25 April decides "That the paper now read to be sent to the Dutch Ambassad.^rs be approved off & sent to Mr Milton to be translated into Latine."[56]

The text of this letter dated and delivered 16/26 April has been unknown to Miltonists and to historians generally. It is now possible to supply for the first time the Council's official letter in English, signed by John Lisle, president for that month, and the official Latin version. Both are done in elegant script by a Council amanuensis, preserved in MS. S.G. 8460, no. 24, with transcripts of both in MS. Aitzema 86, no. 24 (reprinted in Part Two).[57]

Like the two letters dated 29 January 1651 O.S., this

letter was not included in any of the seventeenth century compilations commonly held to derive from drafts retained by Milton. The Council order of 15 April is circumstantial evidence for attributing this letter to him, but the appointments of Rosin and Weckherlin impose caution. Still somewhat unresolved at this time was the question of the letter of 13 April 1652, addressed to the King of Denmark: it is included in *Literæ* and in the Columbia Manuscript (not in Skinner's Transcript, which lacks others from 1652), but was assigned by the Council's order of 7 April to Weckherlin for translation.

This letter of 16/26 April, recovered so late from three centuries of archival entombment, repeats one specifically recognizable Miltonism four times. The English word "treaty" (which in the seventeenth century meant the process of negotiation as well as the final agreed-upon document) is rendered each time by *tractatio*, a term that emphasizes the process: this use of *tractatio* has also been seen in the 29 January *Consilium Status Parlamenti Reipublicæ Angliæ* letter and at the close of the Counter-articles.

There is a sprinkling of late-Latin usages in the 16/26 April letter, but none that constitutes a problem for attribution. *Septimana* is unclassical (because the ancient Romans reckoned by Calends, Nones and Ides, until the introduction of the Sabbath brought a change), but it is compelled by the English word "weeks." *Schedula* is a late Latin derivative from the Greek, but is used three times in the *Scriptum* booklet, page 60 (25 June), page 64 (26 June) and page 67 (27 June), in contexts which are Miltonic on other evidence. *Commissarius* had been standardized by the Commissioners of the Great Seal and it is used by Milton in the heading to the Thirty-Six Counter-articles, as well as in memorials to the Danish envoys later in 1652. The third person singular verb *postulabatur* with the dual subject *jus et satisfactio* was a common usage in that century.

Rather unusual here is *nostro stylo*, with the pronominal

adjective preceding, although there is no absolute rule controlling the placing of *noster*: in one single sentence Milton can be seen dictating *de libertate nostra ... de nostrâ republicâ* (*Defensio Secunda*, 1654, p. 153; Columbia edition, vol. 8, 226). Yet in this letter it seems to register as a precise and literal rendering of the English words *our style* in the word order that would come most readily to a Frenchman who was accustomed to *notre style*.

With *ut* four times in this letter and *uti* not at all, and no other serious element of doubt, it is reasonable to consider this letter as "presumably by Milton," with a possibility that *"nostro stylo"* suggests a final fair copy written out by Rosin.

Since our present interest is to recover the traces of Milton's service in his secretaryship, we continue with this shuffling of diplomatic papers. Nevertheless we are aware that in the shipyards vessels are being fitted for war; in the counting houses, merchants and shipowners are making calculations of risk and gain, and not only in terms of freight charges and marine insurance; and that an intelligent young man, a member of the Dutch negotiating team, close to the realities of the scene, Lodewijck Huygens, at this moment goes off blithely on a holiday jaunt to Oxford, Bath and Wales. About the same time, Vlitius travels off to Northhampton, Lincoln, Nottingham and York, having some private business at the last place; all along the way he passes ruins left by the civil war, in which libraries especially had been hurt, the one at Cambridge almost deserted.[58]

On 21 April/1 May, the Dutch replied to the British letter of 16/26 April with their *Scripto ab Excell^{iis} V^{is} decimo sexto*, and in turn the English responded 27 April/7 May with *Postquam quæ ad nos à vobis 21 Aprilis*, "Having received yours of the 21th instant." Council minutes record the steps in its formulation and approval of the Latin translation, but do not indicate by whom. From MS. S.G. 8460, no. 26, both official texts are reproduced in Part Two, and parts of the text lost in their defective margins are supplied from the transcripts in MS. Aitzema 86, no. 26. For this letter we have no reason to assume Milton's translation. Internal evidence distinguishes it from Rosin's style, rather suggesting the alternative, Weckherlin, whose letters have their own intrinsic interest.[59]

At the same time, the Council drew up another, shorter note, addressed to the Dutch ambassadors. This was approved on 28 April/8 May and ordered to be translated into Latin. The Council further directed that the official English copy be signed, but that it still be retained until called for by Whitelocke. Again the translator's name is missing from the Council minutes, but we can read his handwritten Latin version penned onto the same page as the English draft, and from his vocabulary we can infer his identity to be that of the translator of the 27 April letter. Having obtained several holograph letters of his from the shire archives at Reading, we confirm both as the work of Weckherlin. This paper is also now included in Part Two.[60]

3

May & June 1652: More Negotiations and the Onset of War

❧ Milton's Time of Trouble

Four months of diplomacy had so far accomplished one aim for each side: each had made a paper case for blaming the other. This was of some importance vis-à-vis their own peoples, and vis-à-vis opinion in certain other states. Neither side could have had any realistic expectation of gaining its ends at the conference table, and so now, on the high seas, the ship captains were receiving their signals.

On 6/16 May, Van Vliet submits a complaint: five Dutch ships have been seized under cover of letters of marque nominally issued against the French. On 12/22 May, Captain Anthony Young, with an English flotilla, descries a Dutch convoy homeward bound from Genoa. He calls on the Dutch Vice Admiral Joris van der Zaaen to "strike his flag," and thereby acknowledge English dominion in those waters. Van der Zaaen bids him come aboard and strike it, and soon the guns are blasting. Word of this clash was just beginning to circulate through the taverns of London and Amsterdam when news came of a vastly more serious collision between the English fleet under Blake and the Dutch Navy under Tromp, 18/28 May. From the commanders on both sides, dispatches come full of charges and countercharges, accusation, denials and recriminations.

Confronted by the rising power of England, the Dutch policymakers are not willing to back down, but at least some of them suspect they might come out second best in the trial of arms, despite the confidence of their sea captains. For the time being, however, they continue in the role of peaceseekers.

From the date of the Blake-Tromp encounter until the recognition of a state of war at the end of June, Dutch affairs are the daily concern of the Council of State. During those days their Order Books record intensive activity in other foreign affairs: attention to Aitzema, the Hanse agent, 6 May; a letter to be signed and sent to the "Emperor" of Morocco, 7 May; a newly arrived Swedish envoy, Harold Appelbom, 12 May; a letter to the "Grand Turk," and a possible change of envoys, 14 May; a letter ordered to Tuscany (which will be Milton's work, but perhaps not done till July), 18 May; a letter to Sweden (which will go out 2 June, and which shows clear signs of Weckherlin's style); a communication from Spanish Ambassador Alonso de Cardenas (this will lead to a Milton state paper in August); a letter to the "King" of Tunis, 26 May; and everyday involvement, from the second half of May, with a major Danish embassy.[61]

For Milton these same weeks are a time of terrible tribulation. His young wife Mary dies on 5 May, three days after giving birth to their baby Deborah. Milton is suddenly left with four little children to care for, at the time his blindness has become final and total. He tries to make proper arrangements for the care of his children, but these turn out to be unsatisfactory. In June, his little boy dies,

And such a son as all men hail'd me happy:
Who now would be a father in my stead?[62]

During these weeks, Milton's name is absent from Council minutes, but also absent is Weckherlin's and Rosin's; and Thurloe's is there about twice. More meaningful may be the fact that, with all the foreign affairs activity in progress, no state paper dated in those weeks is included among the collections attributed to drafts retained by Milton.

On 19 May 1652, the committee on foreign affairs was directed to prepare a paper to the Dutch envoys on the case of Captain John Green, whose ship and crew were detained in the Netherlands, but the matter seems to have been sidetracked in the press of events (*CSPD, 1651–1652*, p. 248). Potentially it would have been work for Milton or his colleagues.

One incident that may show how Milton was coping at his public post during these weeks of personal pain and anguish relates to the arrival about 10/20 May of an intermediate envoy from the Dutch, Willem Nieupoort. What little we know of this episode comes from a vague note, added in 1694 at the end of the *Life* composed by Milton's nephew Edward Phillips. This is inserted in smaller type, as if added, late, to the page proofs, from garbled recollections mentioned to him at that moment by the other nephew John Phillips, the "kinsman that was then with him":

> Before the War broke forth between the States of *England*, and the *Dutch*, the *Hollanders* sent over Three Embassadours in order to an accommodation; but they returning *re infecta*, the Dutch sent away a *Plenipotentiary*, to offer Peace upon much milder terms, or at least to gain more time.
>
> But this *Plenipotentiary* could not make such haste, but that the Parliament had procured a Copy of their Instructions in *Holland*, which were delivered by our Author to his Kinsman that was then with him, to Translate for the

> Council to view, before the said *Plenipotentiary* had taken Shipping for *England*; an Answer to all he had in Charge lay ready for him, before he made his publick entry into London.[63]

We find no clear record that Milton is handling any of the day-to-day paperwork in the continuing negotiations with the Dutch envoys. We do have this peculiar reference, dictated two years later, concerning attentions received from Adrian Pauw, the final ambassador sent from the Netherlands in June:

> Tuos verò nefas sit præterire manes, Adriane Pauui qui legatus ad nos summo cum honore missus, Hollandiæ decus et ornamentum, summam in me ac singularem benevolentiam tuam, etiamsi videre nuaquam contigerit, multis sæpè nuntiis significandam curasti.
>
> [It would be truly unthinkable to overlook your departed spirit, Adrian Pauw, sent to us as ambassador with the highest honor, the glory and ornament of Holland, who took the trouble to signify often by many messages your high and particular good will towards me, even if it never worked out to see me.][64]

During the 22 days when Pauw was in England in June 1652, busy as he was with daily conferences, audiences, drafting of papers and speeches, even on Sunday, how "many messages," *multis nuntiis*, sent "often," *sæpe*, could Pauw have passed to Oliver Fleming or to Lewis Rosin, "Give my greetings to Mr. Milton?"

During these same weeks, Milton the political poet was speaking out on public affairs. It was in May of 1652 that Milton sent his powerful sonnet to Cromwell *On the Proposals of Certain Ministers at the Committee for the Propagation of the Gospel*, hailing the hero who brought victory to the Commonwealth on the field of battle, and now emphatically urging comparable generalship against plans for what Milton perceived as a new established church. There is much more to be considered regarding the occasion for this sonnet: how Milton was interrogated by a committee of Parliament for helping the heretical Racovian Catechism appear in print; how that episode led to those ministers' proposals; what Cromwell may have said about the sonnet and what he was in fact doing about those proposals; and then why, when war with the Dutch was on in earnest, Milton sent on 3 July his alternate sonnet to Vane, commending his statesmanship in peace and in war, but focusing again in separation of church from state. For the "practical" rulers of an unsettled land, the war was primary—for the command of the seas, for merchant marine supremacy, for the control of trade routes and the spice islands. Neither Cromwell nor Vane was likely to forget the issues of religious tolerance, but amidst the distractions of the war, it was precisely Milton the poet's duty to draw attention to the principles of religious freedom, for fear they might be forgotten.

There is one written testimony available to us indicating that Milton was back at work in his official capacity in early July. Until now it has been *inferred*, and by some *denied*, that Milton had a share in England's major *Declaration* of self-justification on the outbreak of the war, in its Latin version, the *Scriptum* and its related papers. These mutually excluding judgments are both derived from the Council minutes of 20 July 1652: "Mem. send to Mr Dugard to speake with Mr Milton Concerning ye printing ye Declaration."[65]

In Leo ab Aitzema's unpublished journal, date unclear but after an entry for 9/19 July 1652, this entry is found:

> de declaratie wet in 't Frans
> gestelet deur Rosins
> ende in 't Latijn deur Milton[66]

> [The Declaration enactment was set into French by Rosin, and into Latin by Milton.]

With these items the only direct evidence available, we can proceed to review the further record of the Anglo-

Dutch parleys. We touch on the main events only insofar as these may elucidate the papers that will end up in the Latin *Scriptum* version of the *Declaration*, and its versions in other languages.

✒ The Answer and the Narrative

News of the Blake-Tromp duel at sea reached the Council on 19/29 May. The Dutch ambassadors first became aware of that clash on the following day when a military guard was posted at their Chelsea residence by the Council, as a precaution against any mob violence.[67]

On Friday, 21/31 May, the ambassadors sent Van Vliet and Huygens to deliver a note to the Council. They offered thanks for the guard, discounted the report of the battle as a mere rumor, and insisted that, if something untoward had happened, it was not with their own foreknowledge nor by decision of the Dutch government. After a busy day of hurrying back and forth, Nieupoort, Van Vliet and Huygens reached Sir Henry Vane (president of the Council for that month) to request an audience for the ambassadors.

Saturday, 22 May/1 June. The Council meets and attends to disposition of ships and naval stores, while Van Vliet and Huygens walk up and down Whitehall in company with a much distressed Oliver Fleming until Thurloe comes out and tells them that the envoys may come Monday morning, 24 May/3 June, for their audience. The same Saturday a letter has come to the ambassadors from Tromp, giving *his* version of the duel, blaming the English fleet for the fracas.

Sunday, 23 May/2 June is a day for sitting at sermons, for both Dutch and English. Ambassador Cats prepares his presentation for Monday morning, in Latin, and Lodewijck Huygens is trusted with the chore of turning it into English.

Monday, 24 May/3 June. The three ambassadors are accorded a less than cordial reception at Whitehall. In a quarter of an hour, Cats has read his statement, *Ob casum infelicem*: "We are here by reason of an unhappy and unexpected mischance"; transcripts of the letters from Blake and from Tromp are exchanged; Cats's emotional plea to continue negotiations is brushed aside, and the meeting is terminated.[68]

The Council concentrates on the navy, its disposition and its needs, but later that day their minutes record the peculiar item: "That ye Councell both declare That it is ye pleasure of this Councell That nine of ye Members thereof to speake wth the Haer Newport lately come from Holland or hold any correspondence wth him." The manuscript clearly reads *nine*: was it really intended to be *none*? Nieupoort seems to have brought unofficial answers from the Dutch East India Company with regard to claims and counterclaims, and some instructions on the Thirty-six Articles. But he was without formal accreditation, so he had been quite at loose ends. He was not even housed with the Triple Embassy, but was staying elsewhere. Most of the later references to him in the 1652 Council minutes deal with which ship will carry him home.

The next item on that 24 May agenda directs

> That Mr Thurloe doe prepare an Extract of ye severall Letters which have come to ye Councell giveing an Acc^t of ye Dutch Fleete and ye English Fleete in ye Downes as also of y^t made by Capt Yongue of Plymouth and bringe ye same to ye Committee of forreigne Affayres to morrow morneing who are to sitt for that purpose.[69]

John Thurloe is rather a busy chief secretary, so that order has to be repeated as item 6 on the agenda for 25 May. He does get to it, or his aides do, composing *A true Relation of the late Engagement between the English Fleet, under the Command of General Blake, and the Holland Fleet, under the Command of Lieutenant Admiral Tromp near Dover.*[70]

Thursday, 27 May/6 June. Having received no reply

to Cats's proposals of the preceding Monday, the ambassadors send another paper, *Quemadmodum præterito die Lunæ*. It appears on the Council agenda, 28 May/7 June, but there is no haste to reply.

A week later, on Thursday, 3/13 June, the Dutch ambassadors are still seeking to head off the full outbreak of hostilities. They send a third appeal, *Quemadmodum Illustrissimo Senatui*. This paper is translated and read in Council on 4/14 June (earlier in the day, Vane read the first two in Parliament), and a reply is now authorized. This response is prepared by a committee that includes Vane, Cromwell and Bradshaw, but perhaps—we may guess—drafted for them by Thurloe. On 5 June it is reported to Parliament by Vane as *The Answer of the Parliament of the Commonwealth of England to Three Papers*. This reply still speaks "peaceably and friendly," but it rejects the Dutch position, charges them with planned aggression evidenced by the program for 150 more ships, and demands reparations.[71]

Vane also reads to Parliament the (Thurloe) document, *A true Relation of the late Engagement*. Both the *Answer* and the *Relation* are approved, with some amendments (not specified in the Commons' Journal, but the title *A true Relation* is modified to the more restrained *A Narrative of the late Engagement*).[72] The Commons further resolves that the *Answer*, the *Narrative* and copies of letters from Captain Young about his sea battle and from captains who were at the Downs on 18 May should be printed, together with the three papers from the Dutch ambassadors, with testimony taken from captured Dutch officers, Tromp's letter, and a summary of a Dutch government letter to the Evangelical Swiss Cantons. This publication soon issued from the press of John Field, printer to the Parliament.[73]

Pursuant to Council orders, on 7/17 June Thurloe and Fleming deliver this collection of papers to the Dutch envoys—the *Answer* in its official English signed by Henry Scobell, Clerk of Parliament, together with a Latin translation; the *Narrative* and the other papers apparently in English only.[74] They also deliver Nieupoort's passport for his return home, and he starts out.

❧The Mission of Adrian Pauw

Later that same day, 7/17 June, word comes that Adrian Pauw has arrived at Gravesend, having sailed from Holland only the previous Saturday, 5/15 June, presumably with new instructions and new powers. The ambassadors send a messenger to summon Nieupoort back, and themselves hurry to meet Pauw.[75]

Tuesday, 8/18 June. In the Commons, Vane reports on this new envoy, and the House gives its pro forma authorization for his reception. The next day had already been appointed by the English for "Fasting and Humiliation," and the Dutch followed suit; Pauw's credentials are therefore not proffered to Speaker William Lenthall until 10/20 June. He is received in formal audience by Vane, Strickland and Mildmay in Parliament on 11/21 June.[76]

Huygens's diary for 11/21 June tells us that Pauw wrote out his speech that morning in Latin, and that his going to Parliament was delayed *a cause que la translation de son harangue n'estoit pas preste encore ... Rosin la translatoit en Anglois par faute d'autre*: "because the translation of his speech was not yet ready ... Rosin translated it into English, for want of another."

We know that Pauw was lodged at the mansion rented by the Commonwealth from Sir Abraham Williams for short-term entertaining of distinguished guests, so the ambassadorial staff staying in Chelsea was not available. Rosin may perhaps have been sent ahead to let Pauw know that the committee to escort him to Parliament was on its way. The House of Commons Journals for 11 June record that Pauw spoke in Latin, and delivered copies in Latin and in English translation.[77] On this occasion, Rosin translated Latin to English, which must lead us to ask whether or not there were other such occasions.

Pauw was a supremely capable diplomat. He could generate position papers with great speed, receive rebuffs and parry instantly with new position papers. Between 11 and 30 June, he delivered no fewer than 17 speeches and papers of his own, besides documents from his home office and a couple from the three ambassadors. Consequently, the minutes of the Council of State are replete with orders to consider, to formulate and to return replies, although the replies are fewer by far in number. We need to understand this complicated sequence, not so much because of what each side had to say, but because these exchanges and orders will end up as part of the British *Declaration*.

On 12/22 June at nine o'clock in the morning, the Council hears Pauw in *its* official audience. On this occasion he speaks in French. On Monday, 14/24 June, a seven-man Council committee meets with him at four o'clock, to assure him that they want a speedy issue to their negotiations, but still must demand that he show what powers and authority he has been granted. Pauw is well aware that he bears no powers of any consequence. He waits a day, and on 15 June sends a paper asking for a speedy and favorable answer to the two addresses he has made to Parliament and to Council. Again Council insists on seeing his powers, whereupon he turns over his credential letter and three passport forms issued to him at The Hague. These documents will go into the *Declaration*, with a *Summary* of his remarks at the 24/14 June meeting and his paper of 25/15 June.[78]

The Council feels confirmed in its judgment that Pauw's authorizations are inadequate to conclude any agreement acceptable to them. Herbert Morley and Bulstrode Whitelocke are directed to make such a report to Parliament, 16/26 June, where it is requested "That the Counsell of State doe send into the Parliament to-morrow morning, all the Papers that they have in *French* from the Lords Ambassadors Extraordinary of ye States Generall, with the Translation of them in English." Always abiding by strict formalities, the Council in its minutes of 16 June registers the order that the papers of Lord Pauw be translated from French to English. We must assume that Lewis Rosin is being kept busy.

Another paper comes from Pauw that day, enclosing a letter from the three Dutch ambassadors, who submit themselves to Pauw's superior jurisdiction and insist on the validity of his credentials.

Resuming the discussion in Parliament on Thursday, 17/27 June:

> The Earle of Pembroke reports, from the Counsell of State, the Papers in ffrench, from the Lords Ambassadors Extraordinary from the States Generall, with the Translation of them in English: which were this day read.
>
> He also reports an other paper delivered unto him from the Lord Paw Lord Ambassador Extraordinary from the States Generall of the United Provinces in French, and a Translate thereof in English which was read.
>
> Resolved, that the former Instruction given unto the ffleete be vigourously prosecuted.
>
> Resolved, That upon Consideration of the Report made from the Councell of State The Parliament doeth think fitt and Order that the Councell of State doe proceed with the Lord Paw Ambassador Extraordinary from the Lords the States Generall of the United Provinces according to former Directions.[79]

Up to this point, there have been verbal exchanges and messages from the British to Pauw, but no formal written response. On 17/27 June, among other decisions on political and naval strategy, the Council directs

> That it be referred to the Comittee of forreigne affaires to draw up an answere to the severall papers wch the Lord Paw Extraordinary Ambassadr: of the united provinces hath delivered in either to the Parlt of Councell, keeping close to the former Answeres and Declarations the parlt hath made and to report the same to the Councell wth all speed.

Meanwhile Pauw requests an immediate meeting. The commissioners meet him at six o'clock; he submits another paper, which is also referred to the foreign affairs committee for answer. Vane reports these proceedings to Parliament, 18/28 June.[80]

The committee's written reply to Pauw is reviewed by the Council, and approved to be fair copied in English, signed by the president and delivered to Lord Pauw by Oliver Fleming.

Regrettably, from the moment when the three ambassadors yielded primacy to Pauw, their files, transmitted with their report to The Hague, cease to be complete. Most of the papers exchanged between Pauw and the British are preserved as printed in the *Declaration* and its *Scriptum* version, but these lack the clues that tell so much in original manuscripts. From the Council Order Book it is not clear in what languages this 19 June reply was brought by Fleming to Pauw, but the transcribed texts preserved in MS. S.G. 12589.62 show that it was transmitted in English and in French. Pauw's *Sommaire* and his reply were in French. The English text of that Council response appears in the *Declaration* as *The Answer of the Councel of State to the Summary of the Lord Adrian Pauw*. In the *Scriptum* it is given in Latin as the *Responsum Concilii Status ad Summarium D^{ni} Adriani Pauw*.

This moment is one of many in Milton's biography where gaps in information are most vexing. This state paper was adopted by the Council during one of those days when Milton's little boy lay dying, "about six weeks after his mother." We do not know where the child was, nor where he was later buried.[81] We can be reasonably sure, from its text, that this *Answer of the Council* was not given to Milton to put into the Latin *Responsum Concilii* during that week.

One other fragment from that June has come down to us, a personal letter by Milton, responding to a letter from Athenian-born Leonard Philaras, then serving Parma as a diplomat in Paris. Philaras fancied that the rising power of England could supply armies and fleets to free Greece from the Ottoman Empire. Milton answers warmly. He is all for a free and independent Hellas, which might revive its ancient glories. But Milton's head is not in the clouds. He knows—although from this letter Philaras would not guess—that England's navy is far too engaged in a life and death confrontation with the Dutch on their own coasts to think of grappling with the Turks on the faraway Aegean. Milton courteously thanks Philaras for a gift portrait he cannot see and just as discreetly suggests that the first motion ought to come from the Greeks themselves.[82]

On Monday, 21 June/1 July, in "a paper...desiring a conference" Pauw asks a meeting to respond to the Council's *Answer*. The meeting is held, and he submits "another paper... of the 21 of June" citing all the instances of good behavior by the Dutch and inviting the English to make some proposals. Two days pass with no word, so he sends yet another paper, 23 June/3 July, urging response.

The fact is that both Council and Commons have been in earnest debate over policy. On Thursday, 24 June, a motion is formulated to demand money reparations on account of the new damages sustained by the English in the late events. (This demand was separate and apart from the previous four-part *Paper of Demands*.) On the question in Parliament of whether to vote approval "now" on this proposal, the House divides, 47 *noes* and 28 *yeas*, which gives some measure of their vacillation and disagreements at the approach of war. Nonetheless, the House resolves the next day to "assert the Right of this Commonwealth in the Sovereignty of the Seas," and adopts three articles: the Dutch must agree to pay in full for the current damages an amount which will be later specified, then there will be a cessation of hostilities, after which a treaty will be contracted. These three articles are transmitted to Pauw the same day.

A new paper from Pauw on Saturday, 26 June/6 July

asks a meeting to discuss these new articles. The meeting is held, and he submits another paper of the same date, suggesting that the Dutch also have claims for current damages, and that it is hardly reasonable to agree to pay an unspecified future demand for reimbursement of current damages, after which they will draw up the specific bill.

The intransigence of the English war party is matched by their Dutch counterparts. On the morning of that Saturday, 26 June, two messengers arrive from The Hague with orders recalling all their envoys and ending the talks. Exactly when the Council learns of their coming is not clear. Early on 27 June, although it is on Sunday, Pauw sends to ask for a meeting to continue yesterday's discussion; but when the meeting is held, by another paper dated 27 June he asks for the formality of a farewell Council audience and passports for himself and the Triple Embassy.

On Monday, 28 June, Pauw, still the masterful diplomat, sends in "a paper" and "another paper of the same date," declares his intention of reporting to his superiors in the Netherlands in favor of still seeking an agreement and fair settlement of issues, and asks that the door remain open for some other Dutch representative to resume the talks. The same day, the three ambassadors write to request their official leavetaking.

In Parliament, Tuesday, 29 June, Speaker Lenthall reports a letter from Pauw. The Earl of Pembroke adds Pauw's letters of 28 June and others not previously read there, presumably in English translation, while the letter from the three ambassadors is described as "in Latin." It is resolved to accord the Dutch envoys a farewell audience in full honor and courtesy Wednesday at eleven o'clock, and to provide for their safe transit home. Provision is also made for certain documents:

> Resolved, That it be referred to the Counsell of State to prepare Letters recreditive to the Lords the States Generall of the United Provinces, and report them to the Parliamt.

Resolved, That it be referred to the Counsell of State to cause the severall Papers which have passed between them and the Lord Paw Extraordinary Ambassador from the Lords the States Generall in the late Treaty, to be put in order together, and give order for the printing of them.

Recreditive letters were formal papers of fair dismission, given to an envoy to carry back to his sovereign. The most recent such letter we have seen was prepared in February 1652 for Hermann Mylius, deputy from the Count of Oldenburg, written in English by the then secretary Gualter Frost and later put into classical Latin by Milton and revised by his colleagues into neo-Latin. Of these *recreditifs* ordered for the Dutch, no texts are known to survive, and no record of who may have prepared them.

The second Resolve will add up to the 70-page *Declaration* in English, and its Latin, French and Dutch versions.

On 30 June/10 July the four envoys are received in the House of Commons with stiffly formal honors, all the members standing up, with their hats off. (Nieupoort is again somewhere else, out of the picture.) Pauw delivers a farewell oration in Latin, handing over a copy in writing. "The Oration made by the said Lord Paw was read and Englished by the Clerk," Henry Scobell, most probably from a translation previously ready.[83]

4

Milton at Work: Identifying More Milton Compositions

ᴥ*The* Declaration / Scriptum: *How Milton and His Colleagues Did Their Work*

Each side—English and Dutch—wanted, and needed, to publish its version of the break. Captain William Penn from his ship the Tryumph wrote in a letter to Cromwell, 2 June 1652:

> My Lord, I find the most, and indeed, those that are best principled and most conscientious of our commanders, doe much desire some information of the justness of our quarrell with the Hollander, which they do not in the least doubt of; yett I find them somewhat troubled and dejected for theyr ignorance in that poynt.[84]

Including the Pauw mission exchanges, as directed by the House on 29 June, the *Declaration* in its English form was ready by 7 July. In the House of Commons,

> The Lord Com. Whitelock Reports from the Comittee of Members of Parliament of the Counsell of State, the Declaration of the Parliam^t of the Comonwealth of England, relating to the Affaires and proceedings between this Comonwealth and the States Generall of the United Provinces of the Low Countries, and the present differences occasioned on the States part, as the same is, by the said Comittee altered and amended, wch Declaration so altered and amended was this Day read: And, after divers Amendments at the Table
> Resolved, That this word (Declaration) doe stand in the Title.
> The said Declaration, so amended, being put to the Question, was assented unto.
> Ordered, That the Papers, to wch this Declaration doth relate, be printed together wth this Declaration, and that the Clerk of the Parliament give Order for the Printing thereof, accordingly.
> Ordered, That it be referred to the Counsell of State, to see that this Declaration be translated into Latine, Dutch and ffrench; and into any other Language, as they shall thinke fitt.[85]

The *Declaration* so voted and the associated papers assembled by the Council staff were turned over by Henry Scobell, Clerk of the Parliament, to John Field, official printer to the Parliament, with grant of sole copyright dated 9 July, as printed on the title page. (That same day, official manuscript copies of the English-language *Declaration* proper were delivered to the Danish envoys then in London, Erik Rosencrantz and Peter Reedtz, with a cover letter dated 8 July, also in English. This was accompanied by a Latin translation of the cover letter, which can be safely attributed to Milton (see below). The following Tuesday, 13 July, the Council entered into its minutes "That Mr Thurloe doe appoint fitt persons to translate ye Parl^{ts} Declaration into Latine ffrench and Dutch" (PRO, SP 25/30, p. 29).

These translations of the full sets of papers were done by 20 July, when Dugard was directed to confer with Milton about printing the French and Latin texts. The Dutch had been assigned to John Field. On 29 July the Council ordered that copies of the printed *Declaration* be sent to each foreign ambassador and minister in England, and to the diplomatic agents of the Commonwealth who were stationed abroad (PRO, SP 25/30, p. 90).[86]

This publication, the final diplomatic document in the 1651–1652 Anglo-Dutch negotiations, is a *collection* of diverse papers: the *Declaration* proper adopted by Parliament, 7 July; its *Answer* of 5 June to the three ambassadors; the Thurloe *Narrative* of the Blake-Tromp sea fight; 17 speeches and papers by Pauw, plus his credentials and passes from the States General; papers from the three ambassadors; and interspersed chronologically among all of those, orders and responses by Parliament and the Council.

Some major contributors to Milton studies have described this entire collection, loosely termed the *Declaration* (and in it, specifically the battle narrative), as a Milton work, both in English and in Latin. Other scholars who are just as highly regarded have rejected the entire *Declaration* a priori, without investigation, as not being by Milton.[87]

The English-language publication can now be ruled out; it is not Milton's composition. Those papers that emanated from the Council or Parliament—the *Declaration* proper, the *Answer*, the *Narrative* and the sundry responses and orders—in English, we know were not the work of Milton. Huygens has told us that it was Rosin who turned Pauw's 11 June Latin speech into English. The English translations of that first address by Pauw and the English translation of Pauw's last Latin address of 30 June are such literally precise versions of the translations given in the French edition of *La Declaration* that they are arguably the work of one hand—Lewis Rosin's. By the same test, Rosin is most likely the precisely literal translator—

into English for the English edition, and into French for the French edition—of the Latin letter submitted 28 June by the three ambassadors giving notice of their departure. Rosin is also plausibly the translator into English of those papers that were submitted in French. The English language publication is therefore made up of the original official English texts and *Rosin's* translations into English from Latin and French.[88]

The French edition, *La Declaration*, may also be mainly attributed to Rosin. He was, after all, appointed to be the official translator for French, and Aitzema's diary recorded that Rosin had done the French version (at least of the *Declaration* proper). Much of the material was originally submitted by the Hollanders in French. In its translations from English and Latin, the French is faithfully literal; this is Rosin's style. And what we have inferred until now from reading his work is confirmed by a notice *Au Lecture*, prefixed to the French edition:

> Les Copies de la Harangue du Sr Ambassadeur Pauw, & de ses Memoires presentés au Conseil d'Etat, ont esté transcrites des Originaux, donnés en cette langue, és mesmes termes, mot pour mot.[89]
>
> [The texts of the Address of Lord Ambassador Pauw, and of his memorials presented to the Council of State, have been transcribed from the originals, rendered into this language, in the same terms, word for word.]

The Dutch edition required an interpreter, someone other than Milton. Roger Williams, and perhaps some others, read him some Dutch, but mastery of that language has not been recorded among Milton's attainments. Theodore Haak had been assigned to translate the declaration on the Scots into Dutch in 1650, and he may have been the most likely choice for this Dutch translation in 1652.[90]

What remains to be examined, then, is the Latin version, the *Scriptum Parlamenti Reipublicæ Anglixæ* of July 1652.[91]

Its first component is the Latin *Scriptum* version of the *Declaration* proper. Unlike Rosin's French version, it does not closely follow the English original. It is often a paraphrase rather than a translation. For example, the English original reads, "the Principles and Spirit which then acted in them"; this becomes *quibus rationibus adductus, quo ardore animi ad libertatem aspiraverit—*"by what principles moved, by what ardor of spirit aspired to liberty." The phrase "all different persons" is rephrased into "quibus veri et *æqui studium est—*"who seek truth and fairness." And so it goes throughout.

Scanning the text, we find two occurrences of a significant formula: *liberi commeatûs*, once translating "passes for his Transportation" and once "to take their leaves." Not only is this formula not a literal translation, but these two Latin words are the expression Milton had been trying, a few months before, to substitute for the current but unclassical *Salvaguardia* in the Oldenburg negotiations. There he had been overruled.[92] Milton the purist lexicographer is seen again in the passage *Literas tantum commendatitias sive credentiales* where the English uses only "Crendential Letters." Milton could not avoid having to use the unclassical *credentiales*, but he made his point by prefixing his preference, the classical *commedatitias*.[93] An even more striking, because exclusively Miltonic, usage seen here is his nonconformist substitution of *Potestates Generales* nine times in various grammatically inflected forms in place of the universally used *Ordines Generales* for the "States General" of the Netherlands; only once is *Ordines* used for the central government of the United provinces, and once for the "States" of a province.[94] Another Miltonic usage is the word *primores*, used repeatedly for the English noun "superiors"; Adam Littleton and other contemporaries admitted *superior* as a noun in Latin as in English, but Milton adhered strictly to *primores*, using *superior* only as an adjective in its ancient senses. These usages, which can be confirmed from other documents translated by Milton, are hallmarks of authenticity for his work.

At the same time, peculiarities in the treatment of proper names make for questions. Isaac Dorislaus becomes subject to inflection in Latin in both names, *Isacium Dorislaum* (the first name may be a misprint for *Isaacum*), but among the family names of the three Dutch envoys in 1645—*Borele, Renzwo, Joachimum*—only the third is so inflected. On page 7 *Caroli Stuarti* is treated as Latin, but on page 8 *Capitaneus Young* is not. For reasons that are not clear, a similar inconsistency affects about one-fifth of the family names in the Columbia Manuscript and *Literæ* versions of the state papers.[95]

A pattern of such inconsistencies—inflected Latin first names and vernacular family names, interspersed with fully Latinized forms—might be regarded as conformity with the state papers pattern. But the variants in the Latin *Scriptum* are more complex. In the English *Declaration*, we encounter first a reference to "him whom they call Lieutenant Admiral Trump," followed soon by "that action of Trump"; in the Latin these are *quem appellant Legatum Admirallum Trump*, and *facinus illud Admiralli Trump*. No given name is used in either language text, while the neo-Latin naval title varies with the grammatical case, and the family name is vernacular. Later in the same document, "under the command of Trump" becomes *Duce Trumpio*, "by Trump" becomes a *Trumpio*. In between the two Latin-inflected *Trumpio* family names, there appears the name of Ambassador Pauw—*Adrianus Pauw, Adriani Pauw, Adriano Pauw*—inflected only in the given name, with the vernacular family name. The question arises: was Milton interrupted, dictating at different times, disregarding one day a usage he had dictated a day before? Or did another hand touch the text here?[96]

Passing to the Latin *Responsum* Parlamenti, Parliament's *Answer* to the three June papers of the Triple

Embassy, we can observe several indications of authentic Milton work. Its expansions are in eloquent contrast to Rosin's stark literalness:

> *English*: a good correspondence.
> *French*: une bonne correspindance.
> *Latin*: quod firmæ iis concordiæ, liberoque commercio.

Miltonic vocabulary is conspicuous. Twice, in the heading and in the text, *Potestates Generales* (in inflected forms) stands for "States General," twice *primores* translates the noun "superiors," and *tractatio* renders treaty "negotiation." Nothing in these two pages suggests a contrary evaluation. This *Responsum Parlamenti* is Milton's, likely done about 6 June.[97]

The Latin *Narratio* version of Thurloe's "Narrative," like its English original, is a bare factual account in technical terminology, without the rhetoric of the Commonwealth politicians arguing their case as in their *Declaration* and their *Answer*. Consequently, the text presents difficulties in attribution.

In assembling the English-language (Field) edition, the editor(s) responsible simply included the English text of the "Narrative" for reprinting, verbatim, from the previously published *The Answer of the Parliament*, out by 17 June. Somewhat later, the editor(s) preparing the translations realized that two phrases were no longer appropriate, "all which are hereunto annexed" and "hereunto also annexed." Changes were therefore made, which are reflected in both the French and Latin versions, identical in meaning: "d'autres ecrits cy-devant publiés" and "qui a aussy este cy-devant publiée"; "chartulis denique ex aliis hac de re vulgatis" and "quæ et pridem vulgatæ sunt."

In this one instance, the French version, "La Relation," is not a closely literal translation of the printed English-language text. It seems rather to conform to a prior draft, closer to its sources in the letters from the fleet commanders. Whereas the English and Latin texts credit Blake with having "twelve or thirteen ships," the French has "treize ou 14." It is likewise possible that "La Relation" involved the participation of several people, Weckherlin or Fleming, along with Rosin.

The Latin text does follow the printed English (as revised). There are several nuances that attract the Miltonist. The phrase *in procinctu* ("ready for action") is an expansion not in the English text; it recalls "war in procinct," *Paradise Lost* 6.19. The phrases *pro more percontaretur* and *nullâ pro more data salutê* (neither *pro more* corresponding to the English) recall another *pro more* in Milton's 20 January letter to Hermann Mylius.[98] Unfortunately, these are not compelling to the degree that distinctively or exclusively Miltonic usages would be. Others at that time could have remembered *in procinctu* from Cicero, Tacitus, Seneca, et al., and Adam Littleton offered *pro more* for "customably" in his English-Latin vocabulary (1684 edition).

The Latin *Narratio* puts family names into inflected Latin forms, with one exception, *Capitaneus Young* again. Blake becomes *Blacus, Blaco*. Major Bourne becomes *Bornius, Bornii, Bornio,* In the heading caption, perhaps added later, when the translations were assembled, the Dutch admiral is *Legatus Admirallus Trump* (alongside of *Blaco*), but in the text he is *Van-Trumpius, Van-Trumpio, Van-Trumpium*. The *Van* derives from the English text, where it is used, but the inflections tend to send us back to those in the *Scriptum* proper, and that possible "other hand." For "Dutch," *Batavi, Batavica, Batavicus* are seen eight times; those forms are not used elsewhere in Milton's state letters, which use *Belgæ* and its derivatives, but Milton did use *Batavus* and its derivatives several times in his three Latin *Defenses*, 1650–1655. *Uti* does not appear; *ut* appears twice. *Sclopetarios*— "musquetiers"—and *sclopis*—"small shot"—are unclassical neo-Latinisms, but unvoidable, while for "frigates" the translator draws on the very classical *Liburnicis*.

Another peculiarity is *Die Sabbathi* for "Saturday." This was a church Latin usage, seen in the *Journals* of the House of Lords and House of Commons, spelled *Sabbati* during the 1640s, and discontinued by the Commons about 1651 when the English words for days and weeks were substituted. All in all, the evidence for identifying the translator(s) of the *Narratio* is not conclusive. Weckherlin's participation must be included as one possibility.

There remain 11 items to be examined, extracts taken from the official proceedings of Parliament and the Council. These are recorded in their files in English, and turned into Latin in the *Scriptum* with distinctive Miltonic locutions throughout. Here we encounter some new wrinkles. In the Latin version of Henry Scobell's report of Pauw's 11 June audience, the ambassador's name has become *Adrianus Paius* (p. 27). In a Council order of 14 June, six Englishmen are listed with their family names unchanged, but their given names receive Latin inflections—two as *Henrico*, others as *Oliverio*, *Herberto*, *Guilielmo*, and in another context *Oliverius*—while the ambassador is *Adrianum Paium* (p. 33). In both these entries, "States General" is rendered in inflected forms of *Ordines Generales*. On page 34 another Council order of 14 June shows *Adriano Paio* in one sentence with presumably Miltonic *primoribus*, and *Adriano Paio* again on page 39 in yet another Council order of that date. On page 40 in a 15 June item, *Adrianus Paius* is seen in one sentence with Miltonic *credentialibus sive commendatitiis* and with Miltonic *liberi commeatûs*, and another 15 June order has *Adriano Paio* (p. 45). In a Parliament order of 17 June, Paio is in company with *Potestatum Generalium* (p. 48). Parliament's three demands of 25 June are set forth on page 59 to *Adriano Paio* with *Potestates Generales* twice, *Potestatum Generalium* once. A Council order, 25 June, has *Paium* and *Paio*, with *Potestates Generales*. A Council reply of 26 June refers to *Paio* of the *Potestatum Generalium* (p. 64), and again *Paio* (p. 67), on

27 June, while in the heading to Pauw's final 30 June address, he is *Adriani Paii* asking for (Miltonic) *liberum commeatum*.

Apparently, with regard to given names, where classical, medieval and neo-Latin precedent existed, Milton used inflected forms. But with reference to family names in seventeenth century vernaculars, in the texts preserved in the Columbia Manuscript and in the 1676 *Literæ*, he sometimes left the family name unchanged from the vernacular spelling, as in the instance of *Pauw* in the *Scriptum* proper. Why, then, the change to *Paius, Paii, Paio, Paium* later on, in contexts that are so distinctly Miltonic?

A solution to this question may lie in the manner in which the work of editing the composite booklets had to proceed. The English-language edition had to be done first, and this determined the format for assembling the component parts. Immediately available were the English texts of the 7 July *Declaration*, Parliament's 6 June *Answer* to the three ambassadors, and the *Narrative*. Now, the texts of Parliament's and Council's miscellaneous responses and orders needed to be transcribed and assembled, then interfiled chronologically with Rosin's translations into English from the Netherlanders' French and Latin. This was done, and a heading was prefixed: *A Collection of the Proceedings*. Throughout, Pauw's name is spelled *Pauw*.

Rosin next set up the French-language booklet, which is all in French. He headed the pages with miscellaneous documents with his literal translation, *Receuil des procedures*. Pauw's name is again *Pauw*.

Milton's work had to take longer, because of his blindness. It was simplest to start with what was already in Latin; therefore, he first dictated headings for the *Scriptum* proper, for the 6 June *Responsum Parlamenti*, and for Pauw's 11 June speech, using *Adriani Pauw*. With his usual elegance, he expanded the sentence prefixed to the exchange of papers between Parliament and Pauw, still

Adrianum Pauw. These texts are fair copied and go to an amanuensis for transcription. The Latin caption over the *Narratio* had already been supplied by its translator.

Some time later, Milton turns to the 11 miscellaneous items, which still require translation into Latin. An aide (Rosin, presumably) explains the sheaf of papers at hand.[99] He checks off each item, and ends with the last piece, which is Pauw's 30 June speech, in its Latin original, reading its closing signature, *Hadrianus Paius, J. Cats. G. Schaep. Vandeperre.* Whether it was in Rosin's Gallic pronunciation or some Londoner's, the *H* in *Hadrianus* was inaudible, but Milton definitely heard *PAIUS*, and being alerted to Pauw's own personal preference, Milton adopted it for the rest of the booklet.[100]

It is to be concluded that whether Aitzema's informant referred to the *Scriptum* proper or to the entire booklet, he was correct in naming Milton as responsible (with the exceptions noted above). As senior among the staff employed for foreign languages, Milton dealt with the printer Dugard. While there was some effort at proofreading (an incomplete errata page was appended), no one copyedited the booklet for consistency.[101]

For purposes of Milton's bibliography, or complete collected works, only the Latin edition is a proper entry as a Milton work. None of the four officially printed versions is a primary document. Each one was separately edited from the primary manuscripts. The English edition is the only one that reproduces what was originally English, and translates the French and Latin into English. The French edition retains texts originally in French and translates the Latin and English into French. The Latin edition reproduces Latin and French texts, translating the English into Latin. Field's Dutch text derives from the English.

Because of wide interest in the Anglo-Dutch war, translations were also published in German, Danish and Italian. Variant independent versions were also published in Dutch. All of these derive from the English edition, explicitly or in their literal rendition from its title page. None is a translation of a work by Milton. All are derivative versions of an English-language work from which Milton had previously edited and partly translated a derivative work into Latin.[102]

❧ Two More Milton Letters: To the Danish Envoys on the Dutch War

While we have been following Milton in his day-to-day participation in the Anglo-Dutch developments, he has also been continuously involved in handling correspondence with other states. In particular, from March through October 1652, diplomacy with Denmark, then a major power, required a great deal of his attention.

King Frederick III's sympathies were all with his kinsman, the exiled Charles II, but when Cromwell at Worcester confirmed the continuance of the Commonwealth, Denmark joined the procession of continental powers seeking some normalization of state relations. Following up on surreptitious feelers through Oldenburg deputy Hermann Mylius, on 19 December 1651 King Frederick authorized an exploratory envoy, Henry Willemsen Rosenwing de Lysacker. Willemsen first made a long detour into the Netherlands, perhaps to sound out the Dutch on parallel strategy to cope with the rising might of England, and finally arrived at Gravesend on 5 March 1651/52. After the usual round of audiences, Willemsen received a formal reply to Frederick's *creditif* of 19 December in a letter dated 13 April 1652. Council of State minutes show his letter had been assigned to the newly reappointed Weckherlin to translate, but it was ultimately printed in the 1676 *Literæ* editions as by Milton, therefore leaving a question of attribution.

Willemsen stayed on as a resident chargé d'affaires. In May, the major Danish embassy headed by Peter Reedtz and Eric Rosencrantz arrived for six months of haggling with Council commissioners. Neither side was ready to agree to terms before the outcome of the Anglo-Dutch war would determine the future balance of forces.

Milton's intermittent share in these Anglo-Danish exchanges fully merits and requires study on its own account. However, on two occasions these conferees turned aside from Cimbrio-British questions to the effects of the Anglo-Dutch war, and on each occasion Milton was involved.

The rupture in Anglo-Dutch talks on 30 June immediately complicated matters for the Danes. Although nominally neutral between the combatants, Danish policy had been rather more pro-Dutch than pro-English. On Friday, 2 July, the Danish envoys requested audience in Parliament, where Reedtz read an oration in Latin appealing for the maintenance of peace; at the same time, he submitted it in English translation. Parliament, as customary, directed the Council of State to return thanks, to give a civil answer and to reaffirm their justifications for their proceedings. Later that day, at the end of a long agenda, the Council delegated that proposed civil answer to the committee editing the *Declaration*. At the same time, the committee on foreign affairs was readying written responses on several pending Anglo-Danish issues. All of these were read and approved at the Council on 7 July, formally indited 8 July and delivered to the ambassadors on 9 July.

The Council's "civil answer" on the Anglo-Dutch war has survived, in both English and Latin, in file T.K.U.A., A. II. 16, in the Danish archives. The official English text was inscribed in elegant professional calligraphy, dated 8 July, signed by the Earl of Pembroke and Montgomery as monthly Council president, countersigned by John Thurloe. Accompanying it is the *Translatio* into Latin, *Domini Legati*, undated, unsigned, with no designation of official status—all factors that suggest some haste. No external reference to its translator is on record, but the internal evidence is cogent and sufficient to mark it as another recovered state paper by Milton.

Twice this letter uses the distinctive Miltonic formula *Potestates Generales*. The English phrase "of all indifferent persons" becomes paraphrased (as in the *Scriptum* proper) into *omnium quibus æquitatis studium est*. The four uses of *ut*, and none of *uti*, are what we would expect. One striking feature marks this paper as Milton's. The Latin text of the delivered letter was not handwritten by a Council clerk, but by Milton's personal amanuensis, whose script is familiar to us from the Christopher Arnold album, from the Cromwell sonnet in the Trinity College manuscript and from several letters to Mylius.

Peculiarly, the officially delivered English-language text is distinctly shorter than Milton's Latin. Several clauses, some 40 words, in Milton's phrasing, have no equivalents in the English. Our knowledge of the usual practice, seen by comparing extant texts of other Milton translations of extant English-language state papers, precludes the possibility of such an extensive expansion by him. Since Milton's Latin text described the *Declaration* as shortly to be issued, while the English text had it already "published," it would seem that Milton dictated from a proposed draft as on other occasions, and when in the final copy the English-language text was abridged, no one corrected the Latin to coincide.

Some months later, in the midst of other discussions, on 13 September the Danish ambassadors asked for a special audience at the Council. This was accorded on 15 September, when they proffered another appeal for peace in the name of the King of Denmark. Repeating adjurations against the destructive war, King Frederick urged that the Commonwealth not press demands that would impede the resuming of negotiation, and he warned the English of danger to their recent gains from potential disasters ahead. In the scramble of sundry documents going bank and forth, it appears that not until 12 October was the committee on foreign affairs directed to draw up an answer. Its draft, read at the Council on 14 October, at first seemed acceptable, but later in the day

Whitelocke, Vane and Marten were designated to redo the reply. This was apparently approved in Parliament that same day. On 19 October it was delivered to the Dutch ambassadors. Milton's work would have been done on 15 or 16 October.

Again the official letter in English was handsomely inscribed in ornate calligraphy by a Council scribe, dated 19 October, and signed this time by monthly president William Constable. Again the Latin version, *Concilium de ijs*, is undated and unsigned; it is a fair copy in ordinary neat script, by the same nameless amanuensis. Once again the author of the Latin text is identifiable as Milton by its *Potestates Generales*, and by other locutions he favors: *Deo bene juvante*, "with God's assistance," *ex quo* to express time since. *Ut* appears three times, *uti* once.[103]

Both these letters, in their English originals and in Milton's Latin, are now published for the first time in Milton studies in Part Two.

❧Peace Negotiations in 1653–1654: More Milton Letters Found

In the war at sea in 1652 and 1653, fortune somewhat favored the British navy. In the Netherlands, the British blockade quickly brought on economic distress, unemployment and hunger. "There is great lamentation made amongst the women for their husbands, that are either slain or wounded," Dutch diplomats reported from London, August 1653, but the same wailing could then be heard in Amsterdam. Weighing the immediate real costs against the potential benefits, Cromwell spoke for both sides when he said that the world was wide enough for both, that by agreement together they could dictate markets and law to all other competitors.[104]

On the Dutch side, sentiment for negotiating an end to the fighting first crystallized in the provinces of Holland and West Friesland. A letter from their States, *Ordines Hollandiæ & West Frisiæ considerarunt*, intended to be secret, was transmitted to England, dated 8/18 March 1653. On 1/11 April a reply, *Parlamentum Reipublicæ Angliæ literas ad se missas*, was sent in the name of the Rump Parliament, which also sent a letter *Quæ studia sincera* the same day to the States General, throwing responsibility back on the Netherlands. While the Dutch debated strategy, vainly seeking possible allies among the powers of Europe, the course of events produced a shift in influence among the factions in England. On 19 April, Cromwell dismissed the highly unpopular Rump and then summoned the Nominated Parliament, soon to be nicknamed Barebone's. On 30 April N.S., the States General moved with a letter directly to Cromwell, *Ordines Generales Fœderatarum Belgii Provinciarum accepta et lecta*. This was answered by a letter nominally from the new Council of State, signed by John Lambert and John Thurloe, on 6 May O.S., *Literæ . . . quæ a Thilmanno Aquilio*, requiring the Dutch to come back to England. Without much choice, the States General yielded.[105]

These three diplomatic letters of 1 April and 6 May have never been really studied. Who composed the Latin of the British letters?

Milton's secretary-assistant Weckherlin had died on 13 February. Since a Council order to settle his pay is dated 27 January, he may already have been effectively out of service for some time. The status of Lewis Rosin is unclear: on 17 February in the Council minutes, the petition of Lewis Rosin for satisfaction of his public service is referred to Challoner, Strickland and Mildmay for consideration. Perhaps this entry suggests a discontinuation also for him; his name does not show in the payrolls of Thurloe's office establishment, although in 1656 he is serving as a confidential messenger carrying Cromwell's state papers personally to Holland.

We know that on 21 February, Milton sent a letter to John Bradshaw, then his best access to the Council of State, recommending that Andrew Marvell be appointed in place of the late Weckherlin.[106] Milton mentions "this my enforced absence," which might indicate another protracted stay away from Westminster, like the months in 1651 that Mylius described. His nomination of Marvell was not accepted. On 1 December 1652, Thurloe had moved himself into a position in charge of foreign relations, and he will be choosing his aides himself; exactly when, the record does not show.

The three letters of 1 April and 6 May seem to have been translated into Latin by the same person: the phrase *hoc quam minime grato bello* is used in letters to Holland on 1 April and to the States General on 6 May. Although some of the language is duplicated in Milton state papers, none of the three shows any particularly cogent Miltonisms. Instead, the States General are *Ordines Generales*, not *Potestates*. The Latin for Council, *Concilium*, in various inflected forms, as written by an amanuensis, is spelled *concilium* once and *consilium* four times, which would not have passed Milton's ear if read back to him. So the translator remains unidentified.

On 17/27 June 1653 a new embassy arrived at Gravesend, headed by Hieronymus van Beverningh. His colleagues Willem Nieupoort, Paulus van de Perre and Allard-Pierre Jongestaal followed on 20/30 June. They were met by Oliver Fleming, who explained the new forms of address to be used: "Your Excellency" to Cromwell, "Your most illustrious Lordships" to the Council (*Vostre Excellence, Vos Tres-Illustres Seigneuries*). He also gave new rules on who could wear a hat, and when, at formal audiences. A new series of talks ensued, formal and informal, with new exchanges of position papers and responses, but no agreement was reached on a peace treaty. Negotiations were interrupted in August.

In these exchanges, the Dutch envoys address Cromwell and his Council of State in French. When the English respond with a formal written reply, it is with an official text in English signed in the name of the Council, accompanied by a Latin translation. In this July-August

1653 phase, there were eight such papers submitted by the British.

Six of the Latin translations appear to have been done by one person, who regularly translates "Deputy" as *Delegatus;* uses *currentis* for "instant" (month), *Ordines* for "States General," *telonia* for "customs duties," and other choices of wording that are not Milton's style. This translator may likely have been Philip Meadowes, whose first appointment was made official in some decision that has not come down to us. The Council order designating him as aide to Thurloe in foreign affairs, 17 October 1653, describes him as already "now employed by the Councell in Latin translations."[107]

Two of these eight documents, however, are markedly different in their Latin from the other six. One, beginning *Concilium Status de Chartulâ a Dominis,* dated 13 July 1653, uses *Deputatus* for "Deputy," *hujus mensis* for "instant," *primorum* for "superiors," twice injects *vulgo dictis* when referring to *literis Marcæ,* and seven times offers inflected forms of *Potestates Generales* for "States General." The other letter, much shorter, dated 1 August 1653, answers a Dutch complaint of 25 July/4 August on the treatment of prisoners of war. Beginning *Concilium Status ad Chartulam Dominorum,* this letter uses *Potestatibus Generalibus* and *Deputatorum.* These distinctive and now familiar features indicate that these two Latin state papers should now be included in Milton's works, designated as "presumed done by Milton." In the 13 July Miltonic letter, "Council" is consistently *concilium,* ten times, while *consilium* is reserved for the common noun "counsel." In the 1 August Miltonic letter, "Council" is rendered four times as *Concilium.* In Part Two these English originals and Latin versions are reproduced.[108]

More or less during the same weeks when these two letters were done, Milton translated a letter to Duke Frederick of Holstein (for whom a *Safeguard* was being negotiated, text based on the Mylius 1652 *Salvaguardia*), and wrote a memorial to Council member Sir Gilbert Pickering on behalf of the projected Polyglot Bible. He also followed from time to time the complex legal proceedings of his mother-in-law Anne Powell for recovery of her property lost during the civil war, property from which revenues were also due to him. He daily expected a printed counterattack to his *Pro Populo Anglicano Defensio*, till word came of Salmasius's death on 3 September. He also reviewed, with amanuenses, the manuscripts of his shorter poems, in contemplation of a second edition, and translated the first eight Psalms into a variety of meters, seven of these dated 8 to 14 August.

In October 1653 Milton translated a letter to the Protestant Swiss cantons, who all along had been urging peace both on the English and on the Dutch. Finally dated 23 November, in the name of the (Nominated) Parliament, this letter was supplemented by another, not attributed to Milton, issued in Cromwell's name, acknowledging the mission of Swiss envoy Johannes Jacobus Stockarus, 10 January 1653/54.

On 4 November, the Dutch envoys returned to England. Negotiations resumed, continuing laboriously into the spring of 1654, finally achieving a peace treaty as of 5 April. From December 1653 to late in June 1654, there is a long gap in the sequence of the Milton state letter compilations. During these months, Milton was heavily engrossed in his *Second Defence for the People of England*. Like *Eikonoklastes* and the first *Pro Populo Anglicano Defensio*, *Defensio Secunda* was in some manner a duty officially assigned to Milton. Thurloe may have expected that it would be another panegyric on Cromwell, and therefore Milton was released from mere translation work. It turned out to be a rather critical panegyric, and so, whereas the first *Defensio* came out in a handsome quarto and was reissued in enlarged folio form, both by government printer Dugard, *Defensio Secunda* came out privately in minimal format at Thomas Newcomb's (printer of *Mercurius Politicus*), with no publisher named, and not even the address of George Thomason's Rose and

Crown shop, which was the main sales outlet.

From this time period, only one short letter may with some degree of probability be attributed to Milton, the letter of introduction for John Dury, dated 27 March 1654, sent in three variant versions to Basel, to Genva, and to the Swiss cantons.[109] A heavy load of translation was required during the peace negotiations, which coincided in time with diplomatic proceedings with several other countries—enough, it would seem, to overburden Meadowes. Possibly Rosin was still being employed, possibly the younger Dorislaus, possibly others.

At no time, however, is there any recognizable indication to suggest that Milton was taking part. What is clear is that his Latin version of the Thirty-six Counter-articles of 1652 was constantly in use, and much of that text reappears twice: in the draft submitted by the English on 18 November 1653, as their basis for the peace treaty, and again in the finally agreed upon treaty of 5 April 1654. Texts of 13 articles from 1652 were used, all somewhat revised, and some very revised. These revisions were not in Milton's Latin, but done by others, without question. Tabulating corresponding articles:[110]

Milton's 1652 Draft	18 November 1653	5 April 1654
3, 13	13	12
6	9	8
9	19	16
10	20	17
14	21	19
16	22	20
17	23	omitted
23	24	21
24	25	22
25	27	24
25, 26	omitted	26

These relics of Milton's 1652 text are of interest, but they do not render the 1654 treaty eligible for inclusion in his Works, any more than Dryden's adaptation of *Paradise Lost* merits inclusion in the rhyming *State of Innocence*.

Following the conclusion of the treaty, a number of long detailed and technical papers were required for its effectuation. In some of these, there appear peculiar cautionary phrases, which deserve attention, but do not lead us to Milton (see Appendix C for further discussion).

A Postscript: Judging or Understanding

We have been following Milton's participation in the Anglo-Dutch negotiations primarily to ascertain the facts—biographically, concerning what he was doing at the time, and, artistically, to see what his dictated Latin reveals. For a span of 11 years, Milton devoted his best efforts to presenting the voice of England to Europe in terms worthy of a great nation, whether its message treated the highest matters of state or sought to resolve some merely private grievance. In this present book, we have recovered correct texts of documents previously inaccurately known: Milton letters and the Thirty-six Counter-articles; we have recovered letters by Milton hitherto wholly unknown; we have identified some by his secretary-assistant Weckherlin, and we have resurrected his aide Lewis Rosin, tracing his traces in these papers; we have clarified Milton's share in composite documents: the *Paper of Demands* and the *Scriptum* booklet; and we have recovered the English-language originals corresponding to Milton's Latin translations. All of these contributions lead to an augmented, validated and definitive text of the state papers in Milton's works. In developing decisive tests for identifying state papers as being or not being attributable to him, this inquiry has shed new light on Milton's allegiance to classical Latinity and on the kind of thesaurus he hoped to publish.

One last question: what was Milton's attitude toward the Anglo-Dutch War and to the kind of politics it represented?

Years before, in his first pamphlet, *Of Reformation* (1641), Milton argued for close alliance between England and the Netherlands, "whose mutual interest is of such high consequence, though their Merchants bicker in the East Indies."[111] While the war was going on, Milton read a royalist diatribe wish that Holland "may finish off this war as easily and as successfully as Salmasius will finish off Milton," and Mr. Secretary Milton retorted, "To that wish I shall readily agree, and I believe I am neither presaging ill nor praying ill for our successes and the cause of England."[112]

But when that war was over, equally publicly Mr. Secretary Milton declared:

> You are indeed greatly mistaken, if you think there is any Englishman more friendly, more willingly allied to the United Provinces than myself, anyone who thinks more highly of that republic, who prizes more or more often applauds their industry, their arts, ingenuity and liberty; who would less want a war begun with them, who would support it when begun with less enthusiasm, and when ended, who would more sincerely rejoice.[113]

It is not for us to judge, but to try to understand. If Milton shared in the duplicity of the diplomacy, because he shared in the twisted ideals of nationalist patriotism, it was also because it was his belief that the short-term goals of the Commonwealth merchants and shipowners were inseparable from his long-term goals of republican equality, of freedom of inquiry, freedom of speech and freedom of conscience.

Appendix A

The Treatment of Names in Milton's Latin Texts

A careful reader of Milton's state papers soon notices certain peculiarities in the treatment of proper names. Taking the *Literæ* version of the body text of these letters, we derive certain conclusions. The *Literæ* version is preferable because it includes names not found in the Columbia Manuscript. The Skinner Transcript is inappropriate because it made changes in the treatment of names.

All given (first) names are rendered in Latin, or are given Latin terminations, which are inflected according to Latin declensions.

Personal names in the form of titles of nobility, with *Dux, Marchio, Comes,* whether specified or only implied, are given in Latinized form: *Suffolchiensi, Richmondiæ* and the like.

Family names, not titles of nobility, but using particles (*de, ab, van, le*) remain in their vernacular forms: Simone de Petkum (Danish), Henricus Willemsen de Lysaker (Danish), Leo ab Aisema (Dutch, *sic*, spelled phonetically as pronounced), Dominus de Bourdeaux (but the city Bordeaux, and all place names, are Latin in form), Ioannes Rodericus de Saa Meneses (but *Comitem Pennaguiadanum,* with his title); and so others.

"Ordinary" family names fall into two categories. About 76

family names are given Latinized terminations (including such peculiarities as *Clutterbuxi* for "Clutterbuck"), while about 22 family names (some borne by multiple individuals from one family) remain in the vernacular forms, English, German, Italian, French, Dutch, Danish, Spanish. Some appear both ways: *Dethic, Dethicus; Salvetti, Salcettus.* There are other anomalies: *Piggottus* in *Literæ* but *Piggott* in the final delivered letter.

The ratio of Latinized to vernacular names (excluding names with particles) is about four to one, but there is no obvious rationale why one in Latinized and another is not. In letters bearing the same date and similar content, Carolus Vane is vernacular but Antonius Ascamus is Latinized. Richardus Bradshaw from 1650 to 1657 is always vernacular, and so is Philippus Meadowe(s), but Jepsonus and Duningus are Latinized, all four being English envoys. Some alien envoys are in the vernacular, Patrus Spiering silvercroon, Joannes Fridericus Schlezer, Gulielmus Nuport (*sic*), but we have Hermannus Mylius, Laurentius Paulutius, Henricus Oldenburgus, Fridericus Wolisogus, Christopher Gryphiander, Christiernus Bondus, Petrus Julius Coietus (but *Coijet* in the final letter).

Names in the official formulas of complimentary address, which were usually added by the staff protocol personnel after Milton had dictated the body text, are Latinized (except those with the particle: Alphonsus de Cardenas, Dominus de Bourdeaux). Most of these involve titles, Rex, Princeps, Dux, Comes.

Council presidents sign letters with vernacular family names: *Gulielmus Masham,* and so does Commons Speaker *Gulielmus Lenthall.* As Lord Protector, Cromwell signed by his given name alone, *Oliverius,* followed by the initial *P.*

In the Skinner Transcript most of the vernacular family names were changed to have Latinized terminations, except: Weinshinks, Evans, Schlezer, Meadowe, Romswinckel. In the 1674 *Epistolarum Familiarium,* also handled by Daniel Skinner, family names are Latinized to extremes, in the dative case: Young to *Junio,* Jones to *Jonesio, Heimbachio, Millio* (spelled phonetically and not correlated with *Mylius,* as it should have been), but *Henrico de Brass,* with its *de* (again phonetic, properly De Brosse?).

Elsewhere Milton Latinizes family names. While in the state papers Richard Bradshaw is always Richardus Bradshaw, although the first name is not more Latin than the last in its etymology, his more kinsman John Bradshaw is Romanized into *Joannes Bradsciavus* in *Defensio Secunda* (misprinted *Bradscianus* in Columbia edition, Vol. 8, 156), and in *Epistolarum Familiarium* (*Bradsciavi*, Vol. 12, 86).

Appendix B

Milton's Thesaurus Linguæ Latinæ

Throughout our exploration of Milton's state papers, we have been acutely conscious of the purist Latin standards of Milton the lexicographer. It was somewhere along in his teaching years that Milton began to compile his personal Latin dictionary. He worked on it for almost 30 years, to the end of his life. Unfortunately it was never printed, and the manuscripts have not been seen since 1693. Until now we have not known what it was like. From what we have seen in his practice in the state papers, however, we can infer its basic character: not an all-inclusive dictionary, but rather one selectively limited to what Milton judged was the purest Latin used by the best classical writers native to ancient Rome.

Milton's work on this dictionary was recorded from personal knowledge by his friend Cyriack Skinner (presumed author of Bodleian MS. Wood D4), by his nephew Edward Phillips ("Life of Milton," in *Letters of State Written by Mr. John Milton*, 1694), and confirmed by his widow Elizabeth Milton to John Aubrey (Bodleian Library, MS. Aubrey 8, ff 63–68).

From these three sources we have derived some confused and contradictory descriptions. Aubrey in his scribbled notes first tells us, "I heard that after he was blind, that he was writing a *Latin* (inserted by caret) Dictionary. *vidua* (inserted by caret) Affirmat she gave all his papers to his Nephew, that he brought up"—that was Edward Phillips. Above "all his papers" Aubrey inserted in brackets "[among wch this Dict. imperfect]"—after speaking with Phillips, perhaps. But in the margin preceding these entries Aubrey wrote "in the hands of Moyses Pitt"—Pitt was a well-known printer of that time.

Cyriack Skinner also dated the inception of the work to after Milton's blindness. "It was now that hee began that laborious work of amassing out of all the Classic Authors, both in Prose and Verse a *Latin Thesaurus* to the emendation of that done by Stephanus." Anthony a Wood in his *Athenæ Oxonienses* (1691–1692) cribbed from Aubrey and Skinner: he vaguely knew of "the *Latin Thesaurus* in those [hands] of Edw. Phillips his Nephew."

Edward Phillips, who was in a position to have exact knowledge, wrote in 1694 that it was after the three *Defensios* that Milton had leisure for his own studies, and worked on his *History of England*

> "and a New *Thesaurus Linguæ Latinæ*, according to the manner of *Stephanus*; a work he had been long since Collecting from his own Reading, and still went on with it at times, even very near to his dying day; but the Papers after his death were so discomposed and deficient, that it could not be made fit for the Press; However, what there was of it was made use of for another Dictionary."

Phillips was possibly being somewhat coy. In the second edition of Wood's *Athenæ Oxonienses* (London, 1721), 1118, among the publications of Edward Phillips are included:

> *Enchiridion Linguæ Latinæ*: or, a compendious *Latin* Dictionary, equally sufficient, with the largest extant, for all Learners, whether Children, or those of riper Years, &c. To which are added, 1. A collection of the most usitate *Greek* words, &c. 2. A brief *Anglo-Latin* or *English Lat.* Dictionary 3. Another of the most select proper Names, Poetical and Historical, &c. Lond. 1684. oct.
>
> *Speculum Linguæ Latinæ*: or, a succinct and new method of all the most material and fundamental words of the *Lat.* Tongue *Lond*. 1684. oct. These two last were all or mostly taken from the *Latin Thesaurus*, writ by *Joh. Milton* Uncle to *Edw. Phillips*.

Unfortunately no copies of these 1684 octavos are known to exist. On the supposition that they were intended for use in schools below university level, I wrote to all the major schools surviving in England from that era to search their premises: none reported finding any copies, or any record of any copies.

John Toland, "The Life of John Milton," 1698, suggested a different dictionary: "Milton's *Thesaurus Linguæ Latinæ*, design'd as a Supplement to Stephanus, was never publisht, and has bin of great use to Dr. *Littleton* in compiling his Dictionary" (*A Complete Collection of the Historical, Political and Miscellaneous Works of John Milton* (1698), Vol. 1, p. 45 in the first pagination). Toland was not more precise, and Adam Littleton himself left no such acknowledgment.

The 1693 publication *Linguæ Romanæ Dictionarium Luculentum Novum*, based on Littleton's, on its title page acknowledges "a large Manuscript, in three Volumes, of Mr. John Milton" and in its preface the editors state

> "we had by us, and made use of, a Manuscript Collection in three *Large Folio's* digested into an Alphabetical order, which the Learned Mr. *John Milton* had made, out of *Tully, Livy, Cæsar, Sallust, Quintus Curtius, Justin, Plautus, Terence, Lucretius, Virgil, Horace, Ovid, Manilius, Celsus, Columella, Varro, Cato, Palladius*; in short out of all the best and purest Roman authors."

This list reads as if it were taken from a manuscript title page, and tends to confirm that Milton was not concerned to be all-inclusive, but aimed to offer a vocabulary that would come from the "best and purest" Latins. Some of these authors of technical works were textbooks Milton used in his teaching days. The omission of many names may be explained when the missing three folios are recovered. While Milton in his *Accendence Commenc't Grammar* carried over from Lily's Grammar citations to Macrobius, Justinian, Boethius and Erasmus, no citation he added was later than Suetonius.

The 1693 edition preface continues:

> "In using the assistances mentioned, we did not take every, nay scarce any Word, upon trust; but the way we took to make these great mens labors useful to us was this: they seldom omit naming not only the Author, but the place in him whence they fetch their Authorities. This is known to be Stephen's Method, and the same may be seen in Mr. Milton's Manuscript by the curious or doubtful."

Edward Phillips also described the work as "according to the manner of Stephanus." The emphasis is on Robertus Stephanus's practice of giving many citations to Roman authors. However, Cyriack Skinner's word was different: "to the emendation of that by Stephanus." We may suspect, from his practice in the state papers, that Milton would not have retained from Stephanus the Greek loan-word *telonium* with Stephanus's citation to Tertullian, whom Milton regarded as *scriptorem haud orthodoxam, multis erroribus notatum*, "hardly an orthodox writer, noted for his many errors' (*Pro Populo Anglicano Defensio*, Columbia edition, Vol. 7, 246).

Edward Phillips's description of "discomposed and deficient" papers is strikingly different from the 1693 description of "three Large Folio's digested into an Alphabetical order." It would seem that there were two manuscripts, one imperfect given by Milton's widow to Edward Phillips, another "in the hands of Moyses Pitt." Aubrey's scribbles allow that possibility. The printers in 1693 were inviting inspection. Surely the manuscript was not carelessly discarded, and waits to be rediscovered.

Appendix C

A Caveat

When reservations *vulgo dictus* or *quos vocant* are found in state papers that are otherwise known to be by Milton or when they are found in company with other distinctive expressions that characterize his work, they are properly considered as contributory evidence strengthening the attribution to him. They are especially acceptable as "test" evidence when his use of such expressions is in sharp contrast to their total absence from the English text that he is translating, or from related documents submitted by foreign diplomats who use the same terms without any reservations. One other observation: Milton usually uses his cautionary phrase with reference to common nouns. Only in the B4 catalog in the *Paper of Demands* are any associated with proper names, but *vulgo* with place names was not uncommon at that time.

However, the appearance of such a phrase in isolation, without other Miltonisms, cannot be regarded as such evidence or proof. Some such phrases are found among other writers. Milton's political antagonist, Claudis Salmasius, also had strong feelings on Latinity (not always consistently), and in *Defensio Regia* he wrote "quomodo Optimatum consessum abrogaverint, sola relicta plebejorum domo quæ vocatur vulgo *Communium*" (in edition designated Madan 4, pp. 223–24).

Such cautionary phrases are usually used to justify a translation from the vernacular of a technical term or of a common noun adapted to a name. Readers who are sensitive to bibliographical detail are familiar with seventeenth century title pages advertising booksellers' addresses in this style: *sub signo Angeli in vico Lumbardensi (vulgò Lumbard street)* as printed in Theodore Beza's *Jesu Christi Domini Novum Testamentum,* 1642.

Another common instance was in reference to the Company of Merchants Adventurers, who show up as the *Societate Anglorum Mercatorum quos Adventurarios appellamus* in a Cromwell state letter to the Dutch, 24 August 1655, with similar phrasing in letters to the States General, to Holland, to Rotterdam and to Dordrecht, 26 and 27 October 1654, all printed in W.C. Abbott, *Writings and Speeches* none attributed to Milton, and in a letter from Rotterdam to Cromwell, 9 June 1656, printed in *Thurloe Papers*, Vol. 5, 74. None of these can be attributed to Milton's influence: the form may be seen in a petition from the East Frisian town of Emden to Queen Elizabeth, 8 October 1597, *Vestræ Majestatis Subditos Negotiatores, quos Mercatores Adventurarios vocant* (T. Rymer, *Foedera*, Vol. 16, 323.)

On the other hand, when such phrases occur in writers who have come into the magnetic field of Milton's influence, used together with other terms favored by Milton, tantalizing questions arise. From the tone in which Milton (by letter) corrected Mylius on *projecta*, it would not be surprising if the secretary for foreign languages was in the habit of commenting emphatically on the use and abuse of Latinity among his own colleagues and in the hearing of others.

In Leo ab Aitzema's *Historia Pacis*, page 789, misprinted as 689, he refers to the Council of State's demand to seen Pauw's powers to negotiate:

> In primis Angli petierunt ut exhibeat Legatus mandatum, vulgò *Plenipotentiam*, Gallis *pouvoir;* quod Legatis solet dari ultra litteras vulgò *Credentiales*. Legatus solummodo dictas credentiales, & præterea ternas liberi commeatus literas (*Plenipotentiam* illiam solennem, ut supervacum, neglexerat) exhibuit.

This passage appears to echo Milton's 1652 *Scriptum* booklet phrasing, page 40: "instabat credentialibus sive commendatitiis, ternis*que* datis sibi liberi commeatûs literis." It may also be an echo of Milton when Aitzema has Pauw ask *audientiam, transitum, commeatum liberum* (*Historia Pacis*, 792). Aitzema read "The Flye vulgo dictum" in the British *Paper of Demands*

B4 catalog, for his *Historia Pacis*, 767, put the name into Latin but retained the cautionary phrase, *Ostium Flevum vulgo dictum*. In the same book, pages 48–49, Aitzema supplied this heading over a protest prepared by an English councillor in September 1625 against Dutch hostilities in the East Indies:

> Regis Britianniæ Protestationis, quam vocant, argumentum, super violentarum Repetitionum, vulgo Repressaliorum, adversus Indiæ Orientalis Societatem antehac datorum concessorumque annihilatione.

Protestatio is postclassical, *repetitio* is late law-Latin, and *repressaliorum* was definitely *vulgò*. So much of Aitzema's *Historia Pacis* vocabulary is current unclassical: *offendendi er defendendi*, 171; *salvaguardia*, 814. Milton's reminiscing letter of 5 February 1654/55 recalls repeat visits by Aitzema. Might those uncommon conditional phrases in *Historia Pacis* show the after-effects of conversations with Milton?

In *Exposuerunt nuper*, the Dutch envoys' paper of 16/26 January 1652, there occurs the phrase *protentu repressaliarum (quas vocant)*. That is the *only* such instance in all the papers submitted by the Dutch in 1651–1652: could it be the effect of Vlitius's having met with Milton?

The Anglo-Dutch peace treaty negotiations present other problems with regard to these cautionary phrases. Exactly when Milton was released to concentrate on *Defensio Secunda* is unknown, although it was definitely by December 1653. A preliminary, early draft of the treaty Article 3 read *Angustum mare, quo vulgo Britannicum Mare appellatur*, and as of 18 November 1653, Article 17 read *cum Naviculis suis halecariis quas buysen vocant* ([Scheuleer,] *Verbael*, pp. 320, 212), but both reservations were omitted in the final text. Likewise, all those cautionary phrases Milton dictated into his Latin of the Thirty-six Counter-articles, every one, vanished when those sentences were blended into the 1654 treaty.

On the other hand, cautionary phrases do appear in the documents effectuating the treaty. In a paper submitted by the Dutch envoys, 8 April 1654, they wrote *quo | ad summam Millionis, quod vocant, Belgici, aut Centena Millis librarum Anglicarum* (*Verbael*, 346). The document setting up the *Règlement* committee tells them to seet in "*Aula vulgo nuncupata* Guildhall" (p. 369) and the arbitration committee is assigned to "*Aurifabrorum Aula, vulgo* Goldsmith's Hall," (p. 272), both between 5 and 22 April.

The *Règlement* of 30 August 1654 was the report of Dutch and English representatives appointed to settle the claims for damages on both sides (Aitzema, *Saken*, Vol. 3 1069–075; Olive Parry, *Consolidated Treaty Series*, Vol. 3, 319–53). The English representatives used the occasion to rehearse the 1652 *Paper of Demands*, updated and expanded, but revised into a new document, in language no longer Milton's. The British spoke of *navigia, vulgo Gallihorne et Tingans*, and *vasorum, vulgo barills* (i.e., barrels); the Dutch spoke of *scapharum quas vulgo Tingans vocant* and three times introduced the name of a Dutch ship by *vulgo*. These are matters of translation, rather than concern for classicism. We must hesitate to attribute these usages to Milton or his influence, even though they are relatively frequent here. They *are* seen elsewhere, but rarely. Thomas Killigrew, Resident (agent) of Charles II in Venice, addressing the Collegio there 26 April 1650, used these phrases, *decem mille doliorum (uti vulgo loquuntur capacitatem* and *Insulam Cesaream (vulgo Gearsey)*, printed in *Calendar of State Papers, Venetian*, Vol. 28 (1647–1652), pages 143–45.

Some of such cautionary reservations are seen in Cromwell's treaties (with Sweden) and a 1660 agreement with Portugal, and in Milton state letters between 1654 and 1659. In *Petrus Tyson ex Ostendâ* (Cromwell to States General, 12 March 1657/58) the words *arresto quod vocant* are used. The Latin is by someone who liked the word *commendamus* and used it in eight or more letters; his identity still to be determined.

It is notable that the formula *letters of marque and reprisal* was a problem for others, not only Milton. Adam Littleton in his 1684 *Dictionary* offered the ancient classical *clarigatio*, in his Latin-English, and *diploma clarigatorium* in his English-Latin, as approximate equivalents. Aitzema in *Historia Pacis* uses *literæ contramarcæ vel retorsionales* (813) and *literis retorsionis* (815). I have not seen any of these used in Milton or elsewhere. Cf. Hugo Grotius, *De Jure Belli ac Pacis Libri Tres*, Liber III, Caput II, Par. IV: "Alia executionis violentæ species est ἐωεχυπιχτνὸσ sive pigneratio inter populos diversos, quod jus repressaliarum vocant recentiores jurisconsulti, Saxones & Angli Withernamium, & Galli etiam, ubi a rege impetrari id solet, literas Marcæ."

PART TWO

*The New Published Writings of Milton
and Related Documents*

Eighteen documents are reproduced here from the original manuscripts, each in English and in Latin. Some of these have never been published previously; while others, although obscurely printed in seventeenth and eighteenth century books on diplomacy, with no Milton identification, have never been published in Milton studies; some, previously attributed to Milton, have not been published correctly. Two documents, the English-language *Declaration* and its Latin *Scriptum* version with Milton's contributions, are here reproduced for the first time in full from their original 1652 printings.

Those documents that were Milton's work, whether definitely or most probably, whether entirely or partly his, need no justification for their inclusion here. Related papers from 1652 putatively done by his colleagues Lewis Rosin and Georg Rudolph Weckherlin have their own intrinsic interest and are essential to the process of validating what in Milton's work. Since the methodology for authenticating Milton's contributions is fully established through the diplomatic papers of 1652, it is not felt necessary at this point to include full texts of the non-Miltonic British state papers from 1653–1654, done by Phillip Meadowes or others.

It should be borne in mind that Milton prepared his Latin texts of British state papers from English-language interim drafts, not from the final English-language fair copies, so that some discrepancies do occur; and that different amanuenses used a wide variety of scripts and show many individual peculiarities reproducible only by photography.

Van Vliet's *Cum nihil prius*

No official original text is known. The Latin text here is taken from MS. S.G. 8460, no. 15, and MS. Aitzema 86, both transcripts. It is given here, with my translation, in the hope that this may lead to the identification of Milton's English version somewhere. The echoes of Vlitius's phrasing in Milton's Latin *Concilim Status Parlamenti* suggest that the official English original of that letter may echo the English in Milton's translation of Vlitius's text.

For discussion, see pages 13 and 17–18.

Milton's Latin Translation

Ad Consilium Status Reip: Angliæ

Cum nihil prius fuerit Fœderati Belgij Ordinum Legatis, quam omnia discordiæ (quam avertat Deus) irritamenta præcavere, ideo*que* iam aliquoties ab Illustri hoc Consilio petierint, ut ne judicia illa in captas Belgarum naves intentata præcipitarentur: sed donec de summa re inter utram*que* Remp. tractanda aliquid certi constitutum; vel saltem as tot postulata DD. Legatorum ab hoc Illustri Consilio plene responsum fuerit, nihil auribus eorum gravius aut a sincera spe stabiliendi fœderis alieum magis accidere potuit, quam quod tot serijs petitionibus & repetitis indies expostulationibus nihil omnino actum videant; quo minus jussu hujusce Augusti Consessus illæ ipsæ naves Fœderati Belgij subjectorum definitiva sententia hodie lata occupatoribus addictæ et damnatæ sint. Quod quidem eo gravius praedictis DD. Legatis videtur, quod inconsultorum quorundam nautarum, nihil tale quid opinantium aut expectantium & jure dominorum suorum abutentium (absque ullo enim eorum mandato, nescijs DD. Legatis, a privatis et ignaris istud actum est) præposteræ petitioni, quam publico desiderio DD. Legatorum, plus fidei ac ponderis accesserit. Quamobrem ijdem nunc DD. Legati ne rem tanti momenti extra omnem ferendæ opis aut medelæ spem conclamatam relinquerent, usitata appellationis via nautas suos uti jusserunt; interea dum præsentius et salutarius remedium, quo tot inevitabilia damna spoliatorum cervicibus detrudantur, spoliaque omnia restituantur, a prudentia et æquitate vestra serie desiderant atque expectant.

    Subscriptum jussu et mandato DD. Legatorum & signatum
    Janus Vlitius, a secretis DD. Legat:

Reconstruction of the Original English Text

Since nothing could take greater precedence for the Ambassadors of the States General of the United Provinces than to obviate all provocations of discord (which may God avert) they have therefore several times requested from this Illustrious Council that the projected sentences on the captured ships of the Hollanders not be precipitately rendered: but until something definite is settled on the major issues being negotiated between the two commonwealths; or at least until there will be a full response by this Illustrious Council to a number of propositions submitted by the Lords Ambassadors, nothing more grave to their ears, nor more alien from a sincere hope of settling a treaty could happen than that they may see nothing at all done about so many earnest petitions and expostulations repeated day after day; that, absent an order from this August Conclave, those very ships of the subjects of the United Netherlands, could, by definitive sentence pronounced today, be adjudicated and condemned to those who have seized them. What therefore appears even more grave to the aforesaid Lords Ambassadors, is that more credit and weight have been given to an unseasonable petition of certain indiscreet mariners, not such as show judgment or forethought, and abusing the right of their owners (for that was done without any mandate of theirs, by unofficial and inexperienced men, without the knowledge of the Ambassadors), than to the official request of the Lords Ambassadors. Wherefore the same Ambassadors, lest they abandon a matter of such moment beyond all final hope of getting help or remedy, ordered their mariners to employ the customary avenue of appeal; meanwhile they earnestly demand and expect most immediately and salutarily from your prudence and equity that remedy by which so many inevitable damages may be lifted from the heads of the despoiled, and that all spoils be restored.

Written by order and command of the Lords Ambassadors and signed
> Janus Vlitius, Secretary to the Lords Ambassadors

Concilium Status Parlamenti Republicæ Angliæ

The official original English text of this state paper, dated 29 January 1651/52, is here printed for the first time (superseding the inadequate approximation offered by Nelson G. McCrea in 1938), together with the correct text of Milton's Latin version, both taken form MS. S.G. 8460, no. 16.

Significant as an example of Milton's state papers, somehow emitted from all seventeenth century compilations, this text is also a mirror of Milton's character and his unyielding insistence on a purist standard of classical Latinity.

For discussion, see pages 14–16.

OFFICIAL LATIN TEXT[106]

Concilium Status Parlamenti Reipub: Angliæ Authoritate constitutum, acceptis quæ Excellentiæ V^{ræ} Januarij undevigesimo 1651. Scripta exhibuerunt, in quibus tria postulata comprehensa sunt, responsum hoc reddit.

1. Parlamentum sua studia confirmandæ inter hanc Rempub: et Fœderatas Provincias amicitiæ semper manifesta reddidisse, ne*que* se defuturos quo minùs omni justa at*que* honesta ratione eandem conservet at*que* promoveat; cum*que* Excellentijs V^{ris} commodū videbitur, vel ex pactis prioribus vel siquo alio libuerit modo, eas postulationes singillatim ferre, ad præsentem temporū at*que* rerū rationem accommodatas, quas ex vestra parte conferre ad jacienda societatis fundamenta existimabitis, responsa ad eas idonea accipietis. Quod autem ad ea supplenda quæ hujus Reipub: Legati Hagæ Comitis infecta reliquere, censemus ea consideranda non esse, cum tractatio illa nihil protulerit, ne*que* ullus ejus articulus perfectus et conclusus fuerit.

2. Parlamentum cum neccessarium esse duxerit gentem hanc omni justa ac debita ratione ad navigandi studium rém*que* nostram navalem exaugendam incitare, ea gratiâ Edictum promulgavit cujus in secunda V^{ra} postulatione facta mentio est: quod cum justas et luculentas ob causas factum sit, Edicti ejus vel rescindendi vel inhibendi causam nullam videmus.

3. Maximè vellet Concilium, occasionem nullam fuisse datam, literas quas vocant Merc et Represales concedendi contra fœderati Belgij poplum; quod potuit quidem non factū fuisse, si, qui nostrûm ab eo spoliati sunt jus suū obtinere potuissent: qua de re Parlamentum hoc et antea conquestū est et satisfactionem postulavit, id*que* nominatim, quod ad causam attinet Annæ Pawlett Viduæ, cujus maritus a Capitaneo Cornelio Skint in nave quadam, cui nomen Petro Roterodamiensi, direptus est. Quapropter cum is ut bona sibi ablata restituerentur aut satisfactio fieret impetrare non posset, causá*que* ipsa fidem nostrā

atque opē imploraret, suis petentibus datæ sunt ad hac Repub: literæ, quas vocant Represales, utpote Remedium justissimū et maximè idoneū ad eos sublevandos quibus damnū datum est, quae quidem literæ adhuc solæ sunt a nobis in populum ffœderati Belgij concessæ, quanqua multæ sunt aliæ injuriarū et damnorū actiones, et magnæ quidem aestimationis, quæ ad idem remedium et vindicandi rationem jam diu maturuere: Quæ quidem singulæ Excellentijs V^ris exhibebuntur, quo damna reparari, et satisfieri ijs possit, quibus illata injuria est. Quod quidē eorum postulatum, cùm justissimum at*que* æquissimum sit, si ejus et aliorū ejusmodi rationem habebitis, nullo alio modo ijs incommodis, quæ ostenduntur, certiùs occurri poterit: ne*que* enixius expectabit hæc Respub: justitiam ab alijs, quàm similem reddere paratissima erit, quoties quid hujusmodi acciderit: Út*que* plane perspectū sit; quàm nos libenter caveamus, ne qua in re ad extrema deveniatur, ex quo Excellentiæ V^ræ advenerunt, dedimus mandata, ne quæ porro naves capiantur earū authoritate literarū Annæ Pawlett concessimus, quemadmodum V^ris Excellentijis jam prius significatū a Concilio est.

 Quod autem ad navium restitutionem, impensarū et damnorū reparationem eá*que*, si qua sunt, qua perperàm gesta sunt per eas Literas Merc et Represales vulgò dictas contra Francos et alios jam concessas, ex quibus ulla fieri Fœderati Belgij Populo vera injuria apparebit, cùm in curia causarū maritimarū propria ratio juris obtinendi in causis hujusmodi constituta sit; si illic lege agetur, debitæque probationes factæ erūt, cætera*que* exinde rectè at*que* ordine fient, quandoquidem ijs qui quid habent queralæ, illic jus suū persequendi, si videbitur, liberrima facultas est, rectiùs quidem providere non possumus, quàm si eos, quorū id refert, ad remedia tàm jùsta at*que* legitima remittamus.

Textual note: MSS. S.G. 8460 and Aitzema 86 spell *estimationis* with a cedilla to indicate the dipthong. The line over $\bar{a}$, $\bar{e}$, $\bar{u}$ in the manuscript indicates a final *m* is omitted, except in *erunt*. In their 1938 edition Mabbott and French expanded all the abbreviations, but in their notes (vol. 18, 504) they tabulated all the errors, slips and corrections by the amanuensis.

TEXT OF THE OFFICIAL LETTER IN ORIGINAL ENGLISH

The Councell of State appointed by Authority of the Parlament of ye Common-Wealth of England, haveing received your Lordships Paper conteyning Three Propositions exhibited the 19th Day of January 1651, Does make this Returne.

1. The Parlament hath constantly manifested their Desires of a firme Amitie betweene this Common Wealth and the United Provinces, and will not be wanting by all meanes Just and Honourable to continue and improve the same; And when your Excellencies shall be pleased out of former Treaties or otherwise to propose such particulars suited to the Constitution of the present time and Affaires as are intended on yor part to bee the foundation of an Alliance, You shall receive such answers thereunto as shall be fit; And as to the Supplying what the Ambassadors of the Common Wealth left not performed at the Hague, Wee conceive the same to be of noe Consideration, the Treatie there taking noe effect nor any one particular thereof deduced to a conclusion.

2. The Parlament finding it necessarie to give all just and due encouragement to the Navigation and for the increase of the Shipping of this Nation, have in Order thereunto passed the Act in the second Proposition mentioned wch being done upon cleare and just Grounds; Wee see noe reason for the Repeale or suspension of the same.

3. The Councell could have wished no occasion had been given of granting Letters of Marque and Represall against the People of ye united Provinces which might have been prevented if Justice had been done to those of this Nation depredated by them; Touching which former Complaints, have beene made, and satisfaction Demanded by this Parlament; Particularly in the Case of Anne Pawlett Widdow whose Husband had been robbed by Captaine Cornelius Skynt in a Shipp called the Peter of Rotterdam; whereupon noe Restitution or Satisfaction being obteyned, and the Case requireing redresse, Letters of Represall (as

the proper and just Remedie) have beene graunted, by this State for Reliefe of the Parties interessed upon their Petition, which is the only Commission in that kind as yet granted, although there be divers Cases of wrongs and Dammages to a great Value long since fitted for the like Remedie and proceeding; The particulars whereof will be presented to your Excellencies in Order to a due satisfaction and Reparation to the Parties wronged, which being a Demand of Right and Justice, the doeing of it in those and like Cases will bee the only sure meanes of preventing the feared Inconveniencies; nor will this State be more earnest in expecting, than they will be readie to afford such Justice on all like occasions: And for Demonstration of Our willingnesse to prevent extremities, Wee have since your Excellencies comeing suspended the further Seizure of Ships upon the Letters of Represall granted in Pawletts Case, as hath been already signified to your Excellencies from the Councell.

As to the Restitution of Ships, repaireing Costs and Dammages, and touching the Miscariages (if any bee) in any the Commissions of Marque and Represall allreadie granted against the French or Others wherby any reall Injurie may appear to be done to the People of the United Provinces, there being a proper Course for Receiving of Justice in all such Cases in the Admiralty Court upon complaint and proofe thereof made, & due proceeding thereupon had, and where the Complaints have free liberty to prosecute their Interests if they please; Wee connot provide better than to leave the Parties concerned to such just and legall Remedies.

    Signed in the Name and by Order of the Councell of State appointed by Authority of Parlament.
                    Art Hesilrige. Pres[dt.]

Textual note: interessed, miscariages, dammages, graunted/granted, are manuscript spellings. The Dutch form of the Peter's skipper's name was Cornelis 't Kint.

Scriptum ab Excellentijs Vestris

As in the instance of the preceding letter, the official original English text of this letter, also dated 29 January 1651/52, is here printed for the first time, superseding the McCrea translation offered in the 1938 Columbia edition, together with the Latin text of Milton's version, both from MS. S.G. 8460, no. 17.

Notable are the echoes of Vlitius's *Cum nihil prius* and possibly of phrases from Milton's (now lost) English translation; and the anomaly of *Statibus Generalibus*.

For discussion, see pages 17–20.

Official Latin Text

Scriptum ab Excellentijs V^{ris} missum, cui Secretarius V^{er} subscripsit 2do Feb: juxta computum Vestrum dato, Concilij facta at*que* justitiam admodum perstringit, et quibusdam nec rectè perceptis, ac si vera essent, nititur; ubi affirmat, nihil post tot petitiones, tót*que* repetitas expostulationes de ijs navibus agi, quas jussu hujus Concilij ijs adjudicatas esse difinitiva sententiâ quā ceperunt, et condemnatas dicitis, plús*que* fidei ac ponderis Nautarum petitioni quàm publico Excellentiarum V^{rarum} desiderio accessisse. Assequi non potest Concilium quo pacto ea quæ ab se tàm clarè prolata erant, interpretationi tàm incommodæ occasionem darent. Censuit ita*que* petitionem illam, et simul Concilij ea de re consulta ad Ex^{tias} V^{ras} mittenda, quæ ipsa perlegere poterunt et considerare; unde et quid in illo scripto erratum sit Ex^{tiæ} V^{ræ} perspicient et Concilij justitia, qúa*que* se cū æquitate gesserit, arguetur. Jan: hujus 12mo hæc petitio adlata est.

Honoratissimo Concilio Statûs
aliquot Magistrorum Navium quorū nomina
subscripta sunt,
Humilis Petitio,

Humiliter ostendit, Petitores vestros aliquot navium Belgicarum Magistros esse, perductós*que* huc esse literarum authoritate Represalium, quà contra Belgas, quà contra Francos concessarum, quocirca humiliter petunt, vel ut justitia protinus in se fiat, si quid causæ est, vel ut liberi dimittantur, quæ*que* sua ablata sunt bona (ut multa certè ablata sunt) restituantur; et petitores V^{ri} orabunt.

> Petrus Hoveling Magister Navis Hoveling de Enkuysen
> Laurentius Cornelissen Magister Navis St. Mary de Huysduynen.
> Janus Petrus Cocq Magister Navis cui nomen The Cock of Sardon.
> Petrus Clusenes Magister Navis Amstrodamiensis cui nomen hostia Abrahami.

Gulielmus Cornelissen huf Magister Navis cui nomen Piscator de Maseland Sluce.
Cum alijs circiter tredecim.

De hac Petitione consultum hoc factum est, eodem Jan: 12mo 1651.

Die Lunæ 12mo Januarij. 1651

In Concilio Status in Alba Aula. Decretum est, hujus petitionis aliquot navium Belgicarum Magistrorū exemplar hodie recitatū Causarū maritimarū Judicibus mitti, ijs*que* mandari ut quam primùm sententiam ferant, prout petitio ista sibi quærit: Eós*que* interea Concilium certius facere, quo pacto ista res sub eorū cognitione se habeat, et quid in ea Curia factū de illa sit.

Paulo post ad instantiam aliquā Ex^{tiarū} V^{rarū} scripto 15mo Jan: exhibito Concilium in hunc modum decrevit.

Die Veneris 16? Jan: 1651/2 In Concilio Status in Aula Alba.

Decretum est, literas Merc seu Represales in Curia hujus Reipub: maritima, Administratori Annæ Paulet contra Populū Fœderaturū Provinciarū concessas inhiberi, ne quæ amplius naves earū authoritate [literarum] capiantur, donec Parlamentū aut Concilium ulterius quid ea de re præcipiant, Judicés*que* Curiæ maritimæ eam inhibitionem promulgare, eám*que* usitata formulâ significare.

Scriptúm*que* aliud ab Ex^{tijs} Vestris accepimus, hujus mensis 21mo quo postulatur ut sententia in naves jam captas ampliaretur; Concilium cum id quod justum sibi videbatur in illa re egisset, sensum suū exposuit, éum*que* hoc consulto cum Ex^{tijs} V^{ris} communicavit.

Die Jovis Januar. 22do 1651/2 in Concilie Status in Alba Aula. Perlecto Scripto heri in Concilium hoc misso, cui Secretarius Do^{noru} Legatorum ab Excelsis et præpotentibus Dominis, Statibus Generalibus Fœderataru Provinciaru, jussu prædictoru D^{rum} subscripserat. Decretum est responsum hoc reddi, Concilium, hujus mensis 16$^{o}_{\cdot}$ consultu fecisse, quò Judicibus Maritimæ Curiæ mandatur, ut literaru Represalium, quas administratori Annæ Paulet concesserant, contra Fœderatarum Provinciaru populu, inhibitionem edicerent, ne quæ naves amplius earum authoritate literarum caperentur, donec a Parlamento vel Concilio Status mandatum ulterius acceperint, útque judices curiæ maritimæ quam primum id pro usitata formula significarent. Verū non ea sententia Concilij fuit, quod ex disertis verbis ejusdem consulti liquet, intellegi oportere jam captas ampliari, verū eas eidem cognitioni ex lege relinqui, quæ exerceri in alias solita est captas antequā edictū hoc inhibitionis promulgaretur, cum illa re mandatum dederimus hujus mensis 12$^{mo}_{\cdot}$ juxta petitionem aliquot magistroru naviū Belgicarū Concilio oblatum, ut sententiam maturarent, quemadmodu ab ipsis petitu est; cujus exemplar petitionis unà missū est: Ex quo intelligunt Ex^{tiæ} V^{ræ} quod factū a Concilio est, id populi Vestri gratiâ factū esse, ijs*que* petentibus, qui ut nos credere par erat, res suas et rationes probè calluerunt, ne*que* eò factū est, ut causæ condemnatio præcipitaretur (quod vos dicitis) verū ut justitiæ ratio expediretur, quemadmodū quorū id intererat petiverunt. Quod autem affirmant Ex^{tiæ} V^{ræ}, vestri desiderij rationem non esse habitam, quod ad juris inhibitionem in naves captas exercendi, attribuendū illud est istius rei naturæ, quam petistis, quæ quidem concessa nihil aliud re vera fuisset, quam injustitiæ continuatio in eos qui injuriam acceperant, eósque sine ullo remedio quo sua damna reparare possent, destituisset, tàm vestra justitiâ exclusos, quàm hujus etiam Reipub: cujus pars sunt, a qua et tutelam suam et auxiliū expectare debeant. Quod autem ad provocationem, jus id quidem receptū est, in qua si quid vel per errorem vel per injuria commissū est, corrigetur, singulís*que* jus ita reddetur prout causa cujus*que* meruerit.

Textual note: MS S.G. 8460 has *plegere, hostia* for *Hostia*, Amstrodamniensis. The line over *a* and *u* indicates a final *m* omitted, except in callerūt and petiverūt where an *n* was omitted. MS. S.G. 12589.62 reads *petitio allata* for *petitio adlata, indicerent* for *edicerent*, with other minor spelling variants or errors. MS. Aitzema 86 variants are mainly errors.

In their 1938 edition, Mabbott and French misread 1650 for the year 1651; they expanded all the abbreviations, but in their notes tabulated errors, slips and corrections by the amanuensis.

Text of the Official Letter in Original English

Your Excellencies Paper signed by yor Secretary dated the 2^d of ffebruarie, yor Stile, doth much reflect upon ye proceedings and Justice of the Councell, and is grounded upon great Mistakes in alleaging that nothing hath beene done upon soe many Petitions, and repeated expostulations, concerning those Shipps which you say have beene by Command of this Councell condemned by definitive sentence to the takers, and that more beliefe and weight hath been given to yor Marriners Petition than to ye publique desire of yor Lord^{ps}. The Councell cannot Apprehend how their expressions which are soe cleare in themselves should occasion soe great misinterpretations, and have therefore thought fit to offer to yor Ex^{ies} review and Consideration the Petition with ye Councells order upon that Affaire to rectifie the mistakes in yor Lord^{ps} Paper, and to assert the Justice and fairnesse of their owne proceedings. upon ye 12th of this instant Jan: this petition was presented.

> To the Right Honora^{ble} the Councell of State;
> The humble Petition of y^e severall Ma:^{s} of Ships, whose Names are here underwritten;
> Humbly Sheweth; That yor Petitioners are Ma:^{s} of severall Shipps belonging to y^e Dutch Nation, and are brought up some by vertue of L$\overline{res}$ of Represall granted against the Dutch, and others by vertue of L$\overline{res}$ of Represall granted against the French; Therefore they humbly Pray, that either Justice may speedily passe against them if there be cause, or else that they may bee set at Libertie; and that what goods have been taken out (as many have beene) may be restored. And yor Petitioners shall ever pray.

Peter Hoveling, Ma: of ye Ship Hoveling of Enkuysen.
Laurence Cornelienson, Ma: of ye Ship St. Mary of Huysduynen.
John Petersen Cocq, Ma: ye Ship Cock of Sardon.

Peter Clusenes, Ma: of ye Ship Abrahams Offering of Amsterdam.

Wm Corneliouson Huff, Ma: of ye Ship ffisher of Maseland Sluce.

With about 13 more.

Uppon which this Order was made the same 12th of Jan: 1651/2.

Monday the 12th January 1651/2. At the Councell of State at Whitehall. Ordered, That a Coppie of ye Petition of ye severall Ma:^s of Dutch Shipps this day read be sent to ye Judges of the Admiraltie, and they desired to proceed speedily to Justice according to ye Desire of the Petition, and in the meane time to certifie to ye Councell how the same stands before them, and what proceeding there hath been in that Court upon it.

After which upon some further Representation of yor Ex^cies in a paper of the 15th of January, the Councell made ye Order following.

ffriday, the 16th 1651/2. At the Councell of State at Whitehall, Ordered, That the Letters of Marque or Represall that have been granted out of the Court of Admiraltie of this Comon Wealth to the Administrator of Pawlett against ye People of ye United Provinces; As to ye takeing of any more Ships [by vertue of those L̄r̄es,] bee Suspended untill further Order be given therein by the Parlam^t: or Councell: and that ye Judges of ye Admiralty doe forthwith issue that Suspension, and signifie the same according to ye usual forme:

And upon another Paper from yor Lord^ps of the 21th instant desiring a suspension of proceedings against the Ships already taken; the Councell haveing done what they found just in that Affaire expressed their Sense and Communicated the same to yor Lord^ps in this Order:

Thursday the 22th of Jan: 1651/2 At the Councell of

State at Whitehall. Upon reading the paper yesterday sent in to this Councell, signed by the Secretary to the Lords Ambassado^{rs} from the High and Mighty Lords the States Generall of the United Provinces by the Comande of the said Lords Ambassado^{rs} It is Ordered; That it be returned in answer; That the Councell did by their Order of y^e 16th instant give Directions to y^e Judges of the Admiraltie to issue out a Suspension of y^e L$\overline{res}$ of Represall granted to y^e Administrato^r of Pawlett against the People of the United Provinces; as to y^e takeing of any more Ships by vertue of their L$\overline{res}$ untill further Order from the Parlament or Councell of State; and that y^e Judges of the Admiralty should forthwith signifie the same according to the usuall fforme; but it was not their Intention as doth appear by the expresse words of the said Order, that it should be interpreted to suspend proceedings against those allready taken, but to leave them to ye proceedings against such Ships according to Law as have been taken before the date of the said Order for Suspension, haveing in that particular given Order the 12th instant according to the Petition of severall Duch Ma:^{s} of Shipps presented to the Councell, that they should proceed speedily to Justice as was desired; a Copie of which Petition is herewith sent.

Hereby yor Lord^{ps} perceive, that what was done on the Councells Part herein, was in favor of yor People, and upon their Petition, who Wee had reason to believe understood their owne Businesse; neither was it done to precipitate the Cause to Condemnation (as yor expression is) but to expedite Justice according to ye desires of the Parties interested. And whereas yor Lord^{ps} Alleadge, yor Desire was not hearkened unto, as to the Suspension of the Processe against the Shipps taken, it is to be Attributed to ye nature of the Desire, which if granted would have rend'red it selfe in the Consequence; and true Construction of it, a Continuation of the Injustice to the Parties wronged, and have left them without Meanes of

Reparation either from yor Justice which was shut up from them, or from the Justice of this Common Wealth whereof they are Members, and from whence their Protection and ultimate Reliefe was justly to bee expected.

As for the course of Appeale it is the Way of Justice wherein Wee doubt not but if any Errour or Injury hath been in the Proceedings, the same will bee Rectified, and the parties find such Remedie as their Severall Cases may deserve.

Whitehall
29. January
1651/2

Signed in the Name and by Order
of ye Councell of State
appointed by Authority of Parlament.
Art Hesilrige. Pres^{dt}

Textual note: than, Duch, interessed are MS. S.G. 8460 spellings.

The *Paper of Demands*

This complex assemblage of documents is here printed for the first time. It consists of a covering letter, signed by Philip Lisle on the official English copy, and sets of claims in four appendices, B1, B2, B3 and B4. All of the English texts, and all of the Latin texts *except B4* are here taken from the official originals in MS. S.G. 8460, no. 20, while the Latin of B4 is taken from the original official text in MS. Aitzema, no. 20 (which has transcripts of the rest).[114]

All three Latin texts of the cover letter, in MS. S.G. 8460, MS. Aitzema 86 and MS. St. v. Holl. 2813.1, show errors, omissions and variants. Some exercise of editorial judgment has been necessary. The scribe of the official Latin copy spells *cuius* and *cujus*, *præditio* and *preditio*.

The Latin texts of B1 and B2 are final texts revised from the earlier document that was printed as the *Summarium Damnorum* among other Milton state papers in the 1676 *Literæ Pseudo-Senatûs Anglicani*. This 1676 *Summarium Damnorum* is here also included, now designated as the Earlier Text. With our recovery of the entire *Paper of Demands*, the *Summarium Damnorum* will cease to be the puzzle it has been to Miltonists.

B3 includes the 1652 Latin translation of "Fifteen Articles," which is an updated 1652 version in English of a document originally composed circa 1627.

B4 includes the 1652 Latin translation of the English-language "Catalogue" of individual complaints, which in turn is basically a recopying of the English-language tabulation done in 1645.

For discussion and attributions to Rosin and Milton, see pages 21–30, 33.

Latin Text of the Covering Letter

Quandoquidem justitia unicum honestæ, certæ & firmæ pacis & amicitiæ fundamentum est at*que* hæc Respublica talem pacem talém*que* amicitiam cum Fœderatis Belgij provincijs pacisci magnoperè cupit & conservare; Postulatur idcirco nomine Parlamenti Reipub:æ Angliæ,

1. Uti Societati Anglicanæ, quæ in Moscovia mercaturam facit, jus suum reddatur earúm*que* reparatio injuriarum et prædationum, quæ a populo Fœderati Belgij illatæ sibi in Gronlandia vel ejus per oram sunt, anno circiter 1618, quæ quidem damna quemadmodum ab rege Jacobo cum Ordinibus agitatum est, æstimata sunt libris Anglicis 22000; Cujus summæ nulla adhuc pars soluta est.

2. Uti in eos animadvertatur, qui nefariæ illius & crudelissimæ Anglorum cædis in Amboyna factæ ullo modo rei sunt, si quo modo eorum sunt superstites.

3. Uti Orientalis Indiæ Societati Anglicanæ hujúsque Gentis alijs, quibus per cædes illic & publicationes bonorum factas damnum datum est, reparatio fiat magnarum oppressionum illarum, injuriarum & damnorum, quæ apud Indos Orientales Fœderati Belgij populus ijs intulit, post initum fœdus illud año 1619 quæ quidem damna (quemadmodum prædictæ Societatis Indicæ Mercatores ad Nos deferunt, quorum & adjecta recensio est) æstimata sunt libris Anglicanis plus minus 1700,000. Ob quæ satisfactionem nobis dari postulamus.

4. Uti Insulæ Pularon quæ cum fœdus illud iniretur, ab Orientalis Indiæ Societate, possidebatur, & hujus Reipubæ erat, ijs reddatur; Et quæ Puloæ loca tempore illius fœderis isti 1619, ab ijsdem possessa sunt: Útque Orientalis Indiæ Societas Anglicana partem tertiam Specierum omnium eodem precio eodémque solutionis genere sive pecuniâ numerata, sive mercium aut cibariorum comutatione sibi habeat, quemadmodum habent Belgæ in annos, qui adhuc restant, viginti; De quo temporis spacio in illa fœderis transactione convenerat, cuiúsque beneficio per biennium duntaxat uti licuit. Cum ex illo tempre,

fœdus illud modis omnibus a Belgis violatum fuerit.

5. Uti reparatio fiat direptionum illarum & predationum, quibus ad Brasilæam navis Concordia pessimè recepta est, Magistro Gervasio Coachman anno 1648. Et recentius año proximè præterito navis Mariæ & Joannis nomine insignita, cujus Franciscus Hardegge magister est. Duabus hisce navibus damna data libris Anglicis circiter 42000 æstimantur, præter alias navium prædationes a Brasilea solventium, quarum Catalogus ad V^{as} Ex^{tias} mittetur.

6. Cum Scriptum à Parlamento Angliæ año 1645. Legatis Celsorum & Præpotentum D^{rum} Ordinum Fœderati Belgij Extraordinarijs, qui in Anglia tum erant, exhibitum esset, de magnis quibusdam damnis & injurijs, quas Fœderati Belgij populares multis ex Natione Anglica intulerant, quarum Catalogus ad eosdem Legatos simul est missus, satisfactio etiam postulata; Ad quæ Legati responderunt se hæc ad superiores suos esse relaturos. Verùm hactenus satisfactio nulla data est; Exemplar illius Catalogi Excell^{ijs} V^{ris} una cum hisce exhibetur; Ob quæ damna at*que* dispendia satisfactionem poscimus. Hæc primùm sunt in quibus ex jure nobiscum agi postulamus, quod quidem optimum illius pacis & amicitiæ fundamentum erit, quam cum populo Fœderati Belgij continuare cupimus & conservare.

Ne*que* hîc tacendum est, quod Excell^{ijs} V^{ris} in memoriam revocare nos decet quàm iniquo se gesserint Domini Borrel & Reinswoode à Celsis & Potentibus Dñis Dom^s Statibus Generalibus in hunc Statum Legati Annis 1643, 1644, 1645, Qui Legati ausi sunt in ipsis Comitijs Sententiam ferre contra Parlamentum, & de rebus suis injustè judicare. Quâ de causâ Declaratio Parlamentaria transmissa fuit ad dict^{os} Dños Status Anno 1645. Cui velut his insertæ adhuc innitimur unde sensum nostrum fas sit colligere.

Quin etiam non possumus non memorare, Dñum Stricland apud Vestrates tam diu frustrà commorantem, qui licet Residentis Publici titulo insignitus apud Dños

Status, Tamen post frequentes preces audientiam procurandi gratiâ in cassum fusas, nec admitti ne*que* audiri valuit; Cum tamen interea MacDowell hostis notissimi hujus Reipubᵃᵉ causam agens, & fores vestras aperire potuit.

At verò, quod gravius est repetere, nec possumus silere, parricidium istud horrendum & adhuc inexpiatum, quod Dⁿ Dorislaum nuper abripuit, qui cum publⁱ Ministri Charactere designatus, hujus Reipᵃᵉ causâ apud Dominos Vestros ageret, tamen de Auctoribus, Actoribus, vel Assistentibus, tam execrando facinori, ne unum quidem captum audivimus. Quapropter easdem querelas iterare debemus, Mense Majo 1649, Domini Joachimi olim traditas, quò Dⁿⁱˢ Statibus Generalibus innotescerent; Simul & à Dⁿⁱˢ Sᵗ John & Stricland, Ambasciatoribus hujus Reipᵃᵉ nuperrimè explicatas.

Ne*que* nobis est oblectamento refricare injurias & indignitates istas nondum vindicatas, in dedecus hujus Reipubᵃᵉ legatis dictis illatas, dum Hagæ Comitis adessent, ab Edoardo Reginæ Bohemiæ filio juniori, nec non a Tribuno Apsley, in quos varia postulata a dictis Legatis delata fuerant apud Ordines Vestros, quorum jure ac potestate ijdem sisti poterant, quoniam ante & post delationes istas exhibitas, intra limites vestros aliquandiu remanserant. Quandoquidem verò honoris hujus Reipubᵃᵉ multum interest de his injurijs anquirere, Ideo tales processus expectamus, qui rationi et æquitati benè respondeant, & amicitiam istam reciprocam et mutuam benevolentiam inter utras*que* gentes antiquitùs celebratam, promovere possint.

Porro quanquam quod juris est comunis id nos postulatis ponendum esse non censemus, per hæc tamen significatum Vʳⁱˢ Exᵗⁱʲˢ vellemus, expectare nos, uti populi huius Reipubᵃᵉ navigatio libera sit quæcun*que* loca navibus petierint, aut ibi mercaturam fecerint, tam per Indiam, quàm quocun*que* alio orbis terrarum loco, à Belgijs non occupato prius aut possesso, quod quidem illis Comuni Jure liberum esse debet, ut facere possint, ne*que* ullo idcirco est a Populo Fœderati Belgij aut molestia illis exhibenda aut vis inferenda.

ENGLISH ORIGINAL OF THE COVERING LETTER

Forasmuch as justice is the onely foundation of a good, sure & firme peace and amitie, And that it is the earnest desire of this Commonwealth to entertaine & keepe such a peace & amitie with the Unitied Provinces in the Netherlands, It is therefore demanded in the name of the Parliament of the Comonwealth of England,

1. That Justice be done & reparation made to the English Companie trading to Moscovia for depredations & wrongs done to them by the people of the United Provinces of the Netherlands at or about Greenland in or about the yeare 1618. amounting unto as was insisted by King James & the States, the sume of Twentie Two thousand pounds sterling, Of which no part hath yet beene payd.

2. That justice bee done upon those who had any hand in that horrid & cruel murther of the English at Amboyna if any of them bee living.

3. That reparation bee made to the English East India Company & others of this Nation, who have suffered by the murthers & confiscations there, for the great oppressions & injuries done to them, and losses by them suffered by the people of the United Provinces in the East Indies since the Treatie in the yeare 1619. the losse amounting, as the same is represented to us by the Merchants of the said East India Companie, (Where of a copie is annexed) to the summe of near Seventenne hundred thousand pounds sterling, For which We demand satisfaction, to bee given.

4. That Pooloroon, beeing at that time of that Treatie in the possession of the East India Companie & belonging to this Common Wealth bee delivered into their possession, and such part of Poolowey as were in their possession at the time of the Treatie 1619. And that the English East India Companie may have one third part of all the spices at the same rates and species of pay, Whether monie, goods or victualls, that the Netherlanders have them for the terme of twentie yeares to come, Which was the terme

in that Treaty aggreed, & of which they have had the benefit onely two yeares, The said Treatie having been in all points after that time violated by the Dutch.

5. That reparation bee made for spoyles and depredations done at Brasil upon the Ship Concord of London, Gervaise Coachman Master in the yeare 1648. And now in the last yeare upon the ship Marie & John, Where of Francis Hardedge is Master to the value in these Two ships, of above fortie two thousand pounds sterling, Besides several other depredations of ships, comming from Brasil of which a particular shall be delivered to yor Excellencies.[115]

6. That whereas there was a representation made by the Parlament of England in the yeare 1645. to the Ambassad^{rs} Extraord^y of the High & Mightie Lords, the States General of the United Provinces who were then in England, of several great damages & wrongs done to severall of the English Nation by the subjects of the said States, of which a particular was then delivered to the said Amb^s and a demand made of satisfaction, to which these Ambassad^{rs} returned answere they were to represent them to their Superiours. But hitherto Satisfaction hath not beene given. A copie of the said particular is herewith exhibited to yor Excell^{ies}. For which losses and damages We demand satisfaction.

These things Wee demand Justice to bee first done in, as a good foundation of that amitie & good correspondency, Which Wee desire to holde and keepe with the people of the United Provinces.

And here We may not omit to putt yor Excellencies in minde of the unindifferent & evill carriage of Signor Borrell and the Lord of Renswood, Ambassad^{rs} of the High & Mightie Lords the States Generall to this State in the years 1643, 1644, & 1645, Which Ambassad^{rs} tooke upon them to pronounce Sentence against this Parlament, & traduced the Justice of their proceedings, Of which Remonstrance was made by this Parliament to the said Lords the States in the year 1645. Which Declaraōn We hold as here inserted, and thereto for particulars referre Ourselves. And as We can not but call to minde the long stay of Mr Strickland in yor Countries unreceived and unheard though qualified with the Character of a Resident with the Lords the States, to Whome he often made his addresse for Audience, though in vaine, whilest in the meane time MacDowell the Resident of this Comon Wealths Enemie was owned & admitted; So what is more troublesome to Us to remember, is that yet unexpiated horrid murther of Doctor Dorislaus, late publique Minister sent from this ComonWealth to the said Lords of the States, Touching the plotters, authors, actors & abett^{rs} of which execrable fact None of them being yet apprehended.

We renew our former Instances given unto the late Ambassador the Lord Joachimi in May 1649, to bee represented to the Lords of the States Generall & since made to them by the Lord St. John & Mr Stickland, Ambassadors to them from this Common Wealth.

And with as little pleasure doe we mention the late unvindicated affronts done to the [dis]honour of this Common Wealth in the persons of their said Ambassadors during their late Residence at the Hague by Prince Edward the younger sonne to the Queene of Bohemia, & by Collonel Apsley, against whome severall instances & complaints were given in at the Hague by the said Ambassadors to the said Lords of the States, within whose power the said Offendors were at the time of the representation of the said Exorbitances & for some days after. In which particulars the honour of this Comonwealth appearing to bee very much concerned, We expect from the Lords of the States Generall such proceedings & satisfaction as shall bee found just & reasonable, and may become that friendship & reciprocall good respect, which hath formerly beene, and We desire still may bee continued & cherished betweene both Common Wealths.

And allthough we shall not make a demand of that which is of Comon right, yet We doe hereby signifie to yor Lords^{ps} That We doe expect, That the Navigation bee free for the people of this Common Wealth, to saile to and trade with all places, as well in the Indies, and in any other places in the world whatsoever not possessed & kept by the Netherlanders. As by Common right they ought to bee at Libertie, to doe without any lett, molestation, or violence whatsoever from any of the people of the United Provinces of the Netherlands.

Whitehall

Signed in the name & by order
of the Councell of State
appointed by Authority of Parlament.
P. Lisle presdt

Textual note: Parlament, Parliament as in the manuscript.

The Earlier Text (1650–1651), Latin:
The *Summarium Damnorum*[116]

Summarium damnorum singulorum & haud fictorum quibus Societas Anglicana *multis* Orientalis Indiæ *Locis à* Belgica Societate *affecta est*.

£. s. d.

1. Damna illa sedecim Articulis comprehensa & pridem exhibita, quorum summa est 298555. *Regiorum* $\frac{8}{8}$ quæ est monetæ nostræ
74638:15:00

2. De *Pularonis* Insulæ fructibus satisfactionem dari postulamus ab anno 1622. ad hoc usque tempus ducentes* millenum *Regiorum* $\frac{8}{8}$ præter dispendium futurum donec jus ditionis in illam Insulam nobis restituatur eo rerum statu in quo fuit cum erepta nobis est, prout fœdere sancitum erat: quod est nostræ monetæ
50000:00:00

3. Satisfactionem postulamus de omnibus illis mercimoniis cibariis & apparatibus, qui ab Agentibus Societatis *Belgiæ* apu *Indos* ablati sunt, aut iis traditi aut ulli ex eorum navibus eo cursum tenentibus aut inde redeuntibus, quorum summa est 80635. *Regiorum:* nostræ monetæ
20158:00:00

4. Satisfactionem postulamus ob portiora *Mercium Belgicarum* quæ in *Perside* aut navibus impositæ sunt aut in terram expositæ ab anno 1624. prout

---

* Correct Latin would read *ducentes*.

nobis à Rege *Persarum* concessum erat
quæ minoris æstimare non possumus
quam Octogies millenis *Regiis*   20000:00:00

5. Satisfactionem postulamus ob quatuor ædes malitiosissimè & iniquissimè *Joccatræ* incensas, unà cum
mercium Apothecis repositoriis &
apparatibus, cui rei Prætor illic *Belgicus*
occasionem dedit, de quibus omnibus
ex eo ipso loco certiores postea facti
sumus quam priores quærelas exhibueramus cujus damni summa est
ducentius millenum *Regiorum*   50000:00:00

6. Satisfactionem postulamus ob 32899
Libras peperis ex nave *Endimione* vi
ablatas *anno* 1649. cujus damni summa
est   6000:00:00

                                       220796:15:00

Summarium Damnorum aliquot particularium quibus etiam à Belgica Orientalis Indiæ Societate *affecti sumus.*

£. s. d.

1. Propter damna quæ per eos fecimus qui *Bantamum* obsederunt, unde factum est ut per sex annos continuos eo commercio exclusi simus & consequenter occasione sexcenties mille[nos] Regios in coëmendo pipere locandi pro rata nostra portione, quo multas naves nostras in reditu onerare potuissemus, quo onere cum carerent passim per *Indiæ* littora cariem traxere: interea sors nostra apud *Indos* quæ vel pecuniæ vel bonorum erat stipendio nautico commeatu alioque apparatu imminuta & exhausta est adeo ut prædictæ Jacturæ haud minoris æstimari queant vicies centies et quater millenis Regiis id est nostræ monetæ   600000:00:00

2. Plura etiam propter damna ex amissa parte nostra debita fructuum in *Insulis Moluccis, Banda & Amboyna,* ex quo tempore per cædem nostrorum ibi factam pulsi inde sumus ad usque illud tempus quo de jactura hac atque dispendio nobis satisfiat, quod spatium temporis ab anno 1622. ad hunc annum Præsentem 1650. pro reditu annuo 25000. *Librarum,* annis 28. Summam conficit.   700000:00:00

3. Reparationem insuper postulamus centies & bis millenum nongentorum quiquaginta novem *Regiorum Surattæ* à Populo *Mogulli* nobis ablatorum, quos

Belgæ eum in modum tutati sunt ut neque ex pecuniis neque ex bonis ejus populi quæ in ipsorum *Juncis* seu Navibus erant damna nostra resarcire possemus, quod quidem perficere & conati sumus & in manu nostra situm erat, nisi eos *Belgæ* iniquissimè defendissent, quæ pecunia amissa ad impensas faciendas jamdudum in Europa triplum peperisset: Quod Nos æstimamus 77020:00:00

4. Ob Portoria *Persidis* quorum dimidia pars ab rege *Persarum Anglis* concessa est Anno 1624. quæ usque ad Annum 1629. supputata æstimatur octies millenis *Regiis*, quemadmodum prius exponitur qua ratione subducta quatuor mille Librarum in annos singulos præbere tenentur ab anno 1629. à quo unus & viginti anni sunt, atque indè summa conficietur 84000:00:00

Ab altera Pagina	220976:15:00
Summa totalis	1681996:15:00

Locus Figuræ
Regii

Debitum ab eo tempore fœnus Sortem ipsam longè superabit.

The Official Final Text, 1652, Latin: The *Summarium Damnorum*[117]

Summarium Damnorum singulorum et haud fictorum, quibus Societas Anglicana multis Orientalis Indiæ locis a Belgica Societate affecta est

£. s. d.

1. Damna illa quindecim articulis comprehensa et pridem exhibita, quorum Summa est nostræ monetæ   48900. 15. 00

2. De Pularonis Insulæ fructibus satisfactionem dari postulamus ab Anno 1622 ad hoc us*que* tempus ducentis millenum regiorum $\frac{8}{8}$ præter dispendium futurum donec jus ditionis in illam Insulam nobis restituatur eo rerum Statu in quo fuit, cum erepta nobis est prout fœdere sancitum erat. Quod est nostræ monetæ   50000. 00. 00

3. Satisfactionem postulamus de omnibus illis mercimonijs, cibarijs, et apparatibus, qui ab Agentibus Societatis Belgicæ apud Indos aut ablati sunt, aut ijs traditi aut ulli ex eorū navibus eo cursum tenentibus, aut inde redeuntibus: quorū Summa est 80635 Regiorum, quod est monetæ nostræ   20158. 00. 00

4. Satisfactionem postulamus ob portoria Mercium Belgicarū quæ in Perside aut navibus impositæ sunt, aut in terram expositæ, ab Anno 1624. prout nobis a Rege Persarum concessum erat; quæ minoris æstimare non possumus, quam octogies millenis Regijs   20000.00.00

5. Satisfactionem postulamus ob quatuor ædes malitiosissime et iniquissime Jaccatræ incensas una cum mercium Apothecis, repositorijs, et apparatibus, cui rei prætor illic Belgicus occasionem dedit: de quibus omnibus ex eo ipso loco certiores postea facti sumus, quam priores querelas exhibueramus: cuius damni summa est, ducenties millenum Regiorum   50000. 00. 00

6. Satisfactionem postulamus ob 32899 libras piperis ex nave Endimione vi ablatas, anno 1649 cuius damni sumā est   6000. 00. 00

        195058. 15. 00

Summarium Damnorum aliquot particularium, quibus etiam a Belgica Orientalis Indiæ Societate affecti sumus.

£. s. d.

1. Propter damna quæ per eos fecimus qui Bantamum obsederunt, unde factum est ut per sex annos continuos eo commercio exclusi fuerimus, et consequenter occasione sexcenties millenos Regios in coëmendo pipere locandi, pro rata nostra portione, quo multas naves nostras in reditu onerare potuissemus, quo onere cum carerent, passim per Indiæ littora cariem traxere: interea sors nostra apud Indos quæ vel pecuniæ vel bonorum erat, stipendio nautico, commeatu, alio*que* apparatu imminuta et exhausta est adeo ut prædictæ iacturæ haud minoris æstimari queant, vicies centies et quatermillenis Regijs id est nostræ monetæ   600000:00:00

2. Plus etiam propter damna ex amissa parte nostra debita fructuum in Insulis Moluccis, Banda et Amboyna, ex quo tempore per cædem nostrorum ibi factum pulsi inde sumus, ad illud us*que* tempus, quo de iactura hac at*que* dispendio nobis satisfactum erit: quod spatium temporis ab anno 1622 ad hunc annum præsentem 1650 pro reditu annuo 25000 librarū annis viginti novem summam conficit   725000:00:00

3. Reparationem insuper postulamus centies et bis millenum nongentorum quinquaginta novem regiorum Surattæ a populo Mogulli nobis ablatarum, quos

Belgæ eum in modum tutati sunt, ut ne*que* ex pecunijs ne*que* ex bonis eius Populi quæ in ipsorum Juncis seu navibus erant, damna nostra resarcire possemus, quod quidem perficere et conati sumus, et in manu nostra situm erat, nisi eos Belgæ iniquissime defendissent, quæ pecunia amissa ad impensas faciendas iam dudum in Europa triplum peperisset: quod nos æstimamus   77200:00:00

4. Ob Portoria Persidis, quorum dimidia pars ab rege Persarum Anglis concessa est, anno 1624 quæ us*que* ad annum 1629 supputata conficit octies millenos regios quemadmodum prius exponitur, qua ratione subducta, quatuor mille librarum in annos singulos præbere tenentur ab anno 1629 a quo duo et viginti anni sunt, at*que* inde summa conficietur   88000:00:00

	£	s	d
Ab altera Pagina	195058	15	00
Summa totalis	1685258	15	00

Debitum ab eo tempore foenus sortem ipsam longè exsuperabit.

The Final *Summarium Damnorum*, 1652, Official Text in English

An abstract of the particular and reall Losses which ye English Company have sustayned in divers parts of the East Indies by the proceeding of y^e Netherlanders Company

1 The severall Losses Comprised in fifteen Articles formerly delivered amounting to the Summe of 48900:15: Sterling
    48900:15:00

2 Wee demand satisfaction for the fruits upon the Island of Polloroone from 1622 untill this present, of two hundred thousand Rialls of $\frac{8}{8}$ besides damage for the time to come, untill the Right, Title and Interest of the Island it selfe shall be restored, in the same state and Condition it was taken from us, as it was ordered by y^e Treaty; which is sterling
    50000:00:00

3 Wee demand satisfaction of all such Wares, Victualls, and Provisions as hath either been taken, or delivered unto the Agents of the Netherlanders Company in the Indies, or to any of their Shipping bound thither, or returning from thence, amounting to 80635 Rialls, Sterling
    20158:00:00

4 Wee demand satisfaction upon the Customes of the Wares of the Netherlanders, which have been Laded or Landed in Persia from the year 1624 according to a Grant made unto us

from the King of Persia, which wee cannot value to be lesse then eighty Thousand Rialls   20000:00:00

5 Wee demand satisfaction for the most malitious and uniust burning four dwelling Howses, Ware-Howses, Stoares, and provisions, in Jaccatra, occasioned by the Dutch Generall there, of all wch wee have received certaine Advice from thence, into the exhibiting our former grievances, the losse whereof doth amount into two hundred thousand Ryalls   50000:00:00

6 Wee demand satisfaction for 32899 l. [pounds] of pepper taken by force out of the Ship Endimion in Anno 1649 the damage of which amounts to   6000:00:00

                      Sum:is   195058:15:00

B No. 2

An Abstract of some particular Damages, which Wee likewise have received from the sayd Netherlanders East India Company

1 For the damages Wee have sustained by them, in the blocking up of Bantum, whereby for six yeares together, wee have been kept from that Trade, and soe consequently, from the imployment of six hundred thousand Rialls, in Pepper for o^r proportion, which would have reladen manie of o^r Shipps, which for want thereof have rotted in India, while in the meane time, o^r stock of Money and Goods have been wasted and consumed in the Indies, in Marriners wages and victualls, and other Provisions, soe that the sayd Damages, cannot be estimated less than two Millions and four Thousand Ryalls; which is sterling   600000:00:00

2 More for the Damages for the proportions for the ffruits of the Islands of the Moluccoes, Banda, and Amboyna, from the time Wee have been expelled by murther of o^r People there, untill the time this Losse and Damage shall be fully satisfyed and restored unto us, which being from Anno 1622 to this present yeare 1651, at 25000: per Annum, in twenty nine yeares is   725000:00:00

3 More Wee demand Damages for one

hundred and two thousand, nine hundred ffifty and nine Ryalls of 8⸳ taken from us at Surrat by the Mogulls People, whom the Dutch protected in such manner as wee could not right ourselves, either upon the Money or goods of the sayd People, in the Juncks or Ships which wee attempted and had power to doe, if the Dutch had not most uniustly protected them, the losse of which Money towards charges would have long since yeilded in Europe, three for one, which wee esteeme or estimate at   77200:00:00

4 ffor the Customs of Persia, for the Moity which was granted to y^e English Nation, by the King of Persia in the yeare 1624 and accompted to the yeare 1629 to amount unto eight thousand peeces of $\frac{8}{8}$ as formerly it is set downe, according to which proportion they are to allow 4000 £ per annum since 1629 which is twenty two years and consequently will amount to   88000:00:00

      Brought from y^e other side   195058:00:00
           Summa totalis   1685258:15:00

Interest for the time since due will amount unto farr more [than]* the Principle.

---

* Scribal oversight.

B3, The *Fifteen Articles*, Official Latin Text, 1652[118]

1 Martij 20, 1621. Supputando impensas in Moluccis, Amboyna, Banda, primi anni quo nostra cum ijs illius commercij societas mansit pro 3ᵗⁱᵃ parte nostra ad Gallihorne, Tinganos, scholas, Hospitia, dona, sumptus*que* alios effuse factos, quorum partem nullam suppeditare tenebamur; eorum etiam militibus etalijs cum stipendia panno et vestimentis, id*que* immensis pretijs solverentur, nos tertiam partem nostram pecunia numeravimus, unde primo illo anno plus nostra parte 3ᵗⁱᵃ impensarum communium solvimus us*que* ad sūmam quadragies millenum Regiorum

Rˢ 8ᵗ
40000

2 Martij 20, 1621, ex Regijs vicies et quater millenis sexcenis quinquagenis quos ad Ædificia et munimenta reficiendum per Insulas Moluccas, Bandam et Amboyna, Angli pro sua tertia parte solverunt, ubi annum duntaxat unum frui comercio licuit cum prædictæ reparationes in multos annos sufficere ac durare possint. Ita ex quatuor partibus tres ad minimum sunt Anglis restituendæ; decies octies milleni quadringenti octoginta octo

18488

3 Martij 20, 1621. Ex Regijs mille centenis at*que* senis ab Anglis in Moluccis et Amboyna ob porteria charijophijlorum alias*que* Belgarum exactiones contra fœdus

1106

4 Januarij 20, 1622. Ex Regijs tricies et sexies millenis nongentis sexaginta quin*que* octonis vulgo dictis quos in Moluccis et Amboyna numeravimus, pro ratione impensarum et specierum anni secundi quem porro continuasse sperabamus, in eadem cum ijs ad Insulas illas commercij Societate. Verum oppressiones eorum cum non remitterentur sed indies potius ingravescerent commercio supersedere nos coegerunt; donec Regiæ Ma^{tis} subditos in Insula Pularone crudeliter sævirent, et paulo post in Amboyna adversus Anglos; donec funditus nos ab illo commercio pepulerunt: quapropter illos regios reddi nobis postulamus, ob quos nihil dum nobis restitutum est aut satisfactum   36965

5 Societas Anglicana solvit primo anno ad impensas domesticas, sumptus communes ædium conductiones, dona, impensas deni*que* Mercium, in Moluccis, Banda et Amboyna, vicies et ter millenos quingentos et septem regios octon: quorum Societas Belgica duas 3^{tias} partes numerare debet, quindecies mille sexcentos septuaginta unum   15671

6 Augusti 25, 1622. Belgarum populationibus in Insula Pularone, Angli debita omnia perdiderunt, quæ sibi ab Oranckis, alijs*que* indigenis debebantur, us*que* ad quinquies mille septingentos viginti quin*que* regios octonos   5725

7 Ex munimento cui nomen Nelacca

in Insula Pularone ceperunt vi unum et viginti Servitia quæ Anglorum legitima præda erant et si vænum issent, valebant bis mille centenos Regios   2100

8 Vi etiam retinuerunt, 3.^{tiam} nostram servorum quadringentorum partem, alia*que* bona, quæ bona erant ab illis Tinganis prædando capta, pro quibus solvere nos prius coegerant, Pretium tertiæ partis mancipiorum, erat novies mille nongenti septuaginta quin*que* regi, quo pretio ipsi eos vendidere: quin etiam pars tertia bonorum et vasorum mille reg: octon: 10975

9 Mense Septembris 1622. Ex decies sexies mille centum octoginta duobus Regijs Octonis quo pretio bona æstimata Fiscalis Belgicus ex Apothecis Anglicis Jaccatræ vi abstulit, dum sententiam iniquam exequeretur in gratiam quorundam Sinensium, quamvis Præses Anglicus ad Europam provocaret, iuxta fœderis tenorem   16182

10 Feb: 20, 1622. ex tricies millenis et quinquaginta octo Reg: Octon: quos viceperunt et occuparunt, eodem tempore quo nostros in Amboyna crudelissime trucidarunt   300058
[30058]

11 Feb: 20, 1622, ex quater mille ducentis sexaginta sex Reg: Octon: quos ab Anglis acceperunt, in varia ædificia impensos in prædictis Insulis Molluccis et Banda quibus ædificijs pulsi sunt   4266

12 Ex quatuor mille septigentis septuaginta quin*que* Regijs octon: quos Angli portoriorum nomine aliarum*que* exactionum Jaccatræ numerabant contra fœdus   4775

13 Ineunte Aprile 1627, ex Regijs septem mille ducentis quadraginta duobus, quos Argenti Japonici ex Apothecis Anglici Jaccatræ ffiscalis Belgicus vi accepit, dum sententiam iniquam exequeretur in gratiam Joannis Mariæ Moretti Itali   7742

14 D^{num} Richardum Welden, Agentem nostrum in Banda postquam Daux Anglum fame propè necassent, pro eo redimendo solvere coegerunt   50

15 Eundem etiam Agentem nostrum coegerunt ut partem tertiam solveret ducentorum nitrati pulveris doliorum qui insumptus at*que* displosus est cum Præses illic sæpe festa et convivia ageret. Dolia autem singula valent triginta regios octonos; unde summa conficitur duorum mille Regiorum   2000

	£ s d
Nostræ monetæ sūma est	48900:15:00

Textual note: Article 4, *Januarij* (error for *Junij*); article 7, *vænum issent*; article 8, *regi* (for *regij*); article 10, *300058* (for 30058) are MS. S.G. 8460 readings, reproduced here though manifest errors. In article 4, *remitteretur* has been corrected to the plural.

B3, THE *FIFTEEN ARTICLES*, OFFICIAL TEXT IN ENGLISH, 1652

1 The 20 March 1621. By putting to Accompt in the Muluccoes, Amboyna, and Banda, the Charges of the first, wherein wee continued Partners with them in that Trade; for our third part of the Gallihorne, Tingans, Schooles, Hospitalls, Guifts, and other Exorbitances whereof wee ought to pay noe part, as alsoe their Souldiers, and others; we payd their wages in Cloth and Apparrell, at excessive Rates, whereas wee payd our third part in Money; whereby wee have payd in that first yeare more than our third part of the generall Charges, to the value of fourty thousand Ry:^{s} of 8^t

Rs of 8t
40000

2 The 20 March 1621. By R:^{s} Twentyfour Thousand, six hundred and ffifty, payd by the English, for the third part of Buildings, and Repayving of the fforts of the Islands of the Muluccoes, Banda and Amboyna, where they have enioyed the Trade onely one yeare, whereas the sayd Reparations will serve for many yeares continuous soe there ought to be restored to the English 3/4 thereof at least, Eighteen thousand, four hundred, eighty eight

18488

3 The 20 March 1621. by R:^{s} eleven hundred and six taken from the English in the Muluccoes, and

Amboyna, for Custome of Cloves, and other Exactions by the Netherlanders contrary to Treaty   1106

4 The 20 June 1622, By thirty-six thousand, nine hundred threescore and five R:^{s} of 8^t which Wee payd them in the Molluccoes, and Amboyna upon Accompt of the Charges, and Spices of ye second yeare, which wee well hoped to have continued in Partnership with them, for the trade of those Islands, but their oppressions & exorbitances, not ceasing but daily encreasing upon us, brought us to a Demur, untill such time as they executed their Cruelties upon his Maties Subiects at Polloroone, and shortly after at Amboyna upon the English to our utter extirpation from that Trade, wherefore Wee demand Repayment of the sayd R:^{s} for which as yet Wee have received no restitution or satisfaction   36965

5 The English Company payd in the first yeare in Houshold Expenses, generall Charges, Howserents, Guifts, and Charges of Merchandizes, in the Moluccoes, Banda, and Amboyna, twenty-three thousand five hundred and seaven R:^{s} of 8^t whereof the Netherlanders Company are to pay two thirds thereof fifteen thousand six hundred, seaventy and one   15671

6 The 25 August 1622, by depopulating and wasting the Island of Polloroone the English have lost all their

debts which were owing unto them by the Orankaies and other Natives of the place, to the value of five thousand, seaven hundred, seaventy five R:ˢ of 8ᵗ   5725

7 They took violently out of the Fort Nelacca on this Island of Polloroone twenty one Slaves, which were the English lawfull Prize, and were worth them to be sould, two thousand and one hundred R:ˢ of 8ᵗ   2100

8 They alsoe forceably deteyned from us our third part of four hundred Slaves, and other goods which were Prizall goods taken by those Tingans, which they had formerly forced us to pay for the Price of the third part of the Slaves, amounted to nine thousand, nine hundred seaventy and five R:ˢ as they themselves sould them for. alsoe the 1/3 part of the goods and vessels were by Estimation worth one thousand R:ˢ of 8ᵗ   10975

9 September 1622, by sixteen Thousand one hundred eighty two R:ˢ of 8ᵗ that the Dutch ffiscal took forceably in goods out of the English Warehowses at Jaccatra, in Execution of an uniust Sentence, on the behalfe of certaine Chineeces, notwithstanding our English President's Appeale for Europe, according to the Tenor of the Treaty   16182

10 The 20 February 1622. By thirty

thousand and fifty eight R:ˢ of 8ᵗ which they tooke from the English and seized upon at the cruell Murther of our People at Amboyna 30058

11 The 20 February 1622. By four Thousand two hundred sixty and six R:ˢ of 8ᵗ which they have taken from the English in the value thereof expended by them in sundry buildings of Howses, Warehowses and the like upon the sayd Ilands of Moluccoes and Banda from which Buildings they are expelled 4266

12 By four thousand, seaven hundred, seaventy and five R:ˢ of 8ᵗ payd by the English at Jaccatra in Customes and other Exactions contrary to the Treaty 4775

13 About the beginning of April 1627 By R:ˢ seaven thousand two hundred ffourty and two, that the Dutch ffiscal tooke forceably (in Japon Silver) out of the English Warehowses in Jaccatra in Execution of an uniust Sentence of Gio Maria Moretti an Italian 7242

14 They fforced our Agent Mʳ Richard Welden at Banda, to pay for Dawkes his releasement out of Prison, after they have almost starved him. 50

15 They also fforced our sayd Agent to pay for 1/3 part of two hundred Barrells of Powder, which was spent

and shot away at severall ffeastes made
by the Governor, at thirty R:ˢ of 8ᵗ per
Barrell amounting to R:ˢ   2000

                                £   s   d
           In Sterling am: 48900 15 00

B4, THE 1645 CATALOGUE OF COMPLAINTS, OFFICIAL VERSION IN LATIN, 1652

Summarium querelarum particularium a multis Anglicæ Nationis hujus regni subditis de injurijs at*que* damnis quibus affecti sunt a subditis Fœderati Belgij quæ querelæ juxta aliquot utrius*que* Domus Parlamenti edicta ad Commissarios *Dominorum & Communium Parlamenti* delatæ sunt, quibus datum negotium erat, uti cum Legatis Ordinum *Belgij* de navium & bonorum retentione agerent, ob quas omnes injurias et damna, nomine *Dominorum et Communium Parlamenti Angliæ*, postulatur ut debita reparatio detur, juxta singulorum petitiones.

Gulielmus Curteen Armiger queritur, navem suam *Bonam Esperanzam Londinensem*, bonis prædicti *Curteen* onustam, certis*que* alijs bonis et pecunijs *Lusitanorum* (cum quibus prædicti Ordines pacem in India tubarum et tympanorum sonitu promulgaverunt secundum fœdus diu antea initum in *Europa* inter Regem *Portugalliæ* et prædictos Ordines) 26 Junii 1643 a *Goa* ad *Sinarum* regionem in freto *Malachensi* cursum tenentem, a duabus Orientalis Indiæ Societatis Belgicæ navibus fuisse oppugnatum; post pugnam cruentam, multos*que* navis *Bonæ Esperanzæ* socios occisos, navem ipsam cum toto ejus onere ac bonis, ijsdem oppugnatoribus prædæ fuisse, qui*que* in ea erant inhumanissime habitos, quod nisi accidisset, potuit navis illa in Angliam redijsse, libras*que* ad minimum sexaginta mille ad petitorem hunc retulisse.

Robertus Moulton de Redriff ... *Clench de Ipswich* ... *Gosnall de Ipswich* ... *Chaplaine de Ipswich* aliique aliquot navis illius Domini de suæ navis amissione haud minus queruntur. Navis æstimatur quin*que* millibus librarum merces*que* amissæ alteris quin*que* millibus.

Gulielmus Penoyer et *Ricchardus Hill*, Mercatores ambo *Londinensis*, queruntur, se cum ex pacto cum *Dominorum et Communium* commissarijs ad incolumitatem regni constitutis, Decemb. 27, 1642 in ditione *Legiensi* certum armorum numerum, quibus usus *Parlamento* erat, coëmissent quem navigijs secundo flumine ad portum *Dunkirkensem* subvexerant, mense Julio 1643, unde in Angliam asportarentur a D^no *de Witt*, qui tum Classi Belgicæ præfectus erat, et ad oppidum *Dunkirkam* in anchoris stabat, quamquam is de re tota certior factus esset, prohibitos fuisse quo minus ex portu solverent, qui et eos aut capturum se aut depressurum minatus est, si id tentassent, quamvis et literæ ad eum a D^no *Admirallo Angliæ* datæ essent, quibus libera eorum dimissio peteretur, et in quibus etiam confirmatum esset ea arma *Parlamenti* usibus coëmpta esse. Post hoc prædictus D^nus *Admirallus Angliæ* de eadem re ad D^num *Harpason Trump*, Classis Belgicæ illo tempore *Dunkirkam* obsidebat, Admirallum denuo literas dedit, quibus rursus et arma illa dimitterentur petebat; verum hoc nullo modo impetrare potuit: immo plane contra at*que* prædictus D^nus Admirallus petierat, eadem arma duobus Anglicis navigijs liberis imposita Londinum asportanda, a prædicto D^no *Harpason Trump* circiter 12 superioris Maij capta sunt at*que* in Zelandiam abducta, ibi*que* retenta, quamvis Communium Domus per literas et agentem suum et Commissarij *Parlamenti* utrius*que* regni et *Statibus Generalibus* et *Zelandij Statibus* declarassent, eadem arma ut supradictum est, ad usum hujus regni fuisse coëmpta. Pretium armorum erat octo mille librarum; impensæ retentionis causa, 1500, fœnus 700.

Vincentius de la Barr Londinensis pro se sua*que* societate queritur, se circiter mensem Julium 1639, cum ejus navis, cui nomen *nigro Damæ Londinensi, Canarias* versus Insularum *Maderæ* oram legeret, a Capitaneo *Henrico Claessenswaert* ejus*que* socijs, Belgis omnibus, in navi quadam cui nomen *Spei Amsterodamiensi*, hostiliter oppugnatum, vi*que* captum et abductum fuisse, & quamvis tam in *Hollandia* jus suum persequendo, sollicitationibus insuper ab hac Repub: aliquoties adhibitis summam suam operam dederint, omni*que* ope annixi sint, ut suas res reciperent, omnino tamen nihil ijs restitutum est, cum æstimatur damnum duodenis millibus librarum.

Capitaneus Whetstone queritur, se circiter Feb. proxime elapsam 1643. cum in alto nimirum, intra Indices quos *Boyos* vocant, prope oppidum *Brillam*, longius tamen quam ut ab ulla nave aut munimento Belgicæ ditionis ictu Bombardæ peti posset navem *Scarburgensem*, cui nomen Margeriæ erat, Magistro *Gulielmo Cooper*, cepisset, quæ navis *Scarburgo* solverat, *Roterodamum* versus, plumbo, panno, pellibus ovinis, aliquanto etiam pecuniæ onusta, postquam eam cepissent navem, duas *Hollandiæ* naves bellicas, jussu Admiralli Belgici *Van Trump*, subito adortas esse, illam*que* navem captam prædicto *Capitaneo Whetstone* vi ademisse, navem*que* ipsius propriam *the Cygnett* vulgo dictam, intra molem *Brillensem* abduxisse, ibi*que* vela antennæ dempsisse, clavum*que* sustulisse, post susceptam duorum mensium molestiam et moram dimissa tandem navis Signetta est, nulla ob navem captam satisfactione data, quod damnum sex millibus librarum æstimatum est.

Capitaneus Zachary queritur, se, cum circa initium Martij 1643 ad locum in *Hollandia the Flye* vulgo dictum sua in navi esset, cum antea duas naves Anglicas cepisset (altera, cujus Capitaneus erat...*Hickson, Scarburgo* solverat, *Amstelodamum* versus, & pannum, plumbum, lanas, non nullam etiam pecuniam portabat, quæ omnia æstimata sunt septies millenis libris, altera navicula erat armis et instrumento bellico onusta *Scarburgum* tendens, quo ex portu primum exierat, quinquaginta libris æstimata, a tribus Belgarum navibus bellicis oppressum fuisse, quarum omnium præfectus erat Capitaneus *Ioannes Van Gal*, qui quadraginta bombardas in eum displosit, et uti ad se in naves suas veniret imperavit, ejus deinde vela antennis ademit, secumque in locum illum, *the Flye* vulgo dictum, abstulit, ipsum vero *Amstelrodamum* abduxit, ibi*que* in custodia arcta per septimanas undecim habuit, sine captarum navium restitutione, aut ulla prædæ ullius parte.

Oppidum Jarmutha queritur, Tres Belgarum naves bellicas Julij superioris 2° 1644 Navem quandam *Dunkerkensem*, cui *Petrus Carline* præfuit, cum in fugam dedissent, eam in portum *Jarmuthensem* impulsam insequutas, multis bombardarum ictibus petisse, duos in ea homines interemisse, plures consauciasse, pilas etiam quasdam ad littus emissas unum ex oppidanis confecisse, multisque alijs discrimen attulisse, et post hoc navem prædictam in illo portu occupasse, eam*que* cum præfecto illius omnibus*que* socijs in Stationem Navium *Jarmuthensem* abduxisse, uti eam postmodum una ex navibus *Parlamenti*, quæ tum forte aderat, adjuvantibus ex oppido quibusdam, *Belgarum* ex manibus recuperavit.

Anna Paulet, *Roberti Paulet* Generosi vidua, queritur,* prædictum Robertum Paulet socios*que* ejus nave quadam Minheadensi, cui nomen Columbæ, nave etiam altera *Portugallensi*, quæ cum præda opulenta ceperat, fuisse a quodam Capitaneo *Cornelio Skint* pyratico more spoliatos, cui navi, cui nomen *Petro Roterodamiensi*, præfuit, eos*que* Roterodamum abduxit, bonis omnibus ademptis, et quamvis prædictus Robertus Paulet, tam lege agendo quam solicitationibus Agentium hujus Reipub. regiæ Ma[tis] nomine abhibitis, alijs*que* modis summam operam dederit, ut sua recuperaret, nulla tamen restitutio, nulla satisfactio impetrari potest.

Rogerus North Armiger querit!, Quod cum quidam *Henricus Jacobson Flissingæ* moreretur, et prædicto *Rogero North* debitor esset, viduæ prædicti *Jacobson* coram *Flissingensium* magistratibus litem intendit, sibi*que* deberi ducentas et decem libras, cum quindecim solidis, septem*que* denarijs apparebat, quæ summa ad prædictos Magistratus allata est, verum antequam prædictus *North* eam pecuniam adipisci potuerit, *Arausionensis Principis* Balivus eam retentavit, ea*que* prædictum *Rogerum* privavit, hoc solum obtentu, quod cum prædictus *Jacobson* intestatus moreretur, prædicta pecunia ad dictum principem

---

* Date missing. Given in English as January 1630.

pertineret, at*que* ita Magistratus ille sententiam tulerit.

Mercatores Dorovernienses queruntur, Quod cum mense Septembri 1644 navigium quoddam, cui nomen *Fortunæ Doroverniensi, Laurentio Browne* Magistro, diversorum quorundam bonorum justum onus *Ostendæ* accepisset *Dorovernij* reddendum, ea*que* navis in itinere esset cum altera hujus Reipub. nave præsidiaria, capta tamen in mari est, ab nave quadam Ordinum *Hollandiæ*, cui præfuit *Adrianus Galine*, et *Roterodamum* abducta, ubi et ipsa navis et bona et omnes nautæ sine ulla restitutione etiamnum retinentur, quamvis D^{nus} Admirallus Angliæ ea de re ad Do*mi*na*t*iones V*es*tras questus, responsum retulerit velle vos diligenter ad Ordines *Hollandiæ* scribere, ut satisfactio abunde detur; tamen et nautæ in Custodia illic sunt, minæ etiam adjectæ, illic permansuros, nisi affirmare voluerint, navem illam ac bona ad *Flandros* pertinere, ita affirmantibus præmia etiam proposita sunt. Navis et bona æstimantur quindecies millenis libris, damna bis millenis.

Joannis Marston Londinensis mercator queritur, Quod Septembris 26, 1639 cum duæ Anglicae naviculæ in *Margaretæ Statione* sub Munimento illic intra ictum sclopi in Anchoris starent, Magistris *Rogero Joyner* et ... *Sturgeon* utræ*que* ex mandato ejusdem Marston Hispanis militibus confertæ, circiter horam ejusdem diei duodecimam, venit in eandem stationem navis quædam bellica Fœderatorum Belgij, cujus *Capitaneus Petrus Johnson. Roterodamus* insigne regis Angliæ in puppi posuerat, Unionis vexillum ad proram, pendens*que* ab extremo malo Aplustre, cum*que* intra ictum sclopi minusculi esset in eas naviculas sclopos duos displosit, eas*que* extemplo vi ingressus, anchoras earum tolli jussit, naves in suam potestatem redegit, milites in suam navem deportavit, cum naviculas illas dimisisset, ipse eadem nocte *Zelandiam* versus vela fecit. Damnum quod prædicto *Marstono* inde datum est, æstimatur mille sexcentis libris.

Jacobus Gibbons, mercator Adventurarius, queritur, Quod cum mense Novembri 1637 pervenisset ad eum

Londino Roterodamum in nave *Elizabetha Londinensi*, *Gulielmo Atkinson* Magistro, sarcina una in qua panni Anglici colorati septendecim fuere, qui ut allati sunt in Telonio sine fraude sunt conscripti; cum autem altera in ea nave sarcina esset, quæ *Jacobo Velthusen* mercatori *Roterodamiensi* consignata erat, qui eam noctu ex illa nave clanculum subduxerat, ut rempub. suo jure fraudaret; Magister propterea ab Advocato Fiscali in curia maritima insimulatus est, et curiæ sententiæ mulctam ei crimini irrogatam damnatus tulit: postea sarcinam prædicti *Gibbons* pro sarcina prædicti *Velthusen* prædicta Curia nave exemit, eam*que* magna cum jactura divendi jussit, inaudito prædicto *Gibbons*, ne*que* ex eo tempore impetrare potuit prædictus *Gibbons* ut sua sibi restituerentur.

Joannes Wood, mercator *Londinensis*, queritur, quod, cum anno superiore navem *Stellam* ad oram *Guineæ* profecturam instruxisset, mercator in ea nave præcipuus, dum illud iter faceret, ad *Cormantini* portum contendit, qui in aureo Guineæ littore est, ubi statim comperit, *Belgas* cum ejus regionis indigenis conjurasse de expellendis ab omni suo illic negotio *Anglis*, quod et ad exitum perduxissent, magno cum dispendio et prædicti *Joannis Wood* et totius *Guineanæ* societatis, nisi navis illa eo ipso die ad portum illum appulisset; quæ cum postea ad sanctæ *Thomæ* Insulam profecta esset, ad exigenda quædam debita prædicti *Joannis Wood* quibis illam navem redeuntem onerari oportebat, qui *Fœderatorum* Ordinum nomine Insulæ illi præfuit *Lusitanos* debitores vetuit, ulla *Anglis* debita solvere quamvis et facile possent et parati essent, quo factum est un[a] Navis illa incassum redierit.

Textual Note: Italicized names represent large script in the manuscript, MS. Aitzema 86. Some losses in text at margins are supplied from MS. St. v. Holl. 2813.1, whence also, under *Jarmutha, multisque* before *alijs* (as required by the English text); under *Whetstone*, less correctly, *stabat* for *starent*, which is required by the English text; under *Wood, sancti Thomae* (so also in Aitzema's *Historia Pacis*, which has other variants).

B4, The 1645 *Catalogue of Complaints*, Official Text in English, 1652

An Abstract of the particular Complaints from divers of the English Nation, subiects of this Kingdome, of the Injuryes, wrongs & damages done unto them by ye Subjects of the United Provinces, wch Complaints have been according to severall orders of the Houses of Parlam^t presented to the Comittee of Lords & Comons of Parlam^t appointed to treat wth the States Ambassadors touching detaining of Shipps and goods, for all wch wrongs & damages it is demanded in the names of the Lords & Comons of Parlam^t of England, that due restitution & satisfaction bee made according to the severall petitions.

William Courteen Esq: that his ship the Bona Esperance of London being laden wth the said Courteens goods, and wth certayn other goods & moneyes of the Portugalls wth whom the said States had proclaimed peace in India wth Drum & Trumpett according to the agreement made long before betweene the King of Portugall and the said States here in Europe, was upon the 26th of June 1643 sailing upon her voyage from Goa to China in the straights of Malaca assaulted by two Shipps belonging to the Dutch East India Company and after a bloody fight & divers of the Company of the said Bona Esperance slayne, shee and all her said lading & goods was seized upon by the said Assaultors to their owne use and the men in her most unhumanly used, which Ship might else have returned into England and might have been worth to the petitioner at least sixty thousand pound.[119]

Robert Moulton of Redriff, ... Clench of Ipswich, ... Gosnall of Ipswich ... Chaplaine of Ipswich, and some others all owners of the said ship the Bona Esperance, make the same complaint for the losse of their Ship 5,000^li and for the losse of their freight which comes to 5,000^li more.

William Pennoyer & Richard Hill both of London, Merchants, that according to an Agreement made by them wth the Comittee of Lords and Comons of Parlam^t for the safety of the kingdom of [27th of] Decemb: 1642 they bought for the service of the Parlam^t in the territory of Leidge a parcell of Armes which they brought downe in vessels unto the port of Dunkirck in July 1643 from thence to be transported into England but the then Admirall of the States ffleet Mīn Here de Witt then riding before Dunkircke being informed of the premises refused to let them passe but threatned to take or sincke them if they offered notw^thstanding Letters delivered to him from the Lord Admirall of England to the said Admirall of ye States ffleet to procure their free passage avowing the Armes to bee for the use of the Parlam^t: after this the said Lord Admirall of England writt other Letters to the same purpose to Sr Harperson Trump then Admirall of the States ffleet lying before Dunkircke to procure the free passage of the said Armes but could by noe meanes effect it, but quite contrary to the desire of the said Lord Admirall of Englad, the said Armes then laden in two free English Bottomes & bound for London were taken by the said Sr Harperson Trump about the 12th of May last and sent into Zealand and there deteyned notw^thstanding the House of Comons by their Letters and Agent And the Comittee of Parlam^t of both Kingdomes declared to the States Generall and to the States of Zealand that the said Armes were as aforesaid for the service of this Kingdome, the value of the Armes eight thousand pounds, the charges occasioned by the stay of them 1500 ^li the interest money 700 ^li.

Vincent de la Barr of London in behalfe of himselfe & Company that about July 1639 their Ship the Blacke Buck of London being then neere the Isle of Maderaies sailing towards ye Canaryes was in Hostile manner assaulted and forceably taken and carryed away by Captayne Henrick Claessen Swaert & Company being all Dutch in a Ship called the Hope of Amsterdam and notw^thstanding they have both by legall proceedings in Holland and by severall intercessions from and by this state done their best indeavours and used their best meanes yet they have received no restitution at all, the losse amounting to twelve thousand pounds.

Captayne Whetstone that about ffebruary last 1643 he haveing taken at Sea viz: w^{th}in the boyes neere the Brill but out of Comand of any Shipp or ffort of the States, a Scarborow ship called the Margery, Master William Cooper wch Ship sayled from Scarborow bound for Rotterdam laden wth lead[,] Cloth[,] Sheepskins[,] and some money; after they had taken her, two Holland men of Warre ordered by the Dutch Admirall Van Trump soe to doe tooke the prize Ship from Captayne Whetstone, carryed his Ship the Cignett into the Brill Peere and there took his sayles from the yard and carryed away the rudder, after two moneths trouble and attendance the Cignett was discharged w^{th}out any satisfaction at all for the prize the value whereof was 6000 ^{li}.

Captayne Zachery that about the beginning of March last 1643 he riding wth his Ship at the ffly in Holland and having before taken two English prizes viz: one whose Captayne was ... Hickson wch came from Scarborrow, and was bound for Amsterdam laden wth Cloth, lead, wooles & some moneyes all to the value of seven thousand pounds, the other a ketch laden wth amunition bound for Scarborrow from wch port she first came, to the value of fifty pounds was surprised by three States men of Warre Capt. John Vangall being Comander of them all who shott forty peeces of ordnance at him, and comanded him aboard their Shipps and tooke his sailes from his yards and carryed them ashoare to the ffly and carryed him to Amsterdam and there kept him close prisoner eleven weekes w^{th}out restitution of the said prize or any part of them.

The Towne of Yarmouth that the second of July last 1644 three States men of Warre gave chase to one Peter Carline Captayne of a Dunkirkir and drove the said ffrigott into the Haven of Yarmouth and followed them into the said Haven & there made severall shotts at the said ffrigott and killed two of her men & wounded more and divers of the shott comeing on shoare killed one of the Townsmen of Yarmouth and like to have spoyled many more and after this boarded the said Vessell in the said Haven and carried her wth her Comander & all his Company into the Road of Yarmouth where she was afterwards rescued by one of the Parlam^ts Ships being at that tyme in the said Road wth some helpe from the said Towne.

Anne Powlett Widdow of Robert Powlett Gent: that in January 1630 the said Robert Powlett and his Partners were Pyratically Rob'd of a ship called the Dove of Minehead, and alsoe of a Portugall Prize wth store of rich goods by one Captayne Cornelius Skint in a Ship called the Peter of Rotterdam & carried thither and there disposed, And notw^thstanding the said Robt Powlett used his best endeavours both by legall proceedings, and by intercession of Agents of this State in his Majesties name & otherwise yet noe restitution or satisfaction can be obteyned.

Roger North Esq., That one Henry Jacobson dyeing in fflushing and being indebted to him the said North, He commenced a suit against the Widdow of the said Jacobson before the Magistrates of fflushing and there appeared due to him two hundred & ten pounds fifteen shillings & seaven pence which Sume was brought in before the said Magistrates, but before the said North could obteyne the said money, the Bayliffe of the Prince of Orange arrested the same and keepeth the same from the said North, upon this only pretense that the said Henry Jacobson dyeing intestate, the said money belonged to the said Prince, and soe it was by the said Majestrates sentenced.

The Merchants of Dover, That in September 1644 A Barque called the Fortune of Dover, Lawrence Browne Master haveing taken in her full ladeing of peice goods at Ostend to be delivered at Dover, the said Ship & Goods comeing from Ostend wth the safe [conduct of a] Convoy ship of this State was notw^thstanding surprized at Sea by a Ship of the States of Holland, whereof Adrian Galine was Comander and carried to Rotterdam, where the said Ship, Goods, & her Marriners remayne wthout restitution, although the Lord Admirall of England making complaint thereof to y^r Lord^{ps}, received answere, That you would write effectually to the States of Holland That satisfaction might bee given to content, yet are the Marriners there imprisoned, and threatned to continue soe unlesse they will affirme the Ship & Goods to belong to fflemings & promised reward if they will soe affirme. The value of the Ship & Goods is fiveteene thousand pounds, and damages two thousand pounds.

John Marston of London Merch^t That upon the 26th of September 1639 there was riding at Anchor in the Road at Margaret wthin Musquett shott of the ffort there, two English Ketches, Masters Roger Joyner & ... Sturgeon, both fraighted by order of the said Marston wth Spaniards, and about 12 a Clocke of the same day there came into the same Road a ffrigott or Ship of Warre belonging to the States Captayne Peter Johnson of Roterdam haveing the king of Englands Ensigne on the Poope, the union fflagg on the Bolt sprit end, and a Pendent on the Maine Mast end, and being wthin pistoll shott of the said ketches, did then and there discharge two musquetts and forthwth boarded them, and haveing entered, his men weighed their Anchors and did violently carry the said Ketches & Souldiers aboard his own ship discharged the Ketches, and that night set sayle for Zealand, the damage susteyned thereby by the said Marston is valued at one thousand six hundred pounds.[120]

James Gibbons Merch^t Adventurer, that in November 1637 there was consigned unto him from London to Roterdam in the Elizabeth of London, William Robinson Master one pack conteyning seventeen English coloured Clothes, which being arived, were truely entred into the Custome House, and there being in the Shipp an other pack directed to one Jacob Velthusen a merch^t of Roterdam who haveing secretly unladen the same by night out of the said Ship to defraud the State of their due, the Ship Master was thereupon accused by the Advocate fiscall in the Court of Admiralty was by sentence of Court condemned in the forfeiture thereunto belonging, after which the said Court did take the said Gibbons his pack out of the said Ship, instead of the said Velthusens, and caused the same to be sold wth great losse, wthout hearing the said Gibbons nor could the said Gibbons ever since procure restitution of the same.

John Wood of London Merch^t, That he haveing this last yeare set out for the Coast of Guinny the Ship Starr, the Cape Merchant of the said ship in prosecution of the Voyage, went to the Port of Cormantine, on the Gold Coast of Guinny where he found the Dutch had combined wth the natives of the Country, to have cleane expelled the English from their owne ffactory, which had beene effected to the very great damage of the said Wood, and the whole Guinny Company, had not that ship arived that very day at that Port, and afterwards the said Ship comeing to the Islands of St Thome to recover certayne debts due to the [said] Wood, wherewith the Ship was to be reladen. The Governor of the Island for the States Generall Comanded the Portugalls debtors not to pay any of their debts unto the English, although they were both able and willing thereunto, whereby the said Ship returned home dead fraight.

Textual Note: It is unreasonable to reproduce all the idiosyncrasies of the 1652 scribe of this B4 English text in MS. S.G. 8460; some have here been corrected, using the 1645 text. Bracketed insertions are from 1645. Among errors corrected: Pennoyer-Hill, 12 May; de la Barr, intersessions; Zachary, ledd; Paulett, 1644 (wrong year; perhaps a reason for the omission of the year in the Latin text). The English ships taken as prizes by Whetstone and Zachary appear to have been royalist. Leidge = Liège. Superscript ^{li} = *libri,* "pounds." Boyes = buoys.

The British Thirty–six Counter-articles

The official original English-language text is here printed from MS. S.G. 8460, no. 21, superseding the translation text offered in the 1938 edition of Milton's *Works*, volume 18. This official text, signed *P. Lisle, presd^t*, has suffered damage at the right margin, with some loss of text. I have supplied letters missing at the end of some words where they unquestionably belong, as well as some missing words (here bracketed) based on the context and the Latin text.

The official Latin text as done by Milton is here printed from the official original manuscript, MS. Aitzema 86, no. 21, with some marginal flaws supplied from the transcript in MS. Arch. St. v. Holl. 2813.1, and without the errors printed in the 1938 edition (some of which derived from the less accurate transcript in MS. S.G. 7329; see textual notes following).

In other Milton state papers, his classical Latinity is seen in contradistinction to the usages of his British colleagues. In this document, the contrasts are to the usages of his Dutch contemporaries.

For discussion, see pages 20–21 and 30–34.

OFFICIAL LATIN TEXT

CONCILIUM Articulos 36 ab Excellentijs Vestris 11/21 Februarij Commissarijs suis exhibitos consideravit, ad eos*que* sequentibus Articulis Respondet.

1° Quod ad primum, fore ab hoc tempore inter Angliæ Rempub: & ffœderatas Belgij provincias, inter*que* eas utrin*que* regiones, at*que* urbes, quæ in societatem cum ijs coiverint, aut sub earum ditione fuerint, inter earum item utrin*que* populos & incolas, quicunque illi demum, aut cujuscun*que* ordinis fuerint, bonam, firmam, synceram, inviolabilem, at*que* perpetuam pacem, amicitiam, comercium, arctiorem, etiam & propiorem societatem, at*que* fœdus quam antehac initum est.

2° Ad secundum, fore eas inter se societate et amicitia conjunctissimas, ad Libertatem utrius*que* Populi, mutuum comercium, rem navelem, mutuas*que* terra vel aqua rationes, modis infra expositis, at*que* expressis, defendendum & conservandum devinctas inter se et consociatas, at*que* ita permansuras contra eos omnes qui in hisce rebus exequendis utrivis Reipub: obstare, & molestiam exhibere conati fuerint.

3° De tertio et decimo tertio assentimur, uti hic proponitur, Rempublicam Angliæ, Populum*que* Anglicanum omnes*que* ejus Reipub: incolas prædictas item ffœderatas Provincias earum*que* Populum, & incolas, cujuscun*que* ordinis qut conditionis fuerint, obligatos fore ad sese mutuo rebus omnibus humaniter at*que* amice tractandum, uti terra vel aqua alterutrius Regiones, oppida, pagos, sive muro cincti sive sine moenibus fuerint, muniti vel non muniti, portus etiam & ditionem universam per omnem Angliam, Scotiam & Hiberniam, per omnes itidem ffœderatas Belgij Provincias libere et secure adire possint, in ijs*que* versari, & comorari quamdiu voluerint, ibi*que* sine ullo impedimento comeatum suis usibus quantum necesse erit, coemere, at*que* etiam negotiari, & mercaturam facere, quocun*que* mercium genere ipsis videbitur, eas*que* advehere suo arbitratu, aut exportare, dumodo quæ statuta sunt portoria, solvant, salvis etiam alterutrius pariter Reipub: legibus & statutis omnibus.

4° Quod ad quartum, assentiri nos respondemus eo quo jam dicetur modo, Respublicas nimirum Angliæ & Fœderatarum Provinciarum, ne*que* palam ne*que* occulte contra se invicem ne*que* facere ne*que* agere ne*que* moliri quicquam ullo in loco, sive terra, sive aqua, in portubas aut fluminibus ad alterutrius ditionem pertinentibus, ne*que* promovere ne*que* agitare, suisve consilijs, aut opibus fovere quodcunque, vel quæcun*que* hostiliter facta erunt, ullamve injuriam inferendam aut faciendam, quæ ad præjudicum aut damnum partis alterutrius possit spectare, ne*que* passuras ut quid ejusmodi a populo aut incolis alterutris, aut ab ullo qui in earum potestate sit, tentetur aut fiat, ullumve adjumentum, consilium, studium, subsidium ulli homini ad damnum, aut injuriam alterutrius Reipub: earumve populi, aut incolarum præbeatur, verum uti palam, et cum effectu illiusmodi conatus vetent, prohibeant, impugnent et reipsa impediant

5° & 6° De eo quod 5? et 6? continetur, assentimur, quemadmodum in sequente 5° & 6° dictum erit: neutram Rempub: neve ullum ex ejus populo aut incolis, ullumve in earum ditione comorantem alterutrius Reipub: hostes aut rebelles, subsidio, consilio, aut studio adjuvare, imo aperte, syncere at*que* strenue obstare, ne quid auxilij aut adjumenti ab ullo, qui aut ex populo aut incolis aut comorantibus in alterutra Repub: fuerit, ullis ejusmodi hostibus, aut rebellibus prædictis, viri, pecunia, naves, arma, instrumentum bellicum, comeatus, mercesve ullæ publicæ prohibitæ mari aut terra præbeantur: Si quid contra fiat prædictas naves & bona publice prohibita ei Republicæ addici adversus quam parata sunt, contra sensum hujus articuli: qui*que* contra hunc articulum scientes at*que* volentes commisserint, utrius*que* Reipublicæ hostes judicari, in ea*que* Repub: ubi hoc comissum erit, perduellionis pœnas dare.

6° Utras*que* Respub: sibi mutuo, syncere & fideliter, prout opus fuerit, contra alterutrius hostes & rebelles terra mari*que* opem ferre viris & navibus ea proportione, eo*que* modo, ijs*que* conditionibus quibus postmodum conventum fuerit, prout necessitas et rerum alterutrius ratio tulerit, sumptu tamen at*que* impensis hoc fore illius partis, quæ auxilium postulaverit.

7° De septimo assentimur, si vel Angliæ Respub: vel ffœderatæ Belgij Provinciæ cum ullis Rebuspub: Principibus, aut potestatibus de amicitia, fœdere, aut societate egerint in ejus fœderis transactione, alteram earum altera comprehendi cum tota alterius ditione; siquidem ita comprehendi volet.

8° De octavo assentimur, quemadmodum hic proponitur, in hac fœderis transactione comprehendi amicos etiam omnes, fœderatos, et socios alterutrius, qui cum illud fœdus ratum habebitur utrin*que* nominabuntur de*que* ijs inter utras*que* convenerit si ipsi deni*que* in eo comprehendi voluerint.

9° Quod ad nonum, sequentem articulum pro responso exhibemus, Si acciderit ut quandiu fœdus, amicitia & societas hæc durabit ab ullo ex populis aut incolis alterutrius prædictæ Reipub: contra hoc fœdus, aut ullam ejus partem mari, terra aut alijs aquis quicquam fiat, aut tentetur, amicitiam hanc fœdus et societatem inter hasce Respublicas non idcirco interrumpi aut infringi, verum integram nihilominus durare plenam*que* vim suam obtinere, tantummodo illos ipsos, qui contra fœdus prædictum comisserint, singulos puniri, alium*que* neminem, justitiam*que* reddi, satisfactionem*que* dari illis omnibus, quorum id interest, ab ijs omnibus, qui terra, mari, aut alijs aquis contra hoc fœdus quicquam comiserint ulla in parte Europæ, aut ubivis locorum intra fretum Gaditanum, sive in America, vel per Africæ littora, ullisve in terris, insulis, æquoribus, æstuarijs, sinubus, fluminibus ullisve in locis cis Caput Bonæ Spei intra anni spatium quàm Justitia postulabitur, In omnibus autem uti supradictum est ultra prædictum Caput locis intra menses octodecim quàm Justitia prædicto modo poscetur, si fœderis ruptores non comparuerint ne*que* se judicandos permiserint, ne*que* satisfactionem dederint intra hoc vel illud temporis spatium pro loci longinquitate modo constitutum, prædicti illi utrius*que* Reipub: hostes judicabuntur, eorum*que* bona, facultates, & quicun*que* reditus, publicabuntur, plenæ*que* ac justæ satisfactioni impendendi erunt earum injuriarum quæ ab ipsis illatæ sunt, ipsi*que* præterea cum in alterutrius Reipub: potestate fuerint ijs pœnis obnoxij erunt, quas suo quis*que* crimine comeruerit.

10° Anglos omnes & qui sub eorum ditione fuerint posse libere, tute ac secure in ffœderati Belgii Provinciis per*que* eas terra, vel aqua ad ulla in ijs loca, vel extra eas iter facere, per*que* ulla earum oppida, præsidia, munimenta, quæ ullis in locis Fœderatarum Belgij Provinciarum quibuscun*que* erunt, mercaturam in omnibus illic locis facientes, eorum*que* negotiatores, institores, famulosve armatos sive inermes, armatos autem non amplius quadraginta simul tam sine bonis suis & mercimonijs quam cum ijs, quocun*que* ire voluerint. Poterit item Populus & incolæ Fœderatarum Belgij Provinciarum eadem libertate frui omnibus ullisve per Angliam Scotiam aut Hiberniam locis dumodo in hujus modi Comercio, & mercatura ab utra*que* parte singuli alterutrius Reipub: Legibus et Statutis pareant, morem*que* gerant.

11° Quod ad undecimum, respondemus, cum Reipub: Angliæ popularibus præcise vetitum sit in omnibus colonijs & locis ad Populum Fœderati Belgij pertinentibus, quæ intra fines Belgij non sunt, negotiari, in eo acquiescemus, eas*que* colonias adnavigare, aut cum illis comercium habere supersedebimus ne*que* ijs illic navigantibus impedimento aut molestiæ erimus, & illi vicissim ne in ullis Anglorum Colonijs negotia habeant nupera lege cautum est qua exaugendæ hujus gentis rei navali consulitur, ab qua recedendū esse non Censemus.

12° Ad duodecimum respondemus, Anglos in Septentrionale Americæ continentē primos omniū colonias deduxisse ibi*que* habere ab ea Virginiæ Plaga, qua longissime in Austrum vergit ab gradu nimirum latitudinis Aquilonaris 37 us*que* ad Terram Novam, gradum*que* secundū et quinquagesimū, cum*que* haud sciamus an ulla illic Belgarum Colonia sit præter paucos admodū ad flumen Hudsoni accolas, haud duximus in præsens necesse esse fines constituere quod idoneo dehinc tempore fieri poterit.

13° Ad hunc in 3° articulo respondetur.

14° De quarto decimo assentimur in sequentibus, mercatores, naucleros, gubernatores, et nautas alterutrius Reipub: eorumve naves, bona aut mercimonia in terris, portubus, navium stationibus aut fluminibus alterius neutiquam retentari ex edicto quovis generali aut speciali sive ad bellum sive alium quemlibet ad usum, nisi summa necessitate id cogente, justa autem satisfactione ob id data; ita tamen ut retentionibus et publicationibus quæ ex jure et legibus alterutrius Reipub: rectè at*que* ordine fiunt, nihil hic derogatum sit.

15° De quinto decimo assentimur, ut sequitur, Populares et incolas terrarum prædictæ Reipub: Angliæ et Fœderatarum Belgij Provinciarum in terris alterutrius, ut supra dictū est, negotiantes, non obligari in posterum, ut plus portorij, censûs, vectigalium aut pecuniæ quæ ob speculatorios ignes dispositos exigitur, aut aliorum tributorum solvant quam pro rata portione, quam nunc solvunt, cum alterutrius populo collata.

16° De sexto decimo assentimur, posse utrin*que* mercatores eorum*que* institores, et famulos, uti etiam naucleros alios*que* nautas tam eundo et redeundo navibus per maria, aliás*que* aquas, quàm in portubus alterius utrius, aut in terram egressos, gestare at*que* uti, sui suorum*que* bonorum defendendi causa, armorum omni genere, quibus aut se protegere, aut vim propulsare possint; verum ubi ad sua quis*que* hospitia ac diversoria pervenerit ibi arma sua deponere, at*que* ibi relinquere, donec rursus ad navem se receperit aut eò commeare velit.

17° Ad septimum decimum dicimus, quo utræ*que* Reipub: arctiùs quàm unquam antea consociari et coalescere possint, licere cuivis ex populo, indigenis aut incolis Fœderatarum Belgij Provinciarum, aut ullorum intra septendecim provincias locorum, quæ aut in earum vel societate vel ditione sunt, siquidem reformatam religionem sequuntur, et cum sua familia et facultatibus in Angliam commigraverint, liberè illic permanere, habitare, mercaturam facere, agros etiam at*que* ædes mancipio accipere, hæreditates adire, sibi*que* et hæredibus possidere, omni*que* ea libertate, ijs*que* privilegijs et immunitatibus frui, cuiuscun*que* generis, quibus ullus huius Gentis indigena vel natali jure, vel ulla lege, consuetudine, ullove alio ex jure frui queat ac debeat, modo omnibus in rebus huius gentis legibus et receptis moribus pareant, quemadmodum ipsos indigenas parere æquum est; pari*que* libertate ac privilegijs quemvis ex populo huius Reipub: quibusvis in terris, urbibus, oppidis, alijs*que* locis vel Fœderatarum vel septendecim provinciarum, quæ in earum vel societate vel ditione sunt, itidem frui posse.

18° Ad octavum decimum dicimus, salvo huius Reipub: jure, illud*que* asserentes ad eas pactiones de piscatu accedere non gravabimur, quæ ob æquitate et ratione alienæ non fuerint.

19° De undevigesimo sequentem in modum assentimur, quo navigandi, et commercij habendi liberior facultas sit, ne*que* prædictam Angliæ Rempub: ne*que* Fœderatus Belgij Provincias in suas terras, portus, urbes, aut oppida recipere, aut sinere ut ullus ex populo aut incolis alterutrius recipiat Pyratas aut Prædones, ijsve hospitium, auxilium, aut commeatum præbeat, verum operam dare ut prædicti pyratæ, prædones, eorum*que* pyraticæ participes, conscij et adiutores in aliorum terrorem investigentur, capiantur, et merito supplicio puniantur, omnès*que* naves, bona, at*que* merces pyraticè ab ijs captas, at*que* in portus alterutrius Reipub: advectas, quae quidem inveniri poterunt, immo etiamsi venditæ sint, iustis dominis restitui, aut satisfactionem dari vel eorum dominis vel ijs qui per literas procurationis eas res vendicaverint, modo jus domini debitis ex lege probationibus in curia causarum maritimarum appareat.

20° De vigesimo sequentem in modum assentimur, omnes utrius*que* partis qui accepto speciali diplomate in altum proficiscentur, priusquam diplomata acceperint, oportere vades idoneos dare, et eorum quidem neminem qui ex illius navis contubernio est, coram illius Curiæ judicibus, unde illud diploma emis sum est, observaturos se esse illa mandata, quibus ex illius diplomatis authoritate, quo pacto se gerere debeant sibi præcipietur.

21° Rempub: Angliæ eam curam sui maris tuendi, in eo*que* liberum commercium præstandi suscepturam esse, quæ par erit.

22° Ad 22^(dum) dicimus, si quis intra illa maria molestiæ, impedimento, aut oneri cuiquam erit mercaturam liberè exercenti, quod possit iure suo facere, hanc Rempub: omnes justas at*que* honestas inituram esse rationes, quibus omni commercio legitimo sua libertas per illa maria restituatur et conservetur.

23° De 23ᵗⁱᵒ assentimur, alterutrius reipub: naves præsidarias, si quam in mari navem aut naves mercatorias quæ ad alterum vel ad alterius populum aut incolas, aut ad ullos sociorum hoc fœdere comprehensos pertineurint, eundem cursum tenentes, idemve iter facientes, obviam habuerint, aut assecutæ erunt, obligari ut illis præsidio sint at*que* defendant, quandiu eundem cursum teneurint, contra omnes et singulos, qui eas vi adorientur.

24. De 24ᵗᵒ assentimur, si qua navis aut naves, quæ populi aut incolarum alterutrius Reipub: aut neutrius fuerint, in alterutrius portubus a quovis tertio capiantur, qui ex populo aut incolis alterutrius Reipub: non sit, illos quorum in portu, aut ex portu, aut quacun*que* ditione prædictæ naves abductæ fuerint, pariter cum altera parte obligari, uti dent operam, ut sint qui prædictam navem aut naves captas insequantur et reducant, suis*que* dominis reddant, verum hoc totum fieri dominorum impensis, aut quorum id interest.

25 Si quæ naves mercatoriæ, quæ populi aut incolarum alterutrius Reipub: fuerint, si tempestatis vi, sive pyratis insequentibus, sive casu quovis alio aut necessitate in portum quemlibet alterutrius prædictæ Reipub: delatæ fuerint, licere ijs suo arbitratu liberè discedere suis cum navibus et bonis, nulla portoria solventes, ita tamen ut earum mercium, quibus navis oneratur ne quid attingant, aut venale proponant; ne*que* ulli cuivis molestiæ aut scrutationi obnoxios fore, modo ne quos homines aut bona in navem recipiant, ne*que* contra leges, statuta, moremve, eius loci quicquam faciant, quo in loco, quemadmodum supra dictum est, portum capesserint.

26 De 26ᵗᵒ assentimur ut sequitur, neutram partem alterius regionis portus intrare, aut ibi commorari cum eo numero navium bellicarum et militum, qui suspicionem evidentem afferre possit, nisi impetrata prius ab ijs venia, ad quos portus illi prædicti pertinuerint, nisi

si tempestate, vi aliqua, aut necessitate compulsa illuc sit, quo maris pericula effugiat; quod cum acciderit, Præfectum ejus loci aut summum Magistratum statim de causa sui adventus certiorem facere debere, ne*que* illic diutius hærere, quam illis a præfecto, ut dictum est, aut a summo Magistratu permissum erit.

27.28. Ad 27. 28. dicimus, naves bellicas ab alterutra parte, si eo numero non sint, ut suspicionem, ut dictum est, afferre queant, posse in alterutrius partis navium stationes, portus et flumina venire, ibi*que* in anchoris stare, aut inde exire, abs*que* ulla molestia aut impedimento, dummodo ita se gerant ut contra leges et mores illorum ne quid committatur; ne*que* naves illa bellicæ partis alterutrius in portus alterius ullas merces advexerint aut exportaverint, aut aliud quicquam quod vetitum erit, aut ullos ex populo aut incolis illius reipub: cuius in portubus sunt, nisi qui liberum commeatum pro se suis*que* rebus, literis publicis impetraverit, et ne secus quis fecerit, scrutationi in portu erunt obnoxiæ.

29. Ad 29 dicimus, omnes qui diplomata acceperunt, aut qui privatorum naves bellicæ sunt ab hac vel illa parte, eadem libertate pro se suis*que* prædis esse usuros ad eandem*que* regulam se directuros ut in precedenti articulo dictum est.

30 Vestri tricesimi loco proponimus, ut sequitur: quoties ullæ naves hostium alterutrius, quas oportere prædæ esse iudicabitur, a navibus alterutrius reipub: præsidarijs capiuntur, quæ bona in ijs aut merces ad populum aut incolas alterutrius reipub: pertinuerint, ea liberari, ei*que* reddi qui dominum earum se esse probaverit, omnia*que* bona hostium alterutrius reipub: quæ in alterius navibus invenientur, legitimæ prædæ fore, naves autem dimitti, etcaptorum bonorum vecturam solvi, moræ etiam damna pensari si aequum videbitur.

31 Ad 31 dicimus, ne*que* Angliæ rempub: ne*que* Fœderatas Belgij provincias aut ipsas auxilium ferre oportere, ne*que* sinere ut a populo aut ab incolis alterutrius, aut ab aliquo quovis tertio, hostibus aut rebellibus alterutrius ullo sive armorum aut instrumenti bellici cuiuscun*que* generis fuerit, apparatu, terra aut mari, aut commeatibus quibuscun*que* suppeditandis, auxilium feratur, verum omnes cuiuscun*que* generis apparatus, qui ad hostem aut rebelles alterutrius comportandi in navi qualibet reperientur, ei qui ceperit prædam adiudicari quemadmodum et naves ipsas quæ res illas portarunt, omnia item alia bona quæ in ijsdem navibus reperientur, facta probatione debita, prædictos illos apparatus tàm huius quàm illius generis, ut supra dictum est, ad rebelles hostes, ut dictum est, comportari.

32 De Articulo 32 Concilium assentiendum esse non censet.

33 Si alterutrius reipub: naves populive aut incolarum alterius, sive naves illæ bellicæ fuerint, sive mercatoriæ, vi ventorum, aut tempestatis, ullove alio quocun*que* casu ad littus impelli acciderit, aut illic naufragium facere ullis in terris quæ ditionis alterius reipub: erit, prædictas naves cum armamentis omnibus, toto*que* instrumento, bonis*que* omnibus, et mercibus quæ in terram delatæ fuerint, veris dominis restitui, si quidem suum in eas naves, aut bona verum dominum intra anni unius spatium quando illud naufragium factum est, idoneis testibus iuratis ulla in Curia causarum maritimarum quæ in alterutra repub: iam constituta est aut constituetur, probaverint, modo etiam prædicti domini, ijs qui salvas res suas reddiderint et asservaverint mercedem usitatam, salvagium vulgo dictum, solverint, simul*que* eos sumptus, quos illi fecerint, qui eorum bona conservaverint; et si qua ex prædictis bonis eiusmodi erunt, quæ vel sua natura, vel ex naufragio facile corrumpantur, ea bona,

postquam id præconis voce significatum erit, ad lucernam vendi, et quod id efficietur, dominis, ut prædictum est solvi: omnes*que* officiarios, omnem populum, et incolas partis alterutrius, quoties eiusmodi quid acciderit, obligari, uti pro viribus dent operam, ut bona illa ex naufragio ad prædictam restitutionem serventur, et si quæ inter populum huius at*que* illius partis controversia inciderit, bonam et expeditam justitiam fieri, ne*que* litium ambagibus non necessarijs rem in longam extrahi.

34 De 34 assentimur, ut sequitur, scrutationis Commissarios ab utra*que* parte ad legam normam alterutrius reipub: sese dirigere, ne*que* plus imponere aut exigere, ne*que* quam per authoritate sibi commissam, aut accepta mandata licuerit.

35 Ad 35 responsi loco proponimus, ut sequitur, si qua injuria ab alterutra repub: eiusve populo aut incolis, alterius populo aut incolis illata sit, sive contra ullos huius fœderis articulos, sive contra jus commune, uti nullæ literæ represales, vulgo dictæ mercæ, aut contra mercæ, ab alterutra concedātur: donec justitia prius iuxta leges ordinarias postuletur, sin autem illic justitia vel denegetur, vel in longum protrahatur, tum uti summus eius reipub: magistratus, cuius populus aut incolæ injuria affecti sunt, ab illa altera repub: in qua justitia ut supra dictum est, denegatur, aut differtur, aut ab illa potestate quæ huiusmodi postulatis audiendis constituta erit, publice justitiam postulet, ut omnes huiusmodi lites vel amice componantur vel ordinario legum processu; sin autem mora adhuc interposita erit, ne*que* ius reddetur, ne*que* satisfactio dabitur intra dies quinquaginta, quam lata huius modi postulatio erit, tum demum uti literæ represales mercæ vel contra mercæ concedantur.

36 De Articulo 36 Concilium assentiendum esse non censet.

Hæc V^ris Ex^tijs super ijs rebus, quæ a vobis in articulis sex et triginta proposita sunt, vicissim exhibenda censuimus, quod superest nostra ex parte ad consummationem tractationis proponendum id tempore idoneo Ex^tijs V^ris exhibebitur.

Textual Notes:
The Latin text of the British Counter-articles in MS. Aitzema 86 was written by at least two scribes, divided as articles 1–11 and 12–36; they differed in spelling *i* and *j*, etc., and avoided the ligature in *Fœdus* and *Fœderatus*. Obvious errors (*Feoderatarum*) are corrected here, but other peculiarities are retained. For *com̄miserint*, Article 5 has *commiserint*, while Article 9 has *comisserint*. In Article 12, *ē* stands for *-em* in *continentem, Septentrionalem*; in Article 35, *ā* stands for *an* in *concedantur*.

The text was printed by Aitzema in *Historia Pacis*, with variants. Another manuscript copy done by an English amanuensis, with variants, is preserved in the Mylius papers, Niedersächsisches Staatsarchiv, Oldenburg, Best. 20, Tit. 38, Nr. 73a, Litt J, ff. 249–53. (Mylius and Oldenburg had rather cool relationships with the Dutch, and very cool relationships with Aitzema. Their ability to obtain these and other confidential papers for themselves, presumably from contacts in England, is striking.)

The Latin text published by Mabbott and French in the Columbia edition, vol. 18, 94–122, was derived from photostats of MS. S.G. 7329 (commonly misstated as *1329* in American publications), now filed in the Algemeen Rijksarchief as MS. S.G. 12589.62. This 1938 text has these errors, some being in the manuscript itself (errors are here listed first, with the correct form following):

Article 2: societates / societate
Article 4: passuros / passuras; reipse / reipsa; amicitia societas / amicitia & societas.
Article 9: novum / nonum; Africa / Africæ
Article 10: institutores / institores
Article 11: nuper / nupera
Article 12: Septemtrionalis / Septemtrionalem

Article 16: utriusque / utrinque; institutores / institores
Article 17: indigenos / indigenas
Article 21: suscepturos / suscepturam; qua / quæ
Article 23: alteram / alterum
Article 25: capescerint / capesserint
Article 27/28: quo vetitum / quod vetitum
Article 33: reddiderint. Et / reddiderint et
After Article 36: superscriptis / super ijs; super est / superest

ORIGINAL OFFICIAL ENGLISH TEXT

The Councell hath considered the Thirtie-six Articles exhibited by your Lordships to their Commission^{rs} the 11/21 of February and have returned Answere thereunto in the following particulars.

1. To the first, That there shall be from henceforth betweene the Commonwealth of England and the United Provinces of the Lowe Countreys and the respective Countreys & Cittyes associated to them and under their obedience, and the people & Inhabitants of them respectively of what quality or Condition soever they bee, a good firme, sincere, infrangible & perpetuall peace, friendship, amitie & Correspondency, and a further & nearer allyance, Confœderacy and Union than hath formerly beene.

2. To the Second, That they shall be and remayne confœderated friends united and allyed for the defence and preservation of the liberty & freedome of the People of each other, And of mutuall Comerce, navigation & Common Interest by water or by land in manner as is hereunder declared & expressed, against all those who shall attempt or endeavour to disturbe either of the said States therein.

3. To the Third and Thirteenth, Wee agree as here propounded, that the Commonwealth of England & the people and Inhabitants thereof, And the said United Provinces and the Subjects & Inhabitants thereof of what quality or Condition soever they be, shall be bound to treat each other on both sides with all love, & friendship, That they may come by water or by land into each others Lands, Townes & Villages, walled or unwalled, fortified or unfortified, their Havens & all Dominions in England, Scotland & Ireland, and the said Low Countreys respectively, with freedome & securitie, and in them remayne

& sojourne as long as they please, and there without hindrance buy victualls for their necessary use. And may alsoe trade & traffique and have Commerce in any goods or Commodities they please, and the same bring in and carry out at their pleasure, paying alwayes the Customes that shall be setled, and saveing alwayes the Lawes & Ordinances of either Commonwealth respectively.

4. To what is propounded in the fourth, Wee Answere that Wee agree as followeth, That they the said Commonwealths of England, and of the United Provinces, shall [not] either secretly or openly doe, act or attempt any thing against each other, in any place by land or by water in the Havens or Rivers belonging to either of them, nor helpe, Councell, favour or countenance any act or acts of hostilitie, or wrong to be acted or executed, which may tend to the prejudice & damage of either party, nor shall suffer any thing to be acted or attempted as aforesaid, by any of the people or Inhabitants of either, or by any with in or under their power, or that any ayde, Councell, favour or furtherance be given to any by them, to the wrong or injurie of either State, or the people & Inhabitants thereof, but shall expressly and with effect contradict, gaynsay, [oppose] and really hinder the same.

5. To the matter of the fift & sixt, Wee agree as followeth in this fifth and the following Article That neither of the Commonwealths nor any of the people or Inhabitants thereof, nor any abideing or being with in their power, shall give any ayde, Councell or favour to the Enemyes or Rebells of either Commonwealth, And shall expressly really & with effect hinder, that noe ayde or assistance be given [by] any the people, Inhabitants, or any Resident with in the said Commonwealths respectively, to any such Enemyes or Rebells as aforesaid, by men, money, shipping, Amunition, Victualls or other Contraband goods by Sea or land. And in Case any thing be done contrary thereto, the said Ships and Contraband goods ahll be confiscate[d] to that Commonwealth respectively against

which they were provided contrary to the intent of this Article. And the persons that shall wittingly & willingly offend against this Article shall be declared Enemyes to both Commonwealths, and shall suffer the penaltyes of Treason with in the Commonwealth where the said offence is Committed.

6. That the two Commonwealths shall sincerely & truely assist each other as need shall require against the Enemyes & Rebells of each other at Sea & Land with men and ships in such proportion & manner and upon such Conditions as shall be hereafter mutually agreed upon, and as the exigency & constitution of each others affaires require. All which to be at the cost & expence of the partyes requiring the same.

7. To the Seventh, Wee agree, That if either the Commonwealth of England or the United Provinces of the Low Countreys shall hereafter make any Treaties of Amitie, Allyance or friendship with any other Commonwealths, Princes or States, the one shall comprehend the other, and his Dominions therein, if they will be soe comprehended.

8. To the Eight, We agree as here propounded, That in this Treaty shall be alsoe comprehended all the friends, Allyes & Confœderates of each other, who at the Confirmation of the same shall be nominated & agreed on, on both sides and will be comprehended therein.

9. To the Nineth, Wee offer for answere the Article following, That if it shall happen that dureing this Amitie, Confœderation & Allyance, Any thing shall be acted or attempted by any of the people of Inhabitants of either of the said Comonwealths, against this Treaty or any part there of either by land or Sea, or other waters, This Amitie, Confœderation & allyance between the Commonwealths shall not be thereby interrupted or broken off, but shall continue & remayne in its full & whole power, Onely in such Case those particular persons who have offended

against the said Treaty shall be punished and noe other. And that justice shall be done & satisfaction made to all persons concerned with in twelve moneths (after demand thereof made) upon all such persons who shall have done any thing against this Treaty by Land, Sea or other waters, in any part of Europe or any where with in the Streights of Gibralter, or in America, or upon the Coast of Affrique, or in any Lands, Islands, Seas, Creeks, Bayes, Rivers or any other places on this side the Cape of Goodhope, And in all places what soever as aforesaid beyond the said Cape with in eighteene moneths next after demand of justice shall soe as aforesaid be made. And in case the persons soe as aforesaid offending shall not appeare and submit himselfe to justice & make satisfaction with in the termes respectively here before limitted, The said persons shall be declared Enemyes to both Commonwealths, and their Estates, goods and effects whatsoever shall be confiscate[d] & employed to a due & full satisfaction for the wrongs by them done, and their persons be lyable to such further punishment when they shall come with in the power of either State, as the qualitie of their offense shall deserve.

10. That the People of the Commonwealth of England may freely unmolested & securely travell in & thorough the Countreys of the United Provinces by land or water to any parts in them or beyond them, and passe by any of their Townes, Guarrisons or Forts in any places with in the Netherlands whatsoever, to follow their traffique in all places there, as alsoe their factors & Servants, armed or unarmed, but if armed not above fourty men in a Company, as well without as with their goods & merchandize whither they please. And likewise the people & Inhabitants of the United Provinces of the Netherlands may enjoy the same liberties in all or any places with in England, Scotland or Ireland, they and either of them on each side observeing and conformeing in such their Trade & Traffique to the Lawes & Ordinances of each Commonwealth respectively.

11. For Answere to the Eleventh, Wee say, That the people of the Commonwealth of England, haveing beene alwayes strictly forbidden Trade in all plantations & places belonging to the people of the United Provinces that are not with in the Netherlands, Wee shall acquiesce therein, and shall therefore forbeare to sayle to or trade with any of their plantations abroad, And shall not interrupt or disturbe them in their sayling to them, And as for their tradeing to any of the English plantations it is forbidden by the late Act for encrease of the Navigation of this Nation, from which Wee thinke not fit to recede.

12. To the twelvth, Wee say, That the English were the first Planters of the Northern firme land of America and have plantations there from the Southermost part of Virginia, in thirtie seven degrees of north latitude to Newfoundland in fiftie two degrees, And not knowing of any plantations of the Netherlanders there, save a small number up in Hudsons River, Wee thinke it not necessary at present to settle the limits which may be done hereafter in convenient tyme.

13. This is answered in the third Article.

14. To the 14th Wee agree as followeth, That the Merchants, Masters, Pylots, or Marriners of either Commonwealth, their ships, goods, wares & Merchandize may not be seized or arrested in the Lands, Ports, Havens or Rivers of the other by vertue of generall or particular Commands for any warlike or other service, except upon inevitable necessitie, and upon just satisfaction for the same, provided that hereby shall not be excluded the Arrests & Seizures in the Ordinary way of Lawe and justice of each Commonwealth respectively.

15. To the fifteenth Wee agree as followeth, That the Peoples and Inhabitants of the said Commonwealth of England and of the United Provinces of the Netherlands tradeing as is expressed in the former Articles in the Lands of each other, shall not hereafter be bound to pay any

higher or more Customes, Taxes, imposts, Beakon money or other dutyes than according to such proportions as they now pay compared with the people of each.

16. To the 16th Wee agree, That the Merchants on both sides, their factors and servants as alsoe the Ship Masters & other Seafairing men, may as well, travelling & returning by ships over the Seas & other waters, as in the Havens of each other and goeing on shore, carry & use for the defence of themselves & their goods, all sorts of Armes for defence & offence, but being come therewith to their severall lodgings or Inns they shall lay downe their Armes there and soe leave them untill they goe againe to the ship or on board.

17. To the 17th Wee say, To the end there may be a nearer Union & Confœderacy betweene both Commonwealths then hath formerly beene, That any of the People Natives or Inhabitants of the United Provinces, or of any places with in the seventeene Provinces that are associated with them or under their jurisdiction (being of the reformed Religion) who shall transport themselves and families, and transferre their Estates into England may there freely dwell and inhabite, exercise trade & commerce, and may there alsoe purchase have & hold to themselves & their Heires, Lands, Tenements & hereditaments, and enjoy all such other freedome, priviledges & immunities of what kinde soever as any of the Native people of this Nation may or ought to enjoy by vertue of their birth, or by any Law, Custome or other right whatsoever, they in all things submitting themselves to the Lawes & Customes of this Nation as the Native people are bound to doe. And the like freedome & priviledge shall be had & enjoyed by any of the people of this Commonwealth in any of the Lands, Citties, Townes & other places in the United Provinces or any places of the Seventeene Provinces that are associated with them, or under their jurisdiction.

18. To the Eighteenth Wee say, That saveing & asserting

the right of this Commonwealth Wee shall be willing to proceed to such an agreement concerning the fishing as shall be found fit & reasonable.

19. To the Nineteenth, Wee agree in manner following. That for the greater freedome of Commerce & Navigation, the said Commonwealth of England, and the United Provinces of the Netherlands shall not receive into any of their Lands, Havens, Cittyes or Townes, or permit or suffer that any of the people or Inhabitants of each of them respectively, doe receive, keepe, harbour or give any assistance or releife unto any Pyratts or Sea rovers, But shall cause both the said Pyratts & Rovers, and alsoe their Receivers, Concealors and Assistants to be prosecuted, apprehended and condignely punished for terrour to others. And all ships goods & merchandizes by them pyrattically taken and brought into the ports of either State that shall be found in being (yea though they have beene sold) shall be restored to the right owners or made good unto them, or to such as have their Letters of Atturney or procuration to clayme the same, due proofe of the proprietie being first made in the Court of Admiralty according to Lawe.

20. To the twentieth, Wee agree in manner following, That all persons on either side that shall goe out to Sea upon particular Commissions shall be bound before they take out their Commissions, to put in good & sufficient securitie by responsible men, none of the Ships Company, before the Judges of the Court whence the said Commission is issued, that they shall observe the Instructions to be given them for their regulation in their execution of the said Commission.

21. That the Commonwealth of England will take such care for the guard of their Seas and defence of the freedome of Trade & Commerce therein as shall be fitt.

22. To the 22:th Wee say, That if any person shall within these Seas, trouble, hinder or unlawfully burthen any in the exercise of that freedome of Trade which belongs

of right unto them, This Commonwealth will use all meanes just & honourable to restore & preserve freedome to all lawfull Commerce in those Seas as aforesaid.

23. To the 23th Wee agree, That the men of Warre of either Commonwealth meeting or overtaking any Merchant Ship or Ships belonging to the other, or to the People or Inhabitants thereof, or to any of the Allyes comprehended in this Treaty holding both one Course, or goeing both one way, shall be bound so long as they keep one course together to take them under their protection, and to defend them against [each] and every one that shall attempt upon them.

24. To the 24th Wee agree, That if any ship or Ships of the People or Inhabitants of either Commonwealth, or of a Neuter shall be taken in the Havens of either [by] any third partie, being none of the people or Inhabitants of either Commonwealth, They in or from whose Havens or liberties the said Ships shall be taken, shall be bound together with the other partie to endeavour that the said taken Ship or Ships may be followed, brought backe & restored to the Owners, but all at the charges of the Proprietors or [of those] Interessed.

25. That if any Merchants ships of the people or Inhabitans of either Commonwealth shall by Tempest, pursuit of Pyratts or through any other force or accident be necessitated to come to harbour in the Land of either of the said Commonwealths, it shall be lawfull for them to depart againe freely at their pleasure with their ships & goods without paying any Customes or dutyes, provided they breake not bulke nor expose any thing to sale, nor that they shall be subject to any other molestation or search, provided they receive on board noe persons or goods nor Act any thing against the Lawes, Ordinances or Customes of the place where they shall be as aforesaid in harbour.

26. To the 26th Wee agree as followeth. That neither

party may come into or stay in the Havens of each other Country with men of Warre & Souldiers to a number which may cause apparent suspition without consent & leave first had & obteyned of those unto whom the said ports doe belong, unlesse they be driven soe to doe by tempest, [forced by] necessitie to avoyd the dangers of the Sea in which case they shall forthwith signifie the cause of their comeing in to the Governour, or chiefe Magistrate of the place, and shall stay there noe longer then they shall be allowed soe to doe by the Governour or chiefe Magistrate as aforesaid.

27.28. To the 27th and 28th Wee say, That the Men of Warre on either saide, not being in soe great number as to cause suspition as aforesaid, may come into the Roads, Havens & Rivers of either party, and there lye at Anchor, and saile out again without any trouble or hindrance, they regulating themselves according to the Lawes & Customes of the respective places, provided that the said Men of Warre on either side shall not bring into each others ports any Merchants goods, nor carry out any, nor ought else that is or shall be prohibited, or any persons of the People or Inhabitants of that Commonwealth in whose Ports they are, who shall not have a good passe for his transportation, and for prevention whereof they shall be subject to be searched in Port.

29. To the 29th Wee say, That all Commission bearers, or private men of Warre, of the one side or the other, shall have the same liberty for themselves & their prizes, and be under the same rule, as in the precedent article.

30. In place of your Thirtieth, Wee propound as followeth, That upon the taking of any Ships by the Men of Warre of either Commonwealth from the particular Enemyes of each which shall be judged prize, all goods and Merchandizes therein belonging to the people or Inhabitants of either Commonwealth shall be free, and upon proofe of the proprietie be delivered unto them. And all goods of the Enemyes of either Commonwealth found

in the Ships of the other, shall be good prizes, but the Ships shall be free, and have their freight allowed them for the said prize goods, and reasonable demurrage alsoe if there shall appeare cause.

31. To the 31.th Wee say, That neither the Commonwealth of England nor the United Provinces of the Netherlands shall not themselves give, nor suffer that by the People or the Inhabitants of either respectively, or by any other Neuters, any assistance be given to the Enemyes or Rebells of each respectively, by any provision of Armes or Amunition of what kinde soever or any Utensills or Materialls for Warre either by Sea or land, nor by any provisions of victualls whatsoever, but that all such provisions of the one kinde, or of the other, that shall be found upon any ship goeing to the Enemyes or Rebells of the one side or the other, shall be adjudged confiscate & prize to the Taker thereof, as alsoe the Ships upon which the same were borne, and all other goods then found laden aboard the said ships, upon due proofe made, that the same provisions of the one or the other kinde as aforesaid were goeing to the Rebells or Enemy as aforesaid.

32. To the 32.th Article, The Councell doe not thinke fit to consent.

33. That if the Ships of the one Commonwealth or the other, or the People or Inhabitants of either, whether they be Ships of Warre or of Merchandize shall either by storme or tempest, or any other accident whatsoever shall happen to be stranded or cast away upon the shores of the Lands belonging to the one or to the other Commonwealth, the said Ships with all their apparrell & furniture, and all the goods & Merchandizes therein that shall [be] brought or driven on shore shall be restored to the true Owners, they making their proprietie in the said ship or goods to appeare by due proofe upon oath with in the space of one whole yeare after the said Shipwracke in any Court that is or

shall be erected in either Commonwealth for marine Causes, the said Proprietors paying Salvage for the same to such as shall save and deposite them, and paying such charges as those persons have beene at, who have saved and preserved the same, And if any of the said Goods shall be perishable either in their owne nature, or by the accident of the wracke, they shall be sould by the Candle after publique Proclamation thereof, and the provenue to be payd to the proprietors as aforesaid. And all Officers and other people & Inhabitants of the one part or the other shall be bound in such Cases to give their best assistance for the preservation of the said wracked goods in Order to their restitution as aforesaid, and in Case of any Controversy ariseing betweene the People of the one part or the other, good & speedy justice shall be done without drawing the businesse out at length of any unnecessary formality of processe.

34. To the 34th Wee agree as followeth, That the Commissioners for search on both sides shall regulate themselves according to the Lawes of each Commonwealth respectively, and not levie or take more then they are allowed by their Commission or Instructions.

35. To the 35th Wee offer for an answere as followeth. That in case any wrong or injury [be done] by either Commonwealth, or by the people or Inhabitants thereof against the people or Inhabitants of the other either against the Articles of this Treaty or against [common] right, there shall yet noe letters of Represalls, Marque or Counter-Marque be granted by the one or the other Commonwealth, till first justice be sought in the Ordinary course of Law, and in case that justice be there refused or delayed, then that demand thereof be made from the supreame power of the Commonwealth whose people or Inhabitants have suffered wrong to that Commonwealth where justice is as aforesaid denyed or delayed or to [that] power as shall be by them appointed to receive such demands, that all such differences be composed amicably, or in the

Ordinary course of Law, But if there shall be yet delay and that justice be not done nor satisfaction given with in fiftie dayes after such demand made, that then Letters of Represall, Marque or Counter-Marque may be granted.

36. To the 36:th Article, The Councell doth not thinke fit to consent.

These things Wee have thought fit to exhibite to yo:r Excellencies upon those things you propounded in yo:r Paper of Thirtie six Articles, what remayns further to be offered on our part for Consumating the Treatie shall in convenient tyme be also exhibited to yo:r Excellencies.

Whitehall   Signed in the Name & by Order of the Councell of State appointed by Authority of Parlament.
P. Lisle presid.t

Textual Note: In the English text, MS. S.G. 8460, articles 5 and 6 are each numbered 6, and 28 serves for both 27 and 28. *Inhabitans* and other peculiar spellings follow that text.

The Letter of 16/26 April 1652: *Concilium Status postquam*

The official original English-language text, as assigned to Milton to be translated into Latin, and the official Latin translation, presumably completed by him, are here printed for the first time, from a damaged text in MS. S.G. 8460, no. 24, and from a transcript in MS. Aitzema 86, no. 24. Aitzema printed a somewhat variant version in *Historia Pacis*, page 776, with no indication of who might have done the Latin.

For discussion and attribution to Milton, see pages 37–39.

OFFICIAL LATIN TEXT

Excell^mi Domini
 Concilium Status postquam ab Excell^tiis V^ris schedulam accepisset, in qua multæ particulatim magni momenti res propositæ erant, quam mature in re tàm ardua fieri potuit, quantúm*que* per alia gravissima negotia licuit, per Commissarios suos responsum vobis reddidit, per quos etiam eodem tempore scriptum vobis exhibuit, in quo jus et satisfactio postulabatur, ijs in causis quæ sigillatim illic expositæ sunt, quæ*que* dignitatem et rationes hujus reipub: speciali quodam modo attingere videbantur.
 Hoc cum ante aliquot septimanas* factum nequedum ullum a vobis responsum redditum sit, Concilium nihilo minus Excell^tijs V^ris eo us*que* assentivit ut per suos Commissarios proxima septimana semel at*que* iterum petentibus colloquium dederit; expectans et ad ipsius chartam Ex^tum V^rum responsum, et V^rum, cum super ijs quæ a vobismetipsis proposita sunt, tum super nostris ad ea responsis jam pridem datis progressum. Verùm cum ex eorum colloquiorum relatione, necnon in illa charta cui subscriptum quinto et nono hujus Aprilis nostro stylo ab Ex^tijs V^ris est, nullam nostrarum postulationum prædictarum factam mentionem aut rationem habitam reperiamus, cum*que* instarent ipsæ Ex^tiæ V^ræ ut priusquam incœpta pergeretur tractatione, plena at*que* expressa articulorum explanatio fieret, qui ad illum Consummandam nostra ex parte afferrentur: pro responso ad illam.
 Excell^arum V^rarum recordatione dignum censemus, vos hic priores tractationem hanc petisse, cui assensit Parlamentum et in qua us*que* et processum est ut Ex^tiæ V^ræ Concilij Sensum et responsa jam habueritis ad ea singula quae fœderis ineundi vestra ex parte fundamenta esse voluistis; quin et paratos nos esse ijs de rebus vobiscum agere significatum est. Quibus animadversis, et quod illa posita

---

* Late Latin usage; classical is *hebdomas* (Lewis & Short, p. 1675).

a Concilio in responsionis fine ad triginta sex articulos clausula alia non est, quàm quæ in alijs omnibus tractationibus pro concessa tacitè habetur, quá*que* intelligimus vobis æ*que* ac nobis caveri posse, neque utrivis parti ullum ex ea incommodum existere, cui nulli articuli de quibus convenerit, rati erunt, nisi tractatio tota perficietur, nos uti*que* responsiones a Commissarijs nostris illa in re vobis jam datas approbamus at*que* hic rursus profitemur paratos nos esse, ijs singulis de rebus quæ a vobismetipsis proponuntur ad disceptationam debitam vobiscum progredi, haud æquum ducentes parti vel huic vel illi ad proponenda quævis alia, prout res at*que* occasio tulerit, viam præcludi.

Cúm*que* ea quæ tulimus postulata ad jus fás*que* pertineant, sínt*que* ejusmodi ut eorum consideratio cæteris rebus pro arbitrio proponendis meritò anteponenda sit, causæ nihil videmus, quamobrem ab expectando Excell[arum] V[rarum] ad illá responso discedere debeamus, adeo*que* illud etiam at*que* etiam requirimus.

Official Text in Original English

My Lords
The Councell having received your Ex^cies Paper of proposalls conteyning many particulars of weighty Consideration, did with as much expedition as the nature of the Businesse and their other great Affaires would permit, returne you an answer to the same by their Commissioners; By whom also at the same time they presented unto you a paper of Demands for Justice and Satisfaction in the severall Cases therin expressed relateing in a speciall manner to the Honour and Interest of this Common Wealth.

This being some weekes since, and noe answer from you returned to the said Demands; The Councell neverthelesse in compliance with your Ex^cies desires, gave your Ex^cies Meeting by their Commissioners twice the last weeke in expectation both of your Ex^cies Answering their Paper, and of your proceeding upon your owne proposals and our Answeres thereto given in soe long since. But by the Report of those Conferences, and the papers signed by your Ex^cies of the 5?^th & 9?^th of this instant Aprill, our stile, not finding any mention or notice taken of our said Demands, and it being insisted upon by your Excell^cies That before any further progresse in the Treaty now begun, a full and cleare expression should be made of the Articles which on our part should be offered for Consumation thereof. For Answer thereunto.

Wee think fit to remember your Ex^cies That this Treatie was first desired here by You and consented to by the Parlament and soe farre prosecuted as your Ex^cies have the Councells sence and Answer to all the particulars laied for the ground of a League on your part, and their Offer to debate with you thereupon; Which considered, and that the expression of the Councell in the close of their Answer to your 36. Articles is no more then what is tacitly implyed in all Treaties, and which Wee understand to be equallie reservable to you, as to our Selves, and noe inconvenience being thereby to either party to whom noe agreed Articles are to be concluding unlesse the whole Treaty be brought to effect. Wee well approve of the Answers touching that matter allready given you by our Commissioners, and doe hereby againe Declare our readines to proceed with you to a due discussion of the particulars propounded by your Selves not holding it reasonable to foreclose either Party from further Proposalls as occasion or emergencies may require.

And in respect the Demands Wee have made, are of Right and Justice, and in their owne nature deserving priority of consideration before any voluntary Proposalls, Wee see noe cause of receding from our expectation of your Ex^{cies} Answer thereunto and doe insist upon the same accordingly.

Whitehall
16th Aprill
1652

Signed in the Name, and by Order of the Councell of State appointed by Authority of Parlament
John Lisle President

The Letter of 27 April / 7 May 1652:
Postquam quæ ad nos

The official original English text, signed by Henry Rolle, in the ornamental hand of a Council scribe, and the unsigned official Latin translation in a less ornamental fair copy, are printed here from MS. S.G. 8460, no. 26, with marginal text deficiencies remedied from MS. Aitzema 86, no. 26.

MS. S.G. 8460 has *seperari*, corrected to *separari* in MS. Aitzema 86, which has other variants and errors.

For discussion and attribution of Latin text to Weckherlin, see pages 39–40.

Official Latin Text

Excellentissimi Domini

Postquam quæ ad nos à vobis 21 Aprilis stil. nostro accepimus, at*que* ijs persuasi nostrum ad vestras Ex^cias scriptum ultimum revisimus Nos planè nostrum, de libertate proponendi utrin*que* concessâ, ut et nostram vobiscum conferendi de vestris nobis communicatis particularibus voluntatem, déque nostrâ expectatione vestri responsi ad nostrum quæsitorum nostrorum scriptum, sensum exposuisse censemus adeoquidem ut haud necessarium nobis videatur, ut ullam aliam addamus expositionem, Sed potiùs dicto nostro responso inhæreamus. Quoniam tamen Ex^tiæ V^ræ dictum nostrum ultimum scriptum interpretari velle videntur, ac si V^rum responsum ad nostra postulata differre vellemus, donec vestrorum 36: Articulorum sit finita discussio, at*que* ac si istius considerationis prælatio respiceret tantùm ad id quod deinceps proponeretur, non autem quod jam ante fuit propositum, additis simul rationibus et vestris petitis cur eorum respectus postponendus sit, sive ab præsenti Tractatu dividendus: Nobis igitur ad quæcun*que* dubia, at*que* ulteriorem moram quæ inde possent oriri, amovenda, quæ sequuntur addenda esse fuit visum necessarium et requisitum.

Visâ imprimis et perlectâ Ex^tiarum V^rarum Commissione juxta mandatum Parlamenti, ad quod et ipsi scripsistis accepimus à vobis 36. Articulos. Accepimus etiam a nostratibus magnas querelas de injurijs ab incolis vestris huic genti illatis, quibus ipsum Parlamentum tenetur et honore et Justitiâ ut inde satisfiat; Nihilominus tamen ad omnia amovenda impedimenta, et ad fundamenta tractatus unâ cum Ex^ijs V^ris jacienda. Concilium Responsiones distinctas ad omnia vestra proposita praedicta, postulatorum nostrorum charta ipsas comitante, tradidit. In qua V^ris Ex^tijs exponebatur, Cum Justitia sola pacis et amicitia firmæ solidæ*que* Basis sit, Ideo impensum hujus Reipub: animum esse, ut istiusmodi constitueretur pax et amicitia conservaretur; Adeo*que* post plurimas querelas enarratas Justitiam à Vobis in primo loco super ipsis exigi quæ firmum futuræ sinceræ Concordiæ inter hanc Anglicam nostram et illam V^{ram} Rempublicam fundamentum esse queat.

Ex^{mi} Do^{mi} Concilium auctoritate et Postestate à vobis exhibitâ, fine proposito V^{ri} adventus, ad stabiliendum firmā pacem (quæ Justitiâ neglectâ nec obtineri ne*que* conservari potest) at*que* V^{ris} ipsorum actionibus post V^{rum} hanc in Nationem accessum, dum variarum ab V^{ris} Conterraneis ex Commissionibus hinc concessis captarum Navium restitutionem repetijstis, ad qua quidem ea tulistis responsa, quæ erant congrua et idonea probè consideratis non præsumere non potuit, V^{ras} Ex^{tias} jam pridem fuisse ad respondendum nostris propositionibus dispositas, vel ad minimum jam tandem ab Superioribus vestris, quos jam nunc vos informâsse, at*que* quos (sicuti additis) vobis nuperè aliquid præcepisse de alijs rebus expendiundis dicitis; de hoc etiam negotio sententiam suam vobis significâsse, id quod nondum sit factum, Non possumus quin in toto negotio nostrum sentiamus dispendium, dum videtur V^{ris} Ex^{tijs} saltem rogandi et recipiendi, non autem reddendi responsum nec satisfaciendi, in ijs quæ utrin*que* nobis possunt evenire differentijs esse concessum. Quem sanè ex V^{ra} parte defectum requirimus et expectabimus quanto eius et quidem penitus supplendum, ut tandem æquâ transactione ea tractatûs hujus fiat expeditio et conclusio, in quem V^{ræ} Ex^{ciæ} ipsæ (ut quidem verissimè) quam plurimorum oculos defixos esse confitentur.

Quod attinet ad gravissima et plurima petita de quibus V^{æ} Ex^{æ} nunc tandem faciunt mentionem nobis de ijs cognoscendis et æstimandis tum tempus futurum persuasum habemus ubi in scriptis tradita inspexerimus. Interim non observare non possumus, dum anno 1645 legati Dominorum Ordinum Generalium adfuerant résque non adeo magni momenti (de navibus quibusdam captis) postulabant, In quibus a Parlamento summum tulerunt respectum. Nullam tunc temporis eosdem Legatos graviorem conquerendi causam invenisse, ut videre licet ex Parlamenti Declaratione ejusdem anni, ad quam nos etiam referimus in dicto petitorum nostrorum scripto: Neque ad nostram contigit notitiam V.^as Ex.^as de ullius istius modi gravaminibus esse conquestas, ut aliquam hujus vestri adventus causam, dum tamen varia nostra de quibus ut satisfiat; jam quesivimus illis Legatis tum temporis a Parlamento proposita fuerunt, quibus us*que* deest satisfactio, sicuti prius a nobis dictum est, Quæ tamen sicuti et reliquæ injuriæ jam vobis expositæ sint adeo verè adeò*que*, anxiè hujus Reipub: Honorem Justitiam et interesse tangentes, ut jure mereantur, quæ omnium articulorum sive ex nostrâ sive ex vestrâ parte propositorum vel proponendorum considerationi anteferantur, quæ etiam in priori charta plena est Sententia nostra. Harum autem querelarum disquisitio quando responsionem vestram receperimus quantum videbitur necessarium considerari et definiri poterit, sicuti æquum et congruum videbitur; Nec tamen postponi tractatui ab eóve separari aut dividi, cujus quidem totius pars aliqua sunt.

D.^ni Ex.^mi, Perstat nobis sententia nullam pacem esse posse securam aut expectatione dignam, præter eam quæ cum justitia et æquitate sit conjuncta, At*que* Status et Respublicas sine fœderibus, non autem sine justitia subsistere posse. Nos igitur constanter (ut prius) vestrum ad postulata nostra responsum, At*que* ut Justitia fiat requirimus; Dum certi sumus Parlamentum Angliæ æquè ad faciendum ac ad petendum jus paratum fore. Et quandoquidem multum temporis jam est exactum in hoc Tractatu parando, parum autem adhuc profectum; ut studium vestræ Excellentiæ cum nostro, in eo expediendo, contribuere seriò velint expetimus et postulamus: Id quod ex nostrâ parte, et quidem ex Parlamenti decreto et jussu nobis observatur et observabitur. Sic igitur vestrum expectantes responsum, cum libertate utrin*que* concessâ et in superiori nostro scripto expressa, Declaramus, Nostrum V.^ris cum Ex.^tijs per Nostros Commissarios super

36. istos articulos conveniendi et colloquendi perstare semper animum promptum; Adeo*que* ex nostra parte de tempore in tempus progrediendi, ut videbitur fore ex usu utrius*que* partis, at*que* imprimis ut vera nostra voluntas ulterior innotescat; pro æqua et felice hujusce Tractatûs Conclusione ad utrius*que* Reipublicæ at*que* amicorum alterutrius quorum interest, commodum et utilitatem.

Textual Note: The spellings *negotio, negocio* appear in both MS. S.G. 8460 and MS. Aitzema 86.

Official Text in Original English

My Lords,

Haveing received yours of the 21th of this instant Aprill, our stile, and by occasion thereof taken a Review of our last Paper to your Excellcies Wee conceive Wee have therein clearly expressed our sence touching the reserved Libertie of proposeing applicable to either partie, our readines to conferre with you upon your owne particulars communicated to US, and our expectation of your answer to our Paper of Demands, soe as Wee find it, not necessary to make any other explanation thereof, but to adhere to what Wee have already represented, Yet because your Excies seeme to interpret our last paper as if thereby We respited your Answer to our Demands till the close of the discussion of your 36. Articles, and that the preference of the Consideration of it had only respect to what should be newly, and not to what had been proposed, adding withall your desires and Reasons for postposeing the regard of it, or separating the same from this present Treaty, Wee hold it requisite for rectifying of Mistakes and cutting off Delayes which may thereby be occasioned to represent as followeth.

That, this Councell by Direction from the Parlament upon your Addresse to them, haveing seene your Excies Commission, and afterwards received your 36. Articles, and haveing before them Complaints of a high Nature of Injuries done by those of yor Country to this Nation, wherein the Parlament is concerned in Honour & Justice to see fitting Satisfaction given, and yet willing to avoyd Delaies, and to joyne with your Excies in layeing a foundation for a Treaty, Did in Order thereto give in their distinct Answers to all your Proposalls, and accompany the tender thereof with their forementioned Paper of Demands: in which they tell your Excies That Justice being the foundation of a sure, & firme Peace & Amitie, It was the earnest desire of this Commonwealth to entertaine and keepe such a peace and Amitie, and therefore after the enumeration of divers Grievances, Demand from you Justice to be therein first done, as a good foundation for a future good Correspondencie betwixt Our & your Commonwealth.

My Lords, The Councell considering the Powers by you produced, the proposed end of your comeing hither, setling a firme peace (which can neither be attayned nor preserved where Justice is neglected) and your owne practice since your comeing in makeing severall demands for restitution and amends to some of your Country-Men touching Ships taken by Commissions from hence, Whereupon you received such Orders and Answers as were fitt, could not but suppose your Ex^cies quallified long agoe for giving our said Paper some answer; Or that at least by this time your Superiours to whom you now say you gave notice, and who as you alleadge gave you since some late Orders for other things would have Commissionated you for this allsoe; which not being yet done, Wee cannot but upon the whole be sensible of Our Disadvantage, your Ex^cies having, it seemes, a power to demand and Receive but not to give Answer and Satisfaction in the Differences which Occurre betwixt Us, a defect which on your part Wee expect and desire may be speedilie and thoroughly supplyed, as well for the more equall transacting, as expediting of the Treatie, Upon which, as your Ex^cies truly say, Soe many eyes are fixt.

As to the Numerous, and weighty Demands which your Ex^cies mention are to be presented on your Part, Wee conceive it wil be time enough to take an Estimate of them when Wee have them. In the meane while, Wee cannot but observe, That in the yeare 1645 The extraordinary Ambassadors of the Lords the States being here, and takeing occasion to insist upon some small matters touching Prizes wherein the Parlament shewed them full respect, found them noe important Cause of Complaint, as by the Parlaments Declaration of that yeare referred to in our said Paper of Demands appeareth; Nor have your Ex^cies to our Knowledge manifested any such Grievances to be any part of the cause of your comeing hither, whereas many of our particulars for which Wee have Demanded Reparation, were by the Parlament represented to the said Ambassadors in the yeare aforesaid which remayne yet unsatisfied as We have formerly alleadged, and those with the Rest of ye Wrongs laied before you, are of soe reall and tender a Concernment to this State in point of Honour, Interest, and Justice as deserving to be preferred to Consideration before any Voluntary Articles either on Our or your part propounded or to be propounded which is the full sence of our former Paper. The Adjusting of these Complaints soe farre as shall appeare needfull when answer shall be given to them may bee Considered and Concluded of as may be most proper and fit without postposing them unto or separateing them from the Treatie of which they are a part.

My Lords, We are of opinion, That noe peace can be secure, or worth the having, but what is Just & Honourable, and that without Leagues, States and Commonwealths may subsist, but not without Justice. Wee therefore insist as formerly upon your Answer to Our Demands, and that Right be done, and are assured that the Parlament of England will be as readie to doe Right as to Demand it; And in respect much time hath allready been spent in this Treaty, and soe small a progresse yet made, Wee desire your Ex^{cies} endeavours may concurre with Ours in expediting of the same, which on Our part by Direction of the Parlament is to be observed; And in expectation of your said Answer, and with Reservation of such Liberty to each Party as in Our former Paper is specified. Wee declare, that Wee are ready to give your Ex^{cies} Meeting & Conferrence by our Commissioners upon the 36. Articles, and to make such further proceedings on our part from time to time as may be requisite, and may further manifest Our very reall Inclinations to a faire and happy Conclusion of this Treaty for the good of both CommonWealths, and such other Friends of either of them as may be Concerned therein.

Whitehall

27 Aprill

1652

Signed in the Name & by Order
of the Councell
of State appointed by Authority
of Parlament
Hen: Rolle President

The Letter of 28 April / 8 May 1652:
Ut ulterius

This short note, taken from Bodleian MS. Rawl. A2, leaf 416, is written in English at the top of the sheet in one hand, with the Latin version below in other hand. Three corrections (*poterit, reservetur, declaretur*) appear in a third hand.

For discussion and attribution of the Latin to Weckherlin, see page 40.

Draft of Letter, English Text

Ffor the further satisfaction of yor Ex$^{cs}_{.}$ Desires conteyned in yor last paper, and for the prevention of any delay to the carrying on of this Treaty, the Councell have thought fit, to signify and propound unto yor Lord$^{ps}_{.}$, that in the progresse of this Treaty now begunn betwixt yor Ex^{cies} and this Comonwealth there be equal Liberty to this Councell and to yor Lord$^{ps}_{.}$ reserved and declared, to make such further propositions, and Demands, as either party shall thinke fitt untill the whole Treaty be transacted, and concluded, unlesse by mutuall consent it be hereafter otherwise Limited and declared.

Draft of Letter, Latin Text

Ut ulteriùs V.$^{arum}_{.}$ Excell. petitis, in nupero Vestro scripto expositis satisfiat, at*que* ut omnis procrastinatio, quæ huiusce Tractatus promotioni obstare poterit tollatur, Concilium æquum judicavit, ut V$^{ris}_{.}$ Excell. significaretur & proponeretur, Quòd in præsenti, qui jam inter V$^{as.}_{.}$ Ex$^{tias}_{.}$ at*que* hanc Angliæ Rempublicam est inceptu Tractatu, æqua & æqualis tum huic Concilio tum V$^{ris}_{.}$ Excell$^{tiis}_{.}$ reservetur & (quod jam fit) declaretur plena libertas, alias novas propositionibus & postulatis prioribus propositiones & postulata utrin*que* addendi, uti partium alterutri videbitur requisitum & idoneum, donec Totus Tractatus omninò absolvatur & concludatur, nisi pòst ex mutuo Consensu aliter provideatur & utrin*que* significetur.

The 1652 *Declaration* and the 1652 *Scriptum*

Reproduced here are the texts of two Wing tracts, the *Declaration* (Wing no. E 1511) and the *Scriptum* (Wing no. E 2285).

Mabbott and French, editing these publications for their 1938 edition, omitted large portions of the text, apparently misjudging these to be nonessential. Thereby they also denied readers the possibility of making a critical analysis of the text, language and style. Only when the complete texts were subjected to examination did the most significant items of evidence become apparent, particularly with regard to Milton's participation.

These items are reproduced by permission of The Huntington Library, San Marino, California, call nos. RB 57310 and RB 9558.

For discussion, see pages 45–46, 50, 52, 55, 56–67.

A

DECLARATION

OF THE

Parliament of the Commonwealth

OF

E N G L A N D,

Relating to the Affairs and Proceedings between this *Commonwealth* and the States General of the United Provinces of the *Low-Countreys*, and the present Differences occasioned on the STATES part.

And the ANSWER of the *Parliament* to Three PAPERS from the Ambassadors Extraordinary of the *States General*, upon occasion of the late Fight between the *Fleets*.

With a NARRATIVE of the late Engagement between the English and Holland FLEET.

As also

A *Collection* of the Proceedings in the Treaty between the Lord PAUW, Ambassador Extraordinary from the *States General* of the United-Provinces, and the Parliament of the Commonwealth of ENGLAND.

Friday the Ninth of *July*, 1652.

Ordered by the Parliament, That no person Whatsoever, Without particular License from the Parliament, do presume to Print the Declaration (Entituled, A Declaration of the Affairs and Proceedings between this Commonwealth and the States General, &c.) Nor any the Papers therewith printed, either than the Printer to the Parliament.

Hen: Scobell, Cleric. Parliamenti.

London, Printed by *John Field*, Printer to the Parliament of England, 1652.

---

(3)

A Declaration of the Parliament of the Commonwealth of England, Relating to the Affairs and Proceedings between this Commonwealth and the States General of the United Provinces of the Low-Countreys, and the present Differences, occasioned on the States part.

IF the Sufferings of the People of the United Provinces under the heavy yoke of their Oppressions, before their Deliverance from the same by the Mercy of God be remembered, and the Principles and Spirit which then acted in them, and the ready and constant Help which they have had in all times from this Nation, and that with no small Expence of English Blood and Treasure, the Returns which they have made towards this Commonwealth will hardly be believed.

It is not intended to be very particular in mentioning the state of the Affairs of this Commonwealth as it stood when oppressed by a Tyrant, they were necessitated to flie to Arms for Defence of their Lives and Estates; because in Parliament they did but assert and desire the setling of their Just and Native Liberties, wherein by so many wonders, in so many signal Battels, by such a Series of Providence in *England*, *Ireland* and *Scotland*, the Lord was pleased to bless a poor handful, who approved themselves faithful to that Cause.

Neither

A 2

Neither is that Endeavor to divide them in the memorable years of Forty eight, to be admitted, nor the great Preparations made against this Nation in the year One thousand six hundred and fifty, which necessitated their Proceedings in *Scotland*, being refused Satisfaction for forepast Wrongs; and denied Assurance of Peace from them, who had received the Declared Enemy of this Commonwealth from the *United Provinces*, where that mischievous Contrivement was hatched against *England*, and from whence their Enemies had much open and secret Assistance by the Interest of the Prince of *Orange* and others, even at a time when that Prince and his Adherents were contriving, as was most probable, to erect a Tyranny upon those Countreys, and to reduce them to their former Bondage, of which he missed but narrowly, especially in his Attempt upon *Amsterdam*, which things are better known there than here, and are not the purpose of this Declaration.

Neither is it pleasant to remember that cruel and bloody Business of *Amboyna* towards the English, for which no Satisfaction at all hath been given, though often demanded in that Case; and in others not unlike it.

But such was the Affection of this Nation towards the People of the United Provinces, and to the Establishment of Liberty, and the Advantages of Traffique and Strength to both; but above all, to the Advancement of the true Protestant Religion which both propagates, and which in humane probability would receive the greatest Growth by their Friendship; and observing in some of the Governors and People of those Coun-

Countreys an Affection to this Cause, and particularly expressed by them in their free Contribution for the poor Protestants in *Ireland*, that so soon as the Affairs here came by the Blessing of God to any consistency, the Parliament did send a Resident to the States General, who expresly refused to receive him, as themselves very well know.

The Affairs here being yet further prospered by the Almighty, and the Affliction and Judgement the same still in respect of their Neighbors, the Parliament sent again, and joyned with their Resident there another worthy Person Dr. *Dorislaus*, who were instructed and enabled to see if by any good means a right Understanding might be had; but one of these Publique Ministers, Dr. *Dorislaus*, being come upon this publique Imployment to the *Hague*, the place of Residence of the States General, was there most barbarously and openly Murthered; of whose Assassination the world will judge as of an Action most abhorred, against all Rules of National Intercourse, and even Humanity it self; and how little was done there to Attache the Murtherers whilest the business was fresh, or hath been done since; though often called upon from hence, they well know, and must be here remembred.

On the other side, the States having formerly sent their Ambassadors, the Lords, *Borele*, *Renswe* and *Jaunimint England*, in the name of the late Troubles, pretending all good Offices, which proved to be a Correspondence with the Enemy, and a means of Assisting them against those to whom they were sent; This, with Reproaches by them cast upon the Parliament, was the work of those Ambassadors, for which, they lyable

(6)

tyable soever by the practice of Nations they left themselves, yet not the least Incivility was offered to them, but their Demeanor made known to their Superiors, and Repairation desired, but none vouchsafed.

After these Passages, when it had pleased God to put a full End to the troublesom Affairs in *England*, not one Garison upon the firm Land Being in the Enemies hands, nor any Force on foot, but all reduced to Peace and Settlement, the Affairs of *Ireland* in a good condition, most of the Towns and Cities there in the Parliaments power, and their Affairs in *Scotland* not unprosperous, when there was much less cause to apply to the States, for any need the Parliament had of their Assistance, or if they should have looked upon themselves and their Neighbors, as other States use to do, yet still retaining the former Principles of Affection and Judgement of the great Concernment an Union between the two Commonwealths would be to the upholding of the Protestant Interest, so much designed upon by the Enemies thereof, and unto common good and Liberty.

The Parliament did send a solemn Embassy to the States General, the Ambassadors Enabled and Instructed to endeavor to compose former Differences, and to effect a firm and strict Union, as far as might be consistent with Reason and Justice, and the Honor of this Nation, and be for Mutual Good; Nay, they can say, That those Ambassadors from hence were Impowered to make such Tenders unto; and Agreement with the States, as would have demonstrated the Affection of this Commonwealth to the good of the people of the *United Provinces*, the same as to themselves.

How

(7)

How unheartily and dilatorily they were dealt with in relation to their Errand, whereby the Embassy was rendred of no effect; how unsafe (to say no more) they were in their Persons during their aboad in the Netherlands, what Indignities were offered to them and their Followers, and unpunished; and at whose Door the fault hereof doth lie, is too apparent. But these Endeavors for Friendship, by this delay and Averseness on the States part, becoming fruitless, the Honor of this Commonwealth in the Persons of their Ambassadors wounded, and their desires of Amity thus slighted, the Ambassadors were recalled home.

By this appears what hath been done to procure a firm League and Amity with the United Provinces, and what honest and sincere Endeavors have been on the Parliaments part to effect it, who in the mean time proceeding on to conflict with those Difficulties which Providence called them unto in *Scotland* and *Ireland*, and the same gracious hand of God which had gone along with them, having brought their Affairs in *Ireland* to so good a pass, as that little remained there to be done; and prospering the War in *Scotland* so, as that Countrey being in a maner quitted to them; and the Scotish Army under the Command of *Charls Stuart* Son of the late King, marching into *England*, was totally defeated at *Worcester*, and almost all of them killed or taken, except himself and some few others hardly escaping.

Then and not before, the States General thought fit to send an Embassy to this Commonwealth, which was received with such willingness and Affection, as might testifie for them, they stood fixed to their former Principles.

As

As the Treaty went on, having some reason to avoid Dilatoriness and to desire Certainty, when Positive Demands were pressed to the States Ambassadors, they were evaded in things not of the hardest Resolution, with Allegations of want of Power, though their Commission shewed no such Restraint: yet to obtain further Power, Returns must be made to their Superiors; and before Answers could be had, the Provincial States must be Assembled, which gave small grounds of any real amendment of a firm Peace and Amity.

During the time of Treaty also, whilst at the first their Ambassadors Debates seemed to seek no better Props then of Ingenuity and Reason, the Ambassadors of the States acquainted the Parliament, that one hundred and fifty Ships of War were intended to be set out by their Superiors, besides those of their Navy then abroad, and all these pretended for more security of the Sea, and conservation of the Trade and Navigation of the United Provinces, but not to offend *England*.

Whether this were done to Amuse the Parliament or to Denounce against them, is to the States best known, and the Grounds of those extraordinary and great Preparations, when they had no Enemy at all in these Seas.

To these things the Parliament made no other Answer, but quietly intended a Provision for their own just Defence, in case any should Invade them. Nevertheless, not altering their Resolutions more or less as to the things to be insisted upon or granted; having made Justice and Honor, and a mutual Good, in preservation and saving of each Rights to other, the rule to steer their Actions by, who were most willing to come to

to a happy Close of this Treaty, and were not, to their knowledges, wanting in any thing which might testifie their reality to finish the same.

In the mean time the States go on with their Preparations at Sea, appoint their several Rendezvouz of their Fleet tending to a Conjunction of all into one, under the Command of him whom they call Lieutenant Admiral *Trump*; what his Intentions or Instructions were, his own Deportment and some precedent Actions will demonstrate.

Particularly, when amongst others, one of their Ships being met by a Man of War under the command of Captain *Yong*, was in a friendly maner summoned to give the usual Respect to the Ships of War of this Nation, which another of his Company had done before, and which hath been accustomed not onely as a civility and respect, but a principal Testimony of the unquestionable Right of this Nation to the Dominion and Superiority of the adjacent Seas, acknowledged generally by all the Neighbor-States and Princes, and particularly by themselves and their Predecessors, besides many most authentique Records and other undeniable Proofs, together with a constant Practice in confirmation thereof: Yet he refused, affirming that if he did it, he should lose his Head.

Not long after this ensued that Action of *Trump*, the particulars whereof are set down in the *Narrative* herewith Printed; by which that Hostile and injurious Act appears to have been done against Neighbors in Amity, who have so often and earnestly desired and testified their willingness to firm and continue the same: and this also vailed with, and in the midst of

B

of a Treaty of Peace offered by themselves.

Accompanied also with such Arrogancy & Injustice, not onely to the denying of so unquestionable a Right, but usurping upon the same; and in prosecution of that Injury without any provocation, seeking out the ships of this Commonwealth in their own Seas, upon their own Coast, in their own Road, there falling upon them, beginning a War; and thus endeavoring the Destruction of their Men and Ships, even to the beating them out of the Sea, and utter subversion of their Naval Power and Trade of this Commonwealth, had not God by his goodness turned the shame thereof upon the heads of those who were the wrong Doers.

After this long patience of the Commonwealth of *England*, and after these high Injuries and Provocations thus forced upon them, the success at Sea nor answering Expectation, it pleased the States General to send another Ambassador Extraordinary to the Parliament; who, as the former Ambassadors a little before his coming had done, labored to excuse their Superiors from having any Intention, or giving any Instruction to Warrant this Dealing; which, notwithstanding the Preparations, the returning from another Course and seeking out the Parliaments ships in their own Roads, and there falling upon them without the least Provocation, as before is mentioned, was yet by the Ambassador called an Accident, and a thing done by meer Chance, the Action in the name of his Superiors utterly disclaimed, yet the Imployment and the Agent continued by them and reinforced.

And when the clear truth of this unworthy Fact, bearing in it self part of the Proof thereof, by the Fleet under the Command of *Trump*, coming purposely into the Road of *England* unto their Fleet; and the rest thereof being attested, not onely by many eye-witnesses, English men, but also by divers Officers, and others of the Netherlands taken in the Fight, who concur fully in the Testimony; yet a long and intricate way of Examination thereof is propounded, a Cessation of acts of Offence and Hostility in the mean time desired, and a new Proceeding upon the old long Treaty entred into by the former Ambassadors, that time being thus gained, an addition of strength might therewith be provided.

The Powers of this Ambassador being desired to be seen, none but his Credential Letters, and some Passes for his Transportation were produced; but no power to Treat and conclude with the Parliament, for which material Point he referred to the Powers of the former Ambassadors, who had Commission to Treat and conclude upon the former Negotiation, and owned this also; and although they came upon the general business of the Treaty of Alliance between the two Common-wealths, and the Lord *Pauw* came upon a particular Action done after that Treaty begun and proceeded in, yet such was the continued desire of the Parliament, if possible, to compose the said late Differences in a friendly way, that they proceeded to Treat with the Lord *Pauw*, waving the present Dispute upon his want of Powers.

And when nothing in Particular was tendred by the Ambassador, but the Generals before recited, and a Proposal, That the Parliament would make their Demands to him; they were contented, not insisting upon the

(12)

the disadvantage thereof, to make their Demands unto the Ambassador for satisfaction for Wrongs past, and security for the future, which are herewith likewise Printed; whereby it was put into the Hands of the Ambassador, to come to an Agreement upon the Demands of satisfactions to be by both Parties moderated and asserted, as was propounded to him in another Paper, and upon such Agreement for satisfaction (the Demand for security being left to after consideration) to have a Cessation of all Acts of Hostility and Offence as he desired, and the Parliament was thus willing to assent unto.

But instead of drawing towards any such Agreement, or endeavoring to come to Particulars therein as was offered, the Ambassador was not pleased at all to second or pursue his former earnest desire of a Cessation, though it were thus in his own Power to accomplish, but wholly declined the same; and for himself and the other Ambassadors, desired speedy Audience to take their leaves, and to depart into their own Countrey, being expressly commanded (as they affirmed) so to do; and in that they were not denyed any Respect or Accommodation, nor used, during their abode here, as the Publique Ministers of this Commonwealth had been in the *United Provinces*; and by this Departure, they were pleased to put a period both to the one and the other Treaty.

At their last Audience in Parliament, much was recited of the same matter contained in the former Papers; and as to that which they then urged concerning Acts of Hostility not looked for, neither at any time before declared; and that their ships (brought into the

(13)

Ports of *England*, and there detained of late against their thought; and before any Declaration of Hostility issued out, and whereof the Commanders are unaware and guiltless, having nor given the least, nor to no body occasion of Disputes) might be released; the Parliament therein need but refer to the Narrative by them published, and delivered to the Ambassadors of the Lords the States General, before the arrival of the Lord *Pauw*, and seen by him at his first coming.

And although that first Breach and high Injury done by *Trump* was on the Parliaments part altogether undeserved and unlooked for, yet after the same committed, a Prosecution against the Wrong, does could not in probability but be looked for from the Parties injured, to whom no Satisfaction hath yet been offered, unless the Parliament should quietly and tamely have laid themselves down at the feet of those who have thus endeavored the Ruine of them, and have betrayed into those hands the Rights and Safety of the People of this Nation, which few would have esteemed agreeable to the great Trust in them reposed.

By these Proceedings faithfully represented to the view of the World, it will be more then evident with what Affection and Constancy the Parliament have labored for the Friendship of the *United Provinces*: how carefully they avoided all Differences and Occasions of a War between the Nations, though all such Overtures of Amity and nearest Alliance have been rejected.

At last, when this Commonwealth was assaulted and invaded, their Ships torn, their Men slain, without the least colour of any Offence given; upon which Attempts and the Consequences thereof had the same

succeeded,

succeeded, not onely the Rights, Honor and Traffique, but even the very Being of this Commonwealth had been highly endangered; The Parliament held it their Duty, thus compelled and necessitated into a most unwelcome War begun upon them, to defend themselves, and whilest a just Satisfaction and Security cannot otherwise be had, To endeavor the gaining thereof by such ways and means wherewith the Lord shall enable them.

And herein, as the Parliament doth rest abundantly comforted in the Integrity of their own Proceeding, and faithful Discharge of their Duty, so they assure themselves that all indifferent persons will entertain this clear Testimony of the Justness of their Cause; for the issue whereof they depend not upon any Policy or strength of Man, but onely upon the Goodness and Assistance of that Righteous God who hath hitherto in so wonderful a maner appeared for them, and who never failed those that seek him, and with uprightness and sincerity of Heart attend upon him.

Hen: Scobell, Cleric. Parliamenti.

The A n s w e r *of the Parliament of the Commonwealth of* England, *to Three Papers presented to them by the Councel of State, from the Ambassadors Extraordinary of the Lords the States General of the United Provinces, upon occasion of the late Fight between the Fleets.*

THe Parliament of the Commonwealth of *England*, calling to minde with what continued Demonstrations of Friendship and sincere Affections, from the very beginning of their intestine Troubles they have proceeded towards the Neighbors of the United Provinces, omitting nothing on their part, that might conduce to a good Correspondence with them, and to a growing up into a more near and strict Union then formerly; Do finde themselves much surprized with the unsuitable Returns that have been made thereunto, and especially at the acts of Hostility lately committed in the very Roads of *England* upon the Fleet of this Commonwealth, the matter of Fact whereof stated in clear Proofs is hereunto annexed; Upon serious and deliberate consideration of all, and of the several Papers delivered in by your Excellencies to the Councel of State, the Parliament thinks fit to give this Answer to those Papers:

The Parliament, as they would be willing to make a charitable Construction of the Expressions used in the said Papers, endeavoring to represent the late Engagement of the Fleets to have hapned without the knowledge, and against the minde of your Superiors; So when they consider how disagreeable to that profession

sion the Resolutions and Actions of your State and their Ministers at Sea have been, even in the midst of a Treaty offered by themselves, and managed here by your Excellencies, the Extraordinary Preparations of One hundred and fifty sail of Men of War, without any visible occasion, but what doth now appear (a just ground of Jealousie in your own Judgements, when your Lordships pretended to excuse it) and the Instructions themselves given by your said Superiors to their Commanders at Sea, Do finde too much cause to believe, That the Lords the States General of the United Provinces have an Intention, by force to usurp the known Rights of *England* in the Seas, to destroy the Fleets that are, under God, their Walls and Bulwarks, and thereby expose this Commonwealth to Invasion at their pleasure, as by this late Action they have attempted to do: Whereupon the Parliament conceive they are obliged to endeavor, with Gods assistance, as they shall have opportunity, To seek Repairation of the Wrongs already suffered, and Security that the like be not attempted for the future.

Nevertheless, with this minde and desire, That all Differences betwixt the Nations may (if possibly) be peaceably and friendly composed, as God by his Providence shall open a way thereunto, and Circumstances shall be conducing to render such Endeavors less dilatory, and more effectual then those of this kinde heretofore used have been.

Hen: Scobell, Cleric. Parliamenti.

A Narrative of the late Engagement between the English Fleet under the Command of General Blake, and the Holland Fleet under the Command of Lieutenant Admiral Trump near Dover.

UPon Tuesday the Eighteenth of *May* 1652. in the morning, General *Blake* being gone to the Westward as far as *Rye* Bay eight days before with twelve or thirteen ships, leaving Major *Bourn* in the *Downs* with eight ships onely, there appeared upon the backside of the *Goodwin* a *Holland* Fleet of Men of War consisting of two and forty ships, one whereof had a Flag on the main-top-Mast head, the rest Jacks and Ancients; and being come unto the South-sands head, two of them bore up towards the English ships in the *Downs*, whereupon Major *Bourn* sent out the *Greyhound* to examine them, and to know the reason of their so near approach, who answering, That they had a Message to the Commander in chief in the *Downs*, were permitted to come in; and having saluted the Flag, the two Captains named *Tyson* and *Aldred* came Aboard the said Major *Bourn*, and acquainted him that they were sent by *Van Trump*, to let him know that he had been Riding about *Dunkirk* with his Fleet, where by reason of foul Weather they had lost many of their Cables and Anchors, and the wind being Northerly, were driven fur-

(18)

ther to the Southward then they intended, which *Van Trump* thought fit to signifie to prevent any misapprehensions or jealousies. And having said this, and received for Answer, That the Reality of what they said would best appear by their speedy drawing off from this Coast, they departed to their Fleet; and immediately upon their arrival with them, the whole Fleet stood up to *Dover*, and came to an Anchor within little more then shot of the Castle the same day in the afternoon. Upon their coming before *Dover* Castle; and Riding there with Flag in the Main-top, without saluting the Castle, the Castle made three shot at them; notwithstanding which, the Dutch Admiral kept up his Flag, and rode there at Anchor until the next day noon, and exercised his Musquetiers, by discharging Volleys of small shot many hours together. Upon Wednesday about twelve a clock the Dutch Fleet weighed Anchor and stood off towards *Calice* some four Leagues into the South-east; about the same time the English Fleet under General *Blake* coming from the West towards the *Downs* discovered them, and supposed by their course they had been going back; Major *Bourn* likewise was in sight, coming from the *Downs* to joyn with General *Blake*. About an hour or two after, the *Holland* Fleet altered their course, came back again, made all the Sail they could, and bore directly with General *Blake*, *Van Trump* the headmost with his Flag in the Main-top, and being come within shot, the General shot a Gun at his Main-top, and then two single shot more: whereupon *Trump* shot a single shot through the Generals Flag, and then immediately gave the first Broad-side and took in his Pendants, and hung out his Red Flag under

(19)

the *Holland* Colours, which was the signal on their part for the whole Fleet to ingage; and so the Fight began, which happened between four and five a clock in the afternoon, and continued until nine of the clock. In the Fight the English took two of the *Holland* Fleet, one whereof having six foot water in the Hold they left, taking the Captain and Officers aboard, the other being a Ship of thirty Guns. General *Blake* lay all night where the Fight began, or near thereabouts, and the *Holland* Fleet was espied about four Leagues distant towards the Coast of *France* next morning.

The truth of this Relation appears in the Letters of General *Blake*, Major *Bourn*, and others in the Action, by the Examinations of the Dutch Captains, and other Officers taken in the Fight; the Instructions given to the Dutch Captains and Commanders, and other Papers, all which are hereunto annexed.

And whereas *Van Trump*, in the account he gives of this Action, makes the occasion of his coming back upon the English Fleet, the guarding of some Merchant men richly laden from the *Streights*, which had been in fight with some of our Friggots; That action is set down in a Letter written by Captain *Yong* (hereunto also annexed) whereby the occasion, beginning and ending thereof is declared: And besides, those very Ships which he pretends to come to preserve or relieve, upon Saturday before had past by General *Blake*, and were gone to the Eastward.

G 2

(20)

A Collection of the Proceedings in the Treaty between the Lord Pauw, *Ambassador Extraordinary from the States General of the United Provinces, and the Parliament of the Commonwealth of* England.

The Lord Pauw's Speech at his Audience before the *Parliament*, the Eleventh of *June*, 1652.

Right Honorable,

THe Publique Testimonies and manifest Tokens of a sincere Benevolence, pure Love and true Friendship, which the Universal State and Subjects of the United Provinces have always shewed to the English People, and principally to the Parliament of the Commonwealth of *England*, now prosperously and happily Governing, are so notorious and known to the whole Christian World, that no body can doubt of it; much less of a true Faith and long used Observation of Friendship, of the States General of the United Provinces.

But, forasmuch as by reason of the Variety and Inconstancy of Worldly things, sometime happen those things which do dark the Exterior Face with Clouds, and are like to shew a Distraction of mindes: But when these things are prevented by time, and all Contrarieties taken away, they will serve more to conserve and confirm,

(21)

firm, then to dissolve the Bonds of mutual Friendship: Therefore it hath pleased the States General of the United Provinces, my Superiors, notwithstanding they doubt not of the singular Wisdom and Diligence of their Extraordinary Ambassadors here, staying about great and weighty Business, to send me in an extraordinary Embassage to the Parliament of the Commonwealth of *England*, To present clearly and sincerely their Wishes for the Publique Safety and happy Government thereof, with proffer of all their good Offices, as I, being so lately come from their Honorable Assembly, can testifie out of my certain knowledge, That nothing is more in their Hearts and Wishes, Then that not onely a firm and constant Friendship be Religiously kept between both States; but that it may daily grow, and by all means be consolidated, and nothing may happen which may break or any way disturb the Bars of mutual Safety, Profit and Friendship, between so Neigbor-Nations: And that therefore they have received with great astonishment and sorrow of Heart the News, of what, contrary to all expectation, hath lately happened between the Admirals of both Commonwealths. But forasmuch as this unlooked for and unexpected case might not onely raise new Troubles, but also give occasion of Suspition, as if the present Treaty for a mutual Alliance, and a straighter Corroboration of the old Friendship was not earnestly prosecuted, and therefore we should labor in vain to come to a happy end: My Superiors have not thought amiss, but rather convenient, even necessary, that at this time and upon this unhappy case fallen out, I should above the ordinary use and custom, and therefore

Declaration and Scriptum 207

(22)

fore superabundantly, (seeing that by reason of my Office I have been in all their Councils) reprefent openly and fincerely to the Parliament of the Commonwealth of *England*, all the Particulars which have happened, as well before as after that Fact, as they are come to their knowledge, to remove all things out of the way which might breed any grudge or breach of Friendship between both States, or caufe the leaft difturbance or delay to the Treaty.

Therefore, by virtue of the Credential Letters of the faid General States, and in their name I do Proteft and Declare to the Parliament of the Commonwealth of *England*, That they have never entertained in their thoughts, never acted, much lefs commanded any thing which might offend the Dignity of this Commonwealth, leffen the common Friendfhip and good Correfpondence which hath endured for fo many years, or under any pretence whatfoever fow any feed of Mifunderftanding; But rather that the faid States have intended with all their hearts, and endeavored by all their power, That the faid Friendfhip and Alliance might be perfected in the beft way; and fpeedily, and might be folemnly eftablifhed for ever for the Safety and Advantage of both Commonwealths. It is very true that a great Fleet hath been prepared in the Low-Countreys, but that the States General have by the continual Complaints of their Subjects been forced to confent to it, is alfo a thing moft certain and known; as alfo, that they have Ordered, That notice thereof fhould be given to the faid Parliament; which was done and fignified to no other intent, then that the Subjects of the United Provinces which had fuffered great Damages

(23)

mages at Sea, and loft feveral ships, fhould be fecured and protected by juft and ordinary means, and that no Wrong or Offence fhould be offered to any, much lefs to undertake any Difpute againft the Fleet and Ships of the fame Parliament, upon the Controverfies and Differences of the Sea. All which being done and performed in that maner, and neverthelefs being accidentally happened of both fides a great Debate and Controverfie between both Fleets, the States General have thought fit to acquaint the Parliament of *England*, with the Relation fent to them in writing by their Admiral, and approved and witneffed by their Captains and other faithful perfons, That the Admiral *Trump*, more by neceffity then other reafons, is come nigh the Fleet of this Commonwealth, and hath firft fent his civil Salutation to the Commander *Bourn*, and having afterwards met accidentally with the Admiral *Blake*, put out his Boat to fend fome Deputies unto him, and to Declare the Reafons of his coming, and befides that, commanded to take down his Flag; but when he faw, that he againft all expectation was unhappily falured by him with a Broad-fide, and thereupon he difcarged his Guns, not to offend but to defend himfelf; and that from thence by meer accident, rather then purpofely, was arifed a Fight amongft thofe Fleets, which by the Lords Bleffing fhortly after was ended: Which, forafmuch as it was begun by an unexpected Salutation, and not continued with earneftnefs by ours, nor done or committed by alienated mindes, or any Reafons known before, but by Chance; Therefore the States General do friendly defire, That the PARLIAMENT of the Commonwealth of

England

(24)

England will be pleased to believe and be perswaded, That nothing was done with a consulted purpose or forgoing command, but meerly by a casual chance, and perhaps by reason of the Fragility and Inconstance of the worldly things; and so much the more direct their Counsels and Commissions thither, That all Obstacles, Offences, and further Wrongs may with all speed be removed out the way and prohibited, as the States General on their part are prompt and ready to apply convenient Remedies. They judge that it concerneth much the whole Christian World, and principally the States of the Reformed Churches abroad, That those Misunderstandings do not grow greater between these Commonwealths, and that between Neighbors, partakers of the same Faith, should arise any Dissention which should disturb, interrupt the common and necessary Commerce, and give occasion, as well to their known as to their secret Enemies, to lay waits, or to draw into diverse parts those Commonwealths ready to be United in a common Alliance; and by such means removing from themselves the seat of Calamities and War, to bring (which God forbid) it to their own destruction: To prevent so great a danger, and that the evil may not spread further, I am commanded by times to propound, and do all my best, That by convenient means there may be a speedy Composure made of what is past, and that there may be Order taken, That hereafter such unlucky and unhappy Cases happen no more between the Fleets of both Commonwealths, wherein they desire, the Dignity and the Honor of the Parliament of the Commonwealth of *England* may be conserved.

Whereas

(25)

Whereas then the States General do herewith openly Declare to the said Parliament, That they desire intirely, That all offices of Friendship and Benevolence may be continued, the contrary may be prevented, and that the Counsels of all sides may be directed to the desired End and Conclusion of the mutual Confederacy; therefore, I do earnestly intreat, That it may please the said Parliament to hear and understand me without any delay, by their Deputies or Council of State, and proceed without intermission in the just and amicable former Transactions, to bring the principal Business to an end and conclusion, as the Extraordinary Ambassadors of the States have Charge and are ready to do.

In the same time I do return my Thanks for the singular favor done to my Lord *Newport*, in granting him some days ago one of the Parliaments ships for his return into the *Low-Countreys*; and the said Lord being a Member of the States of *Holland* and *West-Friesland*, I am charged to desire him to stay here, to communicate Counsels and return with me, which I hope will not be displeasing to the Parliament, to whose Benevolence I with all Respect recommend me and all my Offices.

D   A Transf-

Declaration and Scriptum

(26)

A Translation of the Letters Credential to the Lord PAUW.

The States General of the United Provinces *of the Low-Countreys;*

WHereas we have found convenient, even very necessary, in the present Condition of the Affairs in *Europe*, to send to the Parliament of the Commonwealth of *England*, the Lord *Adrian Pauw* Knight, Lord of *Heemstede, Hogersmilde, Rietwijck* and *Nieuwerkerk,* Councellor Pensionary of *Holland* and *West-Frieszland*, and Ordinary Deputy in our Assembly, from the said Province, as Our Extraordinary Ambassador, having made election of his person, as of one, of which, for his rare Qualities and long Experience, we make a high esteem, and have a great confidence; being well acquainted with our good and sincere Intentions, which have no other Aim, then the Maintaining, Increasing, Confirming and Strengthning more and more the good Amity, Correspondence and Alliance between both Nations and States, grounded upon common Interests of Religion, of State and Commerce; having such confidence of his Ability, Prudence, Fidelity and Diligence, that we do refer our selves to him to express them *vivâ voce*, to the said Parliament of the Commonwealth of *England,* and chiefly, the Zeal that we do continue to have for all what may concern the common Good and Security of both Nations: Wherefore we intreat with earnestness and with all our Affection, the said Parliament of the Com-

(27)

Commonwealth of *England* by these Presents, That they be pleased to give a favorable Audience to the said Our Extraordinary Ambassador, and to give him absolute Credence as to Our selves, in all that he shall say and propound of Our part in this present condition of the Affairs of both Commonwealths.

Done at the *Hague* in *Holland*, the Fourteenth of *June*, One thousand six hundred fifty two.

To the Parliament of the Commonwealth of ENGLAND.

Friday the 11th of *June*, 1652.

Mr. Speaker by way of Report acquaints the Parliament with what was delivered by the Lord Pauw, *Ambassador Extraordinary from the Lords the States General of the* United Provinces, *at his Audience in the House this day, and presented the Paper delivered in by the said Lord Ambassador Extraordinary, and the Translate thereof in English, which was this day read.*

Ordered by the Parliament,

That these Papers be referred to the Council of State; And that it be likewise referred to the said Council, to hear what the said Lord Ambassador Extraordinary hath further to say, and to Treat with him, they holding close to the former Answers and Declarations the Parliament hath made, and report it to the Parliament with all speed.

Hen: Scobell, Clerc. Parliamenti.

D 2 *The*

The Lord Pauw's Speech at his Audience in the Councel of State.

Right Honorable,

Whereas it hath pleased my Lords the States General of the United Provinces to send me, besides their Extraordinary Ambassadors, in the same quality, to the Parliament of the Commonwealth of *England*, and having yesterday had the Honor to Declare in their full Assembly the true subject of my coming, and the sincere Intentions of my Superiors: Therefore, I think it to be my duty to appear likewise before this Honorable Councel to present my Credential Letters, and with your Honors all felicity and good success in the direction and managing of so great Affairs as are to them committed by this great Commonwealth. And as I have Declared unto the said Parliament, so do I likewise Declare again with truth and certain knowledge, That my Lords the States General have always had, and have at this present more then at any time before, a very great desire to maintain, increase, and keep faithful the good Friendship, straight Alliance, and perfect Correspondence which hath so long endured between both Nations and States, whereof there hath been heretofore many notorious and manifest testimonies: It is most constant, That my Superiors have nothing more in their hearts, then to see a finishing and conclusion of the Treaty of Alliance between both Commonwealths, to the end, That there by a straighter Union and brotherly Concord may be established

established, to subvert and destroy all Plots and Divisions which would trouble and much endanger the one and the other, as also make them less considerable to the Christian world. This is (my Lords) the very aim of the Enemies of the Reformed and Orthodox Religion, making a certain account, That they will be able by such a Disagreement and Division, not onely to weaken both States, but to bring them also to the utmost extremities. But both People being blessed by the Lord with that precious gift of the true Religion, and wonderfully provided, besides the Spiritual, with Temporal Benedictions, by the benefit of Navigation and Commerce in all parts of the World : and my Lords the States General, judging that the first ought necessarily to be conserved, and the other be looked to, the Religion maintained, and the State secured, did believe, That all those Inconveniences can be no better prevented, then by joyning the Souls and Goods of both Commonwealths, and by this means make them able, with Gods assistance, to shun all Mischinations to the contrary. Therefore, the unexpected news of the meeting of the two Fleets, and the Offences given of both sides hath brought no small Trouble amongst the General States, who have thereupon judged most necessary to dispatch extraordinarily and speedily to inform the Parliament of the Commonwealth of *England*, and this Honorable Councel, and to perform such Endeavors, made choice of me that have been admitted in both Assemblies of the States General and of those of *Holland* and *West Friezland*, and acquainted with their most important and most secret Councels and Deliberations, to witness here with most certain knowledge

Declaration and Scriptum   211

(30)

...nowledge of the matter, and no less truth and faithfulness, That no Deliberation was made, no Resolution taken, no Commission directly or indirectly given to displease in any ways the Commonwealth of *England* to offend them, and much less to set upon their Fleet or Ships; but that on the contrary, there was Command given to deal with them in all places as with the best Friends, and to shew them all kinde of Favor and Courtesie. And as in the said unhappy meeting things have been on both sides otherwise, and very unwarily acted, whereof I made yesterday a large Relation, which I do not intend to mention again at this present, nor to revive that which ought to be buried and entirely forgotten: Notwithstanding, having understood out of the last Answer delivered to our Ambassadors, that there is a Satisfaction demanded for what is past, and Security for the future: And my Lords the States conceive it to be necessary, That all Mis-understanding and Mis-construction of what is lately passed in the said Encounter may be taken away, and both States secured from the like Inconveniences hereafter; As also, that it be proceeded without delay in the continuating and perfecting the Treaty of Alliance so far advanced already: And moreover, That it be considered of the most convenient and reasonable Means which may remove the shadows of all Suspition and Mistrust; and that such Orders be made which the Fleets shall be bound to follow hereafter; to which purpose I have sufficient Instructions from my Superiors. I desire therefore that it may please Your Honors to commit some of the Members of this Honorable Counsel, with whom I may, as soon as is possible, begin, continue and finish

(31)

finish that which may serve to the satisfaction of both States, and removing of all Differences: To which I must adde here, That my Superiors did never pretend nor shall pretend to dispute the Honor and Dignity of this Commonwealth, which they repute the First and most considerable in *Europe*; and with that by an Union of these two formidable States, they might secure them both, preserve them from the Conspirations of their Enemies, and settle by a perfect Intelligence and Confidence their common Peace and Safety. In the mean time I pray your Honors, That it may please you by your wise direction, to order as speedily as is possible, that the evil may not by reason of this unhappy accident proceed any further, by committing new Offences, pursuits, or taking of Ships, but that all Attempts and such Actions may be interdicted and stopped, and not by making the wound wider, even uncurable, to expose our selves to the will and pleasure of our Enemies; being confident, that we shall be able to finde convenient Remedies to remove friendly and happily the present Differences, to the Confusion of those who wish and expect it otherwise. I shall be exceedingly beholden to this Honorable Council, if your Honors grant me a speedy Answer upon these, that I may without intermission begin so Worthy, Profitable and Necessary work; commending my self in the mean time with all Respects to your Honors Favor.

Pronounced in the Councel of State of the Parliament of the Commonwealth of *England*, the 22 of *June*, 1652.

Monday

(32)

Monday the 14th of June, 1652.

At the Council of State at *White Hall.*

IN pursuance of an Order of Parliament of the 11th of June, 1652 The Councel hath appointed the Lord Commissioner Whitlock, Lord Commissioner Lisle, Lord Vißcount Lisle, Lord Chief Justice St. John, *Mr.* Bond, *Mr.* Scot, Colonel Purefoy, Sir Henry Vane, Sir William Masham, Colonel Martin and Colonel Morley, or any three or more of them to the Commissioners, to meet with the Lord Pauw, Extraordinary Ambassador to the Parliament of the Commonwealth of England, from the States General of the United Provinces, to receive from his Excellency such Overtures as he shall please to make in writing, and to Confer and Treat with him thereupon, and make report thereof to the Councel; and that they do meet with the said Lord Ambassador Extraordinary, at Four of the Clock this Afternoon in the usual place for the purpose aforesaid, and so from time to time as there shall be occasion : And that Sir Oliver Fleming Knight, Master of the Ceremonies, do signifie the same unto his Lordship, and attend him to the place appointed.

Ex: *Jo:* Thurloe Clerk of the Councel.

Monday

(38)

Monday 24. June, 1652.

At the Council of State at *White-Hall.*

Ordered,

THat the Commissioners appointed to Treat with the Lord Pauw, Extraordinary Ambassador of the United Provinces, Do demand of the said Lord Ambassador, a sight of the Powers & Authorities given to him by his Superiors to treat and conclude upon such matters and things as he hath to offer and acquaint him, That the Parliament Desires, That all speed and expedition may be used on his Excellencies part in this present Treaty desired by himself, assuring his Lordship, That nothing shall be wanting on the part of the Councel of State which may be any ways conducing to bring the same to a speedy issue.

Ex: *Jo:* Thurloe, Clerk of the Councel.

A Summary of what the Lord Adrian Pauw, Extraordinary Ambassador of the States General of the United Provinces of the Low Countries, hath propounded to the Deputies of the Honorable Councel of State of the Parliament of England, the 11 of June, 1652.

THe said Lord Ambassador having heretofore abundantly Declared, That the States General (as it
E   will

(34)

will be found and always appear) have no ways deliberated, neither in publique nor in private, much less given any Charge, Order or Commission for committing the least Offence against the Parliament of the Commonwealth of *England*, their Fleets, Ships, Officers or Subjects, but rather they should be met with the usual Civilities and Kindnesses, and with the ordinary Expressions of Friendship; therefore none can any wise call into question their sincere Intentions for the maintaining and increasing of the ancient and common Amity.

For the same reason, That cannot be imputed to the said States General which hapned lately between both Fleets, nor any cause thence arise any Discontent or Offence, nor any cause of attempting against their subjects, being a thing directly contrary to the ancient Friendship and Correspondence between both Nations: And the said Encounter having hapned by meer Chance and without any design, the said Lord Ambassador hath propounded, Whether it were not better to lay aside that which is passed, in so much that it should be taken of both sides as a thing not done, and so all be left as before; and that there might a speedy order be taken for the redress of what hath been done since, in such sort, as no External not Internal mark may remain of the same.

Nevertheless, if the pleasure of this Honorable Council is otherwise, although the said Ambassador hath plainly and sincerely related all which is come to the knowledge of his Superiors concerning what is passed, having received (as also the other Ambassadors) besides the former Informations, before his departing, several

(35)

several remarkable and considerable Attestations *in probantis formis*, and hath heard that there are here quite other and contrary Informations, whence it doth appear, That the parties are disagreeing in their Evidences; and so it is a hard matter to judge clearly of the Fact.

The said Ambassador therefore hath thought fit to propound, That the things passed should be more exactly examined, and necessary Informations made by either of the parties, or conjunctim by both; that after certain knowledge gotten, the truth may be discovered by Commissioners specially deputed of both sides upon this matter, to know which of the two hath made the first attempt, and given cause to the following Disorders.

The said Ambassador doth Declare, That if it may appear that the Admiral of the States General hath made the first Assault, he shall not onely be disowned in the like case, and his Fact disapproved of by the said States General, as having transgressed against their Orders and Commission, but they shall also cause him to be punished for the same, according to the importance of his Attempt, for having disobeyed their Commands, and chiefly for having given just cause of Offence to their good Friends and Neighbors: desiring also of this Honorable Council, that if on the contrary it be found true by the Informations, That the Admiral of the Commonwealth of *England* hath given occasion to the said Encounter, and hath the first Assaulted, it be likewise Declared, That the Parliament will in that case disown the said Admiral, and command the same punishment to be put upon him.

E 2   k

(36)

It is to be believed, That the sincere Intentions of the States General will not onely appear, and all suspitions be taken away, but that the means of a just Reparation and necessary satisfaction will be easily found, other States and Commonwealths having taken the same course and followed the same method with good success, whereof the Lord Ambassador hath produced divers examples.

And to the end that the like Inconveniences may no more happen hereafter, the Lord Ambassador hath Declared, That the States General have never had the least intention, nor have yet any at this time, to lessen in no ways the Honor and Dignity of the Parliament of the Commonwealth of *England*; but that they have given command heretofore, as also since the late unhappy Accident, new Order, That upon meetings and salutings of the Fleets or Ships of War, concerning the striking down of the Flag, and what belong to it, there should be the same Honor done to the Parliament of the Commonwealth of *England* as was formerly done during the other Government, hoping by this means to give and receive contain reciprocally.

And as it is most necessary to confirm the mutual Friendship between both Nations, That the negotiation of the Treaty between both Commonwealths be advanced and brought to an end as soon as can be; the said Lord Ambassador hath represented and earnestly desired, That since the Lords Extraordinary Ambassadors have after divers Conferences, by their last Remonstrance, manifested their Superiors Intention concerning the said Treaty, it should also please the Honorable Council to express and signifie theirs clearly, that

it

(37)

it may appear what Differences are yet to be reconciled, that all Difficulties may be removed, to come the soonner to a good, firm and lasting Conclusion, by which the mindes may be on both sides pacified, and an everlasting and undissoluble good Intelligence established. Moreover, the said Ambassador hath instantly desired, That all ways of Fact and Offences be inhibited and stopped by Order of the Honorable Council, and chiefly, That the Persons, Ships and Goods of the Subjects of the United Provinces, as well Military as others, be indifferently freed and released from their Restraint and Detention, and all that have been or are by Force detained, be set at Liberty; and that the Innocents may receive no more hurt or trouble, as we are ready and resolved to do the same of our part.

The said Lord Ambassador hath also desired it may please the said Honorable Council to make known to him, without loss of time, their good Intentions and Resolution upon what is abovesaid, and chiefly upon the Continuation of the Treaty begun, the Cessation of all ways of Fact upon the relaxation of the Ships detained and arrested persons and goods of the Subjects of the United Provinces, seeing it hath lost no time to Declare sincerely from his Superiors, and assure the said Honorable Council of the continuation of their good Affection and perfect Friendship.

At

(38)

14th of June, 1652.

At the Councel of State at White-Hall.

THat the Commissioners appointed to Treat with the Lord Pauw, Extraordinary Ambassador from the United Provinces, do insist upon a sight of his Authorities before they proceed to this Treaty.

A Paper from the Lord Pauw the 15th of June, 1652.

To the Right Honorable, The Councel of State of the Cr--mmonwealth of England.

THe Extraordinary Ambassador of the States General of the United Provinces having had the Honor to come twice in Conference with your Honors Commissioners, and there to propound several things concerning the quality he cometh in, and the re-establishing the good Friendship and perfect Intelligence of both Nations, intreated this Honorable Councel, That it may please your Honors to consider what the said Commissioners shall Report, that he may receive a speedy and favorable Answer, as also be excused for making so much instance, seeing that he is forced to it by the conjuncture of such pressing Affairs, and for timely preventing of the inconveniencs which might follow.

Where-

(39)

Whereupon a Conference being had, the Lord Pauw, to manifest his Powers to Treat and conclude, insisted on his Credentials and three Passes granted to him, the Copies whereof were by him delivered in, and are as followeth:

The States General of the United Netherlands, To all those that shall hear these Presents read, or see, Greeting;

KNow ye, That we do expedite several Affairs of Importance, found good to dispatch into *England* the Lord *Adrian Pauw* Knight, Lord of *Heemsted, Hogersmilde, Ritwick, Nenkerk,* Counsellor Pensioner of *Holland* and *West-Friesland,* Deputy Ordinary of the said Provinces to our Assembly, and for this present our Extraordinary Ambassador; Therefore we do herewith Command and Require all Lieutenants, Admirals, Vice-Admirals, Commanders and Captains of the Ships of War of these Countreys hereunto Ordained, or by his Excellency to be Ordained and Commanded, That they shall in their respective Ships Receive and Transport the Baggage of the said Lord of *Heemsted* into *England,* and to do therein all what our said Extraordinary Ambassador of them shall require, Accommodating him during his said Passage in their said Ships, and Respecting him according to their duty: And having landed our said Lord Extraordinary Ambassador with his Train and Goods in *England,* to do and perform further what they already may be commanded, or may yet be willed, as shall be required at the hands of those that it concerns, Of all which the said

Lieute-

(40)

Lieutenant, Admirals, Vice-Admirals, Commanders and Captains shall not fail, under pain to incur our highest Indignation.

Done in the *Hague* under Our Seal Paraphure, and the Signiture of our Clerk, this 14th *June*, 1652.

Signed, *BOUCHORST*.

By the Order of the High Lords, the States General,

Signed, *B. RUYSCH*.

The States General of the United Low-Countreys, To all those that shall see or hear the reading of these, Greeting;

Know ye, That having found good, for the dispatch of Affairs of Importance, to dispatch into *England* the Lord *Adrian Pauw* Knight, Lord of *Heemstied, Hogersmilde, Ritwick, Niewkerk,* and Councellor Pensioner of *Holland* and *West-Friesland*, Deputy Ordinary of the said Provinces in our Assembly, going in an Extraordinary Embassy, We therefore Will and Command; thereupon all Lieutenants, Admirals, Vice-Admirals, Commanders and Captains of the Ships of War of these Countreys, That they take in and Transport the Baggage and Goods of the said Lord our Ambassador Extraordinary, in their respective Ships, and Transport the same over into *England*, in maner as the said Lord Extraordinary Ambassador shall desire to Transport, and as his Lordship shall command and desire;

(41)

fire; Accommodating also his Lordship on ship-board and using all Respect to the said Extraordinary Ambassador, his Train and Baggage; and having landed them in *England*, to do further as they shall be commanded, or already are commanded; or may yet be commanded, as appertaineth to all that it concerneth of all the said Lieutenants, Vice-Admirals, Commanders and Captains which shall not perform their Duty, shall be punished according to our highest Indignation.

Given in the *Hague* under our Catchet or Seal Paraphure and sign of our Clerk on the Fourteenth day of *June*, 1652.

Signed, *BOUCHORST*.

By the Order of the said High and Mighty Lords States General,

Signed, *B. RUYSCH*.

The General States of the United Provinces of the Low-Countreys, To all that shall see these Presents, Greetings,

Whereas, for the common good of Christendom, and for the advancement of Affairs of great Confideration, Importance and Consequence, we have found good to send towards the Parliament of the Commonwealth of *England* the Lord *Adrian Pauw* Knight, Lord of *Hemsted, Hogersmild, Rietwick, Nieuwerkirk,* &c. Councellor Pensioner of *Holland* and *West-Freizland*, Deputy in Ordinary from this Province in

(42)

in our Assembly, in quality of our Extraordinary Ambassador, requiring all Lieutenants, Governors, Chiefs, Colonels, Captains, and Men of War, Guards of Bridges, Ports and Passages, all places; and besides, all other Justices, Officers and Subjects of the said Commonwealth of *England*, to suffer him with his Train, Servants, Followers, Goods and Baggage, to go, pass and repass freely, and without trouble both by water and land, without doing him, or giving him, and suffering to be given him, made or done, any trouble, hindrance or disturbance: But rather, all aid, help, favor and assistance necessary and requisite, and that we would acknowledge the same most willingly in time and place.

Given at the *Hague* in our Assembly under our Seal: Paraphure and signing of our Clerk, the Fourteenth of *June*, 1652.

Was Marked *A. BOUCHORST.*

And lower it was Written.

B. RUTSCH.

By Order of the States General was Signed,

With the Signet of the said General States in Red Wax.

Tuesday

(43)

Tuesday the 15th of June, 1652.

At the Council of State at *White-Hall.*

Ordered,

THat Report be made to the Parliament of what the Counsel have Ordered and Directed touching the Conference with the Lord Pauw, Extraordinary Ambassador from the Lords the States General, and of the Papers by him delivered to the Commissioners of the Counsel, That by these Papers it is not appearing to the Counsel that the said Ambassador hath any power to Treat or Conclude, The Counsel have thought fit humbly to present and submit the whole to the Consideration of the Parliaments for their Judgement thereupon.

Translation of the Letter of the Lord Pauw to the Lord President of the Council of State.

My Lords,

HAving communicated to my Lords the Ambassadors Extraordinary of the *United Provinces* to the Parliament of the Commonwealth of *England*, what passed in my Audience and Conference with the Commissioners of the Council of State, and having shewed unto them the Instructions and Orders of my Superiors, they have thought fit to address the inclosed Paper to my Lords of the said Council of State: But for as much as Sir *Oliver Fleming* Master of the

(44)

Ceremonies hath signified unto me, That their Excellencies had thought fit to make a Report of the whole Businesse to the Parliament this morning, I judged it convenient to intreat your Excellency, That the said Paper may be put into the hands of the Reporter, to be communicated (as well as the other Propositions and Papers) to my Lords of the Parliament : Praying God (my Lord) to blesse these Affairs for his Glory and the Prosperity of both Nations, I will remain ever

The 1/16 *June*, 1652.

Your Excellencies most humble Servant,

ADRIAN PAUW.

For my Lord the Earl of Pembroke and Montgomery, President of the Councel of State of the Commonwealth of England.

The Paper of the Three Extraordinary Ambassadors, mentioned in the former Letter.

MY LORDS,

THe Lord *Adrian Pauw*, Lord of *Heemsted*, Ambassador Extraordinary of the *United Provinces* of the Low-Countreys, having communicated to us what passed at the Conferences with the Commissioners; And having shewed unto us his Instructions, and all the Orders of the Lords States General of the said *United Provinces*, We would not omit to assure your Ex-

(45)

cellencies, that we have found the whole in as good Form and as Valid as can be desired; And we are very well content, by vertue of the Powers which have been given us and exhibited and approved, to obliege our selves and subscribe whatsoever the said Lord of *Heemsted* hath Transacted and Negotiated in Prosecution of the said Orders, As also whatsoever he may Transact or Negotiate as above, either by himself or joyntly with us, as shall be thought most conducing to the better perfecting of the Treaty of Alliance between the Commonwealth of *England* and the United Provinces of the *Low-Countreys*.

Given the 26th of *June*, 1652.

Thursday the 17th of *June*, 1652.

Resolved upon the Question by the Parliament,

THat upon Consideration of the Report made from the Councel of State, the Parliament doth think fit and order, That the Councel of State do proceed with the Lord Pauw, *Ambassador Extraordinary from the Lords the States General of the* United Provinces, *according to former Directions.*

Hen: Scobell, Cleric. Parliamenti.

A Pa-

(46)

A Paper received from the Lord PAUW, 17 June, 1652.

To the Right Honorable, The Councel of State.

THe Ambaſſador Extraordinary of the States General of the United Provinces of the *Low Countreys*, findes himſelf neceſſitated to Demand moſt inſtantly another Audience of the Lords Commiſſioners of the Honorable Councel, and that as ſoon as poſſible may be, as well to receive from them the moſt deſired Anſwer upon thoſe things that he hath already propounded in the laſt Conferences; as alſo to make to their Honors, according to the expreſs Charge he hath from his Superiors, others Overtures upon things of ſo high Concernment, that they can ſuffer no Delay; Therefore he deſireth earneſtly, That this juſt Demand be as ſoon as can be granted unto him.

A Tranſlation of the Paper of the Lord Ambaſſador PAUW, *17* June, *1652.*

THe Extraordinary Ambaſſador of the United Provinces hath repreſented to the Lords Commiſſioners of the Honorable Councel of State, in the third Conference held this day, as followeth:

That the States of the United Provinces have ſhewed themſelves, and are yet reſolved to remain faſt to the Amity and intimate Correſpondence with this Commonwealth, as they have yet of late made it appear,

(47)

pear, by granting, during theſe falling out, to the Company of Engliſh Merchants Adventurers ſetled in *Holland*, all the Security and Protection that they have deſired, even with this annexed Promiſe, To continue in the ſame good will towards them, though the Diſtemper ſhould proceed ed further.

That which hapned about *Dover* or the *Downs* ſhould not breed a general Quarrel between the two States, but that the ſame Miſchance ſhould be taken for a perſonal action, for which thoſe are to anſwer who ſhall be found to have exceed their Commiſſion.

And to the end that this buſineſs might be compoſted according to the Fact, and the neceſſary ſatisfaction done, That it were moſt fit and expedient to have it examined by Commiſſioners deputed of both ſides, to have that perſon puniſhed which ſhall be found guilty, according to the uſe and Maxims of all States and Commonwealths; by which means, their quiet and tranquility, as well within as without with their Neighbors, is conſerved.

Moreover, That the ſhips of War meeting at Sea, and behaving themſelves as before and during the time of the former Government, there ſhall be thereupon no more diſpute hereafter.

And that when the Confederation now to be done ſhall be concluded, according to the earneſt deſire of the States General, the Friendſhip between both States and their Subjects ſhall be more perfect, permanent, confident and inviolable, and the truly Orthodox Religion, which they by Gods ſpecial favor do profeſs, ſhall have a moſt potent and ſure protection.

The

(48)

The said Ambassador having again propounded the aforesaid means, and having added to them several Reasons and Arguments of great Strength, hath desired to be informed thereupon of the intent of the Honorable Councel of State, offering to answer and give satisfaction upon the remaining Difficulties.

Or otherwise, That it might please the Lords Commissioners to confer with him upon that matter, or to propound on their part what they may finde to be reasonable and just to compose speedily the unhappy Accident, promising to contribute of his side all that shall any ways be in his power, with his most earnest Intreaties, That the Honorable Councel might be without delay acquainted withal, and that the time and present Affairs might be so well husbanded, that the Businefs might be compounded by convenient ways, and without interruption of the publique Peace and further exacerbation of the Mindes and Spirits of both Nations. All which the said Ambassador hath recommended and offered with much Affection to prevent all Provocations and Inconveniencies.

The Answer of the Councel of State to the Summary of the Lord Adrian Pauw, Extraordinary Ambassador of the States General of the United Provinces, presented to the Councel the 21 of this instant June.

WHat the thoughts and judgement of the Parliament have been concerning the late Intentions

(49)

tions of the Lords your Superiors, and the late Actings of your Fleet within the very Roads of *England*; your Excellency hath understood by the Parliaments Answer given unto the three Papers of the Extraordinary Ambassadors of your State before your Excellencies arrival here; which Answer, together with the state of the Fact, and the Examinations thereupon had, and then given in, your Lordship takes notice of in your Papers now before the Councel; neither doth any cause appear to vary from that Judgement upon any thing since offered by your Excellency. And since the Attempt made by the Fleet of the United Provinces, with the Preparations thereunto (all projected and acted by way of surprise and in a time of Treaty) had the same prevailed, would have highly hazarded the safety of *England*. It cannot stand with reason, That this Commonwealth after such a Warning and great Preservation (which they owe onely to God) should leave it self naked and exposed to the like danger for the future, or suffer it self in a case so evident and notorious, under pretence of more solemn Examinations, or from examples of other States which suit not with this case, to be diverted from applying Remedies agreeable to the nature of this evil. And therefore the Councel cannot admit of what is propounded by your Excellency, either as to the passing by what is done, or attending the way of Examinations mentioned in your Papers, which to them seem needless, dilatory, and impracticable.

Touching the overture of re-admitting the late Treaty begun by the other Lords Ambassadors Extraordinary of your Nation, after so high a breach thereof, we

G   conceive

conceive it cannot be seasonable until the Wound now under Cure be throughly closed and healed.

And whereas your Excellency hath thought fit frequently to assert the amicable Minde and Intentions of the Lords your Superiors towards this Commonwealth, and hath given instances of some late Orders and Acts tending to the expression of the same; specially concerning the Honor and Respect to be paid unto this Commonwealth at Sea (being the ancient and undoubted Right of this Nation) and granting of the Protection desired by the English Merchants now at *Rotterdam* : The Parliament hath not been wanting on their part from time to time to manifest their desires of Amity with the United Provinces of the *Low-Countreys*, nor to afford unto the people thereof residing here all necessary Protection though undesired; Nevertheless, in the present posture of Affairs it cannot reasonably be expected. That this State should forbear the prosecution mentioned in the Parliaments said Answer for the Ends thereing expressed.

White-Hall,
19. June, 1652.

A Transflate of a Paper of the Lord Ambassador *Pauw*, of the $\frac{1\ July}{11\ June}$, desiring a Conference with the Commissioners of the Councel of STATE.

To the Right Honorable Councel of State.

THe Extraordinary Ambassador of the United Provinces, having 22th of this instant about the Evening, received by the hands of Sir *Oliver Fleming*, the Answer which the Honorable Councel of State hath been pleased to give him, upon the Summary of those things by him propounded the $\frac{24\text{th}}{14}$, He findeth himself bound to Demand most instantly another Conference with the Lords Commissioners of the Councel, that he may explain unto them more particularly and more fully his Superiors Intentions, and the better perform the Duty of his Office.

Another Paper of the Lord PAUW of the 21th of *June*, 1652.

To the Honorable Councel of State.

THe Extraordinary Ambassador of the United Provinces having the 22th of *June* in the Evening something late, received by the hands of Sir *Oliver Fleming*, the Answer which the Honorable Councel hath been pleased to give him upon the Summary of the things propounded the 24th of the same Moneth.

He

(52)

He hath thought himself bound, for the better performance of the Duty of his Imployment, to assert again here ingeniously as he hath done before, according to the Notice and Knowledge he hath of the most intimate Deliberations and Consultations of the States General his Superiors, That they having no ways propounded, deliberated nor resolved to give any suspition, or the least occasion of Offence against the Fleet or Ships of this Commonwealth : He did believe, That it would have been sufficient to take away all conceits of the contrary; He hath also truly represented the Accident happened between the two Fleets by *Dover* or the *Downs*, as it came to the knowledge of his Superiors by sincere Attestations of trusty and blameless Persons : And hath, to avoid all further Contestations, in stead of insisting upon those Proofs, opened a way by which the true and infallible knowledge of the same might have been found out, and by that means the satisfaction done that could be lawfully pretended

Therefore that Mischance cannot be any ways imputed to his Superiors, who never had the least thought, not in any sort contributed towards the Infraction of the Friendship, which hath always been most dear to them, and less towards the Interruption of the Treaty of Confederation ; for the perfecting of which they have had, and have still here their Extraordinary Ambassadors.

That may sufficiently appear by the firm and constant Resolution of his Superiors, that have never been willing to grant any Letters of Mart or Reprisal upon the continual Complaints and reiterated Petitions, even the Importunities of the Persons interessed in the
ships

(53)

ships taken, arrested and confiscated here, for fear of giving any occasion of Discontent to this Commonwealth.

The same is clearly seen by the Protection granted to the English Company setled at *Rotterdam* (though *ex superabundanti*, and they had no need of the same) to express more specially their good Intentions, the which may be also justified by all their actions; none of this State having yet to this present received the least Damage, Offence or Injury for all the said Proceedings; even our ships of War having rather suffered themselves to be brought into the Ports of *England*, and there to be detained, then endeavored to defend themselves against those whom they have always made account to be their good Friends, as having never heard of any publication to the contrary.

And to make that Testimony of Friendship the more Authentical to this Commonwealth, His Superiors have sent a second Extraordinary Embassage, to disabuse all those that might be pre-occupated or misinformed, and to help the furthering and perfecting of the said Treaty.

But in case all those Overtures and means of Reconciliation be rejected, and it be resolved here to make use of those ways, which in stead of assuaging shall increase the Evil, and which being against all Maxims of all States and Commonwealths (who never give their Judgement upon Signs, Presumptions and Suspitions, but upon infallible and unreproachable Proofs, and as clear as the Sun is at noon, and who during a Treaty do always command most strictly a cessation of all ways of Fact) shall the more surprize my Superiors, and cause
strange

strange Alarms to their Peoples, by making those suffer which are guiltless and come from far, who never had the least suspition or heard the least rumor of a falling out between both States.

Whereupon, the said Ambassador must needs be very much surprized and sorry, desiring, That the said Lords Commissioners be pleased (that no way for a happy Agreement may be neglected) to propound for on their part some other expedients (seeing they have expressed in their last Answer given to the other Extraordinary Ambassadors, *That the most sweet ways will be always the most pleasing to them*) which may be fit, satisfactory and convenient to compose as soon as can be that unhappy Business, and restore all things in their first temper.

And that in the mean time they be also pleased to inhibit all ways of Fact, and to give Order, That the Ships detained may be speedily set at liberty, praying very earnestly the Honorable Councel to explain their minde thereupon, as also to give an Answer upon the last Articles of the Paper exhibited the 21/31 of *June*, to make him the more able to contribute his best Offices for the good and strengthning of the two Commonwealths.

This $\begin{Bmatrix} 21\ June \\ 1\ July \end{Bmatrix} 1652.$

Another Paper of the Lord Pauw 23 *June*, 1 6 5 2.

To the Honorable Councel of State.

THe Extraordinary Ambassador of the United Provinces considering the importance of the Affairs now in hands, and the eminent dangers that threaten both States, is forced to be importunate with your Honors, in recommending most earnestly the care of your Answer upon his last Conference, and intreating you with all his Affections, That the same may be a convenient and lawful means to assway the Differences and restore the Union and perfect Intelligence between both Commonwealths and their reciprocal Subjects.

This $\begin{Bmatrix} 23\ June \\ 3\ July \end{Bmatrix} 1652.$

The Answer of the Parliament to that part of the Paper given in by the Lord Pauw, *whereby he desires the Commissioners of the Councel to propound what they shall think reasonable and just to compose speedily the present Differences between this Commonwealth and the Lords the States General of the United Provinces.*

Friday *the* 25th *of* June, 1652.

THat the Lords the States General of the United Provinces do pay and satisfie unto this Commonwealth

Another

wealth the Charges and Damages this State hath sustained and been put unto, by the Preparations of the said States General, and their Attempts this Summer; the particulars whereof shall be in due time produced.

II.

That upon the Payment of the Sum to be agreed upon as aforesaid, for Charges and Damages, or securing the same to the satisfaction of the Parliament, there shall follow immediately thereupon a Cessation of all Acts of Hostility, and the Ships and Goods taken since the late Differences shall be released.

III.

The two former Propositions being assented unto, and put in Execution, the security for the time to come, which the Parliament does expect, is by both States contracting a firm Alliance, and consistency of Interest for the good of both; which the Parliament of *England* is willing on their part by all just ways and means to endeavor.

Friday 25° *Junii*, 1652.

At the Councel of State at *White-Hall.*

Ordered,

THat the *Commissioners* appointed formerly to meet and Treat with the Lord Pauw, *Extraordinary Ambassador of the* United Provinces, *Do deliver unto the said Lord Ambassador the Answer of the Parliament of the*

the 25th *of* June instant; *to that part of the Paper presented unto them by the* Councel, *from the said Lord* Pauw, *whereby his Lordship doth desire the Commissioners of the* Councel *to propound what they should: but reasonable and just, to compose speedily the present Differences between this Commonwealth and the Lords the* States General *of the* United Provinces.

Ex: *Jo: Thurloe,* Clerk of the Councel.

A Paper of the Lord *Pauw*, 26 *Iune*, 1652.

To the Right Honorable Councel of State.

THe Extraordinary Ambassador of the *United Provinces,* having yesterday had a Conference with the Lords Commissioners of the Councel, and received from them two Papers upon the same Subject, He desireth earnestly they will be pleased to give again order without loss of time, for a new Conference with the said Lords Commissioners, that some things may be better explained and cleared of both sides, and a speedy Composure made of the Business.

This { 26 *June* } 1652.
     { 6 *July* }

H   An-

Another Paper of the Lord PAUW, the fame day.

To the Honorable Councel of State.

THE Extraordinary Ambaffador of the *United Provinces* hath propounded at a Conference held the 26 of Jan. 1652. with the Lords Commiffioners of the Councel of State the following Articles.

That the States General having been forced for the Reafons already alledged, to make extraordinary Preparations at Sea, have been put to exceeding great charges, which do continue yet at this prefent.

That their Subjects, befide the extream great Loffes they have had heretofore at Sea, have received very great ones by the Letters of Mart granted as well againft the French as againft the faid Subjects of the *United Provinces*, and upon fome other pretences.

That the State and their fubjects have fuffered much, and received great Damages of late by the taking and fpoiling of feveral Ships of War, and by the Arrefting of all the Merchants fhips.

And that if it fhould be thought of a Reimburfing of the Charges and Damages, they fhould be weighed of both fides one againft the other, and that it fhould be confidered, whether they have not been greater on the *United Provinces* fide.

However there muft a reafonable Eftimation be made, and the Bufineís not referred to a production of Accounts, which requireth a long Examination.

And if the faid Commiffioners be pleafed to caufe that Eftimation to be made in moderate Terms on their

Declaration and Scriptum 225

their part, it will appear from thence whether there is at this fide any willingnefs or intent to Compound the things paffed according to reafon and friendly, or whether there is a Defign to propound things impoffible and unfeafible.

As concerning the Confederacy between both Commonwealths, and the mutual Help afflicting one another againft thofe that fhall offend or affault them, the other Extraordinary Ambaffadors have made the true Intentions of their Superiors known thereupon, and are ready to go on in the fame Negotiation, and to bring it to an end without lofs of time.

If the faid Lords Commiffioners do think fit that the faid Confederacy fhould be more ample and more ftrict, that will not onely be more pleafing to the faid Ambaffador, but he alfo entreateth very earneftly, that he may be clearly informed thereupon.

Putting at the fame time into confideration, whether it will not be moft convenient, even moft neceffary to give order, That the Fleets do not come near nor engage any more one with the other; the faid Ambaffador fearing much it fhould foon be commanded otherways at the other fide, chiefly if the aborefaid Order be not fpeedily given here.

And defiring moreover, That the Ships which are arrefted may be fpeedily releafed, and that no Prize may be longer detained, to the end that the Mindes being fomething pacified, they may be rather invited by mutual Friendfhip and Love, and of their own accord, then brought by conftraint to unite again by an undiffoluble Confederacy.

As alfo, That the faid Ambaffador may receive upon

H 2

(60)

on these so speedy and so favorable a Declaration, that he may with more hope of success use his Endeavors with his Superiors, and effect what in this conjuncture of time and Affairs, is most expedient and necessary, and that he may do it without delay, according to the Express Order he hath from his said Superiors, which he is bound to follow exactly.

White-Hall, 26 June, 1652.

The Answer of the Councel of State to the foregoing Paper.

THe *Councel of State having considered of the Paper this Evening delivered in by their Commissioners from the Lord* Pauw *Extraordinary Ambassador of the Lords the States General of the United Provinces, and finding therein no clear or direct Answer to the last paper of Demands tendred unto his Excellency in the name of the Parliament, They do desire a speedy and positive Answer thereunto, at least unto the first Article thereof, especially, because that being assented unto, the Councel might speedily apply themselves to a reasonable and moderate ascertaining the Sum; to the end, That immediately upon performance of the second Article, all Acts of Hostility might be forborn, and restitution made of the Ships and Goods detained: The third Article in the nature thereof not requiring so present a Transaction.*

Ex: *Jo: Thurloe* Clerk of the Councel.

(61)

A Paper from the Lord *Pauw* the 27ᵗʰ of June, 1652.

To the thrice Illustrious Councel of State;

THe Extraordinary Ambassador of the United Provinces having considered the Answer delivered unto him yesterday at evening by Sir *Oliver Fleming* upon the Considerations heretofore by him propounded, doth most instantly crave, That it may please this thrice Illustrious Councel of State to grant him one other Conference this afternoon, that he may more particularly deduct the Intentions of his Superiors, and withal likewise satisfie both their Excellencies and his own duties.

Signed, *Adrian Pauw.*

This {27 *June*}1652.
     {7 *July*}

Another Paper of the Lord *Pauw,* 27ᵗʰ *June*, 1652.

To the Right Honorable, The Councel of State.

WHile the Extraordinary Ambassador of the United Provinces was busied about the writing of the Answer upon the Paper delivered to him yesterday very late by Sir *Oliver Fleming* from this Honorable Councel, he was to his great grief informed, That this Common-

(62)

Commonwealths Fleet was gone to Sea to execute some design.

The said Ambassador hath also by several Letters received Order from his Superiors, That in case he could not obtain, by all possible endeavors, the Cessation of Acts of Hostility, he should with all speed return back again into the Low-Countreys to acquaint them with his Negotiation.

And as the said Ambassador can advance no further in the said Negotiation, of which he was charged to give an Account to his said Superiors with all speed, he therefore desireth to be admitted to morrow to take his leave of this Honorable Council, to go over as soon as can be in the Ship of War whereof *John Vernhef* is Captain, who was commanded to bring him hither and back again, and that he may have a Letter or a Pass of the Honorable Council, to be Transported over without any hindrance or trouble, and without being molested or arrested by the Parliaments ships.

The other Extraordinary Ambassadors having in the mean time informed and shewed him that they had received the like Order and Command, have intreated him to demand in their name, That they may also at the same time to morrow have Audience to take their leave of this Honorable Council; as also be provided of such ships as they shall have need of for the Transport of their Persons, Train and Baggage, as also with such Passes as shall be necessary for the security of their Passage.

The said Ambassador desireth, That he may receive a speedy Answer upon these, being a thing of very great Importance.

27 June,

(63)

27th *June*, 1652.

At the Council of State at *White Hall*.

UPon Consideration of the Report made of the Paper delivered in to the Commissioners this evening by the Lord Pauw Extraordinary Ambassador from the United Provinces, The Council hold themselves obliged to represent the same to the Parliament, which they shall do upon Tuesday morning at their first sitting; and in the mean time can give no other Answer to the said Lord Ambassador upon this subject.

Ex: *Jo: Thurloe* Clerk of the Council.

A Paper of the Lord *Pauw* of the 28th *June*, 1652.

To the Right Honorable Council of State.

THe Extraordinary Ambassador of the United Provinces having seen the Answer of the Honorable Council given upon his Proposition made yesterday, hath thought fit to Declare again, That his Intention is to do his best when he shall be arrived in his countrey, That upon the Overtures made to him, or can be yet made, there may be such convenient means and fit expedients found, chiefly to make all Misapprehensions and

(64)

and alienations of mindes, as well as all Acts of Hostility cease; That a fair Agreement upon the Business passed, and consequently a firm Union and Confederacy between both States, as also a good settlement between both Nations may ensue, from which their own Prosperity and Happiness may flow, and all Inconveniences be prevented for the future.

And as his Resolution is godly, Honest, and if it succeedeth, most conducing to the common safety; as also, that it must be speedily, and before things proceed further, put in execution.

The said Ambassador desireth, That it may please to the Honorable Councel to weigh all these, and to Order, That all may be done that may be for that purpose, towards the promoting of the same.

And as the time is most precious, it will be very necessary, That he may speedily be admitted to his Audiences; as also, he may soon have the fit Expeditions concerning the Ship that brought him, and stayeth for his return at *Gravesend*, to bring him back again into the *Low-Countreys*, with the Pass he hath demanded for his security, and to avoid all Misfortunes that might meet him at Sea.

The said Ambassador doth wholly perswade himself, that the Honorable Councel will be pleased to give Order, That in consideration of his Quality, he be used in the same maner at his departure and taking of his leave, as he hath been at his coming and reception, for which favor he thanketh the Honorable Councel most kindly.

Another

(65)

Another Paper of the same Date.

To the Right Honorable Councel of State.

THe Extraordinary Ambassador hath thought fit to propound here, whether this Honorable Councel could not approve, That after his Report made to the Lords the States General his Secretary, or some other faithful person, should be sent to maintain and foment the mutual Correspondence, and deliver as well as receive from both States; what may serve to the compounding of things passed, and to the re-establishing of the Union and Confederacy.

And whether to this end the Honorable Councel would be pleased to command such Passes to be granted, by vertve of which, he might freely and safely come back and stay here, as long as the Parliament of the Commonwealth of *England*, or the Lords States General may finde it convenient.

Or otherwise, That it may please to the Honorable Councel to name or denote here, some body that be agreeable to them, and fit to receive the Letters that might be written upon that subject, and to solicite the Answers thereunto.

I A Paper

Declaration and Scriptum 229

(66)

A Paper of the three Ambassadors, dated 28 *June*, 1652.

To the Council of State of the Commonwealth of ENGLAND.

WHereas we the Ambassadors of the Lords States of the *United Provinces* of the Low Countries, by their last Letters have received Order, without any delay to make haste again to our Countrey, and there to give an accompt of what we have here done; We therefore do earnestly pray this Senate to suffer us, that we take, as it befits us, leave of this most Illustrious Assembly, and may have ships that may conveniently serve for our own Transportation, and for that of our Train and Goods; and besides, That such safe Conducts or Passes be granted us that may make our Journey safe. Here are some of our ships ready, *viz*. Captain *Jacpden Boer*, with three smaller Vessels of the city of *Dort*.

Signed, I: *Catts. E: Scbuep. Vandeperre.*

(67)

The Lord PAUW's *Speech in Parliament, at his taking leave,* 30. June, 1652.

Right Honorable,

THe States General of the United Provinces of the Low-Countreys, have first sent their Extrordinary Ambassadors to the Parliament of the Commonwealth of *England,* to do their earnest Endeavors for the strengthning and confirming of the ancient Amity and Friendship between both Nations, and for the Establishing of an everlasting Alliance between both States, and to bring those things to a happy conclusion for the common Utility and Security; and afterwards the Lord *William Newport,* a Member of the States of *Holland* and *West-Friesland,* to take away some Doubts, and to witness more fully of the good Incentions of our Superiors concerning the Treaty of Confederacy.

At last it hath pleased the said Lords States to prepare, some few days ago, a new extraordinary Embassage to the said Parliament, and to give me that Imployment, with an express command to bear again over and above, witness of their faithful dealing, and of their most sincere intention towards this Commonwealth, and to dissolve and remove all the strange and unthought of accidents, and all the stoppings and hinderances thereby caused and opposed to their good intent; by which means, I might by all my endeavors promote to a happy conclusion, the Treaty of Alliance already begun.

To what end it hath been propounded amongst other things,

I 2   The

(68)

things, That there should be an Enquiry and Examination made by fit persons of both Commonwealths, of all what lately passed as was done between the two Fleets without any Design, but by meer chance, and a just and lawful Satisfaction stated: For we do witness and protest before God and all the Christian world, as well as in the presence of the Parliament of the Commonwealth of *England*, That the States have not had the least minde of Offending or Troubling this Commonwealth, much less of committing any Hostility against them; but rather that they have had nothing more in their hearts, then to Entertain and Maintain with this State of all true Friendship and firm Peace, even to come to a stricter Union and Confederacy with them.

But as it hath unhappily happened, That after extraordinary pains taken, and all the best Endeavors done of all sides to conserve the common Quiet, and remove all hindrances, both Embassages have not onely missed their Ends, but that to the contrary, not onely great Troubles have been given, extraordinary Losses have been caused, but huge Dangers; as also Acts of Hostility not looked for, neither at any time before declared, are threatned from the English Fleet to the States of the *United Provinces*.

Both Embassage hath thought fit to prevent the ensuing Evils, and upon a business so unusual, to return into their own Countrey to give an Accompt of their Negotiation to their Superiors, and to be acquainted with their further Commands.

To that end we do present our selves together to the Supream Authority of this Commonwealth, declare, That

(69)

That we have a Command to return back, and that we are ready to take our Journey.

We have given notice to the Honorable Council of State of this Commonwealth, of those things that are necessary to us for our Transport, according to our Quality and the season, and do look and wait for an Answer thereupon, hoping that the necessary Expeditions shall be done.

In the mean time we cannot be wanting to our Duty, but are forced again to desire most earnestly, That all our ships that have been brought into the Ports of *England*, & there detained of late against our thoughts, and before any Declaration of Hostility issued out, and whereof the Commanders are unawares and guiltless, having not given the least, nor to no body occasion of Dispute, may be released and suffered to go freely, with their officers, mariners, merchandizes, packs and loads, and the whole company, and to perform their Journey without any Wrong or Injury; which we do pretend to be due to our old Friendship, to the Right of Nations, and have been observed between Christian Peoples, as well as we hope to have it granted by the Justice and Equity of this Great and most Honorable Assembly.

Furthermore, We do intreat with all our hearts the great God of Heavens, who is the Author and Promoter of Peace and Concordance, That he will be pleased to afford such thought and counsel to the Parliament of the Commonwealth of *England*, as may tend to the mutual Peace of both States, to the conservation of the Christian Reformed and Orthodox Religion, which hath no better Foundations then upon Peace, and

and can never better thrive and flourish then by Peace, and will without any doubt be afflicted and destroyed by our Troubles and falling out; As also that he will a his Mercy prevent the Destructions and Miseries of Wars, and bestow abundantly his Heavenly Blessings upon both Commonwealths; We shall end upon these Wishes. And being commanded to Repair in haste into our countrey, we shall with all thankful Acknowledgement for all Favors done to us, as well as with all due Respects, take our leave of this most Honorable and Supream Assembly of the Commonwealth of *England*, with confidence that they will not deny us those things which we have already expressed, and are granted every where to the Ambassadors for their quality and security.

Pronounced and delivered to the Parliament of the Commonwealth of England, *the* 12/10 *July* 1652. *by the Extraordinary Ambassadors of the States General of the* United Provinces.

We do besides deliver a Petition put into our hands by the Dutch Merchants, Desiring they may enjoy the same Security and Protection which hath been lately granted in the best Form to the English Merchants in our Provinces.

We desire also at last, That besides the two Dutch Men of War, there should be another of those that are in the *Downs* granted to us for our Passage, seeing we are a very great Company, wherein are some Women of Quality, with much Carriage, which will put us to great Inconveniences, besides the heat of this season, except we be fitted with the said ship.

F I N I S.

SCRIPTUM
Parlamenti Reipublicæ
ANGLIÆ

De iis quæ ab hac Repub. cum Potestatibus Fœderatarum Belgii Provinciarum Generalibus, & quibus progressibus acta sunt; déque controversiis in præsentia exortis, quibus prædictæ Potestates occasionem præbuere.

Adjicitur & Responsum Parlamenti ad ternas chartulas à D^{nis} Legatis Potestatum generalium Extraordinariis, ex occasione pugnæ navalis inter Anglorum & Belgarum classes confertæ.

Una cum illius pugnæ, sicuti commissa est, narratione.

Postremò scripta illa in unum collata, quæ inter Parlamentum Reipub. Angliæ & D^{num} Adrianum Pauw, Legatum Fœderatarum Belgii Provinciarum Extraordinarium, cum de pace agerent; ultro citróque reddita sunt.

LONDINI,
Typis *Du-Gardianis*, Anno Domini 1652.

SCRIPTUM Parlamenti Reipub. Angliæ, de iis quæ ab hac Repub. cum Potestatibus Fœderatarum Belgii Provinciarum Generalibus, & quibus progressibus acta sunt; déque controversiis impræsentia exortis, quibus prædictæ Potestates occasionem præbuere.

Quanta & quàm gravia Fœderatarum Belgii Provinciarum Populus sub tyrannidis jugo, antequam diviná ope liberaretur, passus sit mala, & quibus rationibus adductus, quo ardore animi ad libertatem aspiraverit, si denique quàm amica atque perpetuá ope, idque haud sine multo sanguine aque opibus Anglorum, ejus saluti impensis, omni tempore sublevatus ab hac gente æque adjutus sit, in memoriam redigatur, credibile vix erit, pro tot acceptis beneficiis,

A 2

Declaration and Scriptum 233

(2)

ficiis, quàm non amica huic Reipub. imò, quàm non æqua reddiderit.

Non est consilium jam nostrum res hujus Reipub. quo loco tum essent, prolixè memorare, cùm tyrannico imperio oppressi, armis necessariò sumptis, vitam nostram atque fortunas detendere coacti sumus; dum jus nostrum natale & libertatem justissimam asserere in Parlamento, & stabilire conaremur, qua in asserenda ac stabilienda tot editis planè miraculis Deus, tot præliis insignibus, tàm continenti per omnem Angliam, Scotiam atque Hiberniam, divinæ suæ providentiæ ductu, contemptissimæ eorum paucitati adesse atque opitulari dignatus est, qui in illa causâ tàm bonâ fidem suam atque constantiam comprobârunt.

Neque verò conatus ille serendæ inter nos discordiæ, quod anno illo memorabili 1648. accidit, omittendus est, neque magnus ille in nationem hanc apparatus belli anno millesimo sexcentesimo quinquagesimo tacendus, qui eas gerendi res, quas in Scotia gessimus, necessitatem nobis attulit, quibus ob injurias priùs allatas satisfactio & futuræ pacis fides denegata est ab iis, qui judicatum hujus Reipub. Hostem ex Belgio venientem ad se receperant; ubi & perditissima illa in Anglorum gentem inita consilia erant; unde & hostes eorum permagna suis rebus subsidia & palàm & secretò, cùm Principis Araussionensis, tum aliorum authoritate & potentiâ consecuti sunt; eo ipso tempore, cùm Princeps ille, ejusque fautores, ut verisimile est, consilia agitarent in illa Repub, tyrannidem occupandi, eásque provincia

(3)

vincias in servitutem pristinam redigendi; quod etiam, quin perficerent haud multum abfuit, tum præfertim, cùm is urbem Amsterodamum repentino impetu adortus est, quæ res & illîc multò quàm apud nos magis notæ sunt, & scripti hujus proposito alienæ.

Sed nec crudelissimi illius Amboyniani facinoris in Anglos perpetrati ullo modo grata recordatio est, ob quod facinus, atque alia haud longè dissimilia, nulla satisfactio, quamvis postulata sæpiùs, data hactenus omnino est.

Verùm Populi Anglicani erga Belgii fœderati populum, tàm propensa voluntas erat, tantum libertatis confirmandæ studium, mutuíque commercii, viriúmque ex eo augendarum, religionis verò Protestantium orthodoxæ potissimùm prolatandæ, quam & utrique profitentur, quæque hac mutuâ amicitiâ, quantum humanitùs conjicere licet, maximè crevisset, quosdam etiam ex primoribus & populo earum Provinciarum usque adeò erga hanc causam benè animatos esse animadvertimus, quod & suâ erga Pauperes in Hibernia Protestantes benigniate ampliter testati sunt, ut quamprimum in Anglia rerum status firmitatis aliquid, Deo favente, haberet videbatur, Parlamentum ad Ordines, Fœderatarum Provinciarum generales Oratorem mitteret, qui eum disertis verbis admittere recusârunt; quemadmodum & ipsi satis nôrunt.

Rebus Anglorum majorem indies in modum omnipotentis Dei nutu prosperè cedentibus, cúmque idem eorum judicium, idem animus erga suos illos vicinos esset, Parlamentum denuo aliam misit,

A 3   suóque

(4)

ſcópè illic Oratori adjunxit, virum eo munere dignum, Dominum *Iſaacum Doriſlaum*, jurisprudentiæ Doctorem, qui eâ autoritate ac mandatis inſtructi erant, uti viderent, ſiqua honeſta ratio mutuam utriuſque Reipub. voluntatem inter ſe rectè intelligendi poſſit iniri. Verùm alter ex illis Oratoribus *Doriſlaus*, cùm ad hoc munus publicè obeundum Hagam veniſſet, quo in oppido Poteſtates Generales ſuos ferè conventus peragere ſolent, eo in loco ſceleſtiſſimè atque palàm truci ſatus eſt; de cujus nefaria cæde totus terrarum orbis proculdubio ita ſentiat, ut de piaculo quàm maximè deteſtando contra omnium gentium, immo ipſius humanitatis jura perpetrato omnes homines ſentire debent; in conquirendis autem & comprehendendis ejus interfectoribus, quàm nihil peri, & tùm maximè, cùm factum recens eſſet, & poſtea, actum fit, quamvis hinc ſæpenumero poſtulatum, & ipſi haud neſciunt, & admoneri hic debent.

Contrà, cùm Poteſtates illæ ſuos Legatos D D. Borele, Renzwo & Joachimum antehac in Angliam, recentium turbarum temporibus miſiſſent, nobiſque illi omnia officia ſua prolixè detuliſſent, compertum eſt, eos cum hoſtibus clam agere, eorúmque operâ hoſtes omnibus modis adjutos eſſe, contra eos ad quos ipſos amicorum ſpecie cum legatione venerant. Et hoc quidem, cum contumeliis inſuper quas in Parlamentum ipſum jacere non dubitabant, Legatorum illorum negotium erat; quas ob res utcunque ſe ex jure gentium reddendæ rationi obnoxios feciſſent, nullum tamen hinc viciſſim aut factum aut dictum aſperius retulerunt; duntaxat ad primores eorum

(5)

eorum delatum eſt, quemadmodum ſe geſſerint, & ſatisfactio uti daretur, poſtulatum; verùm nulla hactenus impertitur.

Hæc cùm ita eſſent, poſtquam *DEO* viſum erat turbulentis Anglorum rebus finem imponere, hoſteſque nullum totâ Angliâ præſidium tenerent, nullaque eorum copiæ reliquæ jam eſſent, ſed pacata ubique omnia & compoſita cernerentur, ejúſque Inſulæ pleraque urbes atque oppida in poteſtate Parlamenti eſſent, cùm & in Scotia Anglorum res iiſdem prope ſucceſſibus non carerent, multóque minùs cauſſæ eſſet cur quiſquam à Parlamento ad poteſtates Fœderatarum Provinciarum Generales, petendi auxilii cauſſâ, proficiſceretur, quamvis & nos & vicinos noſtros itâ aſpexiſſe potuerimus, ut aliæ quæque Reſpub. conſueverunt; eandem tamen ſententiam atque judicium retinuimus, utriuſque nempe Reipub. quàm arctiſſimam ſocietatem ad ſtabiliendas Proteſtantium rationes quibus hoſtes eorum tantopere inſidiantur, necnon ad commune bonum & libertatem permagnum eſſe momentum allaturam.

Parlamentum igitur ad Poteſtates Fœderatarum Provinciarum Generales legationem miſit ampliſſimam, legatos iis mandatis inſtructos, táque poteſtate præditos, ut priores controverſias componere, fœdúſque firmiſſimum atque arctiſſimum ferire conarentur, quatenus id quidem æquitati & rationi, hujuſque gentis dignitati conſentaneum eſſet, & cum utriuſque Reipub. communi bono conjunctum. Immo affirmare poſſumus, Legatos illos plena hinc mandata

(6)

ta atque potestatem accepisse ea proponendi, eáque cum prædictis Potestatibus transigendi, quæ erga populum Fœderatarum Belgii Provinciarum eundem hujus Reipub. animum, eandem atque in suos benevolentiam declarâssent.

Quàm non sincerè, quàm non expeditè cum iis Legatis, de quibus missi erant rebus gravissimis ageretur, unde factum est, ut legatio illa nullius usûs reddita sit, quàm non incolumes, nequid gravius dicatur, in illo munere sanctissimo fuerint, quandiu in illis provinciis commorati sunt, quàm indigna in eos, insque famulos eorum, idque impunè, sint commissa; in quos denique sit hæc culpa meritò conferenda, plùs satis manifestum est. Verùm cum hisce Potestatum prædictarum dilationibus, minimèq; propensis ad amicitiam animis factum esset, uti nullus ex illa Legatione fructus percipi potuerit, læsâ etiam, in Legatis suis contumeliosè acceptis, hujus Reipub. dignitate, suísque amicitiæ studiis pro nihilo habitis, Legati domum revocantur.

Ex his, quæ dicta sunt, intelligi potest, à parte hujus Reipub. quid actum fuerit ad firmissimum fœdus & amicitiam cum fœderatis Provinciis consequendam quámque honestis atque integris rationibus Parlamentum adipisci eam studuerit; cúmque eas interea difficultates in Scotia atque Hibernia exandare pergeret, ad quas divina ipsâ providentia vocare nos visa est, cúmque eadem benignissimi *DEI* manus, quæ perpetuò nos adjuverat, Hibernicas res in eum deduxisset locum, ut quod illic gereretur, nihil penè reliquum fuerit, bellúmque Scoticum ita nobis fortunâsset,

(7)

nâsset, ut ea regio quodammodo relicta nobis esset, Scotorúmque exercitus, ductu Caroli Stuarti, nuperi Regis filii, in Angliam ingressus, Vigoniæ fusus fugatúsque esset, eorum plerisque capris aut interfectis præter ipsum ducem, aliósque perpaucos, qui ægrè ex eo prælio elapsi sunt; Tum demum, neque priùs unquam Potestates prædictæ Generales mittendam ad hanc Rempub. Legationem censuerunt, quæ à nobis eo studio ac voluntate accepta est, quæ testificari possit in eadem nos sententiâ atque judicio de illarum Provinciarum amicitiâ permansisse.

Dum procederent colloquia, cùm optimum nobis visum esset moras inutiles amputare, & certi aliquid habere quò res reditura esset, & postulatis quibusdam perspicuis instaremus, de iis etiam ad quæ facilè responderi potuerit, Legati semper ea declinare, deésse sibi potestatem causantes, quanquam inspecta eorum diplomata nihil iis deésse potestatis arguebant; tamen quò pleniora acciperent mandata, ad Primores suos scribendum sibi esse, quibus antequam rescribi posset, Provinciales Ordines esse convocandos, quæ quidem singula perexiguam nobis fidem faciebant, firmam aliquam pacem aut amicitiam eos ex animo voluisse.

Inter hæc etiam colloquia, cùm Legati eorum in disceptationibus suis primò quidem nullâ re aliâ, quàm ratione & æquitate niti velle præ se ferrent, Parlamentum censius secere, Primoribus suis in animo esse centum & quinquaginta naves armare, præter illas ex classe suâ quæ foris tum erant, hócque eo consilio ab se fieri, ut & mare Britús navigaretur, úsque

B commer-

(8)

commercio Reique Navali Fœderatarum Provinciarum confuleretur, non utique ut Anglis ullo modo incommodarent.

Dixerintne hæc, ut Parlamentum fufpenfo animo tenerent, aut quid illi denunciarent, Generales ipfæ Poteſtates optimè nôrunt, ſicut & cauſas tantæ Claſſis extra Ordinem parandi, cùm hoſtis eorum per hæc maria nullus appareret.

Ad hæc Parlamentum nihil reſpondebat, ſuæ tantummodò juſtæ defenſioni fedato animo proſpiciebat, nè quis nos repentè adoriretur: Neque tamen fententiam ullâ in parte mutavit, quod ad ea, quæ aut poſtulanda aut concedenda erant; cùm ad honeſti atque juſti normam, ad ſalutem etiam utriuſque Reipub. ſuámque jus invicem utrique conſervandum conſilia ſua omnia direxerit, foedíſque hoc in medio poſitum ad felicem exitum perducere etiam atque etiam cuperet. Neque ullâ in re, quantum intelligere potuit, deeſſet, quâ ſtudium fuum teſtificari poſſet ejus fœderis perficiendi.

Interea Poteſtates fœderatarum Provinciarum illos navium apparatus maturare non defiunnt, locum, ubi omnes conveniant atque unam claſſem conficiant, edicunt, fub eo præfecto, quem appellant Legatum Admirallum Trump. Quæ ejus conſilia aut mandata fuerint & ex eo quo ſe modo ipſe geſſit, & ex quibuſdam antea-factis abundè liquebit. Et ſpeciatim, cùm inter alias quædam eorum navis, quæ in navem quandam bellicam, cui præerat Capitaneus Young, inciderat, amicè admonita eſſet, ut honorem hujus nationis navibus præſidiariis tribui ſolitum exhiberet,

(9)

hiberet, quem & altera quâ ſimul navigabat, exhibuerat, idque pro more non ſolùm ſalutationis cujuſdam honorificæ, ſed quod etiam teſtimonio eſt, Anglorum jus atque Dominium in hæc maria vicina indubitatum eſſe. Quod & omnes vicinæ reſpub. atque Principes agnoſcunt, & nominatim ipſæ illæ Poteſtates, earúmque majores agnoverunt, ut monumenta fide digniſſima, aliáque argumenta quæ rejici non poſſunt, quæque ad id confirmandum jam diu invaluit, conſuetudinem taceamus. Navis tamen illius Præfectus hoc facere recuſabat, fibíque capitale hoc fore, ſi feciſſet, affirmabat.

Has res ſubſequutum eſt facinus illud Admiralli *Trump*, cujus accurata narratio huc adjicitur, ex quâ id hoſtiliter fuiſſe factum perſpicietur contra vicinos atque ſocios amicitiâ ac foedere conjunctos, qui id continuandi atque confirmandi ſua, ſtudia toties, támque vehementer teſtati ſunt; fuiſſe etiam hoc facinus fœdere velatum, & inter ipſa de arctiore adhuc fœdere colloquia à ſemetipſis oblata, tanta cum injuſtitiâ atque arrogantiâ conjunctum, ut quod jus nobis tam indubitatum denegabat, id ipſe uſurparet, eámque adhuc injuriâ iterando, nè ipſe quidem laceſſitus, hujus Reipub. naves ſuis in fretis, litoribus, ac ſtationibus quærens, hoſtilem in modum ultrò aggrederetur, bellíque initium faceret, virifque & navibus noſtris perniciem moliretur, uti eos toto mari pelleret, hujúſque reipuƀ commercium, rémque omnem navalem ſubvertere conaretur, niſi *D E U S* propitius faucinoris illius ignominiam ac detrimentum in ipſos injuriarum authores avertiſſet.

B 2   Poſt:

(10)

Post hanc tam diuturnam hujus Reipub. patientiam, acceptáſque injurias tam graves, quibus noſtrorum animos irritari par erat, cùm eorum in mari ſucceſſus expectationi non reſponderent, viſum eſt Poteſtatibus prædictis Generalibus alterum adhuc Legatum Extraordinarium ad Parlamentum mittere, qui, quod & priores Legati ante ejus adventum enixè fecerant, & conſilia & authoritatem, & mandata Poteſtatum ſeſe mittentium hujus facti conſcientiâ prorſus eximere contendebat. Quod, quanquam apparatus illi tanti fuere, Claſsíſque eorum ab incepto curſu divertebat, navéſque Parlamenti in ipſis ſuis ſtationibus quærebat, eáſque illi nullâ re laceſsiti ultrò oppugnabant, ut ſuprà demonſtratum eſt, tamen à Legatis *Caſſus* vocatur, facinúſque illud fortuitò patratum fuiſſe, illúdque Primores ſuos nullo modo approbare aiebant, qui tamen facinoris illius authori munus illud ſuum Claſsis ducendæ prorogârunt.

Et de hoc quidem indigniſſimè facto cùm ſatis conſtaret, ſéque ipſum partim argueret, ipſo claſsis adventu, quæ Duce Trumpio ad claſsem noſtram in ipſis ſtationibus ex compoſito accedebat, partim multis teſtibus oculatis confirmaretur, non Anglis ſolùm, ſed etiam Belgis aliquot præfectis & Claſſiariis & naucleris in ea pugna captis, qui idem prorſus teſtantur; Prolixa tamen quædam & perplexa quæſtionis habendæ ratio nobis proponitur, induciæ poſtulantur, uti armis & hoſtilitate omni abſtineatur, útque de illo vetere & complurium articulorum fœdere quod à prioribus Legatis tractari cœptum eſt, nova rurſus diſceptatio inſtituretur, ſcilicet ut tem
poris

(11)

poris acceſsio novam interim illis virium acceſsionem afferret.

Mandata hujus Legati cum inſpicere poſtularemus, Literas tantum commendatitias ſive credentiales protulit, quaſdam etiam liberi commeatûs; quibus autem poteſtas agendi & tranſigendi cum Parlamento daretur, nullas: quam ille poteſtatem (quod caput rei erat) ut quaſi mutuam ſumeret, ad priores Legatos recurrebat, qui in mandatis habebant, ut de priore illo fœdere propoſito agerent atque tranſigerent, hanc etiam Legationem agnoſcebant, & quamvis illi generatim de ſocietate & amicitia utriuſque Reipub. jungenda veniſſent, veniſſet autem Dnus Adrianus Pauw de ſingulari quodam facto, poſtquam illius fœderis tractatio initium & proceſſum aliquem habebat: Parlamenti tamen tam conſtans erat ſtudium novas haſce controverſias, ſi poſſet fieri, amicè componendi, ut cum Domino Adriano Pauw ad colloquium venire pergeret; omiſsâ in preſens omni diſputatione, quæ de poteſtate ejus non ſatis amplâ meritò naſci potuerat.

Cùmque nihil ſpeciatim ab illo Legato proponeretur, ſed tantum quæ generalia ſuprà dicta ſunt, idque etiam poſceret, ut Parlamentum ſua ei poſtulata proponeret, viſum eſt neutiquam inſtare quàm hoc nobis incommodum eſſet, ſed ſtatim deque ſatisfactione ob injurias jam illatas, déque fide in futurum accipiendâ noſtra ad Legatum poſtulata mittere; quæ hic etiam typis evulgata ſunt, unde in eo ſitum erat, vellétne poſtulatis de ſatisfactione aſſentiri, quam pars utraque & mitigare potuerit & certam

B 3

(12)

tam statuere; quod ei in alia chartula significatum est. Et si hunc in modum de satisfactione convenisset (postulato illo de fide accipienda in aliud tempus dilato) potuerant induciæ fieri, potuerat, omni hostilitate quemadmodum petitum erat, abstineri; cui & Parlamentum ad hunc modum libenter assensisset.

Verùm ille, potiùs quàm ut ad ullam hujusmodi pactioné accederet, aut particulatim ad putandas rationes descenderet, maluit studium illud suum induciarú paulò antè ardentissimum planè remittere, tametsi in manu ejus erat quod petiverat, impetrare, atque ita eam postulationem penitùs dimisit, suóque & reliquorum Legatorum nomine petiit, ut quamprimum audirentur commeatús duntaxat liberi causâ, atque in patriam revertendi, quò se mandatis præsentissimis aiebant revocari: neque iis negatum quicquam erat, quod vel honori vel usui in reditu esse poterat, neque ita quisquam eos tractabat, quandiu hic commorati sunt, quemadmodum hujus Reipub. Ministri in fœderatis Provinciis fuerant tractati, atque hoc suo discessu, tam illi quàm huic fœderi, quorum de conditionibus vixdum omnibus egerant, fidem imposuere.

In Parlamento postremùm auditi, de iis quæ chartulis eorum prioribus comprehensa erant, multa recitârunt: ad illud autem quod tum urgebant, de hostiliter factis æquaquam exspectatis, neque unquam indictis, útque naves suorum (in Angliæ portus abductæ, ibíque, contra quàm opinati sunt, retentæ, antequam ulla hostilitas indicta esset, earum præfectis bellum esse nescientibus, nè sibi quidem consciis ullam ab se offensionum

(13)

sionum datam esse cuiquam occasionem) dimitterentur, de his Parlamentum ad narrationem illam ab se vulgatam tantummodo remittere eos debebit, quæ & Legatis D^{norum} Potestatú Generalium ante adventum D^{ni} *Adriani Paaw* missa fuerat, & ab eodem, primo ejus adventu, inspecta.

Et quanquam priorem illam fœderis violationem, factámque à Trumpio injuriam gravem Parlamentum neque commeruerat, neque exspectaverat, illaâ tamen illâ, exspectari non potuit, quin qui essent injuriam passi, authores persequerentur, quibus satisfactio nondum ulla est oblata; nisi fortè Parlamentum fracto animo ad eorum pedes projicere se deberet, qui interitum sibi hoc facto, & perniciem ultimam moliti sunt, nisi iisdem hujus Gentis jus atque salutem prodere voluisset; quod quidem ab officio suo ac fide alienissimum esse nemo non judicaret.

Ex his rebus perspectis, quas jam in lucem omni cum fide evulgavimus, palàm omnibus erit, quanto cum affectu atque constantiâ Parlamentum amicitiam fœderatarum Belgii Provinciarum quasi ambiverit: quàm diligenter omnes controversias, bellíque cum illa Repub. occasiones vitaverit, quamvis illa omnes hujusmodi vel æquissimas amicitiæ ac societatis ærctissimæ conditiones rejecerit.

Tandem verò, posteaquam hæc Respub.armis petita est, naves laceratæ, suorum aliquot interfecti sine ullo offensionis à nobis datæ vel minimo obtentu (quæ facta & quæ indè sequi potuissent, si illis ex sententia processissent, non solùm jus atque decus & commercium, sed salutem etiam & quasi vitam ipsam hujus

B 4.

Declaration and Scriptum 239

(14)

hujus Reipub. summum in discrimen adduxissent) Parlamentum sui officii duxit esse, ingratissimo sibi hoc bello ab illis exorto, necessitate planè impositâ sese defendere: dùmque justa satisfactio atque fides accipienda nullo alio pacto impetrari poterit, eas conari iis rationibus consequi, quas *DEUS* sibi in manus dederit.

Atque hic quidem Parlamentum, ut se rectèfaciendo, suoque munere fideliter administrando abuncè loquatur, itâ sibi persuadet, causæ suæ justissimæ clarum hoc testimonium omnes, quibus veri & æqui studium est, esse accepturos; cujus exitum non cælicis consiliis, non viribus humanis, sed benignitati atque auxilio illius Dei justissimi commendat, qui Anglorum rebus usque adeò mirandum in modum hactenus semper adfuit, quique se verè colentibus, opémque suam piâ cum fiduciâ, animóque integro expectantibus nunquam defuit.

Hen. Scobell, Cleric. Parlamenti.

Responsum

(15)

Responsum Parlamenti Reipub. Angliæ ad ternas schedulas à D^{nis} Legatis Extraordinariis D^{norum} Potestatû Generalium Fœderatarum Belgii Provinciarum ad Concilium Status redditas, ex occasione prælii navalis inter utriusque Reipub. classes conserti.

PArlamentum Reipub. Angliæ secum reputans, quàm perpetuâ amicitiæ studiique sinceri declaratione, ab ipso domesticarum apud se turbarum initio, sium erga Fœderatas Belgii provincias, vicinas suas animum testatum reddiderit, nihilque ad se quod attinet, prætermiserit, quod firmæ cum iis concordiæ, liberóque commercio, necnon etiam propiori quàm hactenus, & arctiori conjungendæ necessitudini conducere possit, non potest quin vehementer sanè miretur, suis benè meritis tàm dissimilia sibi reddi, præsertim in ipso propè Angliæ littore, ipsísque navium nostrarum stationibus, in Classem hujus Reipub. hostilia nuper fieri; cujus facti narratio clarissimis probationibus confirmata simul huc adjicitur. Parlamentum itaque habitâ de omnibus & singulis illis scriptis ab Excellentiis vestris Concilio Status exhibitis deliberatione perquàm seriâ atque maturâ, responsum hoc reddendum censet.

Se, quanquam in illis chartulis quod expressè agitis, ut inopinatam illam duarum Classium inter se dimicationem, insicientibus vestris primoribus, & planè

C   contra

(16)

contra eorum voluntatem accidisse ostendatis, id æquanimiter & ad normam charitatis interpretari valdè cupiunt, tamen quoties suis cum animis cogitant quantopere ab eo quod vos profitemini, & decreta & facta Vestræ Reipub. vestrisque navibus præfectorum discrepaverint, etiam in ipsa fœderis tractatione à semetipsis oblata, & à vestris Excellentiis illorum nomine apud nos administrata; cùm item naves centum & quinquaginta bellicas extra ordinem, & sine ulla, quæ cerni possit, causâ, nisi quæ jam se aperit, instrui videant (magnum profectò justæ suspicionis argumentum vel ipsarum judicio V^{rarum} Ex^{arum}, dum illud exculare atque diluere contendistis) quin & ipsa mandata à prædictis primoribus vestris ad præfectos vestros in altum proficiscentes data cùm intueantur, satis supérque causæ reperire, cur credant D^{nos} Potestates Generales Fœderatarum Belgii Provinciarum in animo habere jus Angliæ per maria notissimum vi & armis invadere; Classes delere, quæ, secundum DEUM, muri ejus ac munimenta præcipua sunt; eáque ratione Rempub. hanc exterorum injuriis opportunam suo arbitratu reddere; quod & hac nuperâ impressione facere adorti sunt. Quocirca Parlamento videtur sui muneris hoc esse, uti dent operam, DEO bene juvante, prout occasio se obtulerit, ut illatarum jam sibi injuriarum & reparationem adipiscantur, & nequid simile in posterum tentetur, fidem accipiant. Hoc tamen animo atque voto, ut omnes inter utramque Gentem controversiæ possint amicè atque pacatè, si quo id pacto fieri potest, componi, prout DEUS, pro sua summa Providentia, viam ad hanc rem patefecerit,

(17)

fecerit, & circumstantiæ profuerint ad reddendos ejusmodi conatus & minùs tardos & efficaciores, quàm alios ejusdemmodi, qui antehac adhibiti sunt, fuisse constat.

Hen. Scobell, Cleric. Parlamenti.

NARRATIO pugnæ navalis inter Classem Anglicanam sub Prætore *Blaco*, & Classem Batavicam, cui præerat Legatus Admirallus *Trump*, ad Dorobernium nuper consertæ.

DIe Martis, octavo decimo Maii, 1652. manè, cum *Blacus* Prætor ante dies octo cum duodecim aut tredecim navibus Occidentem versùs usque ad sinum Rienfem profectus esset, relicto ad Dunas cum octo solùm Navibus Bornio Tribuno, conspecta est ponè arenas Goduinianas Classis Batavica duarum & quadraginta navium bellicarum, quarum una summo vertice mali vexillum gerebat, cæteræ aplustria tantùm. Cúmque ad Australem arenarum extremitatem pervenissent, earum duæ ad naves Anglicas, quæ in Dunis erant, processere. Quo viso, *Bornius* Tribunus navem, cui nomen Cani-Venatico inditum erat, obviam iis misit; quæ eas & de aliis rebus pro more percontaretur, & cur maximè tam propè ad se accederent. Quæ cum responderent, habere se ad præ-

C 2

Declaration and Scriptum 241

(18)

præfectum Classis in Dunis mandata quædam, admissa sunt, earúmque duo Capitanei, Tysones & Aldredus in Navem prædicti *Bornii* Tribuni, salutato priùs ejus vexillo, transcenderunt, eíque ostendunt, sese ab *Van-Trumpio* missos esse, ut certiorem eum facerent, Legatum suum cum Classe Dunkirkensem oram modò legisse, ubi vi tempestatis multarum navium anchoras & funes amisisrant, seque flante Aquilone, longiùs, quàm volebant, in Meridiem propelli: id *Van-Trumpium* censuisse significandum, nè quam offensionis causam aut suspicionis præberet. Hæc cùm dixissent, responsúmque iis esset, dictorum suorum fidem in eo positam esse, si ab hoc littore quamprimùm recessissent, ad classem suam reverterunt, quo simul ac venerunt, tota confestim classis Dorobernium versùs cursum direxit, eodémque die, post meridiem, penè haud longiùs à Castello quàm emissâ pila tormento perferri possit, anchoras jecit; cúmque è regione illius Castelli, nullâ pro more datâ salute, neque detracto mali vertice vexillo, in procinctu stetisset, Castellum ter in eam displosit. Quod quamvis fieret, Admirallus tamen Batavicus neque vexillum demisit, & eodem loco ad meridiem usque postero die in Anchoris stetit, & Sclopetarios suos complures per horas, sclopis simul omnibus subinde displosis, exercitabat. Die Mercurii, horâ circiter duodecimâ, sublatis anchoris Caletum versùs quatuor Leucas in Euronotum Classis ea abscessit; quam circa idem tempus *Blacus* prætor cum classe Anglicana, dum ab occidente ad Dunas rediret, conspicatus est, eámque est ratus, ex eo quem tenebat cursu, abiisse: Simúlque
Bornius

(19)

Bornius Tribunus in conspectu erat, ex Dunis properè adveniens, ut cum *Blaco* se conjungeret: Unâ aut alterâ post horâ Classis Batavica, mutato cursu, revertit, passísque velis omnibus ad *Blacum* prætorem rectâ contendit. Ante omnes *Van Trumpius* erectum præcelso malo vexillum ferox præferebat. In quod *Blacus*, simulátque intra ictum venisset, excussam tormento glandem intendit, binas deinde singulares. Quo facto, *Van Trumpius* item glande singulari Prætoris vexillum trajecit, totóque primus infesto latere tormenta omnia in eum displosit, demptíque apluftribus, sub insigni Hollandiæ insigne rubrum extulit: quod universæ classi datum committendi prælii signum erat, atque ità ad certamen deventum est, quod inter horam quartam & quintam post meridiem est cœptum, & ad nonam usque duravit. In eo certamine Angli duas naves Batavicas cœpere, quarum unam, quæ aquam senis pedibus altam in alveum receperat, traducto ad se præfecto cæterísque Classiariis, pro derelicto habuere. Alteram, quæ tricena tormenta portabat, abduxere. *Blacus* prætor eodem quo pugna commissa est loco, vel haud longè, totâ nocte stationes habuit: Classísque Batavica circiter quatuor Leucarum spatio disjuncta versùs oram Gallicam postero manè visa est.

Hujus narrationis fides ex literis prætoris *Blaci, Bornii* Tribuni, & aliorum qui in ipso aderant negotio, ipsísque Centurionum & Classiariorum Batavicorum, qui in ea pugna capti erant, testimoniis; ex mandatis etiam quæ præfecti Navium, aliíque
Classiarii
C 3

(20)

Classiarii Batavi acceperant, chartulis denique ex aliis hac de re pridem vulgatis constat.

Quod autem *Van Trumpius* in ea quam reddit hujus rei gestæ ratione, causam cur redierit fuisse ait, ut mercatoris quibusdam navibus à Gaditano freto opulenter onustis præsidio esset, quæ naves cum quibusdam nostris Liburnicis conflixerant, res illa tota in literis à Capitaneo Young conscriptis narratur (quæ & pridem vulgatæ sunt) in quibus & quam occasionem, quod initium, quémque exitum pugna illa habuerit perscribitur. Quinetiam naves illæ, quas vel Sabbathi proximè elapso per eum locum transierant, die ubi *Blacus* prætor tum erat, & Orientis plagam versus jam erant profectæ.

Sequuntur illa Scripta in unum collata quæ inter Parlamentum Reipub. Angliæ & D.num Adrianum Pauw Legatum Fœderatarum Belgii Provinciarum Extraordinarium, cùm de pace agerent, ultro citróque reddita sunt.

✢✢✢✢✢✢✢✢✢✢✢✢✢✢✢✢✢✢✢✢✢

Oratio D.ni *Adriani Pauw*, cùm in Parlamento audiretur, undecimo Junii, M.DC.LII.

Illustrissimi Domini!

TEstimonia publica & signa manifesta sinceræ benevolentiæ, ingenui amoris & veræ amicitiæ quæ ab

(21)

ab universo statu & subditis Fœderati Belgii omni tempore Populo Anglicano, & præsertim inclyto Reipub. Angliæ Parlamento eandem prosperè ac feliciter gubernantis exhibita fuere, toti orbi Christiano tam sunt cognita & aperta, uti de illis nemo hæsitare possit: Multò minùs de Ordinum Generalium Belgii Præfectorum optimâ fide ac inveteratæ amicitiæ observatione dubitare debeat. Cùm verò ex humanarum rerum varietate & inconstantia nonnunquam aliquid contingat, quod externam quidè faciem obnubilet, & animorum distractionem arguere videatur, veruntamen si maturè iis occurratur, ac in contrarium opposita è m odio tollantur, ea ad conservanda & corroboranda magis quàm ad dissolvenda mutuæ necessitudinis vincula quàm plurimum facere soleant. Hanc ob causam placuit Ordinibus Generalibus Confœderatarum Belgii Provinciarum, Superioribus meis, quantumvis de singulari prudentia & industria Legatorum extraordinariorum, ipsorum statûs nemine, circa maximi ponderis negotia hic versantium nihil dubitantibus, nihilominus me novâ extraordinariâ Legatione ad Parlamentum Reipub. Angliæ quàm celerrimè ablegare, Uti præmisso imprimis publicæ salutis & felicis regiminis voto, ex propensâ officiorum omnium oblatione apertè & candidè notum facerem (sicubi tam recenter ex supremo ipsorum con gressu egressus cum certissima scientia testari possum) nihil magis ipsis cordi esse, aut optatius accidere posse, quàm ut firma & constans amicitia inter utrumque statum non religiosè tantùm colatur, verùm indies augeatur atque omni modo consolidetur; adeóque

nihil

C 4

(22)

nihil eveniat quod mutuæ securitatis, utilitatis & necessitudinis repagula inter populos tam vicinos abrumpere aut ex aliqua occasione labefactare possit. Et propterea magno cum attonitu & ingenti animorum mœrore nuncios ad eos perveniffe de iis quæ inter claffes & Thalaffiarchas utriufque reipub. præter omnem expectationem nuperrimè evenere & ab utraque parte commiffa fuere. Quia vero cafus tam fubitus & inopinatus non tantum novas turbas excitare, verumetiam fufpicionibus anfam præbere poffet, ac fi illa quæ de mutuo fœdere ac ulteriori veteris amicitiæ corroboratione jam tractantur, non ferio agerentur, atque ideo in pofterum ad fcopum exoptatum incaffum laboratum iri, exiftimârunt fuperiores mei non fupervacuum, immo huic tempori & infelici rerum fucceffui conveniens atque neceffarium, uti præter Ordinem confuetum, atque adeò ex fuperabundanti per me (cui ratione muneris omnibus confiliis intereffe licuit) Parlamento Reipub. Angliæ tam antecedentia, quàm quæ fubfecuta funt, & ad eorum notitiam pervenerunt, palàm & fincerè exponerentur, & omnia è medio tollerentur, quæ aliquam inter utrumque Statum fimulatem producere aut negotium tractatûs confœderationis remorari aut impedire poffent. Itaque vigore credentialium prædictorum Ordinum Generalium & ipforum nomine huic Parlamento Reipub. Angliæ obteftor & declaro, nihil unquam apud eos meditatum vel ab iis actum, multò minùs in mandatis datum fuiffe, quo dignitas hujus Reipub. læderetur, amicitia & concordia cum eadem à longo temporis tractu ftabilita diminueretur, vel
aliquod

(23)

aliquod difcordiæ femen fub aliquo prætextu injiceretur, immo prædictos Ordines toto ex animo optâffe & omnibus viribus laborâffe, uti amicitia & confœderatio in æternum duratura omni meliori modo, & quanto ocyùs perfici & in falutem & commodum utriufque Reipub. folenni fœdere fanciri potuiffet. Verum quidem eft claffem non exiguam in Belgio inftructam, fed Ordines Generales affiduis fubditorum fuorum querimoniis eò adactos fuiffe tam conftans & notorium eft, uti id etiam prædicto Parlamento fignificandum cenfuerint; quod tamen nullâ aliâ intentione factum, vel denuntiatum fuit, quàm ut Belgii fubditorum, qui magna per mare damna & ingentem navium jacturam paffi fuerant, faluti & protectioni per legitima & confueta media profpiceretur, nemo autem læderetur aut offenderetur, multò minùs uti cum claffe aut navibus antedicti Parlamenti de controverfiis maritimis difceptaretur. Quæ omnia cùm itâ acta & gefta fint, & nihilominus ex fuperveniente inter utramque Claffem cafu undequaque ingens rumor & non exigua controverfia fit exorta, fignificandum inprimis Ordines Generales Parlamento Angliæ cenfuerunt, quæ ad aures ipforum perlata à Thalaffiarcha ipforum Status fcripto confignata, teftimoniis Claffiariorum comprobata, & ex relationibus fide dignorum ipfis notificata funt. Videlicet Thalaffiarcham Trompium neceffitate magis, quàm alia de caufa, claffes navales hujus Reipub. appropinquâffe, Præfectum *Bourn* primo humaniter falutari curâffe, ac deinde cum Thalaffiarcho Blake fortuitò obviàm factus effet, fcapham expofuiffe,

D

(24)

fuisse, ut deputatos ad eundem transmitteret, & adventûs sui rationem redderet, & insuper vexillum superius auferri mandâsse; sed cùm præter omnem exspectationem se toto latere tormentorum bellicorum à navi Prætoria infeliciter salutari & accipi videret, non offendendo sed defendendo tormenta sua bellica iterum explosisse, atque exinde inter utramque classem non ex proposito, sed ex accidenti aliquem conflictum exortum, sed brevi finitum, neque amplius continuatum aut profecutum, verùm Deo propitio breviter extinctum fuisse. Quæ cùm ab inexspectata receptione inchoata, nullo autem fervore à nostris continuata, neque tam ex animorum alienatione vel ob aliquam causam præcognitam, sed magis ex accidenti commissa & perpetrata sint, exponunt Ordines generales, & amicè rogant, ut Parlamentum Reipub. Angliæ credere & assentiri velit, nihil deliberato proposito, vel præcedente mandato, sed casu fortuito & forassis ex Rerum humanarum fragilitate & inconstantia evenisse, atque adeò sua consilia & mandata eò dirigere, ut omnia obstacula, offensiones & ulteriores læsiones, quantò citiùs è medio tollantur & inhibeantur, sicuti Ordines generales ab ipsorum parte prompti & paratissimi sunt convenientia iis confestim remedia adhibere : Judicant sanè Universæ rei Christianæ & præsertim religionis reformatæ Statibus quàm maximi interesse, nè dissensiones inter Utramque Rempub. augeantur, atque inter vicinos amicos & ejusdem fidei consortes populos aliquid sinistri oriatur, quod pacem publicam turbare, commercia utrinque utilia & necessaria intervertere & inimicis tàm

(25)

tàm apertis quàm occultis causam præbere possit, utrique insidias struere, vel Respub. jamjam communi fœdere jungendas in diversas partes distrahere, atque eâ ratione, quod Deus avertat, calamitatum & bellorum sedes à se avertendo in earum perniciem derivare; Quod nè eveniat, & nè malum ulteriùs surgat, in principio proponere, omnéaque industriam adhibere jussus sum, ut de præteritis per media convenientia quàm primùm conveniri, & in futurum præcaveri possit, nè similia sinistra aut funesta ab utriusque Reipub. Classiariis ampliùs perpetrari queant, in quibus dignitatem & honorem Parlamentum Reipub. Angliæ conservatam cupiunt. Cùm ergò Ordines Generales hisce prædicto Parlamento publicè testatum faciant; ipsos unicè desiderare, ut omni amoris & benevolentiæ officia continuentur, adversa impediantur & ad optatum mutuæ confœderationis scopum & conclusionem ab omni parte consilia dirigantur, enixè rogo, ut placeat prædicto Parlamento me per deputatos suos vel per Concilium Status pleniùs sine temporis intervallo audire & intelligere, & cum justa & amicabili ante-actorum transactione ad pertractandum & consummandum negotium principale, ad quod Legati Ordinum Extraordinarii instructi & parati sunt, sine intermissione progredi. Interea gratias ago pro singulari favore D^{no} *Guilielmo Neoporto* ad reditum in Belgium per navim bellicam hujus Parlamenti ante paucos dies exhibito : & cùm prædictus Dominus membrum sit Status Hollandiæ Westfrisiæque, in mandatis habeo, eundem requirere, ut mecum hic remanere, communicatis consiliis agere, ac reverti velit,

D 2

velit, quod prædicto Parlamento non ingratum fore arbitror, cujus Parlamenti benevolentiæ me, meáque officia quàm reverenter commendo.

Pronuntiatum & exhibitum in Parlamento Reipub. Angliæ à Legato Ordinum Generalium Fœderati Belgii extra Ordinē misso. die 21 *Junii.* MDCLII.

Lettres de Creance dud' S.r Pauw.

Les Estats Generaux de Provinces Unies du Pais Bas.

COmme ainsi soit que nous ayons trouvé bon voire grandement necessaire en la conjuncture presente des affaires de l'Europe d'envoyer vers le Parlement de la Republique d'Angleterre le Sieur Adriaen Pauw, Chevallier, Seign.r de Heemstede, Hogersmilde, Rietwyck & Nieuwerkerk, Conseillier, Pensionaire d'Hollande & Westfrise, & de la part de ladite Province, Deputé ordinaire en nostre assemblée, en qualité, de nostre Ambassadeur extraordinaire, ayants faict choix de luy, comme d'une personne que nous tenons pour ses rares qualitez & longue esperience en estime & confiance, estant bien instruict de nos bonnes & sinceres intentions, qui n'ont autre but que d'entretenir, augmenter, confirmer, & corroborer d'avantage la bonne amitié, correspondence & alliance entre le deux Estats & nations

tions, fondées sur des interests communs de religion, d'Estat & de commerce, ayans telle confiance en la suffisance, prudence, fidelite & diligence que Nous nous remettons a luy, de les exposer de vive voix audit Parlement de la Republique d'Angleterre, & particulierement le zele que nous continuons a tout ce que peut estre du bien commun & repos des deux Nations, a raison de quoy nous prions bien instamment & de toute nostre affection par ces presentes ledit Parlement de la Republique d'Angleterre qu'il luy plaise de donner favorable Audience audit nostre Ambassadeur Extraordinaire, & luy deferer entiere creance, comme a nous mesmes en tout ce qu'il dira & proposera de nostre part en la conjuncture presente des Affaires des deux Republiques. Fuict à la Haie en Hollande le 14.me de Juin, 1652.

A. Bouchorst.

Par ordonnement desdits Seigneurs Estats Generaux.

Au Parlement de la Republique d'Angleterre   N. Ruyse.

Dies Veneris 11.mo *Junii* 1652.

DOminus Prolocutor referendi more Parlamento breviter exponit quâ sit usus oratione Dominus Adrianus Paius, Legatus Ordinum Generalium Fœde-

(28)

Fœderatarum Belgii Provinciarum Extraordinarius, cùm hodierno die in Parlamento audiretur; de chartula à prædicto Domino Legato Extraordinario unà cum versione Anglica sibi tradita retulit, quæ etiam chartula hodie recitata est.

Ex quo, consultum Parlamenti est factum, hasce chartulas ad Concilium Statûs remitti, & quæ ampliùs in mandatis habeat prædictus Dominus Legatus extraordinarius, ea uti prædictum Concilium audiat, cúmque eo agat, quæque priùs Parlamentum responsa dederit, quæque declaraverit, ab eorum sententia uti nè discedat, déque his primo quoque tempore ad Parlamentum referat.

Hen. Scobell Cleric. Parlamenti.

Harangue du Sr Pauw à son Audience dans le Conseil d'Estat.

Tres Illustres Senateurs,

AYant pleu à Messeigneurs les Estats Generaux des Provinces Unies du Païs-Bas, outre leur Ambassade extraordinaire, de m'envoier en la mesme qualité au Parlement de la Republique d'Angleterre, & ayant eu l'honneur d'expliquer hier dans leur pleine Assemblée le vray sujet de mon envoy, & les sinceres intentions de Mes Superieurs : J'ay creu estre de mon devoir de me trouver aussy dans ce Tres-Illustre

Senat,

(29)

Senat, y presentant mes Lettres de Creance, & luy souhaitant toute felicité & prosperité dans le regime & maniement de ces grandes affaires, qui luy sont commises de par cete grande Republique. Et comme j'ay declaré aud't Parlement, aussy je declare dereche f avec verité & certaine cognoissance, que Messeigneurs les Estat Generaux ont eu de tout temps & ont encore, plus que jamais, tres-grand desir, d'entretenir, augmenter, & conserver inviolablement la bonne amitié, estroite Alliance & parfaite correspondence qui a esté de long temps entre les deux Nations & Estats, & dont on a rendu des preuves assez notables & evidentes par cy-devant.

Il est aussy tres-constant que mes Superieurs n'ont rien plus à coeur que de voir l'acheminement & la conclusion du Traité de Confederation entre les deux Republiques, afin que par icelle soit establi une union plus estroite & une concorde fraternelle, pour renverser & destruire toutes les machinations & divisions qui pourroyent troubler & grandement nuire aux uns & aux autres, & les rendre moins considerables dans la Chrestienté.

C'est icy Messieurs le vray but de Ennemis de la Religion Reformée & orthodoxe, se persuadans fermement que par cete disunion & division, ils ne pourroient pas seulement affoiblir les deux Estats, mais les reduire aussy aux dernieres extremités. Or le bon Dieu ayant doüé les deux Peuples de ce don precieux de la foy Orthodoxe, & pourveu merveilleusement outre ces benedictions spirituelles aussy de temporelles par l'utilité de la navigation & commerse par toutes

tes les estendues du monde, & Messeigneurs les Estats Generaux jugeant qu'il faut conserver le premier, & veiller pour l'autre, maintenir l'Eglise & asseurer l'Estat, ils ont creu de ne pouvoir mieux obvier à tous inconveniens, que de joindre les ames & les biens des deux Republiques, & ainsi avec la grace de Dieu les rendre capables d'eluder toutes machinations contraires.

Pour cete raison l'inopinée nouvelle de la rencontre des deux flottes maritimes & des offences données de part & d'autre n'a pas apporté un mediocre trouble dans les Estats Generaux, jugeant pour ce sujet tres-necessaire que quelqu'un fust depesché extraordinairement & promptement pour informer la Republique d'Angleterre & le Tres-Illustre Senat, en choisissant ma personne pour rendre ces devoirs, comme ayant entrée tant dans l'Assemblée des Estats Generaux, que des Estats d'Hollande & West frise, & ayant part dans tous leur plus importants & plus intimes Conseils & deliberations, pour tesmoigner icy avec grandissime connoissance de cause, & non moins de verité & de fidelité, que nulle deliberation a esté formée, nulle resolution prise, nulle commission donnée directement, ou indirectement pour chocquer en aucune façon la Republique d'Angleterre, de l'offencer & moins d'attaquer la flote, ou navires d'icelle, mais qu'il a esté commandé au contraire de les traiter par tour en meilleurs amis, & leur tesmoigner toute sorte de bienveillance.

Et comme dans ladite malheureuse rencontre les affaires d'une & d'autre part ayent esté autrement, & tres-

tres-mal gouvernées, dont j'ay faict hier un ample recit, & que je ne veux presentement repeter, ni reveiller ce qui doit estre ensevely & oublié entierement, neantmoins ayant aperceu dans la derniere responce donnée à Messrs nos Ambassadeurs Extraordinaires, qu'on a proposé une satisfaction pour le passé & asseurance pour l'advenir Messeigneurs, les Estats jugent aussy estre necessaire qu'on oste la pierre d'achoppement pour les inconveniens survenus, & establisse les seuretés necessaires & qu'on procede sans intermission à la continuation & perfection du Traité de Confederation desja bien avancé & qu'on advise aux moyens les plus convenables qui pourront effacer l'ombrage mesme de mesfiance, & regler les ordres que les flotes seront obligées de suivre d'oresnavant.

Sur quoy ayant des Instructions requise de Mes Superieurs je say instamme que ce Tres-Illustre Senat ait agreable que quelques Senateurs du milieu d'iceluy soyent deputés, avec lesquels je puisse commencer, continuer & achever le plustost ce que pourra servir pour le contentement des deux Estats & appaisement des differents.

A quoy je doibs adjouster que Mes Superieurs n'ont jamais pretendu, ny ne pretendront de discuter l'honneur & la dignité de cete Republique, l'estimant la premiere & la plus considerable dans l'Europe, & souhaittant que par la jonction de deux puissances si redoutables, on puisse asseurer l'un & l'autre Estat, les garentir des embusches de leurs Ennemis,

(32)

Ennemis, & establir par une parfaite intelligence & confiance le repos de l'un & l'autre.

Cependant je vous prie, Messieurs, de vouloir par vostre sage conduitte donner ordre au plustost que pour le susdit accident les choses n'aillent plus avant par nouvelles offences, courses, ou prises, Mais que toutes voyes de fait soyent defendues & empeschées, pour ne rendre les maux incurables & nous exposer à l'appetit de nos Ennemis, ne doutant pas que par ce moyen nous ne trouvions les remedes convenables pour accommoder ce different amiablement & heureusement, à la confusion de ceux qui desirent & esperent autrement.

I'auray des obligations infinies à ce Tres-Illustre Senat s'il me daigne donner le plustost responce cydessus, & que je puisse sans intermission travailler à un oeuvre si digne, utile & salutaire, me recommendant cependant avec beaucoup de respect à l'honneur de leurs bonnes graces.

Adriaen Pauw.

Prononcé au Conseil d'Estat de la Republique d'Angleterre le $\frac{11}{21}$ de Juin 1652. & en suite exhibé par moy, soubsigné Ambassadeur Extraordinaire des Estats Generaux des Provinces Unies du Pays Bas.

Die

(33)

Die Lunæ 14° Junii, 1652.

In Concilio Status in Alba Aula.

EX Parlamenti consulto 14° Junii mandavit Concilium D^{no} Commissario *Whitlock*, D^{no} Commissario *Lisle*, D^{no} Viccecomiti *Lisle*, D^{no} *Oliverio St-John*, summo Justiciario, D^{no} *Bond*, D^{no} *Scot*, Tribuno *Purefoy*, D^{no} *Henrico Vane*, Equiti aurato, D^{no} *Guilielmo Masham*, Equiti aurato, D^{no} *Henrico Martin*, D^{no} *Herberto Morley* Tribunis, aut eorum tribus quibusvis aut pluribus, uti Commissarii sint, qui D^{num} *Adrianum Pauwm* ab Ordinibus Fœderatarum Belgii Provinciarum Generalibus ad Parlamentum Reipub. Angliæ conveniant, & quæ ejus Ex^{tia} scripto exhibuerit, ea uti accipiant, déque iis & colloquium cum eo habeant & agant, quóque egerint ad Concilium deferant, sirque hora quarta hujus diei post meridiem statutum tempus D^{num} Legatum prædictum conveniendi sit, solito conveniendi loco; idque ut idoneo quoque tempore totics fiat, quoties dabitur occasio; Utque D^{nus} *Oliverius Fleming* Eques auratus, Ceremoniarum magister, id ejus Ex^{tiæ} significet, eúmque ad statutum locum deducat.

Jo. Thurloe,
Cleric. Concil.

E 2   Die

Declaration and *Scriptum* 249

(34)

Die Lunæ, 14° Junii, 1652.

In Concilio Statûs in Alba Aula.

PLacuit, Commissarios, quibus mandatum est, ut agant cum D⁻⁰ *Adriano Pauw*, Legato Fœderatarum Belgii Provinciarum Extraordinario, petere, uti inspiciant diplomata ab ejus prioribus ei data, quibus agendi & transfigendi potestas atque authoritas in eum coetus sit iis de rebus proponendis quas in mandatis habet, Eique significare, gratissimum hoc fore Parlamento, si ab ejus Excellentia in habendo hoc colloquio, quod ipse expetivit, celeritas omnis adhibeatur; Ejusque Excellentiæ demonstrare, nihil quidem à parte Concilii Statûs esse defuturum, quod ullo modo conducere possit huic negotio feliciter conficiendo.

Jo. Thurloe,
Cleric. Concilii.

Sommaire de ce que le S.ʳ Adriaen Pauw, Ambassadeur Extraordinaire des Estats Generaux des Provinces Unies du Pais-Bas a proposé aux Deputés du Tres-Illustre Conseil d'Estat.

L Edit Ambassadeur ayant, par cy-devant, & abondamment remonstré que les Estats Generaux n' ont

(35)

ont deliberé aucunement, (ainsy qu'il se trouvera & paroistra tousjours,) ni publiquement ni secretement, ni en general, ni en particulier, beaucoup moins donné chargé, ordre ou Commission de faire aucun acte offensif contre le Parlement de la Republique d'Angleterre, leur Flottes, navires, officiers & subjects, mais au contraire de les rencontrer avec les civilités accoustumées & tesmoignages ordinaires d' affection; tellement qu'on ne doit nullement douter qu'ils n'ayent des sinceres intentions à conserver & augmenter l'ancienne & mutuele amitié.

Pour cette raison, on ne peut nullement imputer aux Estats Generaux ce que c'est dernierement passé entre les deux Flottes, ni pour cela se mescontenter, ou offencer & attenter contre leurs subjects, comme estant directement contre l'ancienne amitié & correspondence qui a esté entre les deux Nations. Et ladite rencontre estant survenue par accident & sans dessein, ledit Ambassadeur a proposé, sçavoir si ne seroit plus à propos qu'on passa par dessus du passé, & qu'il fut pris de l'un & l'autre costé, comme s'il n'y avoit jamais rien eu, & ainsy tout fut remis, comme il a esté par cy-devant, & que la suitte fut plustost redressée a fin qu'il n'en puisse rester marque exterieure, ou interieure.

Neantmoins si le bon plaisir de ce Tres Illustre Senat est autre, combien que ledit Ambassadeur ait rondement, & sincerement deduit tout ce qui est venu à la connoissance de ses Superieurs touchant le passé & luy soient submistrés comme aussy aux autres Ambassadeurs Extraordinaires (oultre les susdits informations)

E 3

(36)

formations qu'il a eües devant son partement,) diverses notables & considerables attestations *in probanti forma*, & qu'il a entendu qu'il y a icy toutes autres & contraires information, d'ou il paroist que les parties sont discrepantes dans leurs productions, & ainsy on ne peut pas clairement juger du faict, ledit Ambassadeur a voulu proposer que les choses passées fussent plus prez examinées, les informations necessaires de l'un & l'autre costé, ou *conjunctim* prises, & en suite la verité aprez certaine connoissance sur descouverte par des Commissaires qui seront deputés de part & d'autre specialement sur ce sujet pour voir lequel des deux parties a faict le premier l'attaque, & causé les desordres qui sont ensuivis.

Ledit Ambassadeur declare, qui si peut conster que le Lieutenant Admiral des Estats Generaux a faict le premier l'attaque, il ne sera pas seulement en tel cas desadvoué & son faict desaprouvé desdits Estats Generaux comme ayant transgressé leurs Ordres & Commission, mais le feront aussy punir pour cela, selon que l'importance de cet attentat requira comme n'ayant obey a leurs commandement, & principalement ayant donné juste sujet de mescontentement à leurs bons voisins & amis, requirant aussy de ce Tres-Illustre Senat que si le contraire soit averé selon que nos informations portent que l'Admiral de la Republique d'Angleterre ait donné occasion aux susdites rencontres, & ait faict le premier l'attaque, qu'en tel cas il soit donné une pareille declaration de desadvenu du Parlement contre ledit Admiral, & la mesme peine decernée contre luy.

(37)

D'ou il est à croire que les finceres intentions des Estats Generaux, ne paroistront pas seulement, & que tout soubçon pourra estre osté, mais qu'on pourra facilement trouver les moyens pour une reparation, ou satisfaction equitable : Les autres Estats & Republiques ayans suivy la mesme methode & practique avec bon succés d'ont l'Ambassadeur peut alleguer des divers exemples.

Et afin que semblables inconveniens ne puissent arriver à l'advenir, l'Ambassadeur a declaré que les Estats Generaux n'ont jamais eu intention, n'y n'ont encore de diminuer en aucune façon l'honneur & la dignité du Parlement de la Republique d'Angleterre, Mais qu'ils ont commandé par cy-devant, & encor' ont donné nouvel ordre depuis le malheureux accidant, qu'aux rencontres & salutations des flottes ou navires de guerre touchant le baississement du Pavillon & appendances d'iceluy, on fasse le mesme honneur au Parlement de la Republique d'Angleterre, comme on a faict autres-fois & durant l'autre precedent Gouvernement, esperant qu'on donnera ainsy & recevra reciproquement contentement.

Et comme il est tres-necessaire pour confirmer l'Amitié mutuelle entre les deux Nations que la negociation du Traité entre les deux Republiques soit avancée & le plustost que sera possible achevée, ledit Ambassadeur a representé & requis serieusement, que puis que Messrs les Ambassadeurs Extraordinaires, aprez diverses conferences ayent assez faict cognoistre par leur derniere remonstrance l'intention de leurs Superieurs (touchant led[t] Traité) qu'auffy la derniere in-

tention

E 4   D'ou

tention de cet Illustre Senat soit exprimée & notifiée afin de remarquer par là les differens qui resteront encor' & que les difficultés puissent estre ostées, & qu'on puisse tant plustost parvenir à une conclusion bonne, ferme & permanente, que les humeurs puissent estre appaisées pour establir une eternelle amitié & indissoluble Intelligence.

Outre cela ledit Ambassadeur a demandé avec grandissime Instance que tous actes d'offence & de faict puissent cesser & estre inhibés & defendus par ordre de ce Tres-Illustre Senat & principalement, que les personnes, navires & biens des Subjects des Provinces Unies tant militaires qu'autres soyent indifferemment licenciés & de leurs arrests & detentions relaschés, & ceux qui ont esté ou sont retenus par force, soyent mis en liberté, & que les Innocens & non coulpables ne puissent plus recevoir de dommage, & d'incommodité, comme on est tout prest & resolu de faire de nostre costé.

Ledit Ambassadeur a prié aussy qu'il plaise audit Tres-Illustre Senat luy faire sçavoir au plustost leur bonne intention & resolution sur ce que dessus, & principalement sur la continuation du Traité qui est commencé, sur la cessation de toutes voyes de faict, sur la relaxation des Navires detinés & arrestés les personnes & biens des Subjects des Provinces Unies, comme luy a esté prest de declarer sincerement de la part de ses Superieurs, & asseurer ledit Senat de la continuation de leur parfaite amitié & affection.

Exhibé par moy Ambassadeur Extraordinaire le $\frac{14}{24}$ Juin 1652.

Adriaen Pauw.

14° Junii, 1652.

In Concilio Statûs in Alba Aula.

PLacuit, Commissarios, quibus negotium est datum, uti agant cum D° Adriano Paio, à Foederatis Belgii Provinciis, Legato Extraordinario, illud urgere, uti authoritatem ei commissam priùs inspiciant, quàm tractationis hujus initium faciant.

Jo. THURLOE.
Cleric. Concilii.

Memoire du Sr Pauw du $\frac{2\text{me}}{12}$ de Juin 1652.

Au Tres-Illustre Conseil d'Estat du Parlement de la Republique d'Angleterre.

L'Ambassadeur Extraordinaire des Estats Generaux des Provinces Unies du Pays-bas ayant eu l'honneur de tenir deux conferences avec Messieurs les Deputés dudit Conseil & y ayant deduit tres sincerement plusieurs choses concernantes sa qualification, & le restablissement de la bonne Amitié & parfaite intelligence des deux Nations, il prie le tres Illustre Senat de vouloir avoir un tel esguard au rapport que lesdits Deputés feront qu'il

(40)

il puiſſe recevoir au pluſtoſt une favorable reſponſe, & luy pardonner qu'il uſe cete importunité, puis qu'il ſe trouve preſſé dans la conjoinĉture des affaires, preſſantes, & pour obvier de bonne heure les inconveniens qui en pourroyent ſurvenir.

Adriaen Pauw.

Ce 25.me Juin, 1652.

ACceptâ hâc chartulâ, datóque colloquio, D.no *Adrianus Pauw*, ut autoritatem agendi & tranſigendi ſibi commiſſam exhiberet, inſtabat credentialibus five commendatitiis, terniſque datis ſibi liberi commeatûs literis, quarum exemplaria ab ipſo tradita ſunt, & unum Gallicè ſcriptum, bina de Belgico verſâ in hunc modum ſe habent.

Les Eſtats Generaux des Provinces Unies des Païs Bas, A tous ceux qui orront, ou verront ces preſentes, Salut.

SCavoir faiſons, que pour l'expedition de diverſes affaires d'importance, nous avons trouvé bon de depeſcher en Angleterre le S.r Adriaen Pauw, Chevalier Seigneur de Heemſtede, Hogerſmilde, Rietwick, Nieuwerkerk, Conſeiller Penſionaire d'Hollande

(41)

de & Weſtfriſe, Deputé Ordinaire de ladite Province en noſtre Aſſemblée & à preſent Noſtre Ambaſſadeur Extraordinaire. Et pourtant Nous commandons icy & requerons tous Lieutenans Admiraux, Vice Admiraux, Commandeurs & Capitaines des Navires de guerre de ces Païs, ordonnés pour cela, ou qui pourront eſtre ordonnés & commandés par ſon Excellence ; Qu'ils reçoivent en leurs vaiſſeaux reſpeĉtifs & tranſportent le bagage dudit Seigneur de Heemſtede en Angleterre, & de faire en cela tout ce que noſtredĉt Ambaſſadeur Extraordinaire requerra, l'accommodant, durant ſon paſſage, dans leurſdits Vaiſſeaux, & luy portant reſpeĉt ſelon leur devoir, & ayans mis à terre Noſtredit S.r Ambaſſadeur Exraordinaire avec ſon train & baggage en Angleterre, faire & accomplir en outre les commandemens qu'ils peuvent deſja avoir receu, ou qu'ils peuvent encor recevoir, comme il ſera requis de tous ceux qu'il pourra concerner. A toutes leſquelles choſes leſd.ts Lieutenans Admiraux, Vice Admiraux, Commandeurs & Cap.nes ne feront faute ſous peine d'encourir noſtre plus haute indignation. Faiĉt à la Haye ſous noſtre ſeau, paraphure & Signature de noſtre Clerc ce 14.me de Juin 1652:

Signé, *A. BOUCHORST.*

Par ordonance des Haughts & Puiſſants Seig.rs les Eſtats Generaux.

N. RUYSE.

Les

(43)

Les Eſtats Generaux des Provinces Unies des Païs-Bas, *A tous ceux qui verront, ou orront ces preſentes, Salut.*

Sçavoir faiſons, Quayant trouvé bon pour l'expedition d'affaires d'importance de depeſcher en Angleterre le Sr Adriaen Pauw Chevalier, Seigneur de Heemſtede, Hogerſmilde, Rietwick, & Nieuwerkerk, Conſeiller Penſionaire d'Hollande & Weſtfriſe, Deputé Ordinaire de ladite Province en noſtre Aſſemblée en une Ambaſſade Extraordinaire ; Pourtant nous requerrons & commandons à cette fin tous Lieutenans, Admiraux, Vice-Admiraux, Commandeurs & Capitaines des Navires de guerre de ces Provinces, Qu'ils recoivent & tranſportent le bagage & les hardes dudit Sr Ambaſſadeur Extraordinaire, dans leurs vaiſſeaux reſpectifs, & le tranſportent en Angleterre en telle maniere que ledit Sr Ambaſſadeur Extraordinaire pourra deſirer, & que ſon Excellence commandera & requerra, l'accommodant auſſy dans leurs vaiſſeaux, & portant tout reſpect audit Sr Ambaſſadeur Extraordinaire à ſon train & bagage : Et les ayans mis à terre en Angleterre, de faire en outre ainſy qu'il leur ſera commandé, ou qu'il leur a deſja eſté commandé, ou leur peut eſtre cy-aprez commandé, comme choſe qui concerne tous leſdits Lieutenans, Admiraux, Vice-Admiraux, Commandeurs & Capnes leſquels ne s'acquittans de leur devoir feront

(44)

feront punis à la rigueur de noſtre plus haute Indignation. Donné à la Haye ſous noſtre cachet ou ſean, paraphure & ſignature de noſtre Clerc. le 14me Juin, 1952. Signé, *A. Boucheriſt*, & au deſſous,

Par ordonnance deſdits Hauts & Puiſſants Seigneurs les Eſtats Generaux.

N. Ruyſc.

Les Eſtats Generaux des Provinces Unies des Païs-Bas, A tous ceux qui ces preſentes verront, Salut.

Comme ainſy ſoit que pour le bien commun de la Chreſtienté & pour l'advancement d'affaires de grande conſideration, importance & conſequence, nous avons trouvé bon d'envoyer vers le Parlement de la Republique d'Angleterre le Sr Adrian Pauw, Chevalier Seigneur de Heemſtede, Hogerſmilde, Rietwick & Nieuwerkerk, &c. Conſeiller Penſionaire d'Hollande & Weſtfrize, deputé ordinairement de la part de ladite Province en noſtre Aſſemblée, en qualité de Noſtre Ambaſſadeur Extraordinaire. Nous requerrons tous Lieutenans, Gouverneurs, Chefs, Colonels, Capnes & Vaiſſeaux de guerre, Gardes de Ponts, Ports & Paſſages en tous lieux ; Et en outre tous autres Juſtices, Officiers, & Subjects

F 3 de

Die Martis 15to Junii, 1652.

In Concilio Status in Alba Aula.

PLacuit, deferri ad Parlamentum quid Concilium ftatuerit, quidque mandaverit, de ratione habendi colloquii cum Dno Adriano Paio, Fœderatarum Belgii Provinciarum Legato Extraordinario, déque chartulis, quas ille Commiffariis Concilii tradidit; cúmque ex hifce chartulis Concilio non videatur, Prædictum Legatum poteftatem ullam agendi aut tranfigendi accepiffe, optimum vifum eft prædicto Concilio, deliberandam rem integram demiffè ad Parlamentum referre, ut de ea re quæ ejus fententia fit, fignificare velit.

JO. THURLOE.
Cler. Concilii.

Lettre du Sr Pauw au Seigneur Prefident du Confeil d'Eftat.

MONSBIGNEUR,

AYant communiqué à Meffieurs les Ambaffadeurs Extraordinaires des Provinces Unies au Parlement de la Republique d'Angleterre ce qui s'eft paffé dans mes audiences & conferences avec Meffieurs les

de ladite Republique d'Angleterre, de laiffer aller, paffer & repaffer avec fon train, vallets & fuivants, hardes & baggage, librement & fans trouble, tant par eau, que par terre, fans luy faire, ou donner, ni fouffrir qu'il luy foit faict, ou donné, aucun trouble, empefchement, ou deftourbier, mais pluftoft toute aide, fecours, faveur, & affiftance necefsaire & requife, & reconnoiftrons tres volontiers ces bons offices en temps & lieu. Donné à la Haie en noftre, Affemblée fous noftre Seau, Paraphure, & fignature de noftre Clerc le 14e Juin, 1652.

Signé, *A. BOUCHORST.*

Et au deffous,

Par ordonnance defdits Seigneurs Eftats Generaux.

N. RUISE.

Et cacheté du cachet defdit Eftats Generaux en cire rouge.

Die

Declaration and Scriptum 255

(46)

les Commissaires du Conseil d'Estat, & leur ayant faict voir les Instructions & Ordres de mes Superieurs, ils ont trouvé bon d'adresser le Memoire cy joinct à Messeigneurs dudit Conseil d'Estat, Mais d'autant que le Chevalier Fleming Maistre des Ceremonies m'a signifié que leurs Excellences avoyent trouvé bon de faire rapport de toute l'affaire au Parlement même ce matin, j'ay jugé à propos de prier vostre Excellence que le susdict Memoire puisse estre mis ez mains de Monsieur le Raporteur pour estre communiqué aussy bien que les autres propositions & papiers à Messeigneurs du Parlement, Priant Dieu, Monseigneur, de vouloir par la grace benir les affaires pour sa gloire, & la prosperité des deux Nation, Je demeureray tousjours.

Monseigneur,　　　　De vostre Excellence
　　　　　　　　　　　Tres-humble serviteur

Le 16/26 Juin, 1652.　　　　ADRIAEN PAUW.

La suscription est,

A Monsieur, Monsieur le Comte de Pembrocke & Montgomery, President du Conseil d'Estat de la Republique d'Angleterre.

(47)

Le Memoire des trois Ambassadeurs Extraordinaires mentioné en la Lettre precedente.

MESSIGNEURS,

LES Sr Adriaen Pauw, Seigneur de Heemstede, Ambassadeur Extraordinaire des Provinces Unies des Pais-Bas, nous ayant communiqué ce qui s'est passé ez conferences qu'il a eues avec les Commissaires; Et nous ayant monstré ses instructions & tous les ordres des Seigneurs les Estats Generaux desdites Provinces Unies, nous n'avons pas voulu manquer d'asseurer vos Excellences, que nous avons trouvé le tout en bonne forme & aussy valide qu'on le peut desirer. Et que Nous sommes tres-contents en vertu des pouvoirs qui nous ont esté donnés & lesquels ont esté exibés & approuvés, de nous obliger & de signer tout ce que ledit Seigneur de Heemstede a transigé & negocié suivant lesdits ordres ; Comme aussy tout ce qu'il pourra transiger & negocier comme dit est, ou de soy mesme, ou conjointement avec nous, selon qu'il sera jugé expedient pour parvenir plus facilement à la conclusion du Traité d'Aliance entre la Republique d'Angleterre, & les Provinces Unies du Païs-Bas.

Donné ce 26me de Juin, 1652.

G

(48)

Die Jovis, 17° Junii, 1652.

De re propositâ decretum in Parlamento est;

HAbitâ consultatione de re à Concilio Statûs relatâ, censet Parlamentum, adeóque decernit, uti Concilium Statûs cum D⁽ⁿᵒ⁾ *Paio*, Legato Potestatum Generalium Fœderatarum Belgii Provinciarum extraordinario ex prioribus mandatis pergat agere.

HEN. SCOBELL, *Cleric. Parlamenti.*

Memoire receu de la part du Sr Pauw
le 17me Juin, 1652.

Au Tres-Illustre Conseil d'Estat.

L'Ambassadeur Extraordinaire des Estats Generaux des Provinces Unies du Pays Bas se trouve necessité de demander très-instamment & aussy tost que sera aucunement possible une autre Audience auprès Messieurs les Deputés dudit Conseil pour y recevoir la responce tant desirée sur les points qu'il a desja proposés dans les dernieres conferences & pour leur faire encore des autres ouvertures sur des choses tres importantes, qui ne peuvent souffrir aucun delay, & dont il est tres expressément chargé de ses Superieurs, Priant tres-affectueusement que cete juste demande luy puisse estre octroyée.

Ce 17/27 Juin, 1652. Adriaen Pauw.

(49)

Autre Memoire dudit Sr Ambassadeur
Pauw du 17 *Juin*, 1652.

L'Ambassadeur Extraordinaire des Provinces Unies a representé à Messieurs les Deputés du Conseil d'Estat en sa troisieme Conference tenuë ce jourd'huy ce qui sensuit.

Que l'Estat des Provinces Unies s'est monstré tousjours & est encor resolu de se tenir ferme à l'Amitié & intime correspondence de cete Republique, l'ayant faict paroistre encor depuis peu, en accordant à la compagnie des Marchands Anglois advanturiers establie en Hollande toute la seureté & protection (durant ces brovilleries) qu'ils ont de sirée avec cete clausule d'y persister mesmes si les affaires fussent allées plus avant.

Que ce que s'est passé aux environs de Dunes, ou Douvres ne doit former une querelle generale entre les deux Estats, Mais cet accident doit estre pris pour une action personnelle dont les personnes sont responsables, qui seront trouvées d'avoir excedé leur commission.

Et afin que cela soit vuidé selon le faict & que la satisfaction requise s'en puisse ensuivre, il seroit tres-expedient de le faire examiner par des Commissaires deputés de part & d'autre, pour faire chastier celuy qui sera trouvé coulpable suivant les maximes de tous Estats & Republiques, par lesquelles leur repos & tran-

G 2

(50)

tranquillité tant au dedans que de hors avec leurs voifins est conservée.

En outre Les Navires de guerre se rencontrans en mer & se reglans, comme auparavant & durant le temps du precedent regime, il n'y aura plus aucune dispute doresnavant sur ce sujet.

Et quand la Confederation qui est à cete heure sur le tapit sera conclue, ainsy que les Estats Generaux desirent uniquement, l'amitié entre les deux Estats & leurs peuples sera plus parfaite, permanente, confidente & inviolable, & la vraye & orthodoxe Religion dont ils font profession par une singuliere grace de Dieu aura une protection tres-puissante & tres-asseurée.

Ledit Ambassadeur ayant derechef proposé les moyens susd[its] & y ayant adjousté plusieurs raisons & argumens tres valables a prié déstre esclaircy la dessus du sentiment dud[it] Conseil d'Estat avec offre de respondre & satisfaire aux difficultés qui pourroyent rester encore.

Ou autrement qu'il pleust à Messieurs les Deputés de conferer avec luy sur le mesme subject, ou de proposer de leur costé ce qu'ils pourront trouver estre raisonnable & equitable pour sortir au plustost de ce malheureux accident, promettant de contribuer de son costé tout ce qui luy sera aucunement possible avec priere tres-instante d'en vouloir faire rapport sans delay aud[it] Conseil & tellement mesnager le temps & le affaires, d'aujourdhuy qu'on en puisse sortir par des voyes convenables sans interruption

(51)

ruption du repos public, & plus grande alteration des humeurs des deux Nations.

Ce que ledit Ambassadeur a recommandé tres-affectueusement & offert pour obvier à toutes sortes d'aigreurs & d'inconvenients.

Ce $\frac{17}{27}$me Juin 1652.   Adriaen Pauw.

Responsum Concilii Statûs ad summarium D[omi]ni Adriani Pauw Potestatum Generalium fœderatarum Belgii Provinciarum Legati Extraordinarii mensis hujus Junii Concilio exhibitum.

DE Consiliis Dominorum superiorum vestrorum nuper initis, deque iis quæ Classis vestra in ipsis Angliæ Littoribus ac stationibus recens patravit, quæ Parlamenti Sententia fuerit, quodque judicium, percepit Ex[cellen]tia vestra ex Parlam[en]ti responso ad ternas chartulas Legatorum vestræ Reipub. Extraordinariorum, priusquam Ex[cellen]tia vestra huc adveneit, reddito ; Cujus responsi, simulque rei totius, ficui gesta est, narrationis, quæque super ea requesitiones habitæ fuerint, & ad vos tum quidem delatæ, meminit in iis chartulis, quæ jam præ manibus concilio sunt, Excellentia vestra ; neque ex re ulla quam deinceps in medium protulit vestra Excellentia causa quidquam nobis videtur esse, cur eam mutare sententiam debeamus. Cúmque ab illa fœderatarum

Provinci-

(52)

Provinciarum classe quod tentatum est, necnon etiam eam ad rem apparatus illi (erant enim inter ipsa vestra de fœdere nobiscum ineundo colloquia ad repentinum impetum instructa & veluti ex compositio facta omnia) si ex sententia processissent, proculdubio rem Anglicanam in discrimen haud leve adduxissent, æquum videri non potest, hanc rempub. tanto periculo edoctam, tamque insigniter conservatam (quam suî conservationem Soli DEO acceptam refert) velle sè pari periculo obnoxiam atque nudam in posterum relinquere, aut in re tam evidenti & perspicuâ pati, quæstionis habendæ accuratioris obtentu aut aliarum exemplis Rerumpub. quæ huc nihil attinent, abduci se ab adhibendis remediis huic malo accommodatis. Quapropter Concilium, quod ab Excellentia vestra proponitur admittere non potest, vel prætermittendo quod jam factum atque patratum est, vel ineundæ quæstionum rationi immorando cujus in chartulis vestris facta mentio est; quæ sibi quidem & non necessaria & dilationum plena & quæ denique iniri non possit, videtur.

Quod autem deinde proponitur, ut ad inceptam à cæteris vestræ Nationis Legatis Extraordinariis tractationem fœderis redeatur, post tantam ejus violationem existimamus huic quidem reí idoneum tempus non esse, donec vulnus, cui jam medicando laboratur obductâ cicatrice penitùs sanari queat. Dᵒᵒᵒᵘᵐ superiorum Vᵒʳᵘᵐ studium in hanc rempub. atque propensum animum sæpiuscule prædicare, necnon edicta aliquot & acta publica proferre, quibus idem eorum

(53)

eorum animus erga nos declaretur, præsertim quod ad honorem illum in mari nobis tribuendum attinet (quum vetustum hoc & indubitatum Gentis hujus jus atque decus sit) quod etiam ad tutelam illam à mercatoribus nostris Roterodami petitam, atque à vobis concessam, Parlamentum quoque, quod ad se attinet, nullo unquam tempore sua studia amicitiæ cum fœderatis Belgii Provinciis colendæ significare destitit, aut commorantibus apud nos earum civibus tutelam omnem quæ quidem satis esset, etiam non petitam præbere; veruntamen prout res & tempora jam ferunt, non est ut expectari possit, uti hæc Respub. ea persequi omitteret, quorum meminit responsum Parlamenti suprædictum, ob rationes illic allatas.

Ab Alba Aula
19° Junii 1652.

Memoire du Sʳ Ambassadeur Pauw de $\frac{1\text{ Juliet.}}{11\text{ Juin.}}$

Au Tres-Illustre Conseil d'Estat.

L'Ambassadeur Extraordinaire des Provinces Unies ayant receu le soir du 1ᵐᵉ/2 du Courant par les mains du Sieur le Chevalier Fleming la Response qu'il a pleu à ce Tres Illustre Conseil d'Estat luy donner sur le sommaire des choses par luy proposées

propofées le 4me du mefme mois, il fe trouve obligé
de demander tres inftamment une autre audience &
conference avec les Deputés dudit Confeil, afin de
leur expliquer plus particulierement & plus ample-
ment les Intentions de fes Superieurs & s'acquitter
fuffifamment de fa charge.

Le 21 Juin / 1 Juillet 1652.

Adrian Pauw.

Autre Memoire du Sr Pauw du 21 Juin / 1 Juillet 1652.

Au Tres illuftre Confeil d'Eftat.

L'Ambaffadeur Extraordinaire des Provinces
Unies ayant receu le 9me Juin fur le foir affés
tard par les mains du Sieur Chevalier Flemming
la refponfe qu'il a plû au tres Illuftre Confeil d'Eftat
luy donner fur le fommaire des chofes par luy propofées le 4me du mefme mois.

Il fe trouve obligé, pour s'acquitter de fa charge
de reiterer ingenuement derechef icy, comme il a faict
par cy devant que les Eftats Generaux fes Superieurs
n'ayant nullement propofé, ny deliberé ny ordonné
de donner aucun foubçon, ou le moindre Subject
d'offenfe à l'encontre la flotte, ou navires de cette
Republique felon la parfaite cognoiffance qu'il a de
toutes leurs plus intimes deliberations & confultations
il avoit creu que cela auroit efté fuffifant à ofter toutes
autres impreffions contraires.

Il a auffy reprefenté naïvement l'accident arrivé
entre les deux flottes aupres de Douvres, ou Dunes,
felon qu'il eft venu à la cognoiffance de fes Superieurs par des atteftations finceres des perfonnes di-
gnes de foy, & fans reproche : Et pour eviter toutes
autres ulterieures conteftations (au lieu de maintenir
les preuves fufdictes) il a ouvert le chemin par
lequel on eut pû parvenir à la vraye & infaillible
cognoiffance & par mefme moyen à la fatisfaction
qu'on auroit pû legitimement pretendre.

Ainfy cet inconvenient ne peut eftre en aucune
façon imputé à fes Superieurs pour n'avoir jamais
eu la moindre penfée, ny aucunement contribué à
l'infraction de l'amitié (pour l'avoir eu toujours
tres chere) & moins à l'interruption du Traité de
confederation pour lequel ils en ont eu, & ont encor
leurs Ambaffadeurs Extraordinaires par deçà.

Cela fe peut manifefter fuffifamment par la
ferme & conftante refolution de fes Superieurs qui
n'ont jamais voulu octroyer des Lettres de repre-
failles fur des affiduelles plaintes & requeftes (rei-
terées jufques à l'importunité) des Intereffé; dans
les Navires qui ont efté pris arrefté & confifqué par
deçà, affin quon ne donnaffe le moindre Subject de
mefcontentement à cette Republique.

Le mefme fe voit encor clairement dans la protection octroyée à la compagnie des Anglois (eftablie
dans Rotterdam) *ex fuperabundanti*, & combien qu'
elle n'en avoit aucun befoing, pour tefmoigner plus
fpecia-

(56)

specialement leurs plus sinceres intentions lesquelles se peuvent justifier auffy par toutes leurs actions, personne de deça n'ayant receu jusques à present le moindre dommage, offence ou injure, pour toutes lesdites & autres procedures, mesme leurs vaisseaux de guerre & autres ayant mieux aimé se laisser conduire dans les ports d'Angleterre que de se deffendre contre ceux qu'ils ont tousjours tenu pour leurs Amis, comme n'ayant jamais receu aucune denonciation au contraire.

Mesme pour rendre un tesmoignage plus authentique à cette Republique & le faire cognoistre à tout le monde ses superieurs ont envoyé une seconde Ambassade extraordinaire pour desabuser entierement tous ceux qui pourroyent estre preocupés & mal informés & faire avancer & parachever ledict traité.

Mais en cas que toutes ces ouvertures & autres moyens d'accomodement soyent rejetées, & qu'on veuille proceder icy par des voyes qui au lieu d'assoupir ne fairont qu'accroistre le mal, & qui estant contre les maximes des Estats & Republiques lesquels ne jugent jamais sur les indices, presuppositions & suspicion, mais sur des preuves infallibles claires comme le jour en plein midy & irreprochables, & qui durant le traité font tousjours precisément cesser toutes voyes de faict, surprendront d'advantage lesdits Superieurs & donneront des estranges allarmes à leurs peuples & faisant souffrir les Innocens & ceux qui viennent de loing & qui n'ont jamais eu le moindre soubçon, ou entendu le moindre bruict de quelque

(57)

que mauvaise intelligence entre les deux Estats. Ledict Ambassadeur doit estre extremment surpris & marry, requirant (pour tenter toutes fortes de voyes) qu'il plaise auxdicts deputés de proposer de leur part des autres expedients (puis qu'on a tesmoigné dans la derniere response donnée aux autres Ambassadeurs Extraordinaires que les voyes les plus douces leur seront tousjours les plus agreables) qui pourront estre propres, satisfactoires & convenables pour sortir au pluftost de cette malheureuse affaire, & remettre le tout en son premier Estat.

Et cependant qu'on veuille faire cesser toutes voyes de faict & donner ordre que les navires detenus soient le pluftost relaschés priant infamment qu'il plaise audict Conseil de s'expliquer là dessus, & quant & quant respondre sur les derniers articles du memoire presenté le 21 Juin, & le rendre ainsy capable de contribuer ses meilleurs offices pour le bien & affermissement des deux Republiques.

Ce 21 Juin, 1652.
   1 Juillet,

                                    Adriaen Pauw.

H 2   Autre

(58)

Autre Memoire du Sr Pauw du 23me Juin 1652.

Au tres-Illustre Conseil d'Estat.

L'Ambassadeur extraordinaire des Provinces Unies considerant l'importance des affaires qui font presentement sur le tapit, & les dangers eminants dont on est menacé de part & d'autre, a esté contrainct de se rendre encor Importun envers vos Excellances en leur recommandant tres-serieusement la responce sur sa derniere conferance & les priant tres-affectueusement qu'elle puisse estre un convenable & legitime moyen à assoupir les differents & restablir la bone union entre les deux Estats, & la parfaicte intelligence entre leurs Peuples.

A Westmunster
ce 23 Juin / 3 Juillet 1652. *Adrien Pauw.*

Re-

(59.)

RESPONSUM *Parlamenti ad illam partem schedulæ à D^{no} Adriano Paio exhibitæ, in qua petit à Concilii Commissariis, uti proponerent quæ sibi justa & cum æquitate conjuncta viderentur ad controversias, quæ inter hanc Rempub. & D^{nos} Potestates Generales Fœderatarum Provinciarum in præsentia ortæ sunt, primo quoque tempore componendas.*

I.

UTi Domini Potestates Generales Fœderatarum Provinciarum satisfactionis nomine solvant huic Reipub. quas fecit impensas hæc Respub. quæque damna sustinuit propter apparatus prædictarum Potestatum Generalium, quæque ab iis hac æstate tentata sunt, quarum impensarum ratio particularis idoneo tempore in medium proferetur.

II.

Uti factâ illâ solutione, de cujus summâ, ut supra dictum est, convenerit, impensarum atque damnorum nomine, aut eam ob rem datâ fide quâ Parlamento satisfiat, extemplò induciæ sequantur, atque arrnis abstineatur, navésque & bona post nuperam controversiam capta dimittantur.

III. Hisce

H 3

(60)

III.

Hisce duobus postulatis praecedentibus si assensus praebebitur, eáque perficiantur, Parlamentum hanc fidem in posterum dari sibi expectat, uti utraque Respub. firmum foedus inter se & rationes utrarumque bono jungat; Quod ut fiat, Parlamentum pro se quidem testatur omnibus justis atque honestis rationibus se esse libentissimè adnisurum.

Die Veneris 25:to Junii, 1652.
In Concilio Status in Alba Aula.

PLacuit, Commissarios, quibus mandatum priùs erat, uti D^{num} Paium, Foederatarum Provinciarum Legatum Extraordinarium convenirent, cúmque eo agerent, ad illud caput schedulae à D^{no} Paio per Concilium Status ad Parlamentum 25:to hujus mensis Junii delatae, quo in capite praedictus D^{nus} petit à Concilii Commissariis uti proponerent, quae sibi justa & cum aequitate conjuncta viderentur ad controversias quae inter hanc rempub. & D^{nos} Potestates Generales Foederatarum Provinciarum in praesentia ortae sunt primo quoque tempore componendas responsum Parlamenti praedicto D^{no} Legato in manus tradere.

Jo. Thurloe,
Cleric. Concilii.

(61)

Memoire du Sr Pauw du 26me Juin 1652.

Au Tres-Illustre Conseil d'Estat.

L'Ambassadeur Extraordinaire des Provinces Unies ayant esté hier en conferance avec les Seig^{rs} Deputés dudit conseil, & receu d'eux deux memoires sur le mesme subjeĉt, il desire grandement qu'il voulur avoir pour agreable d'ordonner derechef sans perdre du temps une nouvelle conferance avec lesdicts Deputés, affin qu'on s'y puisse expliquer & s'esclaircir d'avantage de part & d'autre & sortir au pluftost de cete affaire.

Ce 26 Juin/6 Juillet 1652.   Adriaen Pauw.

Autre Memoire du Sr Pauw du mesme jour.

Au tres Illustre Conseil d'Estat.

L'Ambassadeur Extraordinaire des Provinces Unies a proposé dans la conference tenue ce jourd'huy le 26 Juin/6 Juillet avec les Seigneurs Deputés du Conseil d'Estat les poinĉts suivants.

Que les Estats Generaux ayans esté obligés par des raisons alleguées de faire un equippage extraordinaire

Memoire

(62)

ordinaire, ont faict des frais excessifs & qu'ils continuent encor presentement.

Que leurs Subjects outre les excessives pertes qu' ils ont eues sur mer par cy devant, en ont receu de tres grandes par des represailles données tant contre les François que contre lesdicts subjects des Provinces Unies, & sur des autres pretextes.

Que l'Estat & leurs subjects ont beaucoup souffert, & ont esté grandement endomagés depuis peu par la prise & ruine de divers navires de guerre, & par l'arrest de tant de navires des marchands.

Et si on vouloit venir au remboursement des frais & dommages qu'on les devroit balancer les uns aux autres & considerer s'ils ne seroyent plus excessif. du costé des Provinces Unies.

En tout cas on doit faire une estimation raisonnable sans la referer à la production & examination des comptes.

Et s'il plaist auditcs Deputés d'exprimer ladicte estimation en termes civils de leur costé, on pourra remarquer si on a envie & si on est intentionné de deça de transiger les choses passées felon la raison & à l'amiable, ou si on voudra propofer des choses impossibles & non faisables.

Sur ce que concerne la confederation entre les deux Republiques & l'adjustance mutuelle pour secourir l'un l'autre contre ceux qui voudront offenser, ou attaquer, les autres Ambassadeurs Extraordinaires ont faict cognoistre les vrayes intentions de leurs Superieurs & font tout prests de continuer & parachever ladicte negociation sans perte de temps.

(63)

Si lesdicts Deputés jugent que ladicte confederation doit estre plus ample, & plus estroicte ledict Ambassadeur ne l'aura pas seulement pour agreable, mais supplie serieusement d'en estre esclaircy là dessus.

Donnant à considerer s'il ne sera pas convenable voire tres-necessaire que les flottes ne puissent s'approcher & s'engager davantage ce que ledict Ambassadeur apprehende grandement & notamment si on n'en donne promptement ordre par deça.

Et requirant aussy que les navires retenus puissent estre relaschés au pluftoft & qu'on ne fasse aucune ulterieure detension des prises affin que les humeurs estant aucunement appaisées, on soit pluftoft par amitié mutuelle, bienveillance & de bon gré que par contrainte induict à s'unir derefchef par une indissoluble confederation.

Et que ledict Ambassadeur puisse avoir icy desfus une si prompte & favorable declaration, qu'il puisse travailler avec plus d'apparance de succés auprez les Seigneurs ses Superieurs, & y effechuer ce que dans cete conjoncture du temps & des affaires est tres expediant & necessaire & s'y employer sans aucun delay selon l'ordre exprés qu'il a desdicts Superieurs, & selon lequel il est obligé de se regler precisement.

Signé

Adriaen Pauw.

I *Respon-*

(64)

Responsum Concilii ad Chartulam praecedentem.

CONCILIUM STATŪS cùm de Chartula à Domino *Paio* Legato Extraordinario D^{norum} Potestatum Generalium Fœderatarum Provinciarum per Commissarios suos hodie vesperi sibi allata deliberationem habuerit, neque responsum in illa perspicuum aut planum ad nostram postulationem schedulam Parlamenti nomine Excellentiæ Vestræ proximè exhibitam reperiat, petit uti responsum ad eam quàm præsentissimum atque planissimum reddatur, saltem ad primum ejus articulum, præsertim quia illi si assensus præbeatur, Concilium sese quàm primum conferre possit ad summam illam, cujus mentio fit, quàm moderatè & æquissimè constituendam, ut, quàmprimum secundus articulus præstabitur, ab omni hostilitate abstineri possit, itaque navium & bonorum quæ retenta sunt, restitutio protinus fiat, quandoquidem tertius articulus ejusmodi est, ut eam tantâ celeritate transigi non sit opus.

Ab Alba Aula 26to
Junii, 1652.

Jo. Thurloe.

Cleric. Concilii.

Memoire

(65)

Memoire du Sr Pauw du 27me Juin 1652.

Au tres-Illustre Conseil d'Estat.

L'Ambassadeur extraordinaire des Provinces Unies ayant consideré la responce qui luy fut delivrée hier au soir par le Sieur Chevalier Flemming sur des considerations par luy proposées par cy-devant, demande tres instamment qu'il plaise au tres Illustre Conseil d'Estat luy octroyer une autre conferance cet apresdisné pour y pouvoir deduire plus particulierement les intentions de ses Superieurs, & pour satisfaire aussy bien à leurs Ex^{ces} qu'à ses devoirs.

Signé

Ce $\frac{27\text{ Juin}}{7\text{ Juillet}}$ 1650.

Adriaen Pauw.

Autre Memoire du Sr Pauw du mesme jour 27me de Juin 1652.

Au tres Illustre Conseil d'Estat.

CEpendant que l'Ambassadeur extraordinaire des Provinces Unies a esté occupé à former la responce sur l'escrit qui luy fut rendu hier au soir bien tard par le Sieur le Chevalier Flemming, il a esté informé (à son grand regret) que la flotte de cete Republique est entrée en mer pour executer son dessein.

Ledict

Ledict Ambassadeur a eu ordre aussi par diverses depesches de ses Superieurs qu'en cas il ne put faire cesser les actes d'hostilité par tous devoirs possibles, il retournast en toute diligence aux Pays-Bas pour leur faire rapport de ce qui luy estoit arriué.

Tellement que ledict Ambassadeur ne pouvant plus faire aucun avancement dans la negociation dont il a commandement de faire rapport à ses Superieurs au pluftoft, il requiert qu'il puisse prendre congé demain dudict Conseil d'Estat pour passer en grande diligence avec le navire de guerre du Cap^{ne} Johan Verhaef qui a eu ordre de le mener & rammener, & qu'il puisse avoir un pasport dudict Conseil, affin de passer la mer sans aucun empeschement, ou destourbier & sans estre molesté ou arresté par les navires du Parlement.

Les autres AmbassadeursExtraordinaires luy ayant communiqué, & faict voir qu'ils avoyent pareil ordre & commandement, l'ont requis de demander de leur part qu'ils puissent avoir audience quant & quant dans ledict Conseil d'Estat & prendre congé d'iceluy comme aussy d'estre pourveus des navires qu'ils auront besoing pour le transport de leurs personnes, train & bagage, & aussy de tels autres pasports qu'il leur faudra pour la seurité de leur voyage.

Et ledict Ambassadeur attendra une prompte responce icy dessus, comme une chose tres-importante. Signé

Adriaen Pauw.

Ce 17/7 me Juin 1652.

27° *Junii*

27° Junii, 1652.

In Concilio Status in Alba Aula.

COnsultatione susceptâ de eo quod retulerunt Commissarii, schedulam à D^{no} *Pauw* Legato Foederatarum Belgii Provinciarum Extraordinario hodie vesperi sibi esse traditam; Concilium sui officii ducit esse, rem ad Parlamentum deferre, quod die Martis, primo confessu facturum se esse recipit, interea responsum nullum, præterquam hoc tantum, prædicto D^{no} Legato super hâc re potest reddere.

Jo. Thurloe,
Cler. Concilii.

Memoire du Sr Pauw le 28me de Juin 1652.

Au Tres-Illustre Conseil d'Estat.

L'Ambassadeur Extraordinaire des Provinces Unies ayant veu la responce dudict Conseil donnée sur sa proposition d'hier, a voulu declarer derechef d'estre grandement intentionné de contribuer tout son possible, estant venu par delà, afin que sur les ouvertures qui ont esté faites, & qu'on pourroit faire encore, on puisse trouver des moyen & expediments convenables pour faire cesser premierement toute alienation d'affections & actes d'hostilité, & ain'y

(68)

parvenir à l'accommodement des choses passées, & ensuitte à une ferme Union & confederation entre les deux Estats, & à un tel reglement entre les deux Nations que par iceluy leur prosperité & felicité puisse estre avancée & tous autres inconveniens à l'advenir destournés.

Et comme cette resolution est saincte, honneste, & (a yant bon succés) tres-salutaire, voire qu'on la doit executer tres-promptement, & devant que les affaires aillent plus avant, ledict Ambassadeur requiert qu'il plaise audict Conseil de considerer tout cecy, & ordonner ce qui pourroit contribuer & servir sur ce subject, & à l'advancement d'iceluy.

Et le temps estant grandement à mesnager, il sera tres-necessaire que ses audiences soyent hastées, & qu' il soit admis à icelles au plustost, comme aussy qu'il puisse avoir les expeditions requises pour le navire avec lequel il est venu, & qui l'attend à Graveland pour le transporter au Pays-bas, avec le passport qu'il a demandé pour passer seurement & eviter tous inconveniens qu'il pourroit rencontrer en mer.

Ledict Ambassadeur se promet qu'il plaira audict Conseil de donner ordre qu'en confederation de la qualité, il soit traité de mesme en sa dimission & congé, comme il a esté en son admission & reception, pour laquelle il remercie tres-affectueusement ledict Conseil. Signé

Adriaen Pauw.

Ce 28 Juin / 8 Juillet 1652.

Autre

Autre Memoire de mesme date.

Au Tres-Illustre Conseil d'Estat.

L'Ambassadeur Extraordinaire des Provinces Unies a creu estre à propos de proposer icy, si ledict Conseil d'Estat ne pourroit approuver, qu' aprés avoir faict son rapport aux Seigneurs les Estats Generaux, on renvoya son Secretaire ou autre personne affidée pour fomenter & entretenir la correspon-:nce, & rendre & recevoir de la part de l'un & de l'autre Estat, ce que pourra servir à l'accomodement des choses passées, & au restablissement de l'union & confederation.

Et si à cette fin on n'auroit pas pour agreable de luy faire depescher des passports pour pouvoir revenir librement & seurement & s'arrester si long temps par deçà que le Parlement de la Republique d'Angleterre, ou lesdits Estats Generaux le trouveroyent à propos & s'en retourner avec la mesme seureté estant rapellé.

Ou autrement qu'il plust audict Conseil de nommer, ou enseigner icy quelqu'un qui leur fut agreable, & propre à recevoir les lettres qu'on pourroit depescher pour ce subject par delà, & en faire avoir la responce. Signé,

Adriaen Pauw.

Ce 28 Juin / 8 Juillet 1652.

Memoire

(71)

Memoire des trois Ambassadeurs daté du 28me de Juin, 1652.

Au Conseil d'Estat de la Republique d'Angleterre

COmme ainsy soit que Nous Ambassadeurs des Seigneurs les Estats des Provinces Unies du Pays-Bas ayons par leurs Lettres venues depuis peu receu commandement de nous haster de retourner en nostre pays sans delay pour leur rendre compte de ce que nous avons fait en ce lieu, Nous prions pour cete cause instamment ce Senat de nous accorder la faveur de pouvoir, comme il nous convient, prendre congé de cete tres-Illustre assemblée, & en obtenir en mesme temps les navires necessaires pour nous transporter commodément avec nostre train & nostre bagage; Affin aussy que les Passeports convenables pour la seureté de nostre passage nous puissent estre accordés. Nous avons icy des vaisseaux de nostre pays tout prests pour cet effect, asçavoir le Capitaine Japden Boer avec trois petits Navires de la ville de Dort.   Signé,

F. Cats. G. Schaep. Vande Perre.

ORATIO

ORATIO Dⁿⁱ *Adriani Pau* in Parlamento habita 30 *Junii*, 1652. cùm discedens liberum commeatum peteret.

Illustrissimi Domini!

MIserunt Ordines Generales Foederatarum Provinciarum Belgii ad Parlamentum Reipub. Angliæ Legatos Extraordinarios, ut de corroboranda inter utrunque populum veteri amicitiâ, & sanciendo inter duos Status perpetuo fœdere serio agerent & pro communi utilitate & securitate convenirent, & insuper D. *Gulielmum Neoportum* Statûs Hollandiæ Westfrisiæque membrum ablegârunt ad tollenda nonnulla dubia & benevolas superiorum nostrorum circa tractatum confœderationis intentiones plenius explicandum;

Ac postremum paucis retro diebus placuit prædictis Ordinibus novam Legationem extraordinariam ad illustre hoc Parlamentum adornare, mihique eam provinciam imponere, cum speciali mandato, ut de optima ipsorum fide, propenso animo, & sinceriffima intentione erga hanc Rempub. superabundans testimonium redderem, omniáque accidentia inopinatà & inde exorta & opposita impedimenta diluerem, & è medio tollerem, eáque ratione inchoatam fœderis tractatio-

K

(72)

tractationem omni modo ad felicem exitum promoverem;

In quem finem inter alia propositum est, uti de iis quæ nuperrimè inter utramque Classem nullo sanè proposito, sed omnino Casu fortuito acta & perpetrata sunt, per utriusque Reipub. viros idoneos, factâ inquisitione cognosceretur, ac de justa & æqua satisfactione statueretur.

Nullo enim offendendi aut turbandi, multò minùs hostili animo Ordines erga hanc Rempub. affectos fuisse, sed veram amicitiam & pacem omnimodam cum ea colere, immo arctius fœdus sancire ipsos in animo habuisse, coram DEO toto Orbe Christiano & præsenti Parlamento Reipub. Angliæ profitemur & obtestamur.

Cùm verò infeliciter acciderit utramque Legationem post tot exantlatos labores & præstita ab omni parte ad conservandam pacem communem, & removenda omnia obstacula convenientia officia, non tantum ad optatum scopum pervenire nò potuisse, verùm ex adverso Statui Belgico non exiguâ incommoda & damna esse illata, immo ingentia pericula, necnon hostilia nunquam expectata neque antea denuntiata à Classe Anglica in altum profecta imminere;

Visum fuit utrique Legationi supervenientibus malis occurrere, & in casu tam insolito secundùm expressâ Ordinum Generalium mandata in patriam reverti, uti rationem à se gestorum Superioribus reddere, & de ulteriori ipsorum beneplacito certiores fieri possint.

Hunc in finem supremo hujus Reipub. Concessui, nomine

(73)

nomine Superiorum nostrorum, nosmet conjunctim sistimus, discessum nobis injunctum denunciamus, & itineri nos accingere paratos esse declaramus.

Ea quæ ad transfretationem, pro munere nobis demandato, & secundùm temporis rationem necesse habemus, Excellentissimo Hujus Reipub. Statûs Concilio indicavimus; super quibus responsum & expeditiones necessarias desideramus & exspectamus.

Nec possumus non denuo & obnixè rogare, uti omnes naves, quæ nuperrimè præter omnem exspectationem, & nullâ præcedente denuntiatione, in portubus Angliæ abductæ vel retentæ sunt, & quarum præpositi inscii & innocentissimi, nulli, aut nullam controversiæ occasionem dederunt, cum Navarchis, mercibus, oneribus & toto comitatu liberè discedere, & iter propositum sine alicujus injuria perficere possint, quod & inveteratæ amicitiæ & juri communi inter populos Christianos observato deberi contendimus, & à justitiâ & æquitate hujus Celeberrimi Concessûs impetratum iri speramus.

De cætero Deum Opt. Max. qui summus Author & Promotor est pacis & concordiæ ex animo precamur, uti cogitationes & consilia ad mutuam pacem & concordiam spectantia Parlamento Reipub. Angliæ suggerere, Christianam, Reformatam & Orthodoxam Religionem, quæ solâ pace nititur & florescet, per discidia verò & turbas sine dubio affligetur & dilaceratur, intemeratam & inviolatam conservare, Bellorum verò clades & miserias benigniter avertere & benedictionem cœlestem utrique Statui abundantor impartiri velit.

K 2   Quo

Quo in voto definemus, & in Patriam properantes ab Illustrissimo Reipub. Angliæ Concessu, debitâ, quâ par est, reverentiâ veniam petimus, eámque, & cætera quæ pro dignitate & securitate Legatis ubique conceduntur & contra malevolorum machinationes & injurias præstari solent, nobis non defutura confidimus.

Pronuntiatum in Parlamento Reipub. Angliæ ac protinus scripto exhibitum, die x° *Julii*, Anni M.DC.LII. per Ordinum Generalium Fœderati Belgii Legatos Extraordinarios.

Nous presentons aussy une Requeste laquelle nous a efté mise en main de la part des Marchands Hollandois, desirans de pouvoir jouir de méme seureté & protection, que celle qui a esté depuis peu accordée en la meilleure forme que faire s'est pû aux Marchands Anglois qui demeurent en nos Provinces.

Nous prions aussy finalement, qu'outre les deux Navires de guerre Hollandois, il nous en soit encore octroyé un autre, de ceux, qui sont aux Dunes, pour nous servir à nostre passage, ayans beaucoup de monde en nostre compagnie avec des Dames de qualité, & force bagage, ce qui nous causeroit de grandes incommodités, outre la chaleur de cete saison, si nous ne sommes accomodés dudit Vaisseau.

Hadrianus Paiw.
  J. Cats. G. Schaep. Vandeperre.

FINIS.

ERRATA sic corrigenda.

PAg. 1. l. 5. imprææsentia *lege* in præsentia p. 9. l. 1. quâ *lege* quæ p. 12. l. 23. fidem *lege* fiæem p. 28. l. 2. de *lege* deque

The Letter of 8 July 1652 to the Danish Envoys: *Domini Legati*

The official original English text, with the curtailed signature of the Earl of Pembroke and Montgomery, in the ornamental hand of an official scribe (who spells *Parlament* in the body but *Parliament* in the close) and the unsigned official Latin translation, in the hand of Milton's personal amaneunsis, headed *Translatio*, are printed here from MS. T.K.U.A., A.II.16, Bilag B, in the Danish Rigsarkivet, by permission of the Danish National Archives.

It is not practical to reproduce in print the scribal idiosyncrasies in the English text (*Ambassadors, endeavor, ye*).

For discussion and attribution of the Latin text to Milton, see pages 68–69.

OFFICIAL LATIN TEXT

Domini Legati Extraordinarij Seren.^{mi} Regis Daniæ cùm prædictæ regiæ Ma^{tis} nomine propensa ejusdem studia conciliandæ pacis inter hujus Reipub: Parlamentū, et Potestates generales Fœderatarum Belgij Provinciarum significaverint, permagnam ejus erga Parlamentū tum benevolentiam et amicum animum, et huic etiam nationi quàm impensè faveat, ex ea re simul declaravere; Quapropter Parlamentum Seren.^{mo} Regi Daniæ quammaximas agit gratias ejús*que* Ma^{ti} confirmat, omnibus in rebus quas hæc Respub: cum potestatibus fœderatarum Provinciarū generalibus, vel egit vel transegit, Parlamentū ad pacem et amicitiam cum illa repub: stabiliendam omni operâ et studio semper incubuisse; id*que* et orthodoxæ religionis promovendæ causâ, et ut communi ac mutuo utrius*que* reipub: bono consultum esset; verū ne*que* pacē, ne*que* amicitiam se dignā at*que* honestam adipisci potuit; quamvis et et omnes, quantum in se erat, offensiones, omnes controversianum occasiones sedulò vitaverit, et tamen in summa pace, cùm et legati eorum de fœdere arctissimo nobiscum agerent, in naves nostras nihil tale expectantes in ipsis stationibus ab eorū classe impetus factus est, qua injuria sane gravissima accepta, impetrare nequivit, vel ut satisfactio sibi in præsens, vel ut fides in posterū daretur nihil istiusmodi hostile posthac sibi illatum iri; Parlamentum ita*que* sui muneris hoc esse existimat, ut denegatam sibi satisfactionem omni honesta ratione, prout deus dederit, consequi nitatur; quod et plenius intellegi poterit ex eo publico scripto, quod vicinarum nationum in gratiam, immo omnium quibus æquitatis studium est, brevi promulgabitur; quod et cum Do^{nis} Legatis Extraordinarijs Regis Daniæ Parlamentum communicari jussit, petit*que* ut Excellentiæ Vestræ dare illud Regiæ Majestati ejus idoneo tempore velitis.

Official text in original English

The Lords Ambassadors Extraordinary from his Matie ye King of Denmarke having in ye Name of ye said King signified his Maties friendly desires concerning Peace betweene ye Parlament of this Comonwealth & ye States Gen^ll of the United Provinces of ye Low Countryes have therein declared verie much affection & respect to ye Parlament & to ye good & happinesse of this Nation, for ye which ye Parlament doth returne their hearty Thankes unto ye King of Denmarke, and doe assure his Matie, that in all ye Transactions betweene this Comonwealth & ye States Gen^ll ye Parlament have most earnestly and constantly endeavored to setle a right understanding & Amity between them, for ye advancem^t of true Religion & mutuall good of both Comonwealths, but could not obteine ye same, & have carefully avoided on their part all provocations & occasions of Difference between them, yet have been lately assaulted & invaded in their owne Roads by the Fleet of the United Provinces, for which high injury they could not procure any satisfaction, nor security for ye Future, They therefore hold themselves oblidged to endeavor ye gaining thereof by such just wayes & meanes as God shall put into their hands, as may bee more fully understood by their Declaration published for ye Satisfaction of their Neighbours and of all indifferent persons, which ye Parlament have Comanded to bee communicated to the Lords Ambassadors of ye King of Denmarke, with a desire that their Ex^cies would bee pleased to present ye same in convenient tyme unto his Majestie.

Whitehall   Signed in the Name & by Order of the
       Councell of State
8º July 1652   Appointed by Authority of Parliament
      Pembe & Montgomery, Presi^dt

ex Jo Thurloe cler
of the Councell

The Letter of 19 October 1652 to the Danish Envoys: *Concilium de ijs*

The official original English text, signed by William Constable, in the highly ornamental hand of a Council scribe, and the unsigned official Latin translation in a simpler fair copy by the same scribe, headed *Translatio*, are printed here from T.K.U.A., A.II.16, Bilag H, in the Danish Rigsarkivet, both for the first time.

Many scribal idiosyncrasies in the English (*your*, *ye* and others) have not been reproduced.

For discussion and attribution of the Latin text to Milton, see pages 69–70.

Official Latin Text

Excellentissimi Domini

Concilium de ijs quæ Excellentiæ vestræ Regis Daniæ et Norweghiæ & nomine, proximi Septembris quinto decimo, exhibuerunt, habita consultatione, de controversijs nimirum quæ in præsentiâ inter hanc Rempub: et Potestates Fœderatarum Belgij Provinciarum Generales ortæ sunt, per*que* eam occasionem acceptâ Excellentiarum vestrarum quam dedistis ad Parlamentum, super eadem re chartulâ, unà cum ejus ad illam responso, scripto*que* publicè edito, quod quidem scriptum Ex^tijs V^ris a certis ex eo Concilio delectis in manus traditum erat, quod*que* ad prædictam Regiam Ma^tem idoneo tempore missum a vobis fuisse, uti par erat, credidit, nitatur nunc sanè, ijs quibus cum hac natione amicitia constat, immo vel ijs etiam quibuscun*que* æquanimitas ulla est; de justiciâ et æquitate Parlamenti in ea re non plenissimè satisfactiō esse, quæ et in eo scripto tàm perspicuè declaratur, ubi et Parlamentum disertis verbis profitetur, se quicquid egerit hac in re dum etiam vel maximè dat operam, Deo benè juvante prout occasio se obtulerit, ut illatatum jam sibi injuriarum et reparationem adipiscatur, et nequid simile in posterum tentetur, fidem accipiat, hoc tamen amino at*que* voto id omne agere, ut omnes inter utram*que* Gentem controversiæ possint amicè at*que* pacatè, si quo id pacto fieri potest, componi, prout Deus pro sua summa providentia viam ad hanc rem patefecerit, et circumstantiæ profuerint ad reddendos ejusmodi conatus et minus tardes et efficaciores, quam alios ejusdem modi, qui ante hac adhibiti sunt, fuisse constat. Qui animus illius ad pacem tam propensus, quem se gerere palam et quasi toto orbe terrarum audiente tam religiose confirmat, testis locuples esse poterit, si hujus discordiæ factus nondum finis sit, id Parlamento imputari merito non posse. Ne*que* intelligit Concilium, quid sibi velint Ex^tiæ V^ræ cum magnas difficultates et graviora postulata a Parlamento ferri dicatis, quandoquidem nullæ a Parlam.^{to} postulationes latæ sint, ex quo Ex^{tiæ} V^{ræ} illa de re quicquam exhibuerunt; quæ*que* prius fuerant latæ et claræ et moderatione erant plenæ, super quibus etiam haud eundem expromere sensum Ex^{tijs} V^{ris} eo tempore videbatur, atque nunc expromitis. Concilium ita*que* iterum rogatas vult Ex^{tias} V^{ras} ut quid in prædicto Parlamenti responso scripto*que* publico dicatur, serio velitis considerare, cui sententiâ quidem Concilij, nihil restat quod adjici possit.

Official Text in Original English

My Lords,

The Councell having taken into their Consideration what your Ex^cies in the name of his Matie the King of Denmark & Norweghen represented unto them the 15th day of September last, touching ye present Differences betwixt this CommonWealth and the States Generall of the United Provinces of the Low Countries, and by occasion thereof having reviewed yr Ex^cies former Addresses to the Parlament relateing unto ye same subject, with their Answer and Declaration thereupon, which was delivered into the hands of your Ex^cies by certaine Members of ye said Councell and which they had reason to believe your Ex^cies would in due time have communicated unto his said Matie Doe find it strange, That there should still remayne with those in Amity with this Nation, or indeed with any equall and indifferent Persons, the least Dis-satisfaction concerning the Justice and Candor of the Parlaments proceedings in that Affaire, soe clearlie expressed in the said Declaration, and where is particularly intimated by ye Parlament, That their deportment in this Matter, even while they endeavour with Gods assistance, and as they had oportunity to seeke Reparation of the Wrongs already suffered, and Security that ye like bee not attempted for the future, is, with this mind and desire, that all Differences betwixt the Nations may (if possibly) be ffriendly & peaceably composed, as God by his Providence shall open a way thereunto, and Circumstances shall be conducing to render such endeavours less Dilatory, and more effectuall then those of this kinde heretofore used have beene, which peaceable and good Minde of theirs soe solemnly professed before the World, doth sufficiently shew, That the continuance of these Differences cannot with Justice be imputed unto the Parlament. Neither doe ye Councell understand what can be intended by your Ex^cies makeing mention of great Difficulties, and aggravating of Demands on ye Parlaments part, whereas none have beene made by them since your Ex^{cies} first Addresse on that subject, and those which were made before, were cleare, & moderate; And concerning which, your Ex^{cies} thought not fitt (at that time) to expresse any such sence, as now you doe.

They therefore desire your Ex^{cies} againe, seriously to weigh what is said in the said Answer and Declaration of the Parlament, whereunto in the opinion of the Councell, nothing remaynes needfull to be added.

Whitehall 19th Signed in the Name and by Order
                      of the Councell of
October. 1652.   State appointed by Authority of
                      Parlament.
                  Wm: Constable presid^{t}

The Letter of 13 July 1653:
Concilium Status de Chartulâ

Milton's Latin text, published here for the first time as his work, is printed from the official original manuscript MS. S.G. 8484, together with its official original English-language text. It is extant in other contemporary manuscripts in Dutch archives and was printed in Scheurleer's *Verbael* (1725), pages 38–40. Scheurleer "edited" the English text.

For discussion, see page 73.

OFFICIAL LATIN TEXT

   Concilium Status de Chartulâ à Dominis Deputatis Dominorū Potestatum in fœderatis Belgij Provincijs Generalium 1:/11:° hujus mensis Julij ad se missâ serio deliberavit; quâ ad chartulam a Commissarijs Concilij 29 Junij/9 Julij prædictis Deputatis in colloquio traditam respondetur. Quæ responsio cùm eò spectet ut ostendat causam suspecta primum fidei, belli deinde inter Anglos et fœderatas Belgij provincias coorti ab hâc Repub. profectam esse, hanc scilicet (ut in illâ chartulâ affirmatur) cùm centum viginti naves bellicas instruxisset; quibus et triginta alias mense Majo Anni 1652 adjungere in animo habuit, quúm*que* innumerabilem pecuniam ad eam rem cöegisset vicinis omnibus, quorum id intererat, sese pariter armandi (cum id ipsum et rerum usus, et Reipub: rectè administrandæ recepta apud omnes gentes ratio moneret) necessitatem attulisse. Potestates ita*que* Generales ob hanc potissimum causam et quòd partìm a prædonibus mediterraneum mare per id tempus latè infestanti*bus*, partìm ex literis, Marcæ vulgo dictis, quas Parlamentum Anglicanum proximè dimissum in populum fœderati Belgij concessit, aliarúm*que* obtentu quas concessit in Gallos, detrimenta planè intoleranda ceperant, coactus demum fuisse, eas copias comparare navales, de quibus socios omnes at*que* amicos certiores fecerant; postulata proinde quæ in prædictâ chartulâ quam Concilij Commissarij sibi proximè tradiderunt, sunt lata, ne*que* justa esse, ne*que* rationi consentanea: quum ne*que* a Principibus, ne*que* a rebuspub: hujusmodi negotia pertractantibus id unquam fieri soleat (quod quidem illic affirmatur) ut damnorum reparatio urgeretur, aut ulla omnino mentio ejus fieret.
   Ad hæc Concilium responsum hoc reddit; Causas et rationes quibus adductum est Concilium ut sui esse officij existimaret; et præsertim damnorum reparationem et securitatem in posterum dandam postulare, partìm in sua chartulâ proximè datâ, at*que* uberiùs, cùm in eo responso

quod Parlamentum superius ad ternas chartulas à Legatis tribus Potestatum Generalium extraordinarijs exhibitas per occasionem prælij inter classes utrius*que* Reip: tum recens comissi reddidit, tum etiam in responso Concilij Status ad summarium Domini Adrian Paw 14/24 Junij 1652 datum expositas esse: Quas si prædictis Dominis Deputatis visum erit percurrere, cum alijs item chartulis in quibus ea quæ Parlamentum et Concilium cum praedicto Domino Adriano transegere, continentur, reperietur rerum status longè se alitèr tunc temporis habuisse, at*que* in supradictâ chartulâ Deputatorum ostenditur, natás*que* suspiciones bellúm*que* cœptum ob causas longè alias quàm quæ ab ijs illic afferuntur. Hæc autem Respub: ab instruendis centum viginti navibus bellicis tantum abfuit (quas prædicti Deputati) paratas at*que* deductas mense Majo 1652 fuisse aiunt, ut Parlamentum ex ijs navibus, quæ maris præsidio destinari solebant, minorem numerum expediri tum jusserit quàm Annis superioribus consueverat quùm et divinâ ope re prosperè domi gestâ et studij Potestatum Generalium in se propensi fiduciâ, minori quàm antea classe opus esse arbitraretur: at*que* hoc verum esse constat, non solum ex mandatis de præsidio maris, eo anno ut dictum est datis, verùm ex eo etiam quod die illius Maji undevigesimo 1652 styli veteris, quo die Trumpius quadraginta amplius navium bellicarum classi præfectus Navarchū nostrum prope Doroberniam adortus est, non erant ex nostris amplius duæ et viginti naves deductæ, quarum Navarchus ipse tredecim duntaxat secum tum habebat, octo circiter aliæ subsidio per opportunè advolabant. Et hæc quidem Respub: cùm a fœderatis Belgij Provincijs vicinis suis, quibus benevolentiam suam at*que* amicitiam totiès compertam, reddiderat, et quibuscum de arctiori fœdere ineundo eo ipso tempore colloquia habebat; nihil hujusmodi inimicum expectaret, us*que* adeo à navibus imparata ad repentinum illiusmodi casum tum erat ut quinquaginta naves mercatorias quam primùm conducere ad supplimentum suæ classis cogeretur. Concilio proinde inopinatum accidit ut in chartulâ

Dominorum Deputatorum scriptum reperiret causas magnorum apparatuum illorum quos fœderatas Belgij Provincias moliri fatebantur, magnæ illi classi, quam hæc Respub: tum parabat, ascribendas esse; præsertìm si memoriâ tenuerint, tres illos Legatos Extraordinarios, suorum jussu primorum 10/20 Martij, 1652, Parlamentum certius fecisse de eo quod Generales illæ Potestates secum statuerant centum quinquaginta naves præsidiarias armare, supra eas quas jam habebant, at*que* etiam postquam ista significaverant, quamvis eo tempore quo Potestates Generales hostem nullum foris haberent, ne*que* ullam sui consilij rationem redderent præter Commercij patrocinium (causam haud quaquam probabilem tantorum extra ordinem apparatuum) cujusmodi et illa est de literis, Marcæ vulgò dictis, ab ijsdem Deputatis commemorata, quandoquidem Parlamentum tales literas uni duntaxat ex multis, qui eas petiverant propter direptiones à popularibus fœderati Belgij sibi illatas concesserat, unde si ad receptas ubi*que* gerenda Reipub: rationes, quarum meminerunt Domini Deputati, recurrendum sit, causæ satis erat, cur Parlamentum ad defendendam rem Anglicanam, suá*que* in mari jura notissima sedulò se compararet; quaé*que* oblatæ sunt ijs suspiciones adeo erant omnìno justæ ut supradicti Legati in suâ quadam chartulâ eas etiam excusare sint conati; quod idem fecit et Dominus Adrianus Paw in eâ chartulâ, quam Concilio exhibuit 11? Junij 1652. Hæc tamen Respub: adeo se lentè et cunctantèr hâc in re gessit, ut antequàm in classem suam a Trompio, ut dictum est, factus ultrò impetus esset, ex eó*que* cur fœderati Ordines tantam vim navium comparassent, causa vera apparuerit, classem suam ne unâ quidem nave auctiorem reddidissent.

Cum ita*que* manifestum sit, non solum Potestates Generales in suis apparatibus priores fuisse, sed etiam classem Anglicanam ante oppugnatam quàm vel minima hostilis animi suspicio ab Anglis præberetur, immò contra omnia sinceri eorum studij indicia constarent suós*que* navales apparatus causam aliam habuisse nullam, quàm suam contra fœderatas Belgij Provincias defensionem, ipsa justitia ac ratio, quam ad norman omnes gentes in suis mutuis tractationibus dirigere omnia debent, postulat, etiam ex ijsdem politicis rationibus quas afferunt ipsi Domini Deputati, ut satisfactio huic Reipub: detur ob impensas quas fecit, tam ante quintum et vigessimum Julij quàm deinceps, quæ quamvis summam bene magnam conficere possint, tamen persuasum hoc habeant Domini Deputati, Rempub: hanc eam adhibere moderationem hâc in re paratam esse quæ sincera sua nec non ardentissima studia testari possit firmam at*que* stabilem instaurandi pacem. Quod ad securitatem im posterum præstandam, multæ rationes allatæ à nobis jam sunt, quæ clarissimè ostendunt, quam iniquum esset, hanc Rempub:, post rem tam prosperè gestam, fusúm*que* tot suorum sanguinem, impressionibus ejus generis quovis tempore faciendis obnoxiam se relinquere; quæ omnia si tam seriò perpendantur quàm verè in nostris chartulis prioribus narrata sunt; facinus illud Trumpij non potest fortuitum dici, verum eo consilio cogitatum at*que* commissum ei*que* fini qui in prædicto Parlamenti responso ad supradictam chartulam trium illorum Legatorum disertis verbis exprimitur; Quod si præsentium rerum facies in fœderatis Belgij Provincijs, quàm*que* illio periculosa factio polleat, penitùs consideretur, haud facilè possit intelligi, quo alio pacto libertas illius populi veræ*que* religionis cultores in ijs Provincijs conservari queant, nisi pace et fœdere ineundo seriò et efficaciter provisum fuerit contra eorum conatus at*que* fraudes qui rebus Dei ac populi sui non in hâc solùm, sed in illâ etiam Repub: adversantur.

 Cùm*que* perspicuum sit, pactiones nudas et fœdera finem hunc non posse adipisci, securitatis rationes aliæ considerandæ sunt; Quarum singula capita quemadmodum et quid sit, quod hæc Respub: reparationis loco acceptura est, Dominis Deputatis tum proponentur, postquam ipsi de reparatione et securitate præstanda responsum plenum at*que* clarum reddiderint; quibus instant Concilium, ne*que* dubitat, quin Domini Deputati, perpensis quæ jam dicta sunt et rationum supradictarum momentis qu*æque* his adjungi possunt, suum assensum haud invitè sunt præbituri; unde si Deus futuris consultationibus propitius adfuerit, huic bello quamprimum finis imponi possit, et utræ*que* Respublicæ multò quàm ante hâc inter se conjunctiores, id*que* rationibus mùlto firmioribus ac potioribus sint futuræ.

Textual Note: The amanuensis wrote the *j* in *Majo* like a *y* with an umlaut, and spelled *supplimentum, vigessimum, im posterum præstandam, instant Concilium* for *instat;* in the phrase *reparationem et fidem,* he deleted *fidem* and inserted *securitatem* above it. *Paw* is omitted before *transegere.* The reading *ope re* is confirmed by MS. Aitzema 86.

Official Text in Original English

The Councell of State have seriously considered the Paper sent unto them by the Deputyes of the Lords the States Generall of the United Provinces, dated the 1/11 July instant, in Answere to the Paper delivered unto the said Deputyes of the Commission^s: of the Councell at the Conference the 29 of June/9 July. And the Scope thereof being to shew, That the first occasion of Jealousie, and of the present Warre betweene England, and the said United Provinces was given by this Commonwealth, who (as is alleadged in the said Paper) by their setting out one hundred & twenty men of Warre with a designe to adde thirtie more unto them in the moneth of May 1652, and by provideing an infinit sume of money in readinesse to that purpose, did oblige the interessed Neighbors, by all the rules and maximes of State to put themselves into a suitable posture, and that hereupon, and because of the pyracies of the Mediterranian, and Letters of Marque granted by the late Parlament of England, against the Subjects of the United Provinces, whereby and under pretence of the like Letters against the French, They suffered intollerable losses, The States Generall were necessitated to make the warlike preparations, whereof they had advertised their friends & Allies, and that therefore the demands made in the aforesaid paper delivered to them by the Commission^s: of the Councell were neither just nor reasonable, Being likewise never practised (as is alleadged) by States and Princes in their Treaties upon the like occasion, to insist upon or make mention of satisfaction for damages.

The Councell returnes this Answere thereunto. That the Grounds and reasons upon which the Councell have found themselves obliged to demand satisfaction and securitie, have beene in part exprest already in their said last paper, and more fully both in the Answere given by the late Parlament to the three papers presented unto them from the three Ambassad.rs Extraordinary of the States Generall upon occasion of the then late fight betweene the two Fleets, and alsoe in the Answere of the Councell of State to the Summary of the Lord Adrian Paw, presented to the Councell the 14/24. June 1652. Which if the said Lords Deputyes be pleased to reveiue with the other papers conteyning the transactions betweene the Parlament, and Councell, and the said Lord Paw, It will appeare, That the affaires in both States at that tyme were much otherwise then they are represented to me in the before mentioned paper of the Deputyes, and the Jealousies to have arisen, and the Warre to be begun from other Causes and upon other grounds then are supposed by them.

This Commonwealth was soe farre from makeing the preparations of one hundred & fiftie ships of Warre (as is mentioned by the said Deputyes) to be put out to sea in May 1652, That the Parlament had lessened their ordinary gaurd [sic], and given direction for setting out fewer ships then they had at Sea the yeare before, haveing through the blessing of God upon their forces, and being confident of the good Intentions of the States Generall towards them, lesse occasion (as they apprehended) of a great Fleet then formerly; And this doth not onely appeare by the directions given for that yeares gaurd [sic]; But in fact, There was not above twenty two Ships of their Fleet at Sea the 19.th of May 1652 old stile, when Tromp with above fourty sayle of men of Warre, assaulted the Generall neare Dover, who had with him but thirteene ships, and about eight more came afterwards to his Assistance. And this State not expecting an Action of this nature, from their Neighbours of the United Provinces, to whom they had given soe great Testimonyes of friendship, and good will, and with whom they were in actuall Treaty for a nearer Union, They were soe unready and unprovided with a Fleet sufficient to answere this exigencie, That they were constreyned to hire into their service above fiftie Merchants ships, to strengthen and reinforce their Fleet; And therefore it is very unexpected to the

Councell to finde that the said Lords Deputyes in their paper should make the reason of those great preparations, which they acknowledge the United Provinces were makeing, to arise from the great Fleet this State was setting out to sea, especially if it be remembred that the three Extraordinary Ambassad.rs by command of their Superiours did the 10/20 March 1652, give notice to the Parlament of the Intentions of the States Generall to equip and set forth with all speed one hundred & fiftie ships of Warre besides what was already in their Service, And alsoe that after this notice, although it was in a tyme, when the States Generall had noe Enemy abroad, nor assigned any other reason for their said resolutions, but the defense of Trade & Traffique (a very unlikely ground for such extraordinary preparations) as alsoe is that of Letters of Marque now mentioned by the said Deputyes, whereas the Parlament had granted such Letters but to one, of many that had demanded them for depredations done by the Subjects of the said United Provinces, and therefore upon the rules and maximes of State (as is observed by their Lord.ps) the Parlament had reason to put themselves into a posture and Condition to defend themselves and their knowne rights at sea, and had soe just a ground of Jealousie given them, that the said Ambassad.rs in one of their papers labour to excuse it, as did alsoe the said Lord Paw in his paper delivered to the Councell the 11.th of June 1652. Neverthelesse this State proceeded soe slowly herein, That untill their Fleet was actually assaulted by Tromp as aforesaid, and thereby the true reason of prepareing soe great a Navy made evident, they had not encreased their Fleet one ship.

It being therefore manifest, That not onely the preparations of the States Generall had their beginning sooner, then those of this Commonwealth, but that their Fleet was actually assaulted, before the least ground of Jealousie was given by them, but on the Contrary all demonstrations of sincere affection, and that their preparations at Sea were made upon noe other ground then for their owne defence against the United Provinces, Justice and reason which ought to be the rule and measure in treaties betweene Nations, doe require, even upon the grounds held forth by their Lord^{ps}, That satisfaction should be given to this State, for the Expences they have beene put unto, as well since as before the 25th July, which although it may arise to a great Sume, yet their Lord^{ps} may rest assured that this State will be ready to use such moderation therein, as may testifie the ardencie and senceritie of their desires to restore a good and lasting peace.

Concerning securitie for the future, severall reasons have beene already given, which doe evince how unreasonable it would be for this State, after soe great a deliverance, and the profusion of soe much bloud, to leave it selfe exposed to the same attempts at any other tyme, The Circumstances whereof being considered, as they have beene truely represented in former papers, That action cannot be esteemed of, as falling out by chance, but as intended for those ends, which are exprest in the said Answere of the Parlament to the paper of the said three Ambassad^{rs} extraordinary: And if the present State of affaires in the United Provinces and the spirit which of late hath beene prevalent there, be considered, It is not easie to see by what other wayes & meanes the libertie of the people, and the professo^{s} of true Religion in that Nation, can be preserved and mainteyned, then by a reall and substantiall secureing the intended peace and agreement against the Attempts and Artifices of those who are Enemyes to the Interest of God, and his people, not onely in this Commonwealth, but in that alsoe; And being now evident, That Treaties of Allyance as heretofore will not attayne those ends, other wayes of securitie are to be considered, which may be more effectuall, The particulars whereof, as alsoe what this State will insist upon for reparation, shall be made knowne to their Lord^{ps}, after they have been pleased to give a satisfactory Answere to the propositions of Reparation and securitie, which the

Councell doth insist upon, And cannot doubt, but that their Lordships well weighing the premises, and the importance of the aforesaid reasons, and what else might be added, will readily consent thereunto, whereby through the blessing of God, upon their future deliberations, a speedy end may be put to the present Warre, and the two Commonwealths united, upon better and surer grounds then heretofore.

Whitehall Signed in the Name & by Order of
13 July 1653. the Councell of State
  Gil Pickering Presd[t]

Textual Note: interessed, Mediterranian, revieue, remembred, bloud, gaurd, senceritie are amanuensis spellings.

The Letter of 1 August 1653:
Concilium Status ad chartulam

Milton's Latin text is known only from the copy in Bodleian MS. Rawl. A4, folio 305, from which it was printed — without any attribution to Milton — in T. Rymer, *Foedera*, volume 20, 666–67, and in the *Thurloe Papers*, volume 1, 354. The manuscript shows seven or eight blottings that seem to be corrections by the amanuensis, who may have been Milton's own, rather than a Council scribe. In this reprinting, his text is followed: ū for terminal *-um*; italics to indicate where he used the seventeenth century squiggle in *-ue* and *-us*, the preservation of his diacritical marks.

Milton's letter should be distinguished from another letter of the same date, submitted by the British, dealing with other matters.

The official original signed copy of the English-language text, for which Milton made this Latin version, is printed here from MS. S.G. 8484 in the Algemeen Rijksarchief. There are other copies in the Netherlands archives.

For discussion, see page 73.

Latin Text, Presumably Milton's Translation

Conciliū Status ad chartulam Dominorū a Potestatibus Fœderatarum Provinciarū Generalibus Deputatorū, de captis utrinque bello, responsum hoc reddit. Remp: hanc, quàmvis delatū ad nos sit tam ab ipsis bello captis quàm ab alijs permultis (quorū pleraque scripta testimonia Concilio ad manū sunt) captos in navibus sive præsidarijs sive mercatorejs a Fœderatarū Provinciarū navibus Anglos duram admodùm & miseram captivitatem esse passos, nonnullos in vincula conjectos, & alioqui multa mala terrâ marìque perpeti coactos, nondum tamen adductam esse ut irritato animo paria redderet; verùm è contrario suis perpetùo Præfectis mandasse, uti captivis prospicerent pro cujusque conditione, & prout cuique opus fuisset; utque ne in arctiorem custodiam darentur, quàm necesse esset, ne aufugerent; neque adeò tamen arctè custoditi sunt quin eorū complures sint elapsi, præter Classiarios & Nautas benè multos quibus & licentia domū abeundi & comeatus insuper sine ullâ permutatione est datus. Qui autem eorū in loca dissita traducti sunt illi quidem cùm propter numerum eorū tum propter morbū quo tentari cœperant in aliū necessarìo locū erant traducendi: in eo itaque comodiori duntaxàt ipsorū hospitio ac valetudini provisum est. Nescitque Conciliū quenquam eorū invitum alias in naves esse deportatū; pro comperto etiam habet neminem prorsùs eorū in naves bellicas imponi multò minùs ad ministeria in ijs vel nautica vel militaria abeunda compelli. Quòd autem ad captorū utrinque dimissionem & rationi convenientiùs & recepti passim moris in bello est, dimissionem, pro cujusque loco & gradu, permutatione potiùs fieri, quàm eo modo quem proponunt Domini Deputati. Quemadmodum igitur Conciliū suis Navarchis mandavit uti eam rationem sequerentur, ita nunc placet eandem ab utraque parte sanciri, ratàmque, haberi; interea captos utrinque hamanitèr tractari prout omnes nationes non barbaras jus belli est.

Textual Note: mercatorejs should be *mercatorijs*. The error is particularly notable because the handwriting does not seem to be that of a Council amanuensis, but perhaps of one of Milton's.

Official Text in Original English

The Councell of State upon the Paper of the Deputyes of the States Generall of the United Provinces touching the Prisoners, doe returne this Answere, That although they have beene informed both by the Partyes themselves, and severall others (many of which Informations are in writeing and remayne before the Councell) that the Prisoners taken by the Ships of the United Provinces, either upon men of Warre or Merchant men, were made to endure a very hard and miserable Imprisonment, some of them in Irons, and otherwise compelled to undergoe much hardship as well at Land as Sea, yet the State hath not beene at any tyme provoked to any returne of that nature, but on the contrary have constantly given Orders to their Officers to provide for them in all things, according to their severall qualities and necessities, putting them under noe further restraynt or imprisonment then was necessary to prevent their escape, in which particular they were not soe strictly lookt to, but that a great number of them get away, besides very many both Officers and Common Marriners, who had liberty given them freely to returne, and money to beare their Charges home, without soe much as Exchanges for them. And for those who are sent into Quarters farre remote, the number of them, and the Contagion which was amongst them did necessitate thereunto, and was done for their Conveniencie, as well in respect of Lodging as preserveing them from sicknesse and diseases; neither doe the Councell know that any of them are transported upon other Ships against their Wills, and are very certaine that none of them are put into or made to serve in any of the Ships of Warre. And as concerning the release of Prisoners on both sides, It is more agreeable to reason, and to the generall practice observed in the like Cases that the Release be by way of Exchange according to their respective qualities rather then as is propounded by the said Lords Deputyes, and therefore as the Councell gave Orders to the Generalls at Sea to observe that Course soe they are willing that the same be now setled and agreed upon, and in the meane tyme that Prisoners on both sides be well used as Prisoners of Warre ought to be by all civill Nations.

Whitehall
1 August 1653

Signed in the Name & by Order of the Councell of State
E. Mountagu Presid[t]

Notes

1. The manuscript Order Books, preserved in many volumes at the Public Record Office, London, offer mainly brief and fragmentary minutes of decisions. These have been partially printed ("calendared") in the serial *Calendar of State Papers, Domestic* (abbreviated *CSPD*) during the nineteenth century, recently reprinted. Where Milton is involved, my quotations are taken from the full texts in the manuscript originals of the Order Books.

2. Two manuscript collections of state letters are extant: the Columbia Manuscript (so-called because it is now at Columbia University), compiled not earlier than 1659 by an unidentified scribe who had access to one of Milton's files; and the Skinner Transcript, now SP 9/194 at the Public Record Office, prepared in 1674 at Milton's request, from another file. From a third manuscript collection, which has not survived, two printed editions appeared in 1676, put out by different continental publishers, but both with the same title, *Literæ Pseudo-Senatûs Anglicani, Cromwellii, Reliquorumque Perduellium nomine ac jussu conscriptæ a Joanne Miltono*. Their texts are substantially the same, but the earlier edition, which has the so-called "Fruit" ornament on the title page, has rather more typographical errors than the later edition, which has the so-called "Face" ornament on the title page. (The typos in the "Face" edition were carried over uncorrected in the Columbia University Press edition of Milton's *Works*, vol. 13, 1937). The two manuscripts and the two *Literæ* are the primary sources, each differing somewhat in contents, and each incomplete. They are supplemented by a number of letters that have survived in their final official form in the chancelleries of the European countries to which they were delivered.

In 1690 Johan Georg Pritius reedited the "Face" text, correcting many of its misprints, at Leipzig and Frankfurt, *Literæ nomie Senatus Anglicani, Cromvvellii Richardique Ad diversos in Europa Principes & Respublicas exaratæ a Joanne Miltono.* In 1692 a selection of 49 letters, all found in the previous compilations, but seeming to have come from manuscripts antedating all of those, were rather inaccurately transcribed by Gregorio Leti in his *HISTORIA, e Memorie recondite sopra alla Vita di Oliviero Cromvele,* Amsterdam. Johan Christian Lünig, *Literæ Procerum Europæ,* 1712, printed a selection of 113 of the above letters, interspersed chronologically among letters of continental rulers, and not identified as being by Milton; these give evidence of deriving from still another manuscript source. Some Milton state letters were printed during the Interregnum era in individual pamphlet format, but only as English government state papers and not identified as Milton works.

3. Thomas Ollive Mabbott and J. Milton French, in the Columbia edition, volumes 13 (1937) and 18 (1938), added much material from various sources, but their editorial comment is now obsolete, largely superseded by my published research. Mabbott, French and Maurice Kelley published additional finds in a series of "Supplements" to the Columbia edition in *Notes and Queries* 177 (1939), 329–30; 181 (1941), 16–17; 195 (1950), 224–46. A "Sixth Supplement" by Maurice Kelley and Leo Miller appeared there, 226 (1981), 43–44. Kelley published "Additional Texts of Milton's State Papers" in *Modern Language Notes* 67 (1952), 14–19. Robert T. Fallon's "Miltonic Documents in the Public Record Office, London," *Studies in Bibliography* 32 (1979), 82–100, is noteworthy; but many of the suggestions offered in his "Filling the Gaps: New Perspectives on Mr. Secretary Milton," *Milton Studies* 12 (1978), 165–95, were superseded by the publication of the Mylius papers in 1985.

Except for quotations from the Council Order Books, the materials on Milton secretaryship in *The Life Records of John Milton* (1950–1958) by J. Milton French are now out of date; they suffer from mistranslations and errors in history. W.R. Parker regrettably made no independent study of Milton's secretarial role; his *Milton, A Biography* (1968) derives this phase from French's *Life Records,* and so is also outdated. *The Miltonic State Papers,* vol. 5, part 2 in the *Complete Prose Works of John Milton* (Yale University Press, 1971), must be treated with utmost caution in regard to factual data, dates, citations and interpretations.

My published studies on Milton's secretaryship include: *John Milton and the Oldenburg Safeguard* (Loewenthal Press, New

York, 1985); and, in periodicals: in *Notes and Queries*, Oxford: "Milton's State Papers: Spirensis Camera, Ann of Foy and Other Obscurities," 1969; "Milton's State Papers: The Lünig Version," 1970; "The Miltonic State Papers," review article, 1972; "Columbia Edition of Milton, Sixth Supplement," with Maurice Kelley, 1981; "Daniel Skinner and Milton's Personal Letters," 1983; "Two Milton State Papers: New Dates, New Insights," 1986; "Milton's Conversations with Schlezer and His Letters to Brandenburg," 1987; "Cromwell's State Letters: Addenda to Abbott," 1988; "The Milton/Cromwell Letter to Transylvania," 1989; in the *Milton Quarterly*, Athens, Ohio: "Milton and Weckherlin," 1982; "Milton on January 8, 1649/50, Before He Was Famous," 1987; in *English Language Notes*, Boulder, Colorado: "Another Milton State Letter Recovered and a Mystery Demystified," 1987; in *Ringing the Bell Backward, Proceedings of the First International Milton Symposium, 1981*, R.G. Shafer, ed., Indiana, Pennsylvania: "Milton in the Mylius Papers," 1982; in *TEXT II, 1983, Transactions of the Society for Textual Scholarship*, D.C. Greetham and W.S. Hill, eds., New York: "Establishing the Text of Milton's State Papers," 1985.

4. Public Record Office, SP 25/65, p. 11, no. 11.

5. This 10 February order (Public Record Office, SP 25/17, p. 59) may have referred only to current meetings with Portugese Ambassador Joâo de Guimarâes, or it may have had more general application, in connection with the above mentioned order of 19 February.

6. Bradshaw meeting: Mylius papers *Niedersächsisches Staatsarchiv*, Oldenburg, Acta Grafschaft Oldenburg, Best. 20, Tit. 38, Nr. 73, Fasc. 13 (*Concept*) and Fasc. 14 (*Reinschrift*) for 29 October 1651; Mylius's audience, ibid., for 20 October; letter to Whitelocke, Whitelocke Papers, Longleat, xii, f 41. All of these are available in: Leo Miller, *John Milton and the Oldenburg Safeguard*.

If Mylius came face to face with Cromwell by chance several times, as he did, Milton must have on many occasions; at the very least, at the formal state funerals for Isaac Dorislaus and Henry Ireton, and at the sermons preached by Hugh Peter to the Council of State.

7. Leo ab Aitzema, draft manuscript diary, Algemeen Rijksarchief, The Hague, Eerste Afdeling, *Collectie Aitzema*, Inv. nr. 45, for 27 February/8 March, 1651/52. The commissioners were, more correctly: John Lisle, Sir John Trevor, the Earl of Pembroke, Herbert Morley, Henry Rolle, Richard Ingoldsby, Sir John Hippesley, Walter Strickland, Henry Neville, Thomas Challoner. Most of Aitzema's original manuscript papers are

now lost. This *Inv. nr. 45* manuscript is a full of "strikeout" lines, leaving doubt as to whether a name or a passage has been transcribed to a (now lost) fair copy, or was meant for deletion.

8. Milton's letter to John Bradshaw, 21 February 1652/53, in the hand of an amanuensis, PRO, SP 18/33, p. 75.

9. I have sought widely for Milton's English version of the *Intercursus Magnus*. The Public Record Office, the House of Lords Record Office (archives of Parliament), the Longleat collection of Whitelocke's papers and the Rijksarchief all inform me that they have no such document.

Seeking to solve the puzzling absence of Milton state papers addressed to the Dutch Netherlands during 1649–1651, I have combed the sources for Dorislaus, Joachimi, Schaep, Strickland and St. John.

Dorislaus was first given a letter of credence to the Dutch dated 20 June 1648, signed for each House of Parliament by the Earl of Manchester and William Lenthall. It is now in S.G. 5898, f 75. It was printed in the *Journals of the House of Lords*, vol. 10, 336–37, done in Latin (presumably by Georg Rudolph Weckherlin, with pre-Commonwealth forms, *ex. Palatio Parliamentaro, curiæ admiralitatis, Proceres et Ordines Communium*). For Dorislaus's later and fatal mission, on 20 April 1649 the Council recorded two orders (*CSPD*, 1649, pp. 100–01):

2. The letter read for a credential to Dr. Dorislaus to be delivered to the 18 sovereignties in Holland to be reported to the House.

3. To request the House that he may have the same credentials as given to Mr. Strickland.

Credentials had been issued to Walter Strickland in the name of the two Houses in August 1642 (*Journals of the House of Commons*, vol. 2, 729, 733; English text, *Journals of the House of Lords*, vol. 5, 316); renewals were issued several times up to 1648, addressed to the States General and to individual Dutch provinces. If the credentials for Dorislaus copied those for Strickland, no draft by Milton was needed. Never delivered to the States General, Dorislaus's credentials are not in their archives, and no copy is known in British sources.

Joachimi had been in England in January 1648/49 to intercede for the life of Charles I and remained there till autumn of 1650. When Dorislaus was killed, the States General hastened to exculpate themselves, writing to Joachimi at once. On 15 May 1649, he submitted statements and on 16 May a letter to Parliament, probably with transcripts of the letters he had received. On 18 May 1649, the Council of State directed:

That the ffrench Letters given into the House by the Dutch

Ambassad^r be translated by Mr. Milton, and the rest of the Letters now in the House be sent for & Translated, and that the Councell doe meet tomorrow at seven in ye morning about it (PRO, SP 25/62, p. 325).

These translations have not been found. On 18 May the British acknowledged Joachimi's communications in two papers, a letter from Parliament signed by its clerk Henry Scobell and a letter from the Council signed by its president John Bradshaw, both in English. These are now in S.G. 5898, with Dutch translations and letters by Joachimi to the States General, but with no Latin version. John Bradshaw's draft letter was also entered into the Council Order Book (PRO, SP 25/62, pp. 332–35). It seems that the Council was eager to retract its first hasty judgments (expressed to Joachimi through Oliver Fleming before word had come from the States General) and did not want to delay by having its reply put into Latin; also, Joachimi was competent in English. When Parliament decided to terminate Joachimi's diplomatic right to stay in England, the letter and pass sent to him on 26 September 1650 were both in English (transcripts in S.G. 5898, f 95, f 98, with no Latin texts known).

Schaep was envoy from Holland and West Friesland, and there are references in *CSPD* to his dealings with the Commonwealth administration, with no mention of Milton. In March 1651 he bought 25 copies of Milton's *Pro Populo Anglicano Defensio* for distribution to Holland officials, and he may have been one of the envoys who at that time offered Milton congratulations (see Leo Miller, "Milton's *Defensio* Ordered Wholesale for the States of Holland," *Notes and Queries* 231 [1986], p. 33).

For the mission of Strickland and St. John in 1650/51, the Order Books indicate three documents were to be prepared: official instructions, commissions and letters of credence (*CSPD*, 5 February, p. 34; 10 February, p. 39; 11 February, p. 41; and 14 February, p. 47). The draft instructions, in English, are now in the Bodleian's Nalson Papers 18: 71. The "commissions" and "letters of credence" require some explanation.

At that time, major English envoys were given *two* documents establishing their official status, a letter of credence and a commission. When this practice began I am uncertain; subsequent to his August credential letter, on 2 December 1642, it was ordered in Parliament "That it be referred to Sir Henry Vane and Mr. Pym, to prepare a Commission for Mr. Strickland, the better to enable him to do service for the Commonwealth and Parliament" in his mission to the Netherlands (*Commons Journals*, vol. 2, 873).

William Prideaux in 1655 explained to the Russian chancellery that such commissions were issued to specify a diplomat's powers, whether plenipotentiary or otherwise (*Thurloe Papers* vol. 3, 711). Such commissions were drafted by the staff of the Commissioners of the Great Seal using repetitive legalistic formulas in turgid Latin. This conventional terminology may be seen in the *Journals of the House of Lords*, vol. 6, 702, empowering Richard Jenks and Thomas Skinner, together with letters of credence to the King of Denmark, 11 September 1644, and in the commission issued to Philip Sidney, Lord Lisle, as Lord Lieutenant of Ireland, *Lords Journals*, vol. 8, 261. Such commissions, *not attributable to Milton*, accompanied the texts of treaties: the Commonwealth treaty with Sweden (Milton's *Works*, Columbia edition, vol. 13, 584–86) and the treaty with the Netherlands (W.C. Abbott, *Writings and Speeches of Oliver Cromwell*, vol. 3, 213–14).

The first ambassador authorized by the regicide Commonwealth was Anthony Ascham, to Spain. His commission was voted in the Commons, 2 February 1648/49, and entered into its *Journals*, vol. 6, 356, as if intended to be a model text adapting the traditional Commissioner of Great Seal legalisms to the new regime. This Latin text is therefore not Milton's (contrary to the allegation in the Yale *Complete Prose*, vol. 5, 509, among other errors there). What Milton did prepare for Ascham's mission were two letters to the King of Spain, an initial request for safe conduct, *Antonium Ascamum virum probum*, and a credential letter, *Quis rerum nostrarum*.

The commission for Strickland and St. John, dated 14 February 1650/51, (Latin draft, Nalson Papers, vol. 18, 71, f 190–90v, now filed in Bodleian Dep. C 171; final delivered document, MS. S.G. 5899) reproduced the Ascham commission text closely, changing names, singular to plurals, adding some few words and one whole sentence. This commission was the responsibility of the Commissioners of the Great Seal (*CSPD*, 5 February 1650/51, p. 34), done first in Latin and then translated into English for the Council's benefit (*CSPD*, 10 February, p. 39). After this draft was prepared by the staff of the Great Seal, it was handled by someone else, who changed the names, *Strictlandij* and *Strictlandium* to *Strickland* by striking out the grammatical terminations (similar to a practice seen in the Columbia Manuscript and *Literæ* texts of Milton state letters, where vernacular forms of family names are sometimes retained in Latin documents); the word *utrius* was corrected to *unius*, this *unius* bearing a tantalizing resemblance to *unius* as written by Milton in his 1639 letter to Holstenius and in his Commonplace Book, page 134, line 11.

Three times—*CSPD 1651*, 5, 11 and 14 February—Council orders refer to a separate and distinct letter of credence for Strickland and St. John, which should have been addressed to the States General. Their "commission" was addressed *Omnibus et singulis*, in English "to all and every one to whom these our letters shall come" (Nalson Papers, vol. 18, 71, f 194–94v), not to the States General. A kind of letter of credence was prepared: English draft in Nalson, vol. 18, 72, f 196, identical with the delivered copy now in S.G. 5899 I, and transcribed, with spelling variants by an amanuensis, into the Strickland-St. John Journal, Rawl. MS. C 129 for 20 March 1651/52. A Latin version should have been Milton's work, but none such is to be found at the Rijksarchief, and none may have been done.

10. *The Anglo-Dutch Commercial Competition*: A trade boom, with national rivalries, followed the ending of the Thirty Years War at the Peace of Weestphalia, 1648. The contemporary observations of Jean Nicolas de Parival are eloquent: "two Commonwealths so near one another, which have but one and the same scope, or ayme, i.e., the Traffick, are less able to agree, then rivals, who court one Mistresse, or two Neighbour Kings" (Prival, *The History of This Iron Age*, in the 1656 English translation by Batholomew Harris, p. 270). On the same question, Parival said (in the revised 1659 edition translated by Harris, p. 277): "to which I answer, that *England* having the same aim and scope, viz. traffick could not endure to see trade of sea ingrossed in the hands of these *Hollanders*, through their bringing of commodities home to their doores, and selling them cheaper than their own merchants could afford, nay buy them, which in time would have ruined all the shipping and trading of the English."

For a recent Dutch study, see Simon Groenveld, "The English Civil War as a Cause of the First Anglo-Dutch War 1640–1642," *The Historical Journal* 30 (1987): 541–66.

Samuel R. Gardiner, *Letters and Papers Relating to the First Dutch War*, Navy Records Society, Publications, Vol. 13 (=Vol. 1 of his six) (London, 1899) pp. 48–53, tried to minimize the effect of the Navigation Act, and thereby to lessen England's share of responsibility for bringing on the war. He emphasized the effects of Anglo-French conflicts at sea, which were, indeed, a real factor, but the Dutch ambassadors put the suspension of the Navigation Act as their first demand. Lorenzo Paulucci, Venetian secretary in England, wrote (8 May 1652) that "the Act of Parliament prohibiting Dutch vessels from bringing foreign goods here is what they most dislike. The damage done to them is manifest, while on the other hand to suspend the Act for their gratification would be most difficult and contrary, I am assured, to the intention of all the members of the Council of State" (*Calendar of State Papers, Venetian*, vol. 28, 231, (1647–52), and a similar report, p. 240, translated from the Italian original in Venice, *Senato Secreta. Dispacci, Francia.*

The heavy investment of both English and Dutch in their combat navies, 1649–1652, the conduct of both sides in the 1651–1652 negotiations, and the provocative behavior of their ship captains show that the commercial and shipping interests of both Britain and the Netherlands were ready to resort to war for their business ambitions.

By letters of marque and reprisal, a shipowner, alleging unsettled claims against a resident of a second country, was authorized to seize any ships of the second country at random and to reimburse himself through his own admiralty court.

11. Vlitius was accompanied and introduced by Johan Oste, Dutch secretary residing in England (Bodleian Library, Nalson Papers, vol. 18, 121, ff 324–25v).

12. The politics of Milton's displacement from his Whitehall apartments have never been clarified. Could it have been partly because he was regarded as Bradshaw's man? Bradshaw was not a member of Parliament and was also being displaced as president of the Council during that time.

13. Hermann Mylius reported that sneer by Samuel Hartlib (*John Milton and the Oldenburg Safeguard*, 116). There are extant many contemporary manuscript and printed versions of Cats's speech, in Latin, English and Dutch. The official Latin text signed by Cats, Van de Perre and Schaep is preserved in the Nalson Papers, vol. 18, 119, ff 312–17v, endorsed "Reported by the Speaker 24 December 1651." The English version, apparently done by a Netherlander, is endorsed "Read the 24 day of December 1651" (Nalson, vol. 18, 120, ff 318–22v). The weekly *Mercurius Politicus*, No. 80, 18–25 December 1651, reported that copies were submitted in Latin and English. Mylius received a very good transcript, now in Oldenburg, Best. 20, Tit. 38, No. 72a, Litt J. ff 190–97v. Aitzema printed the Latin in his *Historia Pacis, a Fœderatis Belgis ab Anno MDCXXI ad hoc usque Tempus Tractatæ*, Leiden (1654), 754–60, and in Dutch in his *Saken van Staet in Oorlogh*, 1669 edition, vol. 3, 699–701 (somewhat different in the peroration).

14. Journals of the House of Commons, manuscript in the House of Lords Record Office, vol. 36, p. 363 (italics where letters are omitted in manuscript); printed in *Journals of the House of Commons From August the 15 1651 to March the 6th 1659. Printed by Order of the House of Commons*, n.p, n.d.;

reprinted London (1813), vol. 7, 64. Dutch embassy commission, French original, Nalson, vol. 10, 71, ff 194-94v; English, vol. 10, 71, ff 195-97; *Mercurius Politicus*, No. 83, 8-15 January 1651, p. 1332.

15. Statement of the Three Ambassadors, 1/11 January, Nalson, vol. 18, 122, ff 326-29v, official originals in Latin and English; Ms. Aitzema 86, no. 8, MS. S.G. 8460, no. 8, Latin transcripts.

16. *Exposuerunt nuper*, transcripts in MS. Aitzema 86, under 8 and 9; MS. S.G. 8460, under 9. Transcripts in Latin of many of the papers submitted by the three ambassadors for 1 January to 30 June 1652, their reports to their home office and related papers are collected in British Library, Add. MSS. 17, 677 U, ff 85-166, but since these are nineteenth century copies they are not cited separately herein, when originals are available.

The skippers' petition, according to Vlitius's *Cum nihil prius*, was prepared without consulting the Embassy. Appeals by Vlitius and Huygens to Admiralty Court against sale of ships appear repeatedly in Huygens's diary. For precision I cite from his diary manuscripts: Dutch text, 20 December 1651 to 2 April 1652 N.S., British Library MS. Egerton 1997; French text, 11 April to 15 July 1652 N.S., The Hague, Royal Library, MS. K.A. LVIII. The diary has been published, with English translation, *Lodewijck Huygens. The English Journal 1651-1652*, edited by A.G.H. Bachrach and R.G. Collmer, Leiden, 1982.

Paulet: In 1630 Robert Paulet (or, Pawlett), under cover of letters of marque and reprisal issued by Charles I, captured a Portuguese ship that was in the service of Spain, but Paulet himself was hijacked by a Dutch sea captain soon after. Five years of litigation before the Rotterdam Board of Admiralty, supported by diplomatic representations, left Paulet unsatisfied, so Charles I granted letters of reprisal against the Dutch. Pursuant to a Council of State order of 7 August 1651, these were renewed to Richard Pettingall as estate administrator for Ann and Mary Pawlett, widows of the owners, 8 October 1651 (for text of order, see Rawl. MS. A 226, f 27-27v, which is more accurate than the report of the Dutch Embassy to the States General, 30 January/9 February, 1651/52 as copied in British Library, Add. MSS. 17, 677, U, ff 104-06v). The account in the Yale University Press edition of Milton's *Complete prose*, vol. 5, 561, is inaccurate. I have found no link to John Paulet, Marquis of Winchester, for whose wife Milton wrote an obituary poem.

17. Mylius's diary, *John Milton & the Oldenburg Safeguard*, p. 146. Frost's original, MS. S.G. 8460, No. 10 (miswritten 19); inaccurate transcript, MS. Aitzema 86, No. 10. Apparently it

was not translated into Latin until later, when it was included as part of Milton's *Scriptum ab Excellentijs Vestris*. Milton was also occupied with letters to Tuscany, 2 to 20 January.

18. Huygens's diary, 23 January/2 February.

19. Council order, 23 January, PRO, SP 25/66, p. 252.

20. *Cum nihil prius*, Latin text, transcribed in No. 15 in both MS. S.G. 8460 (British amanuensis) and in MS. Aitzema 86 (Dutch amanuensis). No English version is known in Dutch or British archives.

Janus Vlitius (Jan van Vliet) was prominent in Dutch intellectual life, an author of scholarly works. His unpublished manuscripts might yield much of value. Twice he wrote to a friend of his desire to visit Milton (letters of 5 December 1651 and 12 January 1652, both N.S., printed by Petrus Burmannus, *Sylloges Epistolarum a Viris Illustribus Scriptarum, Tomi Quinque* (Leiden, 1723, vol. 3, 741–43), but the only report of his actually having been to meet Milton comes from a remote source: Gerhard Feltmann, neighbor and colleague of Vlitius in Breda 1664–1666, in his *Tractatus de Polygamia*, Leipzig, 1677, pp. 214, 227. He writes that the "private secretary" of the Dutch ambassador debated with Milton on the issue of scriptural authority for polygamy, and mentions that a "son of the ambassador" was also present. Huygens did not record any visit to Milton. The "son" may have been Schaep's. For full account, see: Leo Miller, *John Milton among the Polygamophiles*, Loewenthal Press, New York, 1974, 77–78, and *John Milton and the Oldenburg Safeguard*, 314, 339.

21. *Quæ tam a Parlamento*, Dutch envoys' paper, transcribed in MS. S.G. 8460, no. 14. The Yale edition of *The Miltonic State Papers*, in *Complete Prose of John Milton*, 1971, vol. 5, 566, makes the inappropriate statement that "Milton may well have latinized this paper, but there is no evidence that he did so."

22. Council orders, PRO, SP 25/66, p. 232 (20 January), p. 257 (26 January), p. 264 (27 January).

23. On 14 January 1651/52, the Council set as policy "That all Treaties with forreigne States & princes be managed by papers. And that all such papers as shall be given in on the part of the Comonwealth, there be one which is to be the Authentique one signed in English, the other a translate of it in Latine" (PRO, SP 25/66, p. 208). "Treaties," here and often elsewhere in the 1650s, means "negotiations." Official papers of the Council were signed by its president, who from December 1651 to April 1653 was chosen monthly by rotation. Papers in the name of Parliament were signed by the Speaker, William Lenthall, or by its clerk, Henry Scobell. Later Cromwell signed as Protector.

During shifts in the regime, there were other signatories.

All available evidence confirms that English-language texts of Milton's state papers surviving from his time are *not* translations from Milton's Latin. Rather, Milton's Latin texts are his translations *from* English drafts, which (in almost all cases) were drawn up by other persons.

24. Mabbott and French printed the Latin text of *Concilium Status Parlamenti* as State Paper 167C in the Columbia edition of Milton's *Works*, vol. 18, 80–84, from unidentified photostats, but their textual notes show the Dutch source was MS. S.G. 8460. Their edition misprints *pactis* as *partis, censemus* as *consemus* (p. 80, lines 9 and 15). They did not know the official English text, and printed a translation by Nelson G. McCrea, generally creditable, but since he was infamiliar with the historical context, he sometimes failed to grasp the sense of the original. Variant transcripts, which are not authoritative, of the Latin text, include: two copies in MS S.G. 12589.62, by a British scribe; MS. Aitzema 86, no. 16, Dutch scribe; Mylius papers, Best. 20, Tit. 38, Nr. 73, Fasc. 6, ff 17–17v, by his amanuensis.

25. Milton consured the early church fathers for their "knotty Africanisms" (*Of Reformation*, 1641, p. 38; Columbia edition, vol. 3, 34), and he criticized his contemporaries for "their choice preferring the gay rankness of *Apuleius, Arnobius* or any modern fustianist, before the native *Latinisms* of *Cicero*" (*An Apology against a Pamphlet, 1642*, p. 45; Columbia edition, vol. 3, 347). Salmasius and *persona*: in Milton's preface to his *Pro Populo Anglicano Defensio*, 1651. Mylius and *projecta*; see *John Milton & the Oldenburg Safeguard*, p. 84 and elsewhere for many other instances of Milton's conflicts in Latinity with his colleagues on the Council staff.

26. In addressing the Dutch ambassadors here and later, the letter uses the form *Excellentia Vestra*. This form was imposed on Milton by his colleagues. He felt *Amplitudo Vestra* reflected better Latin. These terms, literally "Your Excellency" and "Your Grandeur," are intended to represent the English "Your Lordship." See discussion in Leo Miller, "Two Milton State Papers: New Dates and New Insights, "*Notes and Queries* 231 (1986), 461–64; the unfortunate misprint there of *Vester* for *Vestra* is corrected in 232 (1987), 354.

Admiral and its derivative *admiralty* came into West European languages and neo-Latin from the Arabic *amir-al*, "commander of," confused with *admirabilis*. In his state paper *Graves ad nos* (correct date March 1650/51), Milton used *Curia Navali* for "Admiralty Court," and in his related letter *Cum graves ad nos*, April 1651, he used *maritimarum, causarum curiam.* The form *curia ammiralatus* appears in later Milton state papers—*Literæ Excellentiæ Vestræ* and *Parlamentum Repubilcæ Angliæ literas vestræ Celsitudinis*—both of November 1652, and in *Mercatores quidem,* February 1652/53. Whether this was imposed by colleagues or is to be otherwise explained, the usage is unquestionably anomalous. The diplomatic credentials issued by Parliament, 20 June 1648, to Isaac Dorislaus describe him as one of the judges *Supremæ Curiæ Admiralitatis* (*Journals of the House of Lords,* vol. 10, 337).

27. Council order, 28 January, PRO, SP 25/66, p. 267.

28. *Scriptum ab Excellentijs Vestris* was printed as letter 167D in the Columbia edition, vol. 18, 86–94, from photostats of MS. S.G. 8460, no. 17. The translation by McCrea may also now be discarded, in favor of the official original. MS. S.G. 12589.62 has two copies in a slightly variant Latin text by a British scribe. MS. Aitzema 86, no. 17, lacks the paragraph *Scriptumque aliud.*

29. The texts in the *Literæ* editions represent varying interim stages in the letter drafts, from first rough draft to not-quite final revisions. The Columbia Manuscript, although dating to circa 1659, often represents texts earlier than those in *Literæ.* The Skinner Transcript shows some 1674 revisions, notably in Latin terminations to family names.

Both letters of 29 January use *Francos* rather than the classical *Gallos* for the French nation, but Milton uses both words interchangeably, as in his state letter to Cardinal Mazarin, 25 May 1655. The Kings of England, when they still claimed sovereignty in France, used *Francia* in their titles, and so, at times, did Louis XIV. Milton used *Francia* and *Gallia* interchangeably in chapters 7 and 8 of *Pro Populo Anglicano Defensio* for "France," and also referring to the "Franks," chapter 4 (Columbia edition, vol. 7, 368, 370, 414, 264). He also countenanced *Francos* in the *Responsio ad Apologiam Anonumi Cujusdam tenebrionis pro Rege et Popula Anglicano Infantissimam* of his nephew John Phillips, 1651 (Columbia edition, vol. 18, 452).

30. In Milton's Latin, these phrases echo Vlitius's letter: "petitiones, tot*que* repetitas expostulationes" / "definitiva sententia" / "plus*que* fidei ac ponderis nautarum petitioni quam publico Excellentiarum Vestrarum desiderio."

The corresponding English original has: "soe many petitions and repeated expostulations" / "definitive sentence" / "that more belief and weight hath been given to your Mariners petition than to the publique desire of your Lordships."

If Milton's English version is found, these English phrases may be in it. If found, that translation into English might be a key to resolving many other questions pertaining to Milton's secretaryship.

31. Milton's sensitivity to the usage of *Ordines* seems to have begun at this point. In John Phillips's *Responsio*, written late in 1651, *Ordines* is used for both the joint and the provincial bodies, and that was under Milton's critical eye. In the mid-1640s, when he was reading Thuanus's *Historia Sua Temporis*, Milton copied into his Commonplace Book *Ordines Hollandiæ* and *Ordines Belgii* (pp. 53, 183).

The phrase 2do *Feb. juxta computum vestrum dato* corresponds literally to the primary text in English; but in some 24 or so instances in which Milton state papers acknowledge a letter received, the words *datæ, datas, datis* are in grammatical agreement with the word used for *letter*. In this one instance only is the agreement with the ablative of the day of the month. Is this anomally a Rosin touch?

32. Council order, 29 January, PRO, SP 25/66, pp. 271-72, items 2 and 7, and Huygens's diary, 30 January/9 February. Huygens spent the afternoon transcribing copies to be sent to the home office. The rigidly literal character of Rosin's translation style will be repeatedly apparent from other texts herein. Milton also prepared a letter, officially dated 30 January 1651/52, to Spanish Ambassador Alonso de Cardenas.

33. The *Paper of Demands*, 28 January, PRO, 25/66, p. 268, items 6, 7, 8; 29 January, PRO, SP 25/66, pp. 271-72, items 3, 4 and 8.

34. 25 February order, PRO, SP 25/66, p. 378.

35. *Journals of the House of Commons*, printed text, vol. 4, 26, for 21 January 1644/45. Dr. Eden is memorialized in Thomas Fuller's *The History of the Worthies of England* (London, 1662) and in the *Dictionary of National Biography*. This brief, or part of it, appears to be the 13-article catalog of individual claims that was submitted in writing to the Boreel-Renswoude embassy, and later printed as "An abstract of the particular complaints" on pp. 24–31 of *A Second Declaration of the Lords and Commons Assembled in Parliament; of the Whole Proceedings with the late Extraordinary Ambassadors from the High and Mighty Lords, the States Generall of the United Provinces; concerning Restitution of Ships, and the Course of Trade. London: Printed for Edward Husband, Printer to the Honourable House of Commons. Sept. 18, 1645.* The original document in French and English, signed by William Lenthall for the Commons and by Grey of Wark for the House of Lords, is filed as MS. S.G. 12576, No. 51, in The Hague Rijksarchief. No version in Latin from 1645 has been located in England or in The Netherlands. The

Council order of 26 February 1651/52 specified that it was yet to be translated (into Latin).

36. The concepts of what constitutes "freedom" and "slavery" are not uniformly, absolutely or exclusively defined even today, not even in lands where the degrees of freedom available are higher than anywhere else. In Milton's time, and for Milton also, the enslavement of Africans or other darker skinned peoples (practiced by their own rulers as well) was a fact of life: see his *Of Reformation* (1641), 90. Such slavery was sanctioned by the ethics of the Christian churches (see his *De Doctrina Christiana*, book 2, chap. 15). Enslavement of Christians by Moslems was, however, to be protested: see State Paper of 22 October 1657, addressed to Venice in the matter of Thomas Galilee; but sometimes it was a matter for negotiation, as in Cromwell's April 1656 letter to Algiers (Milton's *Works*, Columbia edition, vol. 13, pp. 332, 502).

37. These texts of the complete *Papers of Demands* have been available to me: MS. S.G. 8460, no. 20: official English text of the cover letter, signed by Philip Lisle, but lacking salutation and date; official English texts of B1, B2, B3 and B4; official Latin texts of B1, B2 and B3, but not B4. These are written in the hands of several different Council amenuenses. MS. Aitzema 86, no. 20: Latin texts only, transcript of the cover letter in the hand of a Dutch amanuensis, transcripts of B1, B2 and B3 by another Dutch hand; the official Latin text of B4, in the hand of a British Council amanuensis. MS. St. v. Holl. nr. 2813.1: transcripts of the Latin text of all parts of the *Paper of Demands* as sent by the three ambassadors to the *Gecommitteerde Raden*, the executive body of Holland, on 27 March 1652. MS. S.G. 12589.62 ("secret case" of Dutch Archives): the original letter sent 27 March to their home office by the three ambassadors, enclosing a transcript of the English-language cover letter (still in that file) and also originally enclosing texts of B1 to B4, but these seem to have been separated. Latin texts of B1 through B4, with Dutch translations, are filed in MS. S.G. 12563, no. 28, Loketkas Oostindische Compagine.

An English-language compilation of documents from negotiations in 1653, PRO, SP 105/98, on pp. 77–90, recapitulates the English text of the *Paper of Demands*, without the cover letter, setting the "Fifteen Articles" first, the *Summarium Damnorum* (English text of the Earlier Draft) and the "Catalogue" for 1645. Spelling differs from 1652 texts, and there are inaccuracies in text and numbers. Another 1653 English-language compilation is in MS. S.G. 8484.

38. Weckherlin appointment, PRO, SP 25/66, pp. 429, 440.

Weckherlin was a German-born immigrant to England. After serving Charles I many years in foreign correspondence, during the civil war Weckherlin adhered to the side of Parliament, and was its secretary for foreign correspondence, equal in status with Gualter Frost. Remaining a royalist in principle, opposed to the regicide, he was dismissed from his post in February 1649, (Milton was his replacement), but Weckherlin remained friends with his former colleagues Gualter Frost and John Dury. He was gracious in his praise of his successor Milton, in a letter to Mylius, 8 October 1651. See Leo Miller, "Milton and Weckherlin," *Milton Quarterly* 16 (1982), 1–2. Weckherlin was also a friend of Oliver Fleming, and among other published poetry had composed an ode to Fleming in sixteen 12-line strophes, saying "Fleming, du bist so erfahren, / So verständig, weiss und klug."

Weckherlin's personal correspondence has been studied by Leonard Forster, *G.R. Weckherlin: zur Kenntnis seines Lebens in England*, Basler Studien zur Deutschen Sprache und Literatur, II, Basel, 1944, and "Sources for G.R. Weckherlin's Life in England: The Correspondence," in *Modern Language Review* 41 (1946): 186–95, and an edition is being prepared by Jill Bepler. Weckherlin's state papers done in the 1640s for Parliament's Committee of Both Houses, and during 1652 for the Commonwealth, have never been studied or even identified, and my own tentative analyses of these are incomplete. On 7 April 1652, the Council ordered "The Answer to the King of Denmark approved off and to be translated into Latine by Mr. Weckerlyn" (PRO, SP 25/66, p. 557, the first and only such order in the Council minutes directed to him). That letter, *Literas Vestræ Majestatis*, officially dated 13 April 1652, is not in the Skinner Transcript but was included in the Columbia Manuscript and in the 1676 *Literæ* with somewhat variant texts, and so it has been accepted as Milton's work by Mabbott and French, and by W.R. Parker following them. My evaluation of internal evidence supports this attribution to Milton, but it needs further study. The letter from the Commonwealth Parliament to Queen Christina of Sweden, 2 June 1652, may with much assurance be attributed to Weckherlin: apart from other evidence, his pet phrase *mente constanti* is conclusive.

39. Rosin appointment, PRO, SP 25/66, p. 287. Compare the Council minutes for 18 May 1649 in note 9 above, when Milton was personally responsible for translation of letters written in French. Also see the order of the Committee of Both Houses, 13 March 1647/48, *Calendar of State Papers, Domestic, Charles I, 1648–1649*, vol. 22, p. 28, on translating the answer to the Scots' Papers upon the late address to the king:

2. That this Declaration be translated into Latin by Dr. Dorislaus and into French by Mr. Rosee.
3. That Mr. Weckherlin be desired to translate the former Declaration into Latin and M. D'Espagne into French.

40. The covering letter shows no specific Miltonisms. It includes words not in Milton's usage: *navigatio* for "navigation," *superiores* for the noun "superiors" (in office). A ship's name is designated *nomine insignita.* "States General" appears twice as *Ordines* and twice in the literal and unusual *Statibus Generalibus.* Other words not common in classical Latin but used in this letter are *charactere, assistentibus, recensio.* The 1645 account of claims in English was headed "abstract," repeated as "abstract" in B4 in 1652; in B1, B2 and B4, "abstract" is translated by (presumably Miltonic) *summarium.* The English-language cover letter uses "particular" instead of "abstract" three times in clauses five and six, and this is rendered in the Latin as *catalogus* each time, a word borrowed from the Greek and rarely found in ancient Latin. Most extraordinary is *Ambasciatoribus,* quasi-Italian with a Latin termination, but it was spelled *Ambassiatoribus* in the transcript in MS. St. v. Holl. 2813.1 and in Aitzema's *Historia Pacis. Ambassiatores* was the title of Henry VII's negotiators in the 1495 *Intercursus Magnus;* it was not used by Milton, who preferred *legatus* and *internuntius.*

41. Apart from revisions in data, there are changes in wording and in verb tenses in the final 1652 text of *Summarium Damnorum* (tabulated below) from the earlier version (March 1651 or earlier). The reasons are not obvious, but neither text has any distinctly non-Miltonic phrasing. The phrase *juncis sive navibus* is a precise rendition of the English "juncks or ships." Seventeenth century names of coins are adaptations of classical terminology: "sterling" is rendered *nostræ monetæ* "rialls" (royals, or pieces of eight) are expressed by *regii, regius* being "royal"; and *libra* serves either for pound sterling or pound of pepper.

The accounts of the *Paper of Demands* and *Summarium Damnorum* in the Yale edition, *Complete Prose,* vol. 5, 599–600, and in J.M. French's *Life Records,* vol. 3, 225–26, are inaccurate.

42. Adam Littleton's 1684 Dictionary does not list *admirallus* in the Latin-English part, nor *archithalassus,* but he includes *thalassiarcha,* "admiral," and *thalassiarchia* for the office. In his English-Latin for "admiral," he offers *præfectus* and *legatus,* appending *admiralis* in bracketed italics; *thalassiarcha* for "Lord High Admiral," *classiarius* and *classis præfectus* for "admiral of a squadron."

43. In *Pro Populo Anglicano Defensio* (1651), Milton uses *ordo plebeius* in various inflections seven times as the equiva-

lent of "House of Commons," and *ordines* for "Houses" of Parliament. Once he refers to the single House (the Rump) Parliament as *curiam supremam populi*. He quotes, without comment, other terms used by Salmasius: *optimates, proceres* for "Lords," *populus* and *plebs* for "Commons," *ordo* and *domus* for "House," and *domo Dominorum et Communium* for "Lords and Commons"; this may explain Milton's one-time use, in addressing Salmasius, of the phrase *utraque Ordinum domo* (chapter 11, Columbia edition, vol. 7, 528) for "each House of the Parliament." In *Defensio Secunda* (1654) he picks up *camera plebis et camera procerum* from [Peter du Moulin's] *Regii Sanguinis Clamor* (1652), 4°, pp. 28 and 55.

In the early years of the civil war, when Parliamentary leaders first began to address foreign states, the Speakers of the two Houses tentatively signed credential letters to the Dutch provinces, 7 December 1643, by authority of the *Proceres et Ordines in Comitiis Parliamentariis legitime congregati* (*Lords Journals*, vol. 6, 331) but presently, with more assurance, adopted the style *Proceres et Ordines Communium Parliamenti Angliâe*, letter to Dutch envoys, 15 August 1645, MS. S.G. 12576.51, where Speaker Lenthall signs as *Prolocutor Dom. Comm.*, and passim in *Lords Journals*. A commission issued to Lenthall on 27 February 1643/44, by the Commissioners of the Great Seal, used *Domus Communis* (*Lords Journals*, vol. 6, 443). On 30 January 1649/50, the Rump voted to adopt the form *Parliamentum Reipublicæ Anglicæ*, and that spelling is seen in its documents thereafter, but from 4 February 1649/50, most Council of State papers spelled *Parlamentum* without the *i*. Apparently Milton overrode the Act of Parliament in regard to this spelling, although he had to bow to their neo-Latin word for "Parliament." He had previously tried to obtain the use of the form *Senatus Populusquae Anglicanus* on the model of the ancient Roman republic, but the lawyers in the Rump were primarily concerned with asserting the legitimacy of their continuing as the uninterrupted Long Parliament.

44. *Of Reformation* (1641), p. 58; Columbia edition, vol. 3, 51. In the 1655 British *Declaration* on the war with Spain, it was charged against Philip II that his Spanish Armada of 1588 was a breach of that long inviolate Burgundian League (Columbia edition, vol. 13, 518–19). When Strickland and St. John commented on the Dutch draft Thirty-six Articles, 16 June 1651, they said the Dutch proposals "did neither agree with our propositions, nor with the old treaty of 1495, whereupon ours are grounded, and which for substance are the same with that" (*Thurloe Papers*, vol. 1, 188–89).

45. Dutch request, Vlitius letter, Rawl. MS. A 2, p. 276,

10/20 February. My Latin text of the Dutch Thirty-six Articles is from S.G. 8460 and Aitzema 86, no. 18 in each. The English translation in Nalson, vol. 18, 90, 233–240v, differs slightly in content, as in Article 30. This English text, articles 1–13, is composed in good English idiom and written by a professional scribe; article 10 appears again on a separate page in what appears to be Thurloe's hand. Articles 14–36 are written by another hand and include such usages as *raisonable, sauvegarde, inhabitans, valable, juges, repurge, represailles, Juin*. It may be inferred that articles 1–13 were Englished by Thurloe, 14–36 by Rosin.

46. Order of 8 March, PRO, SP 25/77, pp. 424–25. Order of 9 March, PRO, SP 25/66, p. 428. Since David Masson's *Life of Milton* it has been assumed that "bee sent to Mr. Milton" indicated his incapacitation by blindness. His blindness is not to be minimized, but that instruction may simply reflect his having moved from Whitehall to Petty France. Compare the Council Order Book, 2 July 1650, directing that a *Declaration* "bee sent unto Mr. Thomas May to bee by him translated into Latine" (PRO, SP 25/64, p. 500).

47. Order of 11 March, PRO, SP 25/66, p. 428.

48. An inaccurate Latin text of the British Thirty-six Counter-articles was printed in the Columbia edition of Milton's *Works* vol. 18, 94–124, from an imperfect source (see Part Two) and with English translation by Nelson McCrea. A different translation was printed in the Yale *Complete Prose*, vol. 5, 588–98. All of these may be replaced by the official original English and Milton's Latin texts herein printed in Part Two.

49. In regard to *telonia* here, *telonium* in B4 and *catalogus* (note 40 above): Adam Littleton thought that the first cause of corruption in classical Latin was the introduction of Greek words (essay headed *Præfatio ad Lectorem*, but printed toward the end of his 1684 Dictionary at sig. Yyyyyyy). Milton expressed similar sentiments in his *De Doctrina Christiana*, vol. 2, chap. 6, (Columbia edition, vol. 17, 158): *incommode fecisse reor atque temere qui exoticam vocem* blasphemiam *in sermonem Latinum introduxerunt* ("they acted unfortunately and thoughtlessly who introduced the foreign [Greek] word *blasphemy* into the Latin language, I think"). Both the King James version, 1611, and Geneva Bible, 1560, translated the Greek *telonion* (Matthew 9.9, Luke 5.27 and Mark 2.14) as "at the receipt of *customs*."

Apotheca, used in *Summarium Damnorum*, came from the Greek but had been naturalized into Latin by Cicero, Horace and Pliny. Milton used it again in his letter to Richard Jones (*Epistolarum Familiarium* (1674), p. 52; Columbia edition, vol. 12, 90).

50. It would not be difficult, although it would be tedious, to offer instances to demonstrate that words Milton used only with cautionary phrases were commonly used by others in diplomatic documents without any question. One example will suffice: *salvagium*, without any qualifying apology, used by Willem Nieupoort in a letter to Walter Strickland and Anthony Ashley Cooper, 21 December 1654 (*Thurloe Papers*, vol. 3, 32–33).

In the 1676 *Literæ*, the overall ratio of *ut* to *uti* is about five to one, but the incidence varies over shorter periods. These distributions do not permit any valid inferences.

51. The preliminary article: official English text signed by Philip Lisle as monthly president of the Council, MS. S.G. 8460, no. 19; official Latin text, and a transcript of the English, MS. Aitzema 86, no. 19. Other transcripts in MS. S.G. 12589.62 and MS. St. v. Holl. 2813.1.

52. Huygens's diary, British Library, MS. Egerton 1997, ff 73v–74, my translation from his Dutch.

53. Huygens and Van Vliet (Vlitius) delivered this notification about the 150 ships to Speaker Lenthall in Latin, signed by the three ambassadors (original, Nalson Papers, vol. 18, 124, ff334–35v, Latin; English version, Tanner MS. 55, ff164–65v). According to Huygens's diary, Lenthall *vraeghde wat de intentie vande Staten daer door was*, "ask what the intention of the States General therein was." (In the Sir Thomas Browne Institute edition of Huygens's diary, p. 99, this is peculiarly mistranslated "asked what the Council of State intended to do with it.") Vlitius discreetly declined to comment. This "notification" was no news to the British Council of State. *Mercurius Politicus*, no. 78, for 27 November to 4 December 1651, p. 1250, printed a dispatch from a Leiden correspondent that the Dutch intended that "a Navy of 150 sail shall be kept up to justifie our way in the British Seas, and to counterbalance your Fleets." Parliament order, *Commons Journals*, vol. 7, 103. On 6/16 March, on 8/18 March and on subsequent dates, Vlitius and Huygens were busy at the Admiralty Court and at the Council of State with reference to specific Dutch ships. The details are not important here, but are recorded in Council minutes. From 15/25 March to 4/14 May, Huygens's diary has no data on diplomatic matters.

54. Council orders, 2/12 April, PRO, SP 25/66, p. 535. *Ut tandem*: Latin transcript in MS. S.G. 8460 and MS. Aitzema 86, both no. 22. There is an English version in MS. S.G. 8460, and also in M.S. S.G. 12589.62, which we may suspect was a sample of Lodewijck Huygens's efforts: "our begonnen treatie ... the preliminair article... the next meeting ["last" *was*

intended] . . . to performe the premises." The discussions in Yale edition, *Complete Prose,* vol. 5, 613, and in French, *Life Records of John Milton,* vol. 3, 216–17, are entirely erroneous.

Huygens's diary, 3/13 April, indicates that a Dutch ship carrying their official letters had been detained by English forces.

55. This paper, prepared by the committee on foreign affairs, is now Bodleian Library MS. Rawl. A 2, f 410, formally and elegantly written by a Council amanuensis, and signed by John Lisle on 9 April, from which it is printed in *Thurloe Papers,* vol. 1, 205, with Thurloe's summary of the four orders. No Latin version is now known; it may have been assigned to Milton or Weckherlin. Committee report on nondelivery, PRO, SP 25/66, p. 570. On 6 April, the Council directed the Admiralty judges to release three Dutch ships and to hear certain other cases.

On 31 March the Council ordered Milton to translate a letter to the Spanish Ambassador (PRO, SP 25/66, p. 523); and on 6 April, referring to letters going to the Hanse towns and to Hamburg (Aitzema's mission), the Council directed: "That copies of the said letters bee sent to Mr. Milton who is to translate them into Latin and bring them to the Councell" (PRO, SP 25/66, p. 549). These letters were officially dated 13 April, as was the letter to the King of Denmark, assigned by the Council to Weckherlin but attributed to Milton in the seventeenth century collections. On 12 and 21 April, the Council authorized a letter to Savoy, which appears to be Milton's *Navis Cujusdam* (*CSPD,* 1651–1652, pp. 215, 223). I have also identified and recovered still another Milton letter to Aitzema, dated about 8 April.

56. *Nos infra Scripti,* Latin transcript of the ambassadors' note, no. 23 in MS. S.G. 8460 and MS. Aitzema 86. Council orders for reply, PRO, SP 25/66, pp. 579, 589, 595, 596. The Council reply of 16/26 April, English text, refers to Dutch papers of 5 and 9 April. The Latin text uses the same dates but refers only to *illa charta,* "that paper." *Ut tandem* is undated in the transcripts available, but would seem to fit 5 April.

57. There is some loss of text in the margins in MS. S.G. 8460, which can be remedied from MS. Aitzema 86, although that shows some variants. Aitzema's *Historia Pacis,* 776, printed the text with other variants.

58. Lodewijck's father, Constantine Huygens, had recommended such a tour. Vlitius's journey is reported in his letter, Burmannus, *Sylloges,* vol. 3, 744.

59. The Dutch reply of 21 April/1 May is transcribed in MS. S.G. 8460 and MS. Aitzema 86, no. 25 in each. The Council minutes for 27 April read (PRO, SP 25/66, p. 639): "That the Paper now read in answeare to ye last paper from ye Dutch

Ambassadors be approved of, faire written and signed. That ye latine Translation of ye Paper now read be approved and sent along wth ye other" (that is, with the English). These letters were delivered 29 April/9 May.

Testing the 27 April letter: *superiorbus* as a noun in this sense is definitely not Miltonic. In contrast to *tractatio* in the 16/26 April letter, five times this translation uses *tractatus* for "treaty" negotiation; in contrast to the simple *scripta* and *postulata*, this one uses ornate expressions—*scriptorum quæsitorum, postulatorum charta* and *petitorum scripto*. Phrases rhyme and alliterate: *rogandi et recipiendi, non autem reddendi nec satisfaciendi, / requirimus et expectabimus*—compare the British letter to Christina of Sweden of 2 June 1652, presumably Weckherlin's: *expositurum et propositurum, audiendi et expendiendi*. Milton permitted some alliteration in his prose, but he regarded rhyming in prose as a fault contemned by the best ancient writers. Nonetheless, some homoioteleuton (rhyming grammatical endings) does occur in Milton state letters. In contrast to the 16/26 April letter, the English words "our stile" are here rendered *stilo nostro*.

60. 28 April letter ordered on 27 April, PRO, SP 25/66, pp. 639, 640, 643. The English draft is on the top half and the Latin version below it, in Bodleian MS. Rawl. A 2, p. 416. This text uses *tractatus* three times, which links it with the translator of the 27 April letter. The Council order and the English text are printed in *Thurloe Papers*, vol. 1, 206. I have not seen a signed English text of this letter, and it is not in MS. S.G. 8460, nor in MS. Aitzema 86. It may not have been delivered.

To be able to authenticate Milton's letters, we must be able to authenticate the work of his colleagues. Weckherlin was himself a significant figure in the literature of that era, and his letters deserve more attention on that score.

During the week of 27 April, Milton may have been preoccupied with caring for the needs of his wife Mary, about to give birth to their fourth child, and for the needs of his other three children.

61. The letters to Morocco, to the "Grand Turk," and to the "King" of Tunis are otherwise unknown at present. Extensive efforts to obtain such data from these regions, including appeals written to North African states in Arabic with the help of Dr. Eid Abdallah Dahiyat, have been unanswered.

62. From Milton's *Samson Agonistes*, 354–55, in another context there, but poignantly appropriate here.

63. Edward Phillips, "Life of Milton," in *Letters of State Written by Mr. John Milton* (1694), xliii–xliv. All Milton

biographers, including David Masson and William Riley Parker, have known nothing of the mission of Nieupoort, who offered Milton congratulations for his first *Defensio*, 1651 (see note 9 above). The only members of the Dutch embassy staff reported to have visited Milton were Vlitius and a "son of the ambassador" (see note 20 above). Milton does not mention ever meeting Albert Joachimi, who left England before *Pro Popula Anglicano Defensio* was published; Joachimi died on 17 May 1654.

In Edward Phillips's *Theatrum Poetarum* (1675), Jacob Cats is named as a poet who wrote on plural marriage; that was a topic of abiding interest for Milton, yet there is no hint of any personal acquaintance, although Phillips was in Westminster during the time of this embassy.

64. Pauw *summo cum honore*: Milton apparently uses *honor* here with its connotation of *status*.

65. Order for printing, PRO, SP 25/30, p. 54. William Dugard at this time was one of the official printers of Parliament documents.

66. Leo ab Aitzema, scibbled entry in his sketch of a diary, following a note dated 19 July, N.S., manuscript in the Algemeen Rijksarchief, Collectie Aitzema, Invent. nr. 45. English translation mine, with the help of archivist Theo Thomassen in deciphering the writing.

67. Official Council order for the guard, signed by Thurloe, MS. S.G. 8460, no. 36, and Huygens's diary for 30 May.

68. My account is based on the Council Order Books, Huygens's diary, MS. S.G. 8460, MS. Aitzema 86, and related Nalson and Tanner Papers: Cats's statement, *ob casum infelicem*. Latin original in Nalson, vol. 18, no. 128, ff 346–47v; English version, likely by Huygens, in a Dutch hand, Tanner MS. 53, ff 39–40 (formerly ff 29–31v)—"Papers delivered in by ye Dutch Ambassadors / Translation of the Proposition / Reported 25 May 1652." Transcripts of Latin only, with some variant phraseology, appear in MS. S.G. 8460 and MS. Aitzema 86, no. 37 in each; *Commons Journals* for 25 May, vol. 7, 135–36.

Cats appears to be sincerely troubled by the naval clash in his speech, in principle entirely opposed to war; it is a pity that diplomats are always under suspicion of double-dealing. One sentence is tantalizing: "Recte (nostro judicio) non infimus vestræ nationis scriptor utrum*que* populum duabus ollis fictibus in mari natantibus assimilavit, additu dicto, Si collidimur, frangimur, rem sane acu tetigit bonus ille." In [Huygens's] English: "An author beeing none of the least amongst yours, hath very wel compared, as wee conceive, both the nations to two earthen pots driving in the zea, with this devise, If we hurt, we breake. He hitted it very well that honest man." Who was this British author? Selden kept aloof from the Dutch envoys. Franciscus Junius may still have been in Holland at that time. Meric Casaubon is a slight possibility. Milton was famous for only one book. Was it Thomas Hobbes, whom Vlitius and Huygens did visit on 2/12 February?

69. Order on Nieupoort, 24 May, and order for Thurloe, PRO, SP 25/67, p. 121.

70. Repeat Thurloe order, PRO, SP 25/67, p. 134. The title is in its first form, as in the manuscript Journals of the House of Commons for 5 June. On 25 May following Vane's detailed report, Parliament voted a carte blanche to the Council of State to reinforce the navy, to raise other forces and to use them "for the honour and safety of the Commonwealth" (*Commons Journals*, vol. 7, 135–36).

71. *Quemadmodum præterito die Lunæ*, Latin official original, Nalson vol. 18, [128] ff 348–49v; English version, Tanner MS. 53, ff 49–50v (formerly 46); Latin transcripts in no. 38 in MSS. S.G. 8460 and Aitzema 86. *Quemadmodum Illustrissimo Senatui*, Latin official original, Nalson vol. 18, [128] ff 350–51v; English version, Tanner MS. 53, ff 47–48v (formerly 39); transcripts of Latin in no. 39 in MSS. S.G. 8460 and Aitzema 86. Both of these English versions are in the hand of the same person, an English hand, and both translations read well in English, not like Huygens's dialect. By whom? We wonder whether the three Dutch ambassadors have been given some helpful advice, or whether someone on the Council staff who was in favor of peace has intervened.

Draft of Vane's *Answer*, Tanner MS. 53, ff 55–56v; manuscript Journals of the House of Commons, 4 and 5 June. Orders by the Council, for the *Answer*, PRO, SP 25/67, p. 204 (4 June), p. 205 (5 June). Another 5 June order, p. 206, directs that informational materials be supplied by Robert Coytmore, secretary to the Council's committee on admiralty matters. Coytmore's business often overlapped the matters in Milton state papers, and his name should be added to the roster of Secretary Milton's staff associates.

72. Manuscript Journals of the House of Commons, vol. 36, p. 816, for 5 June, where it is reported as "A True Relation"; manuscript text of the document, title changed to *A Narrative* (above *true relation*, deleted), endorsed *read 5 June 1652*, in Nalson Paers, vol. 18, 137, ff 368–69). The suggestions (Columbia edition, Milton's *Works*, vol. 18, 502) that Milton "had a hand" in this *Narrative*, and other English-language portions of the *Declaration* booklet, are without foundation.

73. *The Answer of the Parliament of the Commonwealth of England, to Three Papers Delivered in to the Councel of State By the Lords Ambassadors Extraordinary of the States General of the United Provinces. As also a Narrative of the late Engagement between the English Fleet under the Command of General Blake; And the Holland Fleet under the Command of Lieutenant Admiral Trump. And likewise several Letters; Examinations and Testimonies touching the same. Together with the Three Papers aforesaid of the said Lords Ambassadors Extraordinary; And the Letter of Lieutenant Admiral Trump therein mentioned, Translated into English. London, Printed by John Field, Printer to the Parliament of England. 1652.* Whitelocke's *Memorials* (1853), vol. 3, 422, dated the publication 10 June. The copy of collector George Thomason was ink dated 17 *June*.

74. These papers are in MS. S.G. 8460, no. 40, official English text of the *Answer of the Parliament*, and an official Latin translation, which has as a heading *Responsum Parlamenti reipub: Angliæ ad ternas schedulas a Legatis Extraordinarijs Dominorum Potestatum Generalium Foederatarum Belgij Provinciarum ad Concilium Status redditas, quarum prima Junij tertio, secunda Junji sexto, tertia ejusdem mensis tertio decimo styli novi, 1652, est data, ex occasione prælij navalis inter utriusque Reipub: classes commissi*; no. 41, official English text of the *Narrative*; nos. 42–47, transcripts of reports by naval officers. All of these are by English amanuenses, and each paper is signed by Henry Scobell. On the back of the English text in no. 40, there is an unsigned endorsement, *Translatum Responsi Parlti accepti per D. Flemingium & D. Thurloe 7/17 Junij, 1652*: "I have received the translation of Parliament's Answer through Mr. Fleming and Mr. Thurloe, 7/17 June 1652." Another notation says that it was in print 11/21 June. On top of the Latin *Responsum Parlamenti* recto, there is the word *Translate*. This paper was done in Latin about 6 June. The likelihood that the Latin was by Milton is discussed below.

There is a transcript of this Latin *Responsum Parlamenti* in MS. S.G. 5899 I. Omitting the last two words *fuisse constat*, there is a transcript among the Mylius papers, *Niedersächsisches Staatsarchiv*, Best. 20, Tit. 38, Nr. 73a, Litt. J, ff 208–08v, in the hand of an English amanuensis. *Mercurius Politicus*, no. 106, 10–17 June 1652, pp. 1661–662, printed the Dutch *Third paper*, and the *Answer of the Parliament*, pp. 1663–664.

75. Our account for 7/17 June to 30 June/10 July is derived from the Commons' Journals, Council Order Books, the *Declaration*, Thurloe Papers (vol. 1, 207–12), MS. S.G. 8460, MS.

Aitzema 86, Aitzema's *Historia Pacis* and his *Saken*, and sources cited below. Aitzema's *Saken* reflects informed access to the discussions between the Dutch ambassadors and the English commissioners. (On Pauw's departure, Aitzema was designated as the Dutch channel of information). Vlitius and Whitelocke seem to have been the spokesmen on each side. Whitelocke brags of his role in his *Memorials of the English Affairs* (1853, vol. 3, 414).

76. Journals of the House of Commons, manuscript text, vol. 36, pp. 819–29; printed text, vol. 7, 140–42 for 8, 9, 10 June O.S.; and Nalson Papers, vol. 18, 129, ff 352–53; 130, ff 354–55; 131, ff 356–56v; 132, f 358.

77. Pauw's speech, Latin original signed by him, Nalson Papers, vol. 18, 127, ff 340–45v; printed text, *Scriptum*, 20–26; transcript, Mylius Papers, Niedersächsisches Staatsarchiv, Oldenburg, Best. 20, Tit. 38, Nr. 78a, Litt. H, ff 162–63v. English translation, Tanner MS. 53, ff 61–64v, transcribed in a continental (Dutch?) handwriting, shows the haste in which it was translated, in un-English idioms and in French spellings (*Ambassage, dommages*). In the *Declaration*, 20–25, the spelling was somewhat regularized to English printers' practice. Rosin is mentioned five times in Huygens's diary.

78. Pauw had no real powers to show. Johan de Witt, in 1652 a major figure in Dutch affairs, testifies that Pauw was sent simply to strengthen the three ambassadors in carrying out their original instructions (Letter, 5 November 1660, printed in *Brieven, Geschreven ende Gewisselt tusschen de Heer Johan de Witt... ende de gevolmachtigen van den Staedt der Vereenighde Nederlanden*, etc., H. Scheurleer, The Hague, 1724, vol. 4, 42).

79. Parliament minutes, Journals of the House of Commons, 16, 17, 18 June, manuscript text, vol. 36, pp. 836–39, spelling *Counsell* and *Councell*; printed text, vol. 7, 143.

80. Council orders, 17/27 June and 28/18 June, PRO, SP 25/29, p. 27.

81. Son's death, entry in Milton's family Bible, British Library, Add. MSS. 32, 310.

82. Milton's letter to Philaras, *Epistolarum Familiarium Liber Unus* (1674), pp. 34–35; Columbia edition, vol. 12, 54–59. Did Philaras notice that Milton speaks of his respect for the Germans, Danes and Swedes (implication: *Protestants*) but omits the Dutch? Among Milton's personal letters during the Interregnum, this one only is marked as written from London, all the others from Westminister: is there a connection to his family troubles? Neither Philaras nor Milton mentions that Venetian

envoy Lorenzo Paulucci had been in England since April asking for ships and men to wage war against the expanding Turks; his official reception was held up, nominally for lack of proper credentials (*Commons Journals*, vol. 7, 142, for 15 June).

Milton asks Philaras *ut quis antiquam in animis Græcorum virtutem, industriam, laborum tolerantiam, antiqua illa studia dicendo, suscitare atque accendere possit.* Was he thinking of the passage attributed to his favorite Roman historian, Sallust (*Letter to Caesar*): *Sed virtus, vigilantia, labor apud Græcos nulla sunt?*

83. 21 to 30 June, from the *Declaration* booklet; Nalson Papers, vol. 18, 138, ff 370–71v; [?], f 359; 133, ff 360–61v; 134, ff 362–63v; 140, f 379; *Thurloe Papers*, vol. 2, 207–08, 210–12 (= Pauw's texts in *Scriptum* 54–69); Tanner MS. 53, ff 77–77v, 25 June reparations demands; Journals of the House of Commons, manuscript text, vol. 36, 855–66, printed text, vol. 7, 144–47. French, *Life Records of John Milton*, vol. 3, 225–28, inevitably confused the demands of 25 June with the previous *Paper of Demands*, and this confusion has been carried over into W.R. Parker's *Milton, A Biography*, vol. 2, 1015–016, and into the appendix of *Achievements of the Left Hand*, edited by Michael Lieb and J.T. Shawcross, Amherst, 1974. W.C. Abbott, *Writings and Speeches of Oliver Cromwell*, vol. 3, 241–42, knew only the Early Draft of the *Summarium Damnorum*, no. 43a in the Columbia edition, vol. 13, 130–37, not the entire *Paper of Demands*.

Mercurius Politicus, no. 109, 1–8 July, pp. 1711–713, printed a letter said to be from a Dutch correspondent in the Netherlands, conceding that Pauw had no powers to conclude a treaty and had been sent only to make demands and then break off. We wonder whether this letter was authentic, or possibly an early example of journalistic propaganda fabricated by a British organ aimed at its London readers.

84. Penn's letter, in John Nickolls, *Original Letters and Papers of State, Addressed to Oliver Cromwell; Concerning the Affairs of Great Britain. From the Year MDCXLIX to MDCLVIII. Found among the Political Collections of Mr. Milton* (1743), p. 87. In this book, Nickolls printed a random mass of papers believed to have been retained by Milton at the fall of the Commonwealth.

85. Journals of the House of Commons, 7 July, manuscript text, vol. 38, pp. 885–86, slightly modified in printed text, vol. 7, 150; Nalson Papers, vol. 18, 139, ff 372–79, manuscript English text of the *Declaration* as adopted. Council minutes and Commons Journals record details of the progress of the *Declaration* from 1 to 7 July.

86. The printing was done by 25 July. The next day, Lorenzo Paulucci wrote to the Venetian envoy in France: "Yesterday Parliament issued a printed manifesto upon the negotiations of all four of the Dutch Ambassadors . . . " (*Calendar of State Papers, Venetian, 1647–52*, p. 262, translated from Venice. *Senato. Secreta. Dispacci, Francia*).

87. A correct conclusion derived from fallacious method is not valid: such are attributions of the *Declaration* and *Scriptum* booklets to Milton, based on incomplete or incorrect evaluation of evidence even if by able scholars, such as: W.D. Hamilton, *Original Papers Illustrative of the Life and Writings of John Milton*, Camden Society (1859), 20–22; David Masson, who regretted he had not tested their Latinity, *Life of Milton*, vol. 4, 447, 482; Hans Eduard Fernow, *Milton's Letters of State*, Hamburg (1903), p. 21. Mabbott and French, Columbia edition, vol. 18, 502, erred in ascribing English originals and translations from Latin to Milton (reiterated in French, *Life Records*, vol. 3, 230, 232). W.R. Parker's out-of-hand exclusion of the *Scriptum* ("We should not outdo the Council of State in demands upon Milton in this period," *Milton, A Biography*, 1016) reflects his regrettable failure to study the state papers. Commentary in the Yale edition, *Complete Prose*, vol. 5, 620–21, may be discarded.

88. John Field published at least three variant issues of the English version, and another was printed by Evan Tyler at Leith, 1652. The title of one Field issue reads *A Declaration of the Parliament of the Commonwealth of England, Relating to the Affairs and Proceedings between this Commonwealth and the States General of the United Provinces of the Low-Countreys, and the present Differences occcasioned* [sic] *on the States Part. And the Answer of the Parliament to Three Papers from the Ambassadors Extraordinary of the States General, upon occasion of the late Fight between the Fleets. With a Narrative of the late Engagement between the English and Holland Fleet. As also, A Collection of the Proceedings in the Treaty between the Lord Pauw, Ambassador Extraordinary from the States General of the United Provinces, and the Parliament of the Commonwealth of England* (followed by Parliament's order of sole copyright, 9 July).

89. The Title of the French booklet reads *La Declaration du Parlament de la Republique D' Angleterre, Sur les Affaires & Procedures entre cette Republique & les Estats Generaux des Provinces Unies des Pays Bas; et les Differens survenus, dont les Estats ont donné le sujet de leur part. Et la Response du Parlement sur les trois Memoires presentés par les Ambassadeurs Extraordinaries des Estats Generaux, sur l'occasion du*

Combat, qui s'est dernierement donné entre les deux Flotes. Avec la Relation de ce qui s'est passé audit Combat entre la Flote d'Angleterre et celle d'Hollande. Comme aussi, Un Récueil des Procedures du Traité commencé entre le Parlement de la République de l'Angleterre, & le Sr Pauw Ambassadeur Extraordinaire des Estats Generaux des Provinces Unies. Traduits fidelement de l'Anglois & imprimés par Ordre du Conseil d'Estat. (ornament) A Londres, Par Guil. Du Gard Imprimeur dudit Conseil. 1652.

90. Aitzema's diary (MS. Collectie Aitzema, Inv. nr. 45) repeatedly mentions Theodore Haak as accompanying Oliver Fleming in his official diplomatic contact. No copy of John Field's Dutch-language edition of the *Declaration* is now known—not at the British Library, not in the Dutch Central Catalogue, nor in any library in the United States. Copies are extant of three distinct editions in Dutch, printed by different publishers in the Netherlands, each dated 1652, each purporting to reproduce Field's Dutch edition as printed in London, with title pages worded approximately the same in each. One title page (with the "bear" ornament used by more than one Netherlands printer) reads: *Declaratie van't Parlement van Enghelandt, Raeckende De Affairen ende Proceduren tusschen de Republijcke en de Staten General van de Vereenighde Nederlanden, Sampt De Geschillen veroorsaeckt vander Staten zijde. Na de Copye tot Londen, door last van't Parlement, gedruckt by Iohn Fielt, haren Ordinaris Drucker, 1652*. The same text, but spelled differently throughout (e.g., *ghedruckt*) by another printer, has *dese* before *Republijcke* in the title and an abstract geometric title page ornament. These two are available in the New York Public Library. A third similar Dutch printing, in the British Library, has *dese* and spells *Rakende* on the title page. All three print only the *Declaration* proper and omit all the other matter, whereas the French edition included everything in the English-language editions. Much of this other matter was printed separately in other formats in the Netherlands, as were some of the speeches and papers submitted by the three ambassadors and by Pauw. A translation made independently into Dutch from the English, of the *Declaration* only, was published by Lieve de Lange, Amsterdam, and yet another, with two variant title pages, by Ian Gerritz in Rotterdam. Aitzema's *Saken* translation, vol. 3, 722–23, is quite different from the reprints of Field's Dutch; his rough draft *Dagboek* version begins like the *Lieve de Lange* and ends like the *Saken* text.

91. The title of the Latin edition reads: SCRIPTUM | Parlamenti Reipublicæ | ANGLIÆ | De iis quæ ab hac Repub. cum

Pote- | *statibus Fœderatarum Belgii Provinciarum Ge-* | *nerali-bus, & quibus progressibus acta sunt;* | *déque controversiis in præsentia exortis,* | *quibus prædictæ Potestates occasio-* | *nem præbuere.* | *Adjicitur & Responsum Parlamenti ad ternas chartu-* | *las à D^{nis} Legatis Potestatum generalium Ex-* | *traor-dinariis, ex occasione pugnæ navalis inter* | *Anglorum & Belga-rum classes consertæ.* | *Unà cum illius pugnæ, sicuti commissa est, narratione.* | *Postremò scripta illa in unum collata, quæ inter Parla-* | *mentum Reipub. Angliæ & D^{num} Adrianum Pauw,* | *Legatum Fœderatarum Belgii Provinciarum Extraor-* | *dinar-ium, cum de pace agerent, ultro* | *citróque reddita sunt.* | rule | ornamental device | rule | *LONDINI,* | *Typis Du-Gardianis, Anno Domini 1652.* | It is a small quarto, A-K4; title page with blank verso, text on pages 1–74, errata on unnumbered [75], and several blank pages (three, in copies examined). The only reprint of that time that I have seen, which is only of the Latin *Scriptum* proper, is in Aitzema's *Historia Pacis* (1654), 804–10.

92. Milton might have used the classical *indifferens* to translate "indifferent," but he may here have remembered his 1642 resentment against the "wilfulnesse and wantonnesse of a needless and jolly persecutor call'd Indifference" (*An Apology against a Pamphlet* (1642), p. 39; Columbia edition, vol. 3, 338). The bishops' party had argued that the "Puritans" were unjustifiably complaining against conforming to requirements that were essentially "indifferent." For similar attitude, see note 102.

Liber commeatus: for Milton's sometime lack of success in obtaining approval for his preference, see Miller, *John Milton & the Oldenburg Safeguard*, 262, 286. Milton was able to use *liberè commeare* in the passes for Petrus Georgius Romswinckel, 13 June 1656 (original manuscript letter to the Elector of Brandenburg, now in the Zentrales Staatsarchiv, Dienstelle Merseburg, DDR, and similar letters in The Hague Rijksarchief, S.G. 5901, and in the Amsterdam archives, Burgomaster Missiven Portef.; Skinner Transcript, no. 55; Columbia edition, vol. 13, 450).

93. Milton showed the same preference in the letter of 16 December 1650 to the Portuguese envoy, João de Guimarães. The English draft (Nalson Papers, vol. 17, 41, ff 86–87 read "a copie of your credentials," but Milton's Latin, from an apparently revised English draft, has *ex literis quas a rege habes commendatitias sive credentiales*. Present-day printings of Cicero, *Ad Familiares* 5.5 and 13.26 spell *commendaticias*. Milton's spelling may be seen in Robertus Stephanus, *Thesaurus Linguæ Latinæ*, in Adam Littleton's Dictionary, and (in non-Miltonic

passages) in J.C. Lünig's 1712 *Literæ Procerum Europæ*.

94. *Potestates Generales* appears on the title page of the booklet, in the heading of the *Scriptum* proper and nine times in its text. Its use elsewhere in that booklet is treated elsewhere in this study; it also appears in two letters to the Danish envoys, 1652, and two letters to Dutch envoys in 1653. After the 1654 Anglo-Dutch peace treaty, *Ordines* is the term used in Milton's state papers, except once when *Potestatibus* heads a letter to West Friesland, 27 January 1658/59.

95. See Appendix B for analysis of the treatment of personal names in the state papers and in Milton's other writings.

96. In the letter of 11 March 1651/52, from Parliament to Queen Christina, Latin by Milton, her envoy's name is uninflected as *Spiering*, but in Parliament's letter of 2 June 1652 to Christina, where all indications are that it is by Weckherlin, the name is inflected to *Spieringio*. Perhaps *Trumpio* here is from the same hand.

In *Ob casum infelicem*, the three Dutch ambassadors use the form *Admirallum Trompium*. Pauw, 11/21 June, uses *Thalassiarchum Trompium*. Milton would have known of these only if someone read these documents to him.

97. *Circumstantiæ (in this Responsum Parlamenti)* is late Latin, but it is seen in Milton's translation of the letter to Danish envoys, 19 October 1652 (published here in Part Two), and several times in Milton's *Artis Logicæ Plenior Institutio*, printed 1672 but drafted circa 1645–1647, book 1, chap. 10, p. 24 and chap. 11, pp. 33–34 (in Columbia edition, vol. 11, pp. 83, 93, 95); at chap. 11, p. 33, qualified *quæ vulgò circumstantiæ nuncupatur, quia extra subjectum sunt*, "which are commonly called *circumstantiæ*, because they are out of their subject." Compare C. Salmasius, *Defensio Regia*, early in Caput I, *Circumstantiæ vulgo vocant*. Whether *ut* used three times to *uti* once is significant, in a short composition, is debatable.

98. For photo reproduction of the 20 January letter to Mylius and discussion of its *pro moré*, see Miller, *John Milton & the Oldenburg Safeguard*. Also cf. *quasi in procinctu* in Milton's letter to Holstenius, *Epistolarum Familiarium* (1674), p. 26; Columbia edition, vol. 12, 40.

99. These 11 items, with all their Miltonisms, show *ut* six times and *uti* 12 times, so out of line with Milton's habits in his longer works, again suggesting that Rosin may have handled the fair copy.

These 11 items are a powerful demonstration of the need to study Milton's language and Latinity most closely. They are crucial to an analysis of the whole document. Yet, failing to see their importance, Mabbott and French omitted them from the Columbia edition, thereby also throwing later readers off the scent.

100. Peculiarly, in *Defensio Secunda* (1654), p. 129 (Columbia edition, vol. 8, 190), Milton dictated *Adriane Pauui* in the vocative case, or it was so written by his amanuensis.

101. The Errata page lists four corrections, but George Thomason's copy, now in the British Library, shows other misprints: *Isacium*, p. 4; *Federatarum*, p. 60, perhaps corrected in some copies during the press run. In the very literal English translation from the French of Pauw's 14/24 June *Sommaire*, printed in the English-language booklet, there is one conspicuous minstranslation of *peut alleguer des divers exemples* as "hath produced divers examples." In my photocopy, from University Microfilms, of the French *La Declaration*, some long ago reader (of the British Library copy?) entered *a allegué* as if the error were in a translation into French.

To complete the record: at the end of the English, French and Latin booklets, there is printed a petition from some merchants transmitted by Pauw, and a request for additional shipping for the voyage home. These are also mentioned in the Journals of the House of Commons, manuscript vol. 36, p. 866; printed, vol. 7, 147.

102. Giovanni Ambrosio Sarotti, Venetian Resident at Florence, wrote to the Doge and Senate at Venice, 14 September 1652: "Parliament has written to the Grand Duke in justification of their procedure against the Dutch. They have also sent a manifesto to his Highness, which he has caused to be translated and printed as a curiosity" (translated from the Italian, *Calendar of State Papers, Venetian* (1647–1652), vol. 28, p. 281, referring to the *Dichiarazione del Parlamento della Republica D'Inghilterra*, Firenze, 1652). The letter "in justification," dated 29 July 1652, was translated into Latin by Milton, *Concilium Status cum à Carolo Longlando*.

Other translations appeared in Danish, *Den Engelske Repub: Manifest*, and two in German, *Das Manifest, oder Endtliche Crklarung* [sic] *von der Republicq von Engelandt* and *Manifest der Repub: von Engelandt*. These titles are given more fully in John T. Shawcross, *Milton, A Bibliography for the Years 1624–1700*, but items 121–124 in the *Bibliography* should read *Declaratie* for the Dutch versions, and items 134 and 135 (which are copies, not originals) are now filed as MS. S.G. 12589.62. Many items clarified or first identified in this present monograph may now be added to the Milton bibliography.

103. For Willemsen's mission, and for photocopies of the script

of Milton's amanuensis, see Miller, *John Milton & the Oldenburg Safeguard*. Some records of the Reedtz-Rosencrantz mission are preserved in the Danish archives, Rigsarkivet, Copenhagen, file T.K.U.A., A. II. 16; these appear to have been disorganized in recent years and show gaps where materials were formerly available. The file retains the English text of the *Declaration* proper, the 8 July cover letter in the original English with Milton's Latin version, and the 19 October letter in the original English with Milton's Latin translation. PRO, SP 103/3, pp. 239–318, has an English file of these negotiations, with the English texts of the 8 July and 19 October letters on pp. 293–94 and 296–97.

Related Council orders are recorded in PRO, SP 25/29, pp. 77, 88 and 95 for 2, 6 and 7 July; for the 19 October letter, PRO, SP 29/34, pp. 14–41. The pertinent Parliament orders are in the *Journals of the House of Commons*, vol. 7, 149, 190–91. Reedtz's 2 July oration is preserved in Nalson papers, vol. 18, 11, f 29–30 (Latin); vol. 18, 12, f 31–31v, English (also in SP 103/3, 291–92); and in Aitzema's Dagboek papers in the Rijksarchief.

The omitted phrases render the 8 July English text rather abrupt; perhaps there were other interim drafts in English. Note that Milton here also avoided the word *indifferent*, substituting a circumlocution. His use of *Deo bene juvante* (19 October) may be seen in the 6 June *Responsum Parlamenti* and in other state papers (Columbia edition, vol. 13, 164, 348 and 430).

On 9 July the British commissioners submitted to the Dutch envoys a response to an earlier 14-point Danish proposal and a set of British demands in six articles. Both documents use English-language phraseology taken from their Thirty-Six Counter-articles to the Dutch. Consequently the Latin translations show some phraseology seen in Milton's Latin of the Counter-articles, but with more differences than there are between the two sets of English-language documents. The six-article paper was definitely not by Milton; the other seems to me doubtful.

104. This letter of H. van Beverningh and P. van de Perre to Adrian van Hooghe is printed in *Thurloe Papers*, vol. 1, 428, from an English manuscript, now Rawl. A 5, pp. 218–20. Was this one of Thurloe's intercepts, translated from the Dutch original?

Cromwell was quoted by the Dutch envoys who reported back to the Netherlands on 14 July 1653, as saying "dat de Werelt ruym genoegh was, ende dat wy den andern daer in welverstaende alle andern de Marckt ende Wet souden konnen stellen" [Scheurleer, *Verbael* (1752), p. 46]: that the world was wide enough for the English and Dutch to control the markets and lay down the law for the others.

105. The Rijksarchief has in MS. S.G. 12589.66 the official English original signed by Lenthall and the official Latin translation of *Quæ studia Sincera*, 1/11 April 1653; and in the hand of Dutch amanuenses, English and Latin transcripts of *Parlamentum Reipublicæ Angliæ literas ad se missas*, 1/11 April 1653, in Arch. St. v. Holl. 2389. English language drafts of these two letters are preserved in Tanner MS. 52, f 1–2v and 3–3v.

The official English language original of the 6 May letter, *Literæ... quæ a Thilmanno Aquilio*, signed by Lambert and Thurloe, if filed in MS. S.G. 12589.66, together with the official Latin translation. Another copy of the English text, also signed, and in the same handwriting as the Rijksarchief original, is in Rawl. MS. A 3, pp. 33–34, from which it was printed in *Thurloe Papers*, vol. 1, 239 and [T. Rymer,] *Fœdera*, vol. 20, 631–32.

The Holland letter of 18/28 March is extant in what appear to be two originals, in Dutch and in French, Nalson Papers, vol. 18, 135, f 364 and f 365. No original copy of the 30 April letter is reported. Historians seem to have neglected these. Samuel R. Gardiner, *History of the Commonwealth and Protectorate*, vol. 2, 239, and vol. 3, 31, knew only the Dutch versions in Aitzema's *Saken*, vol. 3, 804–12.

These two letters from the Netherlands were translated in England, and the translations are filed in Tanner MS 53, ff 226–27v and ff 235–36v. Latin texts of the two Netherlander letters and the three British letters were printed in Aitzema's *Historia Pacis*, 817–25, and in J.C. Lünig, *Literæ Procerum Europæ*, vol. 1, 486–506, but I do not know whether the Netherlander letters were sent to England in Latin.

For the period June 1653 through 1654, the Dutch documentary sources are MS S.G. 8472, apparently the first provisional report submitted by the Dutch envoys on 27 August 1653, also transcribed into MS. S.G. 8486 and MS. Aitzema 86; and the final report, submitted 4 January 1658, in MS. S.G. 8483 and its supplement MS S.G. 8484, from which variant transcripts were made, MS. S.G. 8485 and MS. S.G. 8473. From one or more of these, there was published by Hendrick Scheurleer at The Hague, 1725, with an editor named, *Verbael Gehouden door de Herren H. Beverningk, W. Nieupoort, J. Van de Perre, en A.P. Jongestaal, Als Gedeputeerden en Extraordinis Ambassadeurs van de Heeren Staeten Generael Der Vereenigde Nederlanden, Aen De Republyck van Engelandt*, xx, 716 pages. This reproduces most of the documents, but "modernizes" the English to 1725 standards.

British records are less complete. PRO, SP 105/98, some 97 pages, is a collection, all in English, of papers from 18 March to 29 December 1653, including an English variant of the *Paper of Demands* from 1651–1652; PRO, SP 103/46 and SP 105/99 have papers from the 1654 negotiations and settlements. Some documents were printed in [T. Rymer,] *Fœdera* (1735), vol. 20.

106. Exactly when Milton and Marvell became acquainted is not known. Marvell's Latin epigram addressed to Oliver St. John in 1651, *In Legationem Domini Oliveri St. John ad Provincias Fœderatas*, suggests that he may have then been soliciting employment in diplomacy. It is not clear why W.C. Abbott (*Writings and Speeches of Oliver Cromwell*, vol. 3, 81) thought that by 1653 Marvell had been "more recently temporary assistant to John Milton."

107. Meadows, as his name is usually given, also signed himself as *Meadowe* and *Meadowes*. Weckherlin in 1652 was designated as *Secretary-Assistant* to Milton, but Meadowes appears to have functioned as Latin Secretary. The number of letters he translated during his tenure of office was much larger than what had been needed during 1649–1652. During six months in 1656 when Meadowes was overseas, Milton did almost 30 letters. Meadowes was again abroad on diplomatic missions from August 1657 to July 1659, and therefore Andrew Marvell was appointed to take his place alongside Milton, September 1657. (Marvell confirms the year in his *The Rehearsal Transpros'd* (1673), vol. 2, p. 127).

Some state papers between 1653 and 1660 may have been translated into Latin by others than Milton, Meadowes or Marvell. (A notable instance is the translation of 22 April 1653, *Declaration of the Lord General and His Council of Officers*, on the dissolution of the Rump Parliament, published in Latin as *Declaratio Oliveri Cromwelli Praefecti Exercituum pro Repub. et Consiliii sui Militaris, Exhibens fundamenta, & caussas Dissolutionis nuperi Parlamenti. Ex Anglicano Sermone in Latinum traducta. Londini, Typis Guilielmi Du-Gard. 1653.* This translation, not mentioned by Abbott, was done by someone whose university training included a heavy emphasis on church-influenced late Latin. William Jessop was also assigned to foreign affairs, 17 October 1653 (Council Order Books, PRO, SP 25/71, p. 118). In 1657 and later, John Dryden and (an otherwise unidentified) "Mr. Sterry" were associated with Milton and Marvell in office.

108. These eight letters are dated 29 June; 13, 21, 22 and 25 July; 1 August; 1 August and 3 August. The official originals in English of these eight letters, and their official Latin

translations—with one important exception—are preserved in MS. S.G. 8484. The same *eight* English letters, and the same *seven* Latin letters as transcribed by Dutch amanuenses are extant in MS. S.G. 8473, 8483 and 8485; in MS. Aitzema 86; and in Gemeentearchief Amsterdam, Archives of the Burgomasters, Lands- en Gewestelyk Bestuur, no. 94.

All the English-language originals of these eight letters are signed by the monthly Council presidents, and are in the handwriting of several Council amanuenses. The seven official Latin translations are unsigned. Five of these were written by Council amanuenses, while two, *Consilium Statûs cùm in prioribus* (21 July) and *Consilium Statûs de chartula a Delegatis* (25 July) appear to be in the handwriting of Philip Meadowes. The script always spells *Consilium* with an *s* for "Council" of State. The Council amanuenses use *s* or *c*, inconsistently, even within one letter, except when they are writing for Milton.

A variant transcript of the English text of the 13 July letter, done in 1653, is extant in PRO, SP 105/98, pp. 26–30; and the same official amanuensis wrote the English text of the 1 August letter (on prisoners of war) on what is now Bodleian MS. Rawl. A 5, pp. 2, 3, 4, from which at some later time MS. PRO, SP 84/159, ff 158–58v, was transcribed, and thereafter printed in *Thurloe Papers*, vol. 1, 395.

109. Letter for Dury, see Miller, *John Milton and the Oldenburg Safeguard*, p. 354. In Aitzema, *Historia Pacis*, 848–50, a long Latin letter, imprecisely datable as November (O.S.), the British reply to a Dutch letter of 2 December (N.S.) uses *Deputatus* twice in referring to the Dutch envoys, but it has no other cogent Miltonic usages and has too many unclassical words to be readily assigned to Milton.

110. The 18 November 1653 treaty draft, introduced by a letter whose Latin is not by Milton, is preserved in MS. S.G. 8484 and printed in [Scheurleer,] *Verbael*, 206–14; the final 1654 treaty, in Latin, 356–67. There were many printings of the Latin in 1654 and thereafter. The final English text, *Articles of Peace, Union, and Confederation* was printed in *A Catalogue and Collection of all those Ordinances, Proclamations, Declarations, &c., which have been Printed and Published since the Government was established in His Highness the Lord Protector, viz. from Decem. 16, 1653 unto Septem. 3, 1654*, which appeared in at least two variant editions; reprinted, with spelling somewhat modernized, in W.C. Abbott, *Writings and Speeches*, vol. 3, 897–906. Only with most stringent qualification may any part of the Latin text be considered for inclusion in Milton's primary bibliography; texts in other continental languages do not belong there at all.

Peculiarly, no copy of Milton's 1 August letter, Latin text, is found in the Dutch archives, which has only the original official signed English letter and its transcripts. I have found Milton's 1 August Latin text only in the draft now filed as Bodleian MS. Rawl. A 4, p. 305, from which it was printed in [T. Rymer,] *Fœdera*, vol. 20, 666–67, and in *Thurloe Papers*, vol. 1, 354, with abbreviations expanded, and, as in the 13 July letter, no indication that anyone recognized that is was by Milton. It is an open question whether the Latin text was delivered to the Dutch envoys, or whether they lost it in the interruption of their negotiations. None of the eight Latin letters are included in Aitzema's 1654 *Historia Pacis*, nor in Lünig's anthology; this suggests that these letters remained restricted until 1658, were first transcribed then, and were effectively buried until Scheurleer printed the seven in *Verbael* (1725), 245–304, still with no knowledge of Milton's connection.

These eight letter were still being completed in accordance with the order requiring the signed authentic text to be in English, with the Latin as an accompanying translation (see note 23 above). Lorenzo Paulucci, Venetian secretary in England, reported 13 December 1653: "The written reply was at length delivered to me last Saturday by Sir [Oliver] Fleming, in both English and Latin, according to their custom" [*Calendar of State Papers, Venetian*, vol. 29 (1653–1654), p. 155, translated from the Italian]. When Cromwell became Protector, procedure changed: the official original texts of letters to European rules were done in Latin and signed by Cromwell in his own hand. Companion English texts appear no longer to have been sent abroad to continental states. Possibly one reason was that (unlike some members of the Commonwealth Council of State) Cromwell was competent enough in Latin to converse with foreign diplomats. He dropped the Commonwealth Council's policy of officially negotiating by written papers only, taking upon himself the prerogative of direct conversations with envoys, sometimes informally and "off the record." Although from the inception of the first Protectorate there was a trend to monarchical forms and procedures in "court etiquette," in regard to state letters, peculiarly, the reverse occurred. The elegant stylized calligraphy affected by the amanuenses under the Commonwealth and the Nominated Parliament from the beginning of the first Protectorate was replaced by informal, neat, very legible but unadorned script.

In preparing the 13 July letter, Milton seems to have had someone read to him to refresh his memory, from a manuscript text of the *Scriptum* proper in his possession and not from the printed booklet, so that *Paius* is forgotten, and that envoy is again *Adrianus/Adrian* (for *Adriani/Adriano*), but *Paw* as in the 1653 official original English texts; Tromp is *Trumpius, Trumpii*.

111. *Of Reformation* (1641), p. 58; Columbia edition, vol. 3, 51.

112. "ut tam facilè, támque feliciter defungantur hoc Bello, quàm defungetur Salmasius Miltonio," adapted by Milton from the address to Charles II, signed by Adrian Vlacq, in [Peter du Moulin] *Regii Sanguinis Clamor Ad Coelum Adversus Parricidas Anglicanos* (1652) 4^0, Sig) (((2v; and "Cui ego voto si facilè assensero, arbitror me nostris successibus Reîque Anglicanæ nec ominari malè, nec precari," both passages in Milton, *Defensio Secunda* (1654), p. 53; Columbia edition, vol. 8, 76.

113. Milton, *Pro Se Defensio*, Typis Neucomianis (1655), p. 71 (Columbia edition, vol. 9, 104): "Falleris tu quidem magnoperè, si quenquam esse Anglorum putas, qui Foederatis Provinciis me uno sit amicior, aut voluntate conjunctior; qui præclariùs de Republ. illa sentiat; qui eorum industriam, artes, ingenium, libertatem aut pluris faciat, aut sæpiùs collaudet; qui bellum incœptum cum iis minùs voluerit, susceptum pacatiùs gesserit, compositum seriò magis triumpharit."

114. Detailed data about many claims involved in these documents may be found in the serial volumes edited by W. Noel Sainsbury, *Calendar of State Papers, Colonial, East Indies* (and other variant titles). The economics of the spice islands is described by John Cartwright, "A brief description of the Islands of Banda, with a short relation of some principal injuries done by the Hollanders in those parts, whereby the Kings Ma*ty* and our whole nation have suffered great damage, but also ignominy & dishonour intolerable," 18 May 1631, in *CSP, Colonial, 1630–1634*, pp. 159–61.

Poolaroon and Pooloway were two of the six Banda Islands, between Celebes (Sulawesi) and New Guinea (Irian Barat), which in the 1620s yielded most of the world production of nutmeg and mace, with some cloves, at that times worth vast sums in Europe. Jaccatra is now Jakarta. Bantam at the west end of Java was a major source of pepper. Amboyna (Ambon) is an island north of the Bandas.

Outside of the documents in these proceedings, Milton does not mention any of these place names, although they were used by Luis de Camoens in his epic *Os Lusiadas* a century earlier. Milton names two of the Moluccas in his simile of a fleet seen far off at sea, *Paradise Lost* 2.636–42, "the Iles / Of *Ternate* and *Tidore*, whence Merchants bring / Thir Spicie Drugs," but Ternate and Tidore are not named in these negotiation documents, and Milton scans them differently than does Camoens.

Amboyna: In February 1622/23 the Dutch forces executed a number of British subjects on Amboyna, alleging a criminal conspirarcy, allegations which the British declared were fabricated by torture of witnesses (*CSP, Colonial, 1622-1624*; British account, pp. 303-20; Dutch account, 339-49). There are many other published accounts from that era. In the settlement after the 1654 peace treaty, in return for some financial compensation to heirs and assigns of the victims, the English agreed to drop the issue and to desist from the accusations, which were deeply resented by the Dutch.

Alexander Gil the Younger, chiefly remembered as Milton's sometime friend, repeatedly harped on his countrymen's bitterness over the Amboyna events in his *Mosae-Trajectum* (1632), and *Skenkiana* (1635), Latin verses to be published in his collected works. Milton himself did not refer to the tragedy; other English authors continued to call the executions a "massacre," particularly during later Anglo-Dutch wars. Abraham Cowley included a long discursive passage on the second Anglo-Dutch war at the end of his Latin *Sex Libri Plantarum*, recalling the *scelus Amboynæ*, rendered as "Amboyna's wickedness" by Aphra Behn in her English translation. In 1673 John Dryden dramatized the tortures and executions in a prose melodrama *Amboyna*; Sir Walter Scott, editing Dryden's works a century and a half later, commented, "This play is beneath criticism, and I can hardly hesitate to term it the worst production Dryden ever wrote."

William Macdowell, named in the cover letter, was Charles II's agent in the Netherlands.

For complaints of the Muscovy Company from 1618, see *CSPD, James I, 1611-1618*, pp. 572-73; King James I's declaration, January 1622/23, claiming £22,000 damages, *CSPD, James I, 1619-1627*, p. 485.

Most of the claims in the *Paper of Demands* were cancelled out or resolved by negotiation after the 1654 peace agreement, which provided for a panel of arbitrators who were to be locked into a room with no necessities of life—no fire, candle, food or drink—until they would emerge with settlements. Details of these settlements are printed in *Verbael* (Scheurleer, 1725), with English text of the arbitral award, 529-34; [S.W.,] *A General Collection of Treatys of Peace and Commerce, Renunciations, Manifestos and other Public Papers from the Year 1642 to the End of the Reign of Queen Anne* (London, 1732) III, 112-35, 144-45. The *Règlement*: see Aitzema, *Saken*, vol. 3, 1069-75; *Recueil des Traitez de Paix, de Trêve, de Neitralité*, Amsterdam,

Chez Henry et la Veuve de T. Boom (1700) III, 659–63 (also the 1619 treaty between the English and the Dutch East India Companies, III, 153–56, Clive Parry, *Consolidated Treaty Series*, III, 319–53.

115. Of the many items in the *Paper of Demands*, only the case of Francis Hardedge (or, Hurdidge) turns up in another Milton state paper, draft text in the Skinner Transcript, 136; in the Columbia Manuscript, no. 21, printed in the Columbia edition, vol. 13, p. 460, no. 149; not in *Literæ*. This letter was apparently drafted shortly after the Anglo-Portuguese treaty of 1656 and addressed to King John IV. He died 6 November 1656, and the letter was held up, not sent until April 1659, so that the surviving text of the draft, redated, retains the original addressee, while the final text most likely was directed to Alfonso VI. (As Francis Hardidge, he had petitioned the Council of State, 20 January 1651: PRO, SP 25/66, p. 230).

116. The Earlier Text of the *Summarium Damnorum*, done March 1651 or before, is here taken from the printed Latin of the 1676 *Literæ Pseudo-Senatûs Anglicani*, "Face" edition, 70–74.

There are printing errors in both "Fruit" and "Face" editions of *Literæ: portiora, ducentius*; in "Fruit," *milenum* in item 3 of second set; in "Face," *peperis*. In his 1690 edition, Pritius corrected "Face" to *portoria, ducenties, piperis* and replaced the upper case in *Jacturæ* (in both 1676 texts) with lower case *j*, but the Columbia editors (1938) retained all four "Face" errors without comment. The money figures are a mess. "Fruit" has the first amount wrong as 74628.15.00; both "Fruit" and "Face" make errors in carrying over from *ad altera pagina* ("from the other page") and end with wrong totals. Edward Phillips in *Letters of State* (1694) miscopied 20000 as 2000 in B1 (4). The Columbia editors (1938) followed "Face" for their Latin text and unhelpfully "corrected" the final total. From the Final Text of 1652, it appears that 77020 in both *Literæ* should have been 77200.

In the 1653 manuscript PRO, SP 105/98, pp. 80–82, an English-language version of the Earlier Text seems to have been anomalously attached to the table of Fifteen Articles; with these differences from the Final English Text (later herein) in B2 (and different totals):

[2] from Anno 1622 to this present year 1650 at 2500 L.p. annum in twenty eight years   700000.00.00

[4] which is twenty one years & consequently will amount to   84000.00.00

Beligæ: The form *Belgia* was admitted by Littleton's Dictionary and not changed by Pritius. Milton used it at least five times in his English prose; and once in his Latin *Elegia* III, for which he was censured in Salmasius's (posthumously printed) *Responsio*. Milton did not accept the criticism and left it unchanged in his 1673 edition; yet at least eight times in the state papers, and in his *Defensio Secunda* and *Defensio Pro Se*, he used the more usual Latin form *Belgium*.

117. The Final Text of the 1652 *Summarium Damnorum* in English and in Latin is taken from MS. S.G. 8460. This text reflects the reduction in B3 from 16 articles to 15, so that the monetary figures are changed. The number of years change from *twenty-eight* to *twenty-nine*, and one of the two *1650* dates is omitted; both should have been. Changes in wording from the Earlier Text: *exclusi simus* to *exclusi fuerimus*; *plura* to *plus*; *satisfiat* to *satisfactum erit*; *æstimatur* to *conficit*; *superabit* to *exsuperabit*. Earlier Text and MS. St. v. Holland 2813.1 have correct *ablatorum*, while (in Final Text) MS. S.G. 8460 and MS. Aitzema have *ablatarum*.

118. The English Text of the "Fifteen Articles" in MS. S.G. 8640 was in 1652 taken almost verbatim, with minor spelling differences, from the text of a memorandum of 16 articles formally written by a professional amanuensis and now filed in East India Company Papers, PRO, E.I., vol. 4, no. 33.

This statement originally dealt with the period March 1621 to February 1622 O.S., items 1–11, and was later expanded to include items up to April 1627. In drafting the *Paper of Demands*, the number of items was reduced to 15 by removing item number 13, which became item three in Part 2 of the *Summarium Damnorum*. The Earlier Latin Text should have changed its reference from 16 to 15 articles, as was done in the Final Text.

For the case of Thomas Dawkes, imprisoned 21 days on bread and water, see *CSP, Colonial, 1617–1621*, 21 September 1621, p. 451; *CSP, Colonial, 1622–1624*, festive waste of gunpowder; *CSP, Colonial, 1625–1629*, passim for the Moretti case, and same volume, 535–37, for the four burned buildings of *Summarium Damnorum*. The Orankays of Orankayenses were local chieftains or officials with whom the English and the Dutch East India Companies made contracts, on occasion under circumstances less than honorable on either side.

119. William Courteen was the son-in-law of John Egerton, Earl of Bridgewater (in whose honor Milton composed the *Mask* of Comus in 1634), and both lost heavily by the Dutch capture of their ship, the *Bona Esperanza* (using the name given to the Cape of Good Hope by its Portuguese explorers). It is not clear

whether there was any connection to the *Bona Esperanza* ship named in Milton's state paper of 31 May 1656.

120. In 1651 John Marston tried to compel redress by taking action against the ship *Water Hound* of Amsterdam (on which Gerard Schaep was due to sail when he fled from London just before the battle of Worcester), but Marston was not upheld by the Admiralty Court (*CSPD, 1651,* 21 October 1651, pp. 484–85, report of Judges William Clark and John Exton).

Index
[Part One only]

Abbott, W. C., 87
Admirallus, 28–29
Admiralty Court, 12, 16, 18, 27
Advocatus fiscalis, 28
Aitzema, Leo ab, *xx, xxiv*, 6–7, 25, 31, 37, 40, 42, 59, 66, 87–89
Amboyna massacre, 24
Amplitudo Vestra, 28
Applebom, Harold, 42
Archithalassus, 29
Armis et instrumento bellico, 28
Arnold, Christopher, 69
Athenæ Oxonienses, 83
Aubrey, John, 82–83, 85

Balivus, 28
Bentinck, Lady Anne, *xviii*
Beverningh, Hieronymus van, 72
Birch, Thomas, *xviii–xix*
Black Monday, 36
Blake, General, 42, 47, 58, 63
Bodleian Library (Oxford), *xviii*
Bombardas, 28
Boreel, Willem, 23, 24
Bourne, Major, 63
Bradshaw, John, 6, 7, 48, 71
British Library (Museum), *xix*
Burgundian treaty. See *Intercursus Magnus*

Cadenas, Alonso de, 42
Calendar, *xvii*

Calendar of State Papers:
  Colonial, East Indies, *xviii*;
  Venetian, *xviii*
Caryophyllum, 27
Cats, Jacob, *xix*, 8, 10–11, 30, 34, 46–48, 66
Challoner (commissioner), 7, 71
Charles I, 12
Charles II, 9, 67, 89
Christina of Sweden, 25
Church-state separation, 44–45
Columbia Manuscript, 38, 61, 65, 79
Concilium de ijs, 70
Concilium Status Parlamenti Reipublicæ Angliæ, 15, 38
Constable, William, 70
Credentialibus sive commendatitiis, 64
Cromwell, Oliver, 6, 9, 44–45, 48, 56, 67, 70–74, 87
Cui nomen, 18, 26–27, 29
Cum nihil prius, xxii, 13, 17, 19
Curia maritimarum (maritima): 18, 29; *causarum*, 16
Cygnet ship, 27

Declaration of July 1652, *xxiv*, 45–46, 50, 52, 55–69
Defensio Regia, 5, 86
Defensio Secunda, 34, 39, 74, 88
Deputatorum, 73

337

Die Sabbathi, 64
Dominationes Vestræ, 27–28
Dominatio Vestra, 28
Domini Legati, 68
Domus Communium, 29
Domus Dominorum, 29
Dorislaus, Isaac, 8, 24, 61, 75
Dugard (printer), 45, 58, 66, 74
Dury, John, 75

East India Company reparation, 24, 47
Eden, Thomas, 23
Eikonoklastes, 74
Elizabeth (Queen), 87
Embassy receptions, 6–7
Endimion ship, 24
Exposuerunt nuper, 12

Field, John, 48, 57–58, 66
Fiscalis, 27
Fleming, Oliver, 6–7, 13, 28, 35, 44, 46, 48, 52, 63, 72
Flye ship, 27, 87
Foedus, Foederatus, xvii
Frederick III (Denmark), 67, 69
French, J. Milton, 15, 18
Frost, Gualter, 5, 12, 18, 28, 36, 55

Gemeentearchief (Amsterdam), xix
Green, Captain John, 43
Gregorian calendar (N.S.), xvii

Haak, Theodore, xxiv
The Hague, xix, 15, 17, 31, 50, 52, 54
Hamburg Senate, 25
Hardedge, Francis, 24
Hardwicke, Philip I., xix
Hesilrige, Arthur, 15, 17
Historia Pacis, xx, 87–89
History of England, 83
Hollandiæ Ordines, 19
Holstein, Duke Frederick of, 73
Hujus [mensis], 18
Huygens, Lodweijck, xix, 12–13, 35–36, 39, 46, 49, 58

Illustrissimi Foederatorum Ordines, 19
Ingelsby (commissioner), 7
Intercursus Magnus, 8, 15, 30, 32, 33
Intra indices quos Boyos vocant, 27
Ipsly (commissioner), 7

Joachimi, Albert, 8
John Milton and the Oldenburg Safeguard, xxi, xxiii, xxv, 5
Jongestaal, Allard-Pierre, 72
Judices maritimarum causarum, 18
Julian calendar (O.S.), xvii

Killigrew, Thomas, 89

Lambert, John, 71
Latin dictionary, xxiii, 16, 82–85
Latin Letters, xix, 17: of 16/26 April 1652, 37–39; of 27 April/7 May 1652, 39–40; of 28 April/8 May 1652, 40; of 8 July 1652, 68–69; of 19 October 1652, 69–70; of 13 July 1653, 73; of 1 August 1653, 73
Lenthall, William, 35–36, 49, 54
Liberi commeatûs, 60, 64
Liburnicis, 63
Life of Milton, xxiv, 43–44
Linguæ Latinæ Liber Dictionarius Quadripartitus, 16
Lisle, Lord Philip Sidney, 6–7, 10, 31, 37
Literæ Pseudo-Senatûs Anglicani, 4, 16, 23, 26, 30, 61, 65, 67, 79
Literas Merc et Represales vulgò dictas, 16
Literas quas vocant Merc et Represales, 16
Littleton, Adam, 16, 27, 33, 60, 63, 84, 89

Mabbott, Thomas Ollive, 15, 18
Marque and reprisal letters, 16
Marten, 70
Marvell, Andrew, 71–72

Mary and John merchant ship, 24
Meadowes, Philip, *xxv*, 73, 75
Mercator Adventurarius, 28
Mildmay (commissioner), 49, 71
Milton, Deborah, 42
Milton, Elizabeth, 82
Milton, John: Anglo–Danish exchanges, 67–70; authenticating texts of, 14–40; blindness of, *xxii–xxiii*, 7, 10, 25, 36, 83; classical Latin preference, *xxiii*, 6, 14–21, 32–33; Commonwealth Council relationship, 5–6; church–state separation belief, 44–45; death of wife and son, *xxiii*, 42–44, 52; exercising personal influence, 6; as foreign correspondence secretary, *xviii*, *xxi–xxii*, 3–13; how he worked, 56–67; moving from Whitehall to Petty France, 10; at Mylius's reception, 6; peace negotiations and, 70–76; on Vlitius's paper, 19; and Westminster negotiations, 12–13
Milton, Mary, 42
Mirk Monday, 36
Morley, Herbert, 6, 50
Muscovy Company reparation, 24
Mylius, Hermann, *xix*, 55, 67, 72: commendation of, 28; diary of, 12; meeting with Milton, 6; Milton's letters to, 6, 69, 87; papers of, *xxi*, *xxii*, 5–6; word usage of, 16, 29

Nalson Papers, *xviii*
Name treatments, 19, 27, 61, 65, 79–81
Naval titles, 28–29
Navarchus, 29
Navigandi studium, 16
Navigatio, 16, 33
Navigation Act, 9, 11, 15, 32
Nevile (commissioner), 7
Newcomb, Thomas, 74
Niedersächsisches Staatsarchiv (Oldenberg), *xix*
Nieupoort, Willem, *xxiii–xxiv*, 8, 43, 47, 49, 55, 72
Nitrati pulveris, 27
Nostræ montæ, 26

Octonis, 26
Of Reformation, 30, 78
Oldenburg, Count of, 10, 28, 55: negotiations, 6, 60
Oldenburg Safeguard, 10, 25. See also *John Milton and the Oldenburg Safeguard*
On the Proposals of Certain Ministers at the Committee for the Propagation of the Gospel, 44, 69
Order Books of the Council of State, 4, 22, 42
Ordines, 19, 29, 60
Ordines Generales, 19, 60, 64, 72
Ordines Generales Foederatarum Belgii Provinciarum accepta et lecta, 71
Ordines Hollandiæ & West Frisiæ considerarunt, 70–71
Ordo plebeius, 29

Paper of Demands, *xxii*, 21–30, 31, 33, 35, 53, 77, 86, 89
Parlamentum Reipulicæ Angliæ literas ad se missas, 71
Paulet Letters, 12, 15, 18
Pauw, Adrian, *xxiv*, 8, 29, 44, 58, 61, 64–65: mission of, 49–55, 66, 87–88
Pembroke, Earl of, 6, 10, 51, 54, 68
Penn, Captain William, 56–57
Perre, Paulus van de, 8, 66, 72
Persona, 15, 26
Philaras, Leonard, *xxiii*, 52–53
Phillips, Edward, *xxiv*, 43–44, 82–85
Phrasings, Miltonic, 16–21, 33–34, 69, 86–88
Pickering, Sir Gilbert, 74
Pitt, Moyses, 83, 85
Polyglot Bible, 74
Poolaroon Island, 24, 27
Pooloway Port, 24

340 Index

Potestates Generales, 19–20, 60, 62, 64, 69, 70
Potestatibus, 21, 73
Powell, Anne, 74
Præfectus, 28–29
Pridem exhibita, 27
Primores, 60, 62
Pritius, J. G., 17
Pro Populo Anglicano Defensio, xxiv, 19, 29, 34, 74
Pro Se Defensio, 34

Quæ studia sincera, 71
Quæ tam a Parlamento, 14
Queritur (queruntur), 30
Quos vocant, 16, 29, 86, 89

Racovian Catechism, 45
Raleigh (commissioner), 7
Recreditif, 28
Reede van Renswoude, Johan van, 23
Reedtz, Peter, 57, 67–68
Renswoude, 24
Res navalis, 16, 33
Rigsarkivet (Copenhagen), *xix*
Rijksarchief (Algemeen), *xix*, 15, 17, 31
Rosenkrantz, Erik, 57
Rosin, Lewis, *xxi, xxiv*, 20, 26, 30–32, 34, 38, 43–45, 49–51, 58–59, 60, 62, 65–66, 71, 75, 77
Rump Parliament, 71

St. John, Oliver, 8, 24
Saken van Staet en Oorlogh, xx
Salmasius, Claudius, 5, 15, 26, 74, 78, 86
Salvaguardia, 29, 60, 73
Samson Agonistes, 36
Schaep, Gerard, *xix*, 8, 66
Sclopus, 28, 63
Sclopus minusculus, 28
Scobell, Henry, 48–49, 55, 57, 64
Scriptum ab Excellentijs Vestris, xxiv, 17–18, 19, 38
Scriptum of July 1652, 45–46, 52, 56–67, 66, 69, 77, 87
A Second Declaration, 27

Second Defence for the People of England, 74. See also *Defensio Secunda*
Skinner, Cyriack, 82–83, 85: Transcript, 38, 79–80
Slave cargoes, 24–25
Societas Adventuraria, 28
Statibus Generalibus, 19, 20, 29
Stephanus, Robertus, 83–85
Stockarus, Johannes Jacobus, 74
Strickland, Walter, 7, 8, 24, 49, 71
Strickland–St. John mission, *xix*, 8, 9, 26, 31, 35
Summarium Damnorum, *xxii*, 23–24, 26–27, 30

Tanner Papers, *xviii*
Telonium, 29, 33
Thirty-six Articles (Dutch), *xxiii*, 31–33, 35, 47
Thirty-six Counter-articles (British), *xix, xxiii, xxv*, 20–21, 30–40, 75, 77, 88
Thomason, George, 74–75
Thurloe, John, *xviii*, 6, 31, 32, 36, 43, 47–48, 57–58, 68, 71–73
Toland, John, 84
Tractatio, 38, 62
Traver (commissioner), 6
Treaty, draft and final peace, *xxv*, 74–76
Trinity College manuscript, 69
Tromp, Lieutenant Admiral, 42, 46–47, 48, 58, 61, 63
Tryumph ship, 56

Ut, 26, 29, 34, 63, 69, 70
Uti, 26, 29, 34, 63, 69, 70
Ut tandem, *xxiii*, 36

Van de Perre, Ambassador, *xix*
Vane, Sir Henry, 8, 45–46, 48–49, 70
Verbael vande Ambassade naer Engelant, xix, xx
Vlitius, Janus (Jan van Vliet), 10, 12–13, 17, 19, 34, 35, 39, 41, 88
Vulgo dictus/dictum, 26, 27, 29, 86–88

War's onset, 41–55
Weckherlin, Georg Rudolph, *xxiii*, 25, 26, 38, 40, 42–43, 63–64, 67, 71, 77
Wentworth, Sir Peter, 10
Westminster talks, 8, 10–13
Westphalia treaty, 33
Whitelocke, Bulstrode, 6, 11, 12, 40, 50, 57, 70
Willemsen Rosenwing de Lysacker, Henry, 67
Williams, Sir Abraham, 49
Williams, Roger, 59
Witt, Johan de, *xix*
Wood, Anthony à, 83

Young, Captain Anthony, 41, 47, 48

Zaaen, Vice Admiral Joris van der, 41

About the Author

Leo Miller (1915-1990) was one of the most respected twentieth century historical Miltonists. This book, *John Milton's Writings in the Anglo-Dutch Negotiations*, represents his last major work before his death. His previous publications include *John Milton among the Polygamophiles* (Loewenthal, 1974) and *John Milton and the Oldenburg Safeguard* (Loewenthal, 1985).

In 1990, Miller was cited as that year's Honored Scholar by the Milton Society of America, recognizing his lifetime achievements in this field of scholarship. And in 1980, he was awarded the James Holly Hanford Award of the Milton Society for the most distinguished article published in that year.